SUNNYSIDE

A British Academy Monograph

British Academy Monographs showcase work arising from:

British Academy Postdoctoral Fellowships
British Academy Newton International Fellowships

SUNNYSIDE

A Sociolinguistic History of British House Names

Laura Wright

Published for THE BRITISH ACADEMY
by OXFORD UNIVERSITY PRESS

Oxford University Press, Great Clarendon Street, Oxford OX2 6DP

© The British Academy 2020

Database right The British Academy (maker)

First edition published in 2020

British Library Cataloguing in Publication Data
Data available

Library of Congress Cataloging in Publication Data
Data available

Typeset by
Keystroke, Neville Lodge, Tettenhall, Wolverhampton

Printed in Great Britain by TJ International Ltd, Padstow, Cornwall

ISBN 978-0-19-726655-7

Albert George Wright
Jeweller, Watch & Clock Repairer
1932–2016

CONTENTS

ILLUSTRATIONS

ACKNOWLEDGEMENTS

My research into historical multilingualism in Britain was initially funded by a British Academy Postdoctoral Fellowship. I thank the British Academy for publication of the present volume, and the Academy of Finland for funding research time. I thank the University of Cambridge, the Marc Fitch Fund and the Scouloudi Foundation in association with the Institute of Historical Research for funding costs of map reproduction.

My particular thanks go to place-name scholars Dr Keith Briggs; Professor Richard Coates, University of the West of England; Professor Richard A. V. Cox, University of the Highlands and Islands; Dr Gillian Fellows-Jensen and Professor Michael Lerche Nielsen, Institute of Name Research, University of Copenhagen; Dr Oliver Padel, University of Cambridge; and Dr Simon Taylor, University of Glasgow. My thanks also to historians Professor Caroline Barron, Royal Holloway, University of London; Professor Tim Hitchcock, University of Sussex; and Professor Derek Keene and Olwen Myhill, Centre of Metropolitan History, University of London. Also my thanks to historical geographers Professor Richard Dennis, University of London; Professor Robert Dodgshon, University of Aberystwyth; and to Philip Stickler, Department of Geography, University of Cambridge; Nick Mann, Department of Geography, University of London; Craig Statham and Christopher Fleet, National Library of Scotland, and Mark Rance, for their advice and technical help with maps. I thank my 'Multilingual Practices in the History of Written English' partners Professor Päivi Pahta, Dr Arja Nurmi, Dr Jukka Tyrkkö, and Dr Janne Skaffari, of the Universities of Tampere and Turku; and my British Academy readers, Professor Peter Trudgill, University of Fribourg/University of East Anglia, and Dr Philip Durkin, Deputy Chief Editor, Oxford English Dictionary. Charles Curran of the Oxford University Computing Service is thanked for creating the medieval abbreviation and suspension font, and archaeologist of abandoned ruins Stein Farstadvoll of the University of Tromsø is thanked for alerting me to sunny farms in Norway. Brigid Hamilton-Jones, Geetha Nair and Graham Bradbury are thanked for seeing the book through the press.

Selections of material herein have been aired, at various stages of development, on BBC Radio 4 (my thanks to presenter Michael Rosen, producer Emma-Louise Williams, editors Beth O'Dea and James Cook); BBC Radio London (my thanks to presenter Robert Elms, producer Sarah Bateson and managing editor David Robey);

at the University of the West of England Linguistics Group, October 2014 (my thanks to Professor Richard Coates); the fifteenth Nordic Theoretical Archaeology Group, University of Copenhagen, April 2015 (my thanks to Dr Guus Kroonen and Dr Rune Iversen); at 'Constructing the self: Linguistic and historical perspectives on identity and authenticity in egodocuments and other writings "from below"', University of Brussels, April 2015, and the Historical Sociolinguistics Network Summer School at the University of Agder's Metochi, Lesbos, August 2015 (my thanks to Professor Wim Vandenbussche and Professor Rik Vosters for both); at the ninth 'Studies in the History of the English Language' conference, University of British Colombia, June 2015 (my thanks to Professor Stefan Dollinger and Professor Laurel Brinton); at the Third Southern Englishes Workshop, University College London, February 2016 (my thanks to Dr Charles Wilson), at the 'Urbanisation in the British Isles: a Historical and Interdisciplinary Perspective' conference, University of Lausanne, April 2016 (my thanks to Professor Anita Auer and Dr Marije van Hattum), at the Twenty-First Sociolinguistics Symposium, University of Murcia, June 2016 (my thanks to Professor Juan Camilo Conde-Silvestre, Professor Juan Manuel Hernández-Campoy and Dr Juan Antonio Cutillas-Espinosa), at the Historical Sociolinguistics Network Conference 'Examining the Social in Historical Sociolinguistics', University of New York and City University of New York (my thanks to the several organisers), and at the Tenth International Conference on Middle English, University of Stavanger (my thanks to Professor Merja Stenroos). I am grateful to everyone who listened, commented, and advised. I single out Peter Gilliver of the Oxford English Dictionary for drawing my attention to Sir James Murray and his Sunnysides, and Mark Rance for pointing out that there was more to Sunnyside than a twenty-minute radio broadcast.

My thanks go to the following archivists, librarians and institutions: Kath Humphries, Crawshawbooth Library; Pamela Hunter, Hoare's Bank at the Sign of the Golden Bottle, Fleet Street; Fiona McIntyre, Community Heritage Manager, Libraries, Museums, Culture and Registrars, Lancashire County Council; Matthew Payne, Keeper of the Muniments at Westminster Abbey; Elizabeth Scudder, Principal Archivist, London Metropolitan Archives; James Wilson, Librarian, the Swedenborg Society, London; Jo Wisdom, Librarian, Guildhall Library (Manuscripts); Philip Curtis and Norman Kirtlan of the Sunderland Antiquarian Society; Andrew Metcalfe, Address Management Unit, Royal Mail, and Carlton Hall, Product/Data Manager, Royal Mail; the Royal Mail Archive; the Institute of Historical Research, University of London; the British Library. Laurence Worms, Ash Rare Books, is thanked for locating the image of George Cargill Leighton. Sue Young, sueyounghistories.com, is thanked for locating the image of Orlando Jones & Co's Rice Starch label. Nadine Licence, Shoe Lane Library, is thanked for help tracing Victorians mentioned in Chapter 4.

Copyright acknowledgements

Images from Ordnance Survey maps, and maps by Robert Gordon, Joan Blaeu, Timothy Pont and John Thomson, are reproduced by permission of the National Library of Scotland.

Images from Roy's Military Survey of Scotland are reproduced by permission from the British Library, © British Library Board: British Library Maps C.9.b 3/4c, 5/5c, 5/6c, 5/6f, 6/4b, 6/5e, 6/5f, 6/6a, 6/6b, 6/7d, 6/7e, 7/1b, 7/5c, 8/5d, 8/5e, 9/2b, 17/5f, 18/1a, 18/2a, 28/3b, 28/3c, 28/3f, 28/4d, 29/2f, 30/1e, 30/2b, 30/2c, 30/3d, 31/1d, 38/2a.

Images from Andrew Armstrong's *A Map of the County of Northumberland: with that part of the County of Durham that is North of the River Tyne also the Town of Berwick and its bounds*, 1769, Sheet 5, Whitaker Collection 538; and from Andrew Armstrong's *The County Palatine of Durham*, 1768, Sheet NE, Whitaker Collection 531, The University Library, are reproduced by permission of the University of Leeds.

Images from John Fryer and sons, *Map of the County of Northumberland including the Town and County of Newcastle upon Tyne, the Town and Bounds of Berwick upon Tweed and those parts of the County of Durham situate to the North of the River Tyne*, 1820, are reproduced with permission from The National Archives, reference MPZ 1/15.

The image from John Rain's *An Eye Plan of Sunderland and Bishop Wearmouth from the South*, 1785, is reproduced by permission of the Sunderland Antiquarian Society.

Quotations from the *17th and 18th Century Burney Collection Newspapers*, © Gale, a part of Cengage, Inc., are reproduced by permission.

Quotations from the *Illustrated London News* Historical Archive, 1842–2003 and the illustration of George Cargill Leighton are reproduced by permission.

Quotations from *The Times* are reproduced by permission of *The Times* / News Licensing.

Quotations from *19th Century British Library Newspapers* are reproduced by permission of the British Library.

I thank the Faculty of English, University of Cambridge, for help financing copyright fees.

Laura Wright
above J. A. Sharwood & Co. Ltd.
Wholesale Grocers and Importers of Foreign Produce
March 2018

ABBREVIATIONS AND SYMBOLS

*	indicates an unattested wordform, either reconstructed, or simply unknown. *kumbos*: unattested but plausibly reconstructed; *Unicornbury*: unattested
(	indicates both with and without final letter-graph. *Green(s* is a conflation of both *Green* and *Greens*
<>	indicates what is visible or barely visible, or illegible if left blank
//	indicates phonemes: sounds which are meaningful in a language
[]	indicates allophones, the sound as uttered. However, in Appendix 1, [] also indicates a house name used as a surname (the context will make clear which is intended).
a.	*ante* (before)
AN	Anglo-Norman
AND	*Anglo-Norman Dictionary*
BL	British Library
ECCO	Eighteenth Century Collections Online
Esawyer	The Electronic Sawyer. Online Catalogue of Anglo-Saxon Charters
HR	London Metropolitan Archives, Hustings Court Rolls, microfilm X109/399–424, Deeds Enrolled in the Court of Husting 1254–1400
K	Kingsford, C. L. 1916. 'Historical Notes on Medieval London Houses.' London Topographical Record 10, 44–144.
	Kingsford, C. L. 1917. 'Historical Notes on Medieval London Houses.' London Topographical Record 11, 28–82.
	Kingsford, C. L. 1920. 'Historical Notes on Medieval London Houses.' London Topographical Record 12, 1–67.
Letter-Books A–H	London Metropolitan Archives, Letter-Books, COL/AD/01/001–8
LMA	London Metropolitan Archives
M	Mason, Emma (ed.). 1988. *Westminster Abbey Charters, 1066–c.1214*. London: London Record Society 25

ME	Middle English
MED	*Middle English Dictionary*
ML	Medieval Latin
OE	Old English
OED	*Oxford English Dictionary*
Plea & Mem	London Metropolitan Archives, Plea & Memoranda Rolls, CLA/024/01/02/002–051
TNA	The National Archives
WAM	Westminster Abbey Muniments

GLOSSARY

bury	manor house
garrett	in the context of towers, a turret; in the context of houses, an upper floor
haw	enclosure
hithe	riverside port
messuage	residence, dwelling house
seld	bazaar, shop containing multiple retailers
soke	local district division
solar	room in an upper storey
steading	farmhouse plus dependent outbuildings

INTRODUCTION

In this book I make the case that house names are worthy of sociolinguistic study. House names have not yet received systematic attention from linguists, perhaps because they have been out of fashion in Britain since the Second World War. The fourth citation in the *Oxford English Dictionary* under the headword naff, *adj.* 'unfashionable, vulgar; lacking in style' is: 'It is naff to call your house *The Gables, Mon Repos*, or *Dunroamin*.'[1] However, house names belonging to the nobility are held exempt from such negative judgement: the name *Buckingham Palace* is not considered to be socially problematic, nor *Chatsworth*, nor *Hampton Court*. Yet house names abound in the English-speaking world, bestowed on large, medium and small homes, and it is largely the British middle classes alone who find *Mon Repos* to be *infra dig*.[2] Essentially the consensus seems to be that all the *Fernleas, Oakdenes* and *Fairholmes* are part of the landscape but insignificant and beneath notice.[3]

How did this situation come about? How, why and when did the social downgrading of house names occur? When was the heyday of house name bestowal? And how, when and where did such names as *The Gables, Mon Repos*, and *Dunroamin*

---

[1] *Sunday Telegraph*, 21 August 1983, 11/3.

[2] The Duke of Edinburgh, Prince Philip, was born at a house named *Mon Repos* in 1921. It was so named in the 1860s by an earlier owner, King George I of the Hellenes, who was born a Danish Prince, William of Schleswig-Holstein-Sonderburg-Glücksburg (Christmas 1914: 141). It was not the first house to be named *Mon Repos*: '"*Ma Favorite* is the Elector's country seat, at some little distance from the city, towards the south. By the name, it is natural to suppose that the Elector François de Shönborn, who gave it that name, preferred it to *Mon Repos*, an Electorial country seat in the neighbourhood of Treves.' (Cogan 1794: 321–2). Nor was it the first to be given a fanciful subjective name: Frederick the Great, King of Prussia, named his favourite retreat *Sans Souci*. The Palace of Sans Souci was so-named in 1746, and by 1747 the name, 'which we may translate "No-Bother"', was 'put upon his lintel in gold letters' (Carlyle 1864: 245–6).

[3] *Fernlea (Fern-lea, Fern Lea, Fernleigh, Fern-leigh, Fern Leigh)*: 2,015 hits in the UK Royal Mail database; *Oakdene (Oak-dene, Oak Dene, Oakdean, Oak Dean)*: 2,040 hits; *Fairholme (Fair Holme, Fairholm, Fair Holm)*: 712 hits, snapshot taken 21 September 2018 (my thanks to Carlton Hall, Licence Development & Implementation Manager, Royal Mail). Not everyone shares this view: projects undertaken at the University of London's Centre for Metropolitan History over the last 35 years have investigated the physical arrangement of London's houses as a primary way into understanding the interactions and influences of residents and visitors, and much of the medieval house name data discussed in these pages was first noticed by historians.

enter the British housing name stock? There is no obvious place to look for the answers.[4] The English Place-Name Society, publishing since the 1920s on the toponomy of England, does not systematically include house names, nor is there a database available other than that held by the Royal Mail. Yet house names are ancient. The oldest work of English literature, *Beowulf,* written some time between the seventh and ninth centuries, tells of a meadhall named *Heorot,* which name is still to be found (usually as the *White Hart*) around the country and throughout the English-speaking world.[5]

This book contains many biographies, because house names result from the experiences of the people who live in them. I begin with my own biography and how I came to study house names, as it caught me by surprise. I started my linguistic studies looking at Middle English vocabulary embedded in Medieval Latin and Anglo-Norman French administrative documents – lost words, essentially. I then analysed the syntax of such documents, particularly the accounts of medieval London Bridge, figuring out the systematicity of mixed Middle English/ Anglo-Norman/Medieval Latin writing. This kind of business and administrative language-mixing has been overlooked, perhaps because documents such as accounts appear to consist of dry, formulaic lists of names as opposed to the imaginative wonders of monolingual poetry, on which the history of English has largely been based so far – even though poetry has never been the main reason people put quill to parchment in any century.

Dry, formulaic lists of names. Names are a quintessential human speech act, bestowed with care and reflecting the values of society. While waiting for manuscripts to be delivered to the counter in archives I would take down historical Post Office directories from the shelves. Selsey, Sussex, 1915: Elsinore, Grasmere, Gunthwaite, Santa Kilda, Glindah, Oakwood, Rose Cottage, Dalmorton, Erivan, Tythe Barn, St Ronan's, The Hut, Verica, The Bungalow, Ingleside, The Barn, Cloverlea, Tamarisk, Island View, Old Farm House, Hazeltryst, Indiana, Ingleton, Ferncroft. None in 1859, few in 1890, efflorescent by 1915 with seaside bungalows. I would keep them on my desk and ponder them in the interstices of my work: why did *Verica* repeat in the plotlands of Selsey in 1915 and Laindon in 1949?[6] Were the only four *Hazeltryst*s known to Google (one in Selsey, three in Croydon) bestowed by owners who knew each other, or did three copy the first, or was there a literary antecedent, as is so often the case?[7] Kelly's directories for Selsey list Major Robert

[4] Miles (2000) is an exception, based on the author's 1979 University of Bristol MLitt thesis ('The naming of private houses in Britain since 1700') covering 19,206 homes in England and Wales, surveyed from telephone directories.
[5] For dating of *Beowulf* see Fulk (1992: 351–62, 286–90), cited in Goering (2016: 180).
[6] Verica was the name of the king of the Atrebates when Britain was part of the Roman empire and coins with his head were found on Selsey beach, but I do not know the link with Laindon. Both were bungalows.
[7] Hazeltryst, Havelock Road, Addiscombe, Croydon, was so-named by 1880 (*Daily News,* 27 October 1880).

J. Lamb as living at Hazeltryst throughout the 1930s. Titles such as 'Major' sound intrinsically pompous, and house names can either bolster or deflate, creating a householder's public identity even though the name was bestowed generations before. As a speaker on BBC Radio London I would select a suburb and pick out older houses named after Victorian battles, because a triangulation of census data, house-name evidence and battle reportage in *The Times* can sometimes pinpoint the original bestower. In more than one case, a young man who won honours in what must have been the most dangerous, frightening and intense experience of his life retired in old age to an ordinary house in an ordinary suburb and named it after the distant patch on earth where he nearly lost his life, or took the lives of others. House names remind as well as proclaim, every time you return to your home and enter your own front door.

While going over the poetry of Stevie Smith for teaching purposes I read her essay on the house names in her North London, outer-suburb locality. She was class-sensitive, noting the naming pretentions of interwar housing and how they differed from the naming practices of older houses. I followed her lead, and came to realise that the naming categories were few: (1) the transferred place-name is the largest (Elsinore, Grasmere, Gunthwaite, Santa Kilda, Glindah, Dalmorton, Erivan, Indiana, St Ronan's, Ingleton), followed by (2) the nostalgically rural (Oakwood, Rose Cottage, Tythe Barn, Ingleside, Cloverlea, The Barn, Old Farm House, Island View), (3) the commemorative (Tamarisk, Indiana, Glindah, Dalmorton, Erivan, often commemorating an Empire experience), (4) the upwardly mobile, and (5) the popular culture one, which was usually literary in pre-cinema days (Ferncroft, Elsinore). These are fluid categories – anything can be commemorative, from a war to your sister. But it was not until I was startled by seeing General Scott, Sunnyside, Ealing Green, in a Post Office directory for 1872, that I researched a name that led back over six hundred years, and into other languages. This was when I realised the lacuna, the scholarly blindness, to house names, from which I was suffering myself. Linguists are not exempt from the taboos of the day, and I too had been regarding house names as trivia, all right for light entertainment on the radio but not for serious academic study. Sunnyside repeats over a hundred times in Scotland as a historic steading name occurring in Latin records,[8] but it has been overlooked by the Scottish Place-Name Society precisely, I imagine, because of this prejudice against the house names of the lower social classes – contrast your reaction (if you are a native English speaker) to 'Ingleside' and 'Hazeltryst' as opposed to 'Buckingham Palace' or 'Windsor Castle', and consider the impossibility of *Ingleside Palace, *Hazeltryst Castle. Over the centuries, Scotland has been particularly multilingual, and during my participation in the Finnish Academy-funded *Multilingual Practices in the History of Written English* project, I came to

---

[8] *Steading* is a northern term for a farmhouse together with dependent outbuildings.

realise that the 'Greens' in Scottish place-names such as Greens of Invermay and Greens of Auchmahoy are not green at all but Scottish Gaelic *grian*, meaning 'sun'.

This, then, is the background to how I came to focus on house names, via a career-long gleaning of multilingual accounts and similar historic administrative documents for the purposes of social history by means of linguistic analysis. The research methods I use are (a) to locate historical house names – on parchment, on gatepost, on the internet – and (b) to arrange them according to date, and then (c) to try to find out who gave the name to the house. Early house names occur in Medieval Latin/Anglo-Norman mixed-language deeds and wills. Eighteenth-century house names occur in historical directories and on trade-cards. Nineteenth-century house names are found in directories, membership lists and, in rural areas, on Ordnance Survey maps. As well as English, Medieval Latin, Anglo-Norman and Older Scots, evidence is also found in Scottish Gaelic.

I start with the earliest house names I can find in London. The first few date from before the Norman Conquest of 1066. I interpret 'house' as a 'building in which people dwelt', because the modern-day notion of a house as a single physical non-commercial building housing a single nuclear family had not yet come into existence. Evidence from before 1300 is scant. I have collected 294 names from before 1400 (listed in Appendix 1), of which 52 names date from before 1300, – but such evidence that I have found is consistent, showing that houses were named after their inhabitants: *Sabelinesbir* 'Sabeline's dwelling-house'; their appearance: *le Brodedore* 'the broad door'; and what went on in them: *le Taninghus* 'the tanning house'. Early second-elements were *haw* ('enclosed space'), *bury* ('large dwelling-house'), *shop* and *seld* ('proto-department-store'), with *haw*, *bury* and *seld* becoming unproductive by the end of the Old English period. This stable pattern had held good for centuries, and it was not until the fourteenth century that a change occurred and heraldic emblems became routinely used as house signs (*le Crowe, le Sterre, le Horn*). This mirrored a shift in the social standing of the more successful merchants and brewers who used such symbols on their seals. Heraldic emblems began to act as a visual signifier of commerce, occurring as names of buildings which also functioned as selds, shops, inns, taverns and brewhouses as well as homes. This is the first sociolinguistic claim of the book: that the new social class of knighthood which emerged in the fourteenth century, and which adopted personal (as opposed to dynastic) heraldic devices of the sort that had formerly been restricted to the nobility, became apparent in heraldic house names signifying commercial enterprise. Again, the history of how pubs came to have names like the *Red Lion* or the *Boar's Head* may not seem to fall within the purview of sociolinguistics (the social activities of drinking and shopping being relative constants across the centuries), but naming practices have undergone sea-changes from time to time, revealing social shifts and affiliations. In this case, the rise of a *nouveau riche* (to borrow a term coined for a different set of people in a different century) merchant class can be identified by heraldic house names. I also borrow the term *punctuated equilibrium* from biology for these sea-changes, by which I mean that house names held steady for long periods of time until a shift in naming trends resulted in the addition of a new category.[9]

London is central to an understanding of later British house names because the metropolis was subject to street laws which had a pivotal effect on the naming of buildings. The London Streets Act of 1762 set in chain a series of events which resulted in the abandonment of most medieval commercial building names (pubs excepted), and the coming of the railways from the 1840s resulted in the erection of new houses in places that had hitherto been too distant from the City of London and the West End for daily commuting. The names of these new houses can be divided into the five main categories just mentioned, illustrated here from *Mason's Court Guide and General Directory for Brentford, Kew, Ealing, Isleworth, Twickenham, Teddington, Richmond, Kingston, Hampton, &c., &c.* of 1853:

1 the transferred place-name (Hanover Lodge, Kew Bridge)
2 the nostalgically rural (Orchard House, Ealing Lane)
3 the commemorative (Wycliffe House, Twickenham, which was home to the Rev. H. H. Campbell at the time and likely to reference the fourteenth-century theologian John Wycliffe)
4 names associated with nobility (Grosvenor House, Butts, Brentford, *Grosvenor* being the surname of the Dukes of Westminster)
5 the latest fashion or fad (Gothic Villa, Woodland Road, Isleworth)

I include *Mon Repos* and *Dunroamin* under (5) as the fashion for subjective house names performing declarative speech-acts expressing their owners' states, attitudes and opinions, either explicitly or implicitly first-person – such as *Chez Nous* (French for 'our place') *Cartref* (Welsh for 'home'), and even verb phrases such as *Bide-a-Wee* – began to snowball in the eighteenth century (cf. *Ma Favorite* in footnote 2).[10] The commemorative category also includes subjective commemorative acts, often of a personal nature, such as Bianca Lodge, Primrose Vale, next to Chalk Farm on Greenwood's map of 1827 (surveyed 1826), where the bestower had some long-lost personal reason for delighting in the Italian feminine adjective for 'white'.

---

[9] For a discussion of the application of the punctuated equilibrium model to language history see Dixon (1997 [2002]: 3—5).

[10] In its current instantiation, that is. There was an earlier medieval usage, exemplified by *Beaurepair, la ffeytishalle* and *le Wynsoler* in Appendix 1, but these names have not remained productive. I include personal names, and all the many made-up names under the 'commemorative' category, since although they are opaque to outsiders they commemorated something meaningful to the namers. Scots *bide a wee* 'stop awhile' reached a wide audience via Sir Walter Scott's novels *The Tale of Old Mortality* (1816) and *Rob Roy* (1817), where characters beseech their interlocutors to 'bide a wee, bide a wee'. As a house name, Bide-a-Wee can be interpreted as 'may you bide a wee time here with us', or as '(this is where we) stop awhile', in which case it is a synonym of *Dunroamin*.

Commemoration is subjective, whether collectively so (*Trafalgar House*) or individually, and the categories of commemoration and latest fashion could overlap if one householder's innovatory act of commemoration became taken up by others.

There was an unusual linguistic consequence to this building boom: whereas the houses of the nobility took their name from the nearest village (such as *Holkham Hall*, a relatively modern eighteenth-century stately home built near the village of Holkham in Norfolk, morphologically transparent as *holk + ham*, regardless of whether anyone knew or cared what *holk* or *ham* originally meant), Victorian newbuild home-owners took morphologically transparent British place-names apart and recombined them into new, previously unattested groupings, which sounded traditional although they were not. A page chosen at random (page 21) of *Kelly's Directory of Middlesex* for 1899 reveals houses in Acton named *Roselea*, *Elm Dene*, *Fernlea*, which were typical house names of the period. *Elm, dene, lea, fern* are Old English words found in place names (although *rose* is rare as a place-name element) but in these specific pairings, they took on a new life.

This is the second sociolinguistic claim of the investigation: that just as new technology in recent decades has resulted in linguistic change in the virtual environment, with a proliferation of new meanings, acronyms and blends; so the coming into being of the new suburbs resulted in linguistic change in the residential street frontage, visible on house signs. That it was a collective linguistic response of a new group of people to a new situation, and that it consisted of a redeployment of onomastic material that had not been productive for centuries in a kind of exaptation, has not, so far as I am aware, been identified before. Yet there is a precedent: Old English personal names were also coined by taking existing words and putting them together in new combinations – although they may have been words current at the time of coining, unlike the denes, leas, holmes and hursts of house names.[11] Morpurgo Davies (2002: 222–3) observed that the same word can behave differently depending on whether it is a noun or a name: Classical Greek does not have a special feminine form for *hippos*, which mean both 'horse' and 'mare', but it does in the feminine name *Xanthippē*. Certainly the denes ('valley'), leas ('meadow'), holmes ('island') and hursts ('wooded knoll') came back into productive life as names long after their original designations as nouns had fallen out of use, and there is a further nuance to this particular piece of exaptation seen in spelling variation. Since the late fifteenth century, the forces of standardisation have ensured that spelling variants have reduced down, not quite to zero (*judgment* v. *judgement, standardise* v. *standardize*), but very nearly so. However, Victorian house names expanded the pool of variants back out again, especially with decorative word-final <-e>, and a predilection for <y> where standard orthography has <i>.[12] Variants such as *dean/*

[11] For a synopsis of whether meaning was of relevance in the pre-Anglo-Saxon period of name formation, see Okasha (2011: 114–17).
[12] Such as *Lyndhurst* (*Kelly's Directory of Middlesex* 1899: 21).

dene, lee/lea/ley/leigh, Lindholme/Lyndholme, had nothing to do with pronunciation but gave a veneer of antique authenticity to newly-coined names for new houses in new suburbs. Around 1960 my grandparents took over the lease of an already-named shop and flat above, Fayre House, 22 High Street, Barnet. This alluded to Barnet Fair, boasting both pseudo-ancient <y> and excrescent word-final <-e>. More is more in house names. *Roselea, Elm Dene, Fernlea,* however spelt, achieved the seeming paradox of proclaiming both last-minute modernity (they were brand new) and genealogical legitimacy (they were grafted from venerable rooted stock).

Subsequent chapters trace the history of one quintessential British house name, *Sunnyside.* The Royal Mail database currently returns 5,439 hits for *Sunnyside* (*Sunny-side, Sunny Side, Sunniside*) in the United Kingdom, largely associated nowadays with interwar suburban houses, and the name occurs all over the English-speaking world.[13] Yet prior to 1859 there were precisely none in London, or none that I can find. In many ways Sunnyside is a typical British house name, a two-element compound, both elements transparent in meaning, both elements high-frequency items, conveying something pleasant to do with the natural world and the local terrain, and expressing a cheery, sunnyside-up opti-mism. Yet the history of the name is quite different, and, working backwards in time from the first London *Sunnyside* of 1859, the hunt for its origin led me away from London around the country, first to the Northern counties, and then into Scotland, and uncovered a boost in the mid nineteenth century from an American celebrity. I have used the methods of social network theory, and the concept of the community of practice, to discover who talked to whom, and in what kind of relationship and social activity.[14] I have constructed biographies of key Sunnyside owners and plotted their interactions, and the social reasons that caused such inter-actions to occur. During the eighteenth century, the scope of Sunnyside usage in England was restricted to a network of Quakers who used the name as an insider shibboleth, a fact which was not lost on the first London Sunnysiders in 1859, who were also of nonconformist bent. The third sociolinguistic claim of the book is that the house name Sunnyside had a life as a code-word signaling firstly the Quaker, and then more generally the counter-establishment values of the house owner, which significance was still operative into the early 1860s.

When tracking the name back to the sixteenth century, it was necessary to cross language boundaries, since much evidence is found for the earlier history of Sunnyside in documents written in Latin, and also in Scottish Gaelic place-names, because the concept of the sunny side as opposed to the shadow side was a routine constituent of Scottish legal land tenure records. The fourth sociolinguistic claim

[13] Snapshot taken 21 September 2018; my thanks to Carlton Hall, Licence Development & Implementation Manager, Royal Mail.
[14] See Milroy (1980) for the concept of the social network as applied to sociolinguistic study, and Eckert and Wenger (2005) for the concept of communities of practice.

of the book is that this common modern house name had an anterior life as part
of a prepositional phrase in Middle English, Older Scots and (as a translation) in
Scottish Gaelic, with manuscript evidence dating to *c.*1200, long preceding its use
as a house name. Knowing which was the sunny side and which the shadow side
of cultivatable plots was part of the ancient collective cultural memory of certain
parts of North Britain.

In what way does such an investigation further the aims of linguistics – is not the
study of house names rather social history, with little implication or application for
the study of language at large? Elsewhere I have set out the case that just as speakers'
repertoires consist of all the languages known to an individual, they also consist of
all the words, even if those words are not known to the dictionary: *mahalla, oktis,
pesco, atbara, zog, komo.*[15] Edwardian shoppers were aware of these words because
they appeared on large colourful advertising posters, as well as on labels on goods.[16]
Weinberg's Mahalla cigarettes, Oktis corset shields, Pesco underwear, Atbara por-
poise laces, Zog cleaner, Komo furniture cream and black enamel – if, in 1911,
one had run out of Zog and Komo, then restocking necessitated asking the person
behind the shop counter for more: *zog* and *komo* formed part of the speaker's active
repertoire. Most marketing words read from advertisements are not spoken aloud
by a given individual, but those that an individual habitually buys are used in the
same way as other nouns. The ulterior history of the word is irrelevant – the speaker
may or may not know or care that Kitchener fought the Sudanese at the Battle of
Atbara in 1898, or that a mahalla is a land-division in Turkey. Like advertisements,
house names are mostly lodged in speakers' passive rather than active vocabularies.

Names are often treated by linguists as separate from the rest of the lexicon, with
their own specialist journals, and there are phonological and semantic reasons for
this.[17] Names do not always participate in sound-changes, nor do they trigger the
same semantic responses as their homophones. But they do form part of cultural
knowledge: which name is apposite for which social circumstance. Being a native
English speaker and belonging to British culture entails knowing that *Fernlea*
belongs to the name-stock of housing whereas *Fido* does not. I draw a distinction between innovation and change: anyone might name their house *Fido* (and
the house lived in by Freddie, Ida, Dolly and Olly might have been particularly
susceptible) but others have not followed suit. The innovator of *Fernlea*, on the
other hand, resulted in the addition of *Fernlea* along with *Ferndale, Fernhurst, Fern
Villa, Fernville, Fern Lodge* and all the other *Fern-* combinations to the housing
name-stock. Who that innovator was, the duration of the Victorian craze for ferns,

[15] For discussion of multilingual historical individuals and deployment of their languages see Nurmi
et al. (2017). For discussion of commercial words see Wright (2017a, 2017b, 2017c).
[16] The posters can be seen in Jubb (1984).
[17] Name theory has been developed by philosophers rather than linguists; for an argument that name
theory should be informed by linguistic part of speech, see Willems (2000).

who the early adopters were, when the name gathered traction, when it reached its heyday, how far its geographical spread, and when the second-element *-ville* became popular, are all sociolinguistic concerns.[18] Names for children, domestic servants, pet animals such as dogs, cats and rabbits, farm animals such as horses, cows and donkeys, racing animals such as horses and greyhounds, houses, businesses, and boats all reflect the values of society. Medieval Britons named their cups and swords, but cups and swords no longer hold social value and are no longer named. Names are initiated by the bestower, and uptaken and interpreted by everyone else. It takes social and cultural knowledge to decode and judge, whether grand, regional, literary, whimsical, sectarian, clever or pretentious, according to circumstance. My first general point, then, is that house names express social affiliations.

> In the straight streets planted with trees and fringed with grass plots stand the modern houses where the families live. These houses have quite different sorts of names from the old houses. The modern names are written on the garden gates or slung in fretwork over the porch. *The Cedars, Cumfy, Dunromin*, the more original *Dunsekin, Trottalong*. There is the house that is called *Home Rails* (a happy investment, fortune-founding?). There is *Deo Data* for the learned, *Villa Roma* for the travelled, *Portarlington Lodge* for the socially ambitious. Ella, Basil and Ronald live at *Elbasron*. There is also *Elasofton* which is 'not for sale' written backwards.
>
> Stevie Smith, 1949, *A London Suburb*[19]

Secondly, names have not always been names. There is a process of conversion in turning the noun *heorot* into the meadhall name *Heorot*, or the Irish peerage of the Earl of Portarlington into *Portarlington Lodge*. *Dunroamin* is a fossilised verb phrase, *Deo Data* and *Villa Roma* are sourced in Latin and Italian, *Cumfy* is a clipped adjective used as a proper noun, *Elbasron* is a twist on the uncoupling and recoupling of placenames.[20] Sunnyside entered the housing name-stock via a prepositional phrase used by a community of practice, farmers living in a specific set of geographical circumstances dividing up their land. In each case a linguistic process is involved in turning something into a name. Nor do names necessarily remain as names; they can become common nouns (*jack, robin, derrick*), or signify things other than, or as well as, the building they denote (*Chatham House*). The phrase *sunny side* was used in various nineteenth-century idioms: 'the sunny side of things' (1831), 'to present the sunny side of the picture' (1840), to live on 'the sunny side of the wall' (1858),

---

[18] Miles (2000: 16–17) dates the fashion for naming terraced houses with second-element *-ville* as apposite for attached houses to around 1900, in response to the prevalence of second-element *villa* for detached houses.

[19] 'Home Rails, which are now in effect British Transport stock' *Railway Gazette International* 87 (1947: 744); The poet Stevie Smith spent almost her entire life in a London suburb at No. 1, Avondale Road, Palmers Green, N13. 'Her own fortune was invested in Home Rails, and most ardently did she beg her niece to imitate her' E. M. Forster (1910: 15).

[20] The Edinburgh and Leith telephone directory of 1926–7 has the as-yet-unclipped form *Dunroaming*. My thanks to Charlie Cook for this reference.

to be 'the sunny side of thirty' (1865), eggs 'sunny side up' (1901).[21] *Sunnyside* was the title of a film of 1919, in which Charlie Chaplin worked in the fictional village of Sunnyside. When Wall Street crashed in 1929, *Keep Your Sunnyside Up, Up* became a hit from the film *Sunny Side Up*, written by Buddy De Sylva, Lew Brown and Ray Henderson, sung by Janet Gaynor. *On the Sunny Side of the Street* was a hit from Lew Leslie's Broadway *International Revue* of 1930, written by Jimmy McHugh and Dorothy Fields and sung by Ted Lewis. The sun-loving 1930s brought into fashion the flat roof on which to sunbathe,[22] the development of sun-tan oil,[23] the lilo, and lidos in which to float on them,[24] and architectural *moderne*'s sunburst motif decorating front-garden gates and doors. Names are not context-free; all the nineteenth-century and early twentieth-century *sunnyside* idioms and associations combined to keep the name Sunnyside buoyant once it had become established as a house name. Becoming a name, and ceasing to be a name, may form part of a word's trajectory over time. The temporal and cultural context is an essential part of the biography.

I fell into the trap of anachronism when I jotted down my perusings of Post Office directories:[25]

Ellis, Charles, Foo Choo Villas, Cambridge Road, Turnham Green (1870)
Archbutt, John, Nutty Hagg, Clapham Road, Wandsworth (1870)
Buonaparte, Prince Lucien, Alder Grove Lodge, High Beech, Loughton (1870)
Scott, General, Sunnyside, Ealing Green (1872)
Whittaker, William James, Wee-Neste, Endsleigh Rd, Ealing (1889)

---

[21] *OED* sunny, *adj.* 5. b.
[22] The word *sunbather* first attested *Daily Express*, 14 January 1929: 19 'The groups of Lido sun-bathers.' *OED* sun *n.*[1] C3.a.
[23] The phrase *sun-tan oil* first attested *Beautycraft*, 19 July 1934: 1. *OED* sun-tan, *n.* (and *adj.*) 1. b.; the word *suntanning* first attested in the Baltimore *Sun*, 5 September 1932 'The millions busy today suntanning themselves'.
[24] *OED* Li-Lo, *n.*, trademark patented by P. B. Cow and Co. Ltd. of Cheapside, 16 September 1936. *OED* Lido, *n.* gives /'liːdəʊ/ pronunciation only, but as a frequenter of Ruislip Lido in the 1970s I can attest 'laɪdəʊ/. *OED* first attestation *Morning Post*, 16 July 1930: 5/4 'The question of the safety of bathers in the Serpentine "Lido" was raised at an inquest'; *Daily Express* 16 October 1931: 8/2 '£60,000 lido for England. The bathing pool and sun-bathing beach which the Hastings Corporation has just decided to construct'. An advertisement in the *Illustrated London News* of 16 June 1928 for the hotels of the Venice Lido says: 'The Lido is well named. It is the perfect natural playground of Europe', showing that by 1928 the word *lido* already signified an outdoor swimming-pool and recreation area.
[25] Foo Choo ('a town of much commercial importance . . . the capital of the province of Fokien . . . the far-famed bridge of *Foo-choo-foo*, of which the splendour and magnificence is celebrated over the whole empire' *The Saturday Magazine*, 4 February 1843, No. 680, 41) is an earlier spelling for Fuzhou. 'Nutty Hagg. – There is a cottage and about 4½ acres, including a new allotment of 1 A. 2 R. 4 P. added thereto in 1807, situate in the township of Byers Green, and called Nutty Hagg' (in Bishop Auckland, Darlington, Mackenzie and Ross (1834: 297); *hagg* is the Northern pronunciation of the Southern *haw*, OE *haga* 'enclosure': 'At Aukland Castle, the park was formerly called the Hagg (*English Dialect Dictionary*, hag (g *sb.*1)). Prince Louis Lucien Buonaparte (1813–91), linguist, was Napoleon's nephew; Bonaparte, Louis Lucien (1813–1891): Geoffrey West, https://doi.org/10.1093/ref:odnb/96959.

My present-day cultural experience led me to regard Sunnyside as a post-war, semi-detached or terraced house name, more aligned with the lower social classes than the higher ones, so I was surprised to find it as early as 1872, and unfitting for someone with as much social gravitas as a General, in so unsuburban a location as Ealing Green, which is picturesque even today. That these assumptions were wrong is demonstrated in the following pages, but the cultural knowledge that led me to make these assumptions is only revealed as transient when it is questioned. Middle-class British native speakers have an unspoken collective cultural understanding that Hampton Court is not naff although Bide-a-wee is, with Fernlea somewhere in the middle. Words only mean what they mean in social context, and the name a person chooses for their home conveys information to contemporaries about social status, values and aspirations. Those social connotations are not obviously appar-ent across time and place, and what follows is my interpretation of the plentiful data still legible on fanlights and doorframes lining the streets of older residential neighbourhoods.

As a final surprise: as well as houses, this is a book of shop and pub names, and also a record of quarrels. Many arguments run through these chapters, from the large-scale, such as the many Christian sects that split off from the established church; to the personal, such as Sir James Murray's irritation with Sir Walter Scott. This too was something I had not expected, but language comes back to usage, and quarrelling is something that people who live in houses are inclined to do.

1

THE EARLIEST LONDON
HOUSE NAMES

I begin with a survey of the earliest London house names, which were quite unlike *Fernlea, Wee Neste*, and *Dunroamin*, and also quite unlike *Holkham Hall* and *Chatham House*. Evidence for the earliest London house names is taken from early wills and deeds and presented in Appendix 1, which contains 294 house names from before 1400 (excluding religious houses, abbeys, churches, monasteries, convents, almshouses and the like, and also excluding livery company halls). Such early wills and deeds were written in Medieval Latin and, to a lesser extent, Anglo-Norman French, although house names began to be written in English in such documents long before the convention of writing the rest of the text in monolingual English. The earliest names are *Ceolmundingchaga* ('Ceolmund's haw') 857, *Hpætmundes stan* ('Hwætmund's stone (house)') 889, *Paules byri* ((St) Paul's dwelling house') 900s, and *Wermanecher* ('Wærman's block') 1044, but these are all copies found in documents written several centuries later. It is not until *Stæninga haga* ('people of Staines' haw') in a document written between 1051 and 1056, that a contemporary witness occurs. The earliest London house names therefore date, strictly speaking, to the eleventh century, but there is no reason to doubt our earliest witnesses.

Garrioch (1994: 21–2), surveying what he calls the 'meagre literature' on the subject, says that the earliest northern European evidence of building names dates from the thirteenth century (I say 'building' rather than 'house' because people lived where they worked, which in an urban environment was above and behind the seld, shop, brewhouse, inn, bakery, mill, tavern, or other commercial premises). Haslam however disagrees, showing that in an English urban context, names crystalised earlier. He demonstrates with *Wermanecher*, which Eilert Ekwall, the great Swedish place-name scholar, assumed was agricultural:

> Ekwall's interpretation of the meaning of Wermanecher as the 'field, arable land' of Wærman (Ekwall 1954, 38) . . . is open to doubt. It had shops and stalls, and was connected to a wharf . . . and was described as a soke (soca) in the 13th century . . . The connotation of 'soke' in this case . . . is supported by several instances in Domesday where various tenants-in-chief held 'acres' in Wallingford . . . all of which contained a number of tenements. In these instances these 'acres' can best be interpreted as high status sokes, and clearly had nothing to do with agricultural activities.
>
> (Haslam 2010: 120)

Wermanecher was the designation of a number of buildings – holdings or 'tenements' – forming a specific commercial unit. But such names are rare. In early wills and deeds the main way of identifying property was by name of the householder and parish alone rather than by name of the house:

> *Robto de Lintoñ domū suam cū omībȝ ptinenī qᵃ m huit ī pochia scī Albañ de Wudestrate*
>
> 1252, HR 1/8

'Robert of Linton his house with all belongings which he has owned in the parish of St Alban Wood Street'

> *Robto le Wirdrawere totam írā suam cū domibȝ supedificat˙ & ptinenī qᵃ m habuerunt in Sopereslane in parochia scī Pancracij*
>
> 1252, HR 1/21

'to Robert the Wiredrawer all his land with the houses built on it and the belongings which they (Sir John and Cristina his wife – LCW) have owned in Sopers Lane in the parish of St Pancras'

Together, citizens' place of origin and occupation were productive in forming thirteenth-century surnames; where they were from and what they did was what was needed for ascertaining rights of ownership:

> *in venella que vocatᵒʳ Cockeslane in poch scī Sepulcri extʳ Neugate Londoñ . . . do lego Witło filio meo domū illam cū ptinent˙ suis in Cockeslana qᵃ m Egelina la wympel wasshestere qᵒndam de me tenuit*
>
> 1301, HR 30/20

'in the lane which is called Cocks Lane in the parish of St Sepulchre without Newgate London . . . I give and bequeath to William my son that house with its belongings in Cocks Lane which Egelina the wimple washer lately held from me'

Robert and Egelina's forenames and their occupations as wiredrawer and wimple washer, together with the name of the street and parish, were the legal requirements for identifying the house in question. The combination of tenant's name, street and parish remained default for several centuries, with the name of the householder and the parish the primary identifiers, the street less essential. In some cases, the name of the dwelling place shifted into becoming the name of the householder:

> *matiłł atte vine vxⁱ quondam Johis atte Rose de Londoñ . . . lego matiłɖ Nepote mee relicte Johis Ram om̄ia & singła teñ mea cū gardinis venellis & cū omibȝ alijs suis ptiñ . . . que heo tam in p̄dcâ poch scī Edmundi de Lumbardestrete qᵃ m in pochia scī Benedicti de Grēschirch Londoñ*
>
> 1349, HR 76/201

'Matilda at the Vine late wife of John at the Rose of London . . . I leave to Matilda my niece widow of John Ram each and every one of my tenements with gardens, lanes and with all their other belongings . . . which I have both in the aforesaid parish of St Edmund Lombard Street and in the parish of St Benet Gracechurch London'

In early deeds and wills, the main terms for buildings that people dwelt in were Latin *domus* 'house', *tenementum* 'freehold house + appurtenances (belongings)', *aula* 'hall'; Anglo-Norman French *messuage* 'house + appurtenances', *rent* 'house + appurtenances yielding income'; Old English *burh, byrig* 'bury, manor house + appurtenances', *heall* 'hall', *haga* 'house + appurtenances', *hus* 'house', *seld* 'bazaar, shop containing multiple retailers', *sceoppa* 'shop'.[1] The Anglo-Norman term *manor* seems to have been a later usage. It occurs with property in rural Westminster rather than the built-up City of London, and is only found in monolingual English contexts after 1300, although it was used earlier in Latin contexts and so this perception might just be due to lack of evidence. The City was an urban environment by the twelfth century but most of Westminster was still agricultural – I have included the Westminster manors of *Eybury, La Neyth, le Hyde* and *Rosemond*, which lie under present-day Victoria and Pimlico. I have deemed relevant everything that was indicated as residential either in the source document or in historians' assessment of a source document, including shops, selds, mills, brewhouses and taverns, as these were also people's homes. It would be anachronistic to exclude *la Stoorhous*, *le Forge, Mewes*, on the grounds that the name expressed a function, or *Peinteselde, la Cornereschoppe, Drinkewaterestauerne*, on the grounds that the name expressed a commercial activity, or *Castle Baynard, Tower of Monfychet, la Tour Servat*, on the grounds that castles and towers were not for commoners, or *Kote, Loge, le Posternehawe* on the grounds that such buildings were subsidiary to the main event (the lodge protecting another building, the back garden having a more important building in front of it). Haws are particularly problematical as they signified ground space as well as the buildings on them, so I have included haws only if a house is mentioned. This has led me to include '*illud teñ quod ħeo in le Portehawe*', for example, but to exclude haws such as '*suū curtilagiū qui Iacet int'<. . .> de la maderhawe*' (HR 16/111 1285–6). This may lead to the exclusion of haws that did in fact have houses, and there are, inevitably, inconsistencies. The requirement that a house be mentioned (or a historian opine that a house was present, as is the case with the early haws) has led to the inclusion of just eight haws, although there were many more in both Westminster and the City.[2]

---

[1] *MED* mesuage (n.) 'residence, dwelling house', and see also *OED* curtilage, n. 'small piece of ground attached to a dwelling-house; the area attached to and containing a dwelling-house and its outbuildings'; *OED* haw, *n.* 1.a. 'messuage, enclosure'; *MED* haue (n.(1))(a) 'enclosure, yard'; Ekwall (1954: 37) translates *haga* directly as 'town house'; *OED* bury, *n.* 'a manor house, or large farm'; borough, *n.* 1. b. 'a court, a manor-house'; *MED* burgh (n.(1.)) 3. (b) 'dwelling, mansion; property within a town'; see also Ekwall (1954: 37 (haw), 194–7 (bury)); *MED* rent(e (n.) 2a. 'a dwelling place for which rent is paid, a tenement'; *MED* maner (n.(1) 'mansion and estate'.

[2] Similarly, buries proliferated outside the City but I have included only non-Westminster/City buries if they were close by (*ffynesbury*) or if their precise whereabouts is uncertain (*Achiesburia, Musterlingebur, Northbī*). From a linguistic point of view ever more distant manorial place-names –

Of the earliest pre-1200 London house names, which are *Ceolmundingchaga,*
Hƿætmundes stan, Paules byri, Wermanecher, Stæninga haga, Aldremanesberi,
Bassingeshage, Blanckesapeltunā, Musterlingebur, Lodebure, Prestbure, three are
haws and five are buries.[3] All eleven pre-1200 house names are qualified by the
names of their owners, Ceolmund, Hwætmund, St Paul's Cathedral, Wærman,
the people of Staines, an Alderman, the people of Basing, Blanck, someone from the
little monastery at Mouster in Brittany, Hlotha, and a priest. The formula [owner's
name + haw/bury] was the predominant way of naming London houses before
1200, so far as can be deduced from the data. The other names conveyed a description of the house (*stan*), the activity conducted there (*apeltun*), and the rank of
the owner (*aldreman, prest*). After the haws and buries came halls and selds: *la*
Blakehalle, Stapledehalle, Redehalle, la Coppedhalle, le Hoppindehalle, la Ledenehalle;
Andoureselde, Tanñselde, Peinteselde, Wyncestre selde, Depeselde, Brantefeld selde, all
attested before 1300. Keene, reconstructing the thirteenth-century shop frontages
on Cheapside, defines selds as bazaars behind the shopfronts in which individual traders kept benches, cupboards, and chests from which they displayed their
wares.[4] Like the haws and buries, early seld names record the name of the owner,
the appearance of the seld, and the activity carried out at the seld.[5] Old English *hus*
'house' occurs as the name of three buildings before 1300, all dating from the 1290s:
Wolhous, Stonhus, le Taninghus. Shops as such are rarely named but *La Corner*
schoppe occurs in a manuscript of 1278–9 and is relatively common thereafter.
Although numbers are low, the picture is steady: haw, bury, seld, hall and house
were the predominant early house-naming nouns, with haw, bury and seld ceasing
to be productive at the end of the Old English period.

Barnsbury, Brondesbury, Canonbury, Gunnersbury, Highbury, leading on to further, non-bury manors
on the outskirts such as *Ruggemere* and *Tothale* – would have resulted in rather more personal names
and landscape descriptors, but their presence would not bring any further naming categories to light.
[3] See Appendix 1 for details of dating; Ekwall (1954: 37, 38, 54, 57).
[4] *OED* seld, *n.*, metathetic form of *setl* 'sitting-place, seat'.
[5] For details of the individual selds, see Keene (1985b: 12–13; 2006: 131–5; 2008: 205, whence the
information below is taken); Harding (2008: 26); also Schofield (1994: 55–6). Cheapside selds extended
to a depth of 30m from the street frontage and were commonly about 7m wide. Shortly before 1250, a
seld on the corner of Cheapside and Soper Lane contained sites for twenty or thirty traders, although
this was probably larger than average. By 1300 there were about four hundred shops in Cheapside with
perhaps four thousand retail units in selds behind them. The trading area of the shop itself consisted of
the window by the door fronting onto the street with a let-down stall in front, and a projecting sloping
pentice roof above it. The shopfront was very small, less than 2m wide and 3m front to back, with a
street door less than half a metre wide. Shoppers would not customarily have entered the street-front
ground-floor room of the house at all, as shopkeepers – especially the female members of the family – sat out by the stall. With regard to the rest of the house, Cheapside's street-front houses around
1300 consisted of two rooms over a cellar, rising to two or three storeys, with selds and outbuildings such as stables and latrines behind. The ground floor housed the shopfront and workroom, the
main living room was on the first floor, and chambers and garrets were above, divided into multiple
occupancy.

The present-day notion of a house does not correspond well to early London building names, where the named unit could be larger or smaller than a single dwelling. Those larger than a single dwelling, of which the most frequent is *tenementum*, are perhaps best translated as a block, a group of contiguous buildings consisting of commercial premises at ground floor and cellar level with dwellings above. Accordingly it is not contradictory to find in a deed of 1331 that *le Brokeneselde* was a tavern, or that in 1399 *le Wellehous* was a brewhouse, or that in 1311–12 *Kote* was a shop, as the tavern, brewhouse and shop in question belonged to larger units. Units smaller than a house were also named, *Rosemunde* being the name of a chamber in the City in 1309 as well as a manor in Westminster in 1333. Cellars (*le Depeceler, Helle, le Holceler*), solars (*le Wynsoler*), garrets (*la West'ne Garite*) and lofts (*la Blakelofte, le Webbeloft*) received names. Indeed the bottoms (cellars), ground floors (shops, selds), middles (solars, cameras), and tops (garrets, lofts) of houses can all be found named in early wills and deeds. Different parts of a holding could be known by separate names, or have alternative names:

> totū tenementū nr̄m̄ cū oībȝ suis p̄tinent' quod vocat'ᵒ Eldehalle cum tribȝ shopis in p̄te occidentali dc̄i tenementi et qᵃ tuor solaria cū duobȝ Celarijs cū p̄tinentijs que vocant'ᵒ le Scot in pochia sc̄i Michis ad Ripâ Regine London

> 1335 HR 63/80

'the whole of our tenement with all its belongings which is called Eldehalle with three shops in the western part of the said tenement and four solars with two cellars with belongings which are called le Scot in the parish of St Michael Queenhithe London'

> totū illud teñ meū vocatū le Depeceler siue le Melle atte hope . . . in vico vocat' Tamysestret' in pochia sc̄i Michis apud Ripam Regine

> 1355–6 HR 83/58

'the whole of my tenement called le Depeceler or le Melle atte hope . . . in the street called Thames Street in the parish of St Michael Queenhithe'

> in venella & pochia sc̄i Laurencij in Iudaismo Londoñ . videłt de teñ cum suis p̄tiñ quod p̄ aliquos vocat'ᵒ la Redebrewehous & p̄ aliquos vocat'ᵒ la Rededore

> 1377 HR 106/142

'in the lane and parish of St Lawrence Jewry London, to wit a tenement with its belongings which by some is called la Redebrewehous and by others is called la Rededore'

The name of the tavern part of a holding often dominated over the whole:

> totam illam tabnam cum omībȝ suis p̄tiñ vocatā le Holceler in pochia sc̄e Margarete de Breggestrete Londoñ

> 1371–2 HR 98/51

'the whole of that tavern with all its belongings called le Holceler in the parish of St Margaret Bridge Street London'

& in vno teñ cum shopis , celar' solar' & suis ptiñ vocato Cherchegatestaú'ne situato in pochia sc̄i Leonardi de Estchep Londoñ

1369–70 HR 97/173

'and in one tenement with shops, cellars solars and their belongings called Cherchegatestauerne situated in the parish of St Leonard Eastcheap London'

It is not until well on into the seventeenth century that evidence for shop names becomes as plentiful as that for tavern names.

Name elements

In terms of internal structure, the earliest house names consisted of a compound of two elements, a personal name + *haw* or *bury*. Pre-thirteenth century compound house-name second elements reference both the construction: *bury* (manor house) (12 examples), *stan* (1) (a stone house), and the plot: *haw* (8), *acre* (1) (a block), *appleton* (1) (an apple orchard). Examples with these second elements in the database of house names before 1400 in Appendix 1 are as follows:[6]

bury:
Paules byri [3]
Aldremanesberi [6]
Musterlingebur [9]
Lodebure [10]
Prestebure [11]
Achiesburia [12]
Northbī [16]
Sabelinesbir' [18]
Bokerelesberi [26]
Blemondisberi [31]

haw:
Ceolmundingchaga [1]
Stæninga haga [5]
Bassingeshage [7]
la Bordhawe [17]
Barndehaw [21]

acre:
Wermanecher [4]

apple orchard:
Blanckesapeltunā [8]

stone:
Hpætmundes stan [2]

The main thirteenth-century second elements in house-name compounds are *house* (34), *seld* (21), *hall* (21), *rent* (8), *door* (5). Examples with these second elements in Appendix 1 are:

---

[6] Compound names are presented in date order as given in the database of house names in Appendix 1, with their database numbers. Ambiguous names are omitted from the analysis.

house:
Wolhous [43]
le Taninghus [48]
Stonhus [50]
la Monetere House [60]
Bonsieshous or *Bousieshous* [61]
la Tau̯nehous [68]
Bordenhous [75]
Bruggehous [82]
ʒylynghous [93]
le Stuſhous [95]
Gladewyneshouse [100]
la Redebakhous [102]
le Tawynghous [105]
le Crokedhous [113]
le Wellehous [116]
Crouchehous [123]
la Newewodehous [130]
la Longehous [141]
le Colebrewous' [145]
Tymbirhous [150]
la Scholdynghous [151]
le Brewehous [153]
le Wachouce [158]
Beuereshous [163]
le Stuwehous [174]
la Weyhous [176]
le Tanhous [178]
le Heghehous [181]
le ffishous [201]
le Thoroughous [224]
la Redebrewehous [225]
Tylhous [244]
Deyhous [246]
la Stoorhous' [280]

seld:
seldā de Andouer' [27]
Tann̄selde [30]
Peinteselde [36]
le Seelde [37]
Wyncestre selde [39]

Depeselde [42]
Brantefeld selde [47]
Seyntemartynseld [53]
Fridayselde [64]
la Brodeselde [78]
Hauerilleselde [94]
Whitawyeresselde [101]
le Brokenselde [107]
Gerdleresselde [109]
Berneselde [119]
Arraces selde [133]
Aerneselde [148]
Anketynesselde [169]
le Whiteselde [179]
le Crowneselde [247]
Godschepsceld [263]

hall:
la Blakehalle [14]
Stapledehalle [33]
Redehalle [34]
Coppedhalle [38]
le Hoppindehalle [41]
la Ledenehalle [45]
Audeleeshalle [55]
la fflint halle [66]
Heyroneshalle [70]
Dyneshemanhalle [74]
Cokedonhalle [76]
la Ryngedehalle [110]
Eldehalle [114]
Giffardeshalle [138]
le Yuyhalle [147]
Seint Nicholas Halle [154]
Pauedehalle [157]
Gysors Halle [160]
Bakkewellehalle [172]
ffeytishalle [174]
le Cornerhalle [256]

rent:
la Newerente [25]
Prestenerente [125]

Pecokkesrente [136]
Paťnosťrent [210]
la Olderente [241]
le Walsherente [257]
le Blakerente [275]
Stonerente [290]

door:
le Brodedore [44]

le Isnendore [73]
le Ernedore [88]
le Rededore [124]
þe lyoun atte Dore [189]

shop:
la Corner<schoppe> [28]

repair (AN, 'home'):
Beaurepair [49]

By contrast with the older second-element nouns, only *inn* 'private residence' (10) and *tavern* (4) showed much productivity:

inn:
Topfeldes In [83]
Pulteneys In [194]
le Newin [198]
Blosmeshyn [213]
Bacūnysyn [222]
Lyncolnesynne [232]
Trompouresynne [262]
Montieofysyn [266]
Topclyuesyn [279]
Greysyn [284]

tavern:
Drinkewaťestauerne [99]
le Newetauerne [191]
Cherchegatestaůne [202]
Colchestrestaůne [248]

porch:
le Ledeneporche [146]
le Longeporche [209]
Spaldyngporche [293]

gate:
le Blakegate [144]
le Brodegate [152]
le Grenegate [294]

loft:
la Blakelofte [67]
le Webbeloft [77]

cellar:
le Holceler [111]
le Depeceler [167]

tenement:
Roustenēmt [134]
lawestenemēt [234]

mill:
Horsmelle [46]
Crachemille [219]

alley:
Leggesaleye [271]
le Kyngesaleye (the name of
    tenements) [278]

harbour:
Coldha<bber> [56]

garret:
la Wesťne Garite [63]

salle ('hall'):
le Rouge Sale [89]

court:
la Bas Court [104]

tower:
Suruetistour [195]

pentice ('lean-to, porch'):
Ye Ledenpentitȝ [129]

solar ('upper room'):
le Wynsoler [184]

entry:
Longeentre [182]

abbey:
le Coldabbeye (the name of a
    tenement) [187]

brewern ('brewery'):
Powlesbrewerne [206]

Compound house names in London house names before 1400 followed one of
four templates:

1. Name of householder + type of house (whether the name of an individual, or
groups of individuals such as priests, merchants from Andover or Winchester, or
corporate owners such as St Paul's Cathedral): 55

Ceolmundingchaga [1]
Hpætmundes stan [2]
Paules byri [3]
Wermanecher [4]
Stæninga haga [5]
Aldremanesberi [6]
Bassingeshage [7]
Blanckesapeltunā [8]
Musterlingebur [9]
Lodebure [10]
Prestebure [11]
Achiesburia [12]
Sabelinesbir' [18]
Castrum de Baynard [22]
Tᵒʳris de Monfychet [24]
Bokerelesberi [26]
seldā de Andoueʳ [27]
Blemondisberi [31]
Wyncestre selde [39]
Brantefeld selde [47]
Seyntemartynseld [53]
Audeleeshalle [55]
Heyroneshalle [70]
Dyneshemanhalle [74]
Cokedonhalle [76]
Topfeldes In [83]
Hauerilleselde [94]
Drinkewatestauerne [99]

Gladewyneshouse [100]
Prestenerente [125]
Arraces selde [133]
Roustenēmt [134]
Pecokkesrente [136]
Eltammismes [137]
Giffardeshalle [138]
Gysors Halle [160]
Beuereshous [163]
Anketynesselde [169]
Bakkewellehalle [172]
Pulteneys In [194]
Suruetistour [195]
Powlesbrewerne [206]
Patʰhostʰrent [210]
Blosmeshyn [213]
Bacūnysyn [222]
Lyncolnesynne [232]
Lawestenemēt [234]
Colchestrestauʰne [248]
le Walsherente [257]
Trumpouresynne [262]
Godschepsceld [263]
Montieofysyn [266]
Topclyuesyn [279]
Greysyn [284]
Spaldyngporche [293]

2. Visual descriptor + type of house: 49

la Blakehalle [14]	*la Newewodehous* [130]
la Newerente [25]	*la Longehous* [141]
Stapledehalle [33]	*le Blakegate* [144]
Redehalle [34]	*le Ledeneporche* [146]
Coppedhalle [38]	*le Yuyhalle* [147]
Depeselde [42]	*Aerneselde* [148]
le Brodedore [44]	*Tymbirhous* [150]
la Ledenehalle [45]	*le Brodegate* [152]
Beaurepair [49]	*Pauedehalle* [157]
Stonhus [50]	*le Depeceler* [167]
la fflint Halle [66]	*ffeytishalle* [174]
la Blakelofte [67]	*le Whiteselde* [179]
le Isnendore [73]	*le Heghehous* [181]
Bordenhous [75]	*Longeentre* [182]
la Brodeselde [78]	*le Wynsoler* [184]
le Ernedore [88]	*le Newetauerne* [191]
le Rouge Sale [89]	*le Newin* [198]
la Redebakhous [102]	*le Longeporche* [209]
le Brokeneselde [107]	*Crachemille* [219]
la Ryngedehalle [110]	*le Thoroughous* [224]
le Crokedhous [113]	*la Redebrewehous* [225]
Eldehalle [114]	*la Olderente* [241]
Crouchehous [123]	*le Blakerente* [275]
la Rededore [124]	*Stonerente* [290]
Ye Ledenpentiȝ [129]	*le Grenegate* [294]

In this second group, the following subdivisions are apparent:

2a. 'approach to the house':

le Brodedore, le Isnendore, le Ernedore, le Rededore, le Blakegate, le Brodegate, le Grenegate, le Ledeneporche, le Longeporche, Spaldyngporche, Longeentre (and *þe lyoun atte Dore* belongs to this group for semantic reasons, although it is not a compound noun): 12

2b. 'building material':

la Ledenehalle, ye Ledenpentiȝ, le Ledeneporche, Stonhus, la fflint Halle, Stonerente, Pauedehalle, Bordenhous, la Newewodehous, Tymbirhous, le Isnendore: 11

2c. 'coloured':

Redehalle, la Redebakhous, le Rouge Sale, le Rededore, la Redebrewehous, la Blakehalle, la Blakelofte, le Blakegate, le Blakerente, le Whiteselde, le Grenegate: 11

2d: 'praise':

> *Beaurepair* (*AND* bel a.1 'beautiful' + repair s.2 'home'), *ffeytishalle* (*MED* fetis (adj.)) 'elegant'), *le Wynsoler*: either Old English *wyn* 'delightful' (*MED* win (adj.)), or possibly Old Welsh *gwyn*, which undergoes frontal mutation to *wyn* 'white'[7]: 3

3. Occupation of householder/purpose of building + type of house: 26

Tanñselde [30]	*le Wachouce* [158]
Wolhous [43]	*Horsmelle* [46]
le Taninghus [48]	*la Weyhous* [176]
la Monetere House [60]	*le ffishous* [201]
la Tauᵒnehous [68]	*le Brewehous* [155]
le Webbeloft [77]	*Tylhous* [244]
le Stufhous [95]	*Deyhous* [246]
ʒylynghous [93]	*le Seelde* [37]
Whitawyeresselde [101]	*le Tanhous* [178]
le Tawynghous [105]	*le Stuwehous* [274]
Gerdleresselde [109]	*la Stoorhous* [280]
le Wellehous [116]	*le Steelyerde* (German merchants'
la Scholdynghous [151]	*stahlhof* 'sample-yard') [249]

4. Locative descriptor relative to something else + type of house: 8

Northbī [16]	*la Bas Court* [104]
la Corner<schoppe> [28]	*le Postᵒnehawe* [108]
la Westᵒne Garite [63]	*Cherchegatestauᵒne* [202]
Fridayselde [64]	*le Cornerhalle* [256]

The compound names in group 2 (visual descriptor + type of house), together with the compound names in group 4 (locative descriptor relative to something else + type of house), make it likely that this sort of visual-descriptor naming came about by public consensus rather than by householder's individual choice. A hall covered with ivy known as *Yuyhalle*, a house with a broad door known as *le Brodedore*, a seld that was deep known as *Depeselde*, a house with a leaden pentice called *Ye Ledenpentitʒ* – these names served as directive addresses and were comprehensible as such to everyone looking at the premises.[8] Only the three names in

---

[7] As in *Sir Gawain and the Green Knight*'s 'wynne halle' (see Meecham-Jones 2018:114) – if so, *le Wynsoler* may be one of the first literary-reference names, or named by someone with Welsh connections.

[8] I have interpreted first elements *aerne, erne*, as 'eagle' (*OED* erne, *n.* 'eagle') rather than 'building' (*OED* earn, *n.1* 'building, house, dwelling'), even though the spellings allow both interpretations. This is because the reflex of OE *earn* largely occurred in second-element position in name compounds: 'In Old English (and Middle English) chiefly as the second element in compounds, as Old English *bæcern* bakehouse' (*OED* earn, *n.1*), attested in the database in Appendix 1 by *Powlesbrewerne*, 'brewhouse belonging to St Paul's Cathedral'. The erne and lion in question are likely to have surmounted

group 2d might convey a more personal subjectivity, expressing the point of view of the owner.

Simplex names

Single-element house names are not found until 1220–2, '*ipsam terram et domum que fuit Diane*', also recorded as 1407–8 '*hospiciū Deane*', 1452 '*Camera Diane*':

> *Diane, Grangia* (a messuage rather than a barn), *Saueye, Wyuelastone, la Burgate* (I interpret both of these as placename/surnames, rather than as two-element compounds), *Helle, le Halles, Mewes, Herlewyne, Rosemunde, Stoples, Kote, le Stokkes, Loge, la Hole, Viene, de Bethlehem, le Bretasse, la Goutere, le Hyde, atte Vine, la Pirie* (a tenement as well as a street), *la fforge, Bekenhᵃm, Littel Watte, le Cage, La Neyth, Parys, Estlandia, Gascoign, Halstede* (I interpret this as a placename/surname), *le Seelde, le Mot, le Caban, le Voute*. (36)

1a. Place-names, either the surname of the householder or a group of merchants hailing therefrom (9):

> *Saueye* (Savoy), *Wyuelastone* (Woollaston, Staffordshire), *Parys* (Paris), *la Burgate* (Burgate, Surrey), *Viene* (Vienna), *de Bethlehem, Bekenhᵃm* (Beckenham, Kent), *Estlandia* (Eastland, the Baltic), *Gascoign* (Gascony, France), *Halstede* (there were Halstedes in Essex, Kent and Leicestershire)

1b. Other surnames (1):

> *Herlewyne*

1c. Forenames (3):

> *Diane, Rosemunde, Litel Watte*

2. Visual descriptor of building (14):

> *Helle, Stoples, la Hole, le Bretasse, la Goutere, atte Vine, la Pirie, le Cage, le Mot, Kote, Loge, le Caban, le Voute*

3. Occupation of householder/purpose of building (4):

> *Grangia, Mewes, la fforge, le Seelde*

Simplex house names expressed the same information as compound ones: personal name of householder, visual descriptors, and occupational terms.

---

the door ring. This was known as a *hagodai* 'have-good-day', Salzman (1952: 299); *MED* hagodai (n.) 'ring forming the handle for raising the latch on a door', as appears in the list of door-furniture bought by the Merchant Taylor's Company in 1399: 'cliefs lacchis cacchis hokis hengis hagodaies' (Guildhall Library, London, MS 34048/1, 1397–1445, *Merchant Taylors' Company Accounts*, fo 7v), presumably so-called after the words said upon opening or closing the door.

Punctuated equilibrium:
a new development in house naming

However this name-stock was to change radically in the fourteenth century, not because the three main categories of householder, house appearance and house usage fell out of use – they did not, but because another category accelerated. Between 1100 and 1300 London grew from being two times more populous than the next city in the kingdom to three or four times greater, and by the early sixteenth century, four or five times more populous. Late thirteenth-century London is estimated at having 80,000 or more inhabitants (Keene 2006: 125; 1995: 12), so it is not surprising that this naming change, which was an expansion of an already-existing low-frequency name pattern, should be visible in its buildings. I have already mentioned the meadhall in *Beowulf* named *Heorot* 'hart'. In eleventh-century Winchester there was a house named *Hauoc* 'hawk', which von Feilitzen notes 'is the earliest example of the name on independent record' (that is, as a simplex name, rather than as one element of a compound place-name such as in Hawkley, Hants).[9] *Heorot* and *Hauoc* align with a category not seen in London until the 1320s, which is houses named after the earthly, celestial and fabulous devices of heraldry. Prior to this date heraldry was the preserve of the nobility, and although the nobility were householders, they constituted a minority of the population. It is therefore to be expected that houses bearing the names of heraldic devices should have been infrequent. Yet fourteenth-century London examples of house names reflecting the sort of emblems found on heraldic devices went from none before 1320 to four in the 1320s: *Croweonethehop* 1323 ('Crow on the Hoop', the barrel-hoop surrounding the inn-sign), *le Kok* 1325 ('the Cock'), *le Meire* 1327–8 (kind of garment used in heraldry), *la Mariole* 1328–9 (figure of the Virgin Mary), with surnames presupposing a heraldically-named house a little earlier: *Atecok* (1282–3), *ate Sterre, atte Swan, atte Ramme, atte Rose* (1319).[10] This fourth category of heraldic names neither replaced the earlier personal, visually descriptive and occupational naming categories nor did it spread to all kinds of dwellings, as I shall show.

Here are the London heraldic house names from the database of pre-1400 house names in Appendix 1, starting from 1323 (79):[11]

---

[9] Two twelfth-century surveys of Winchester list houses named *Godbiete* (analysed by Löfvenberg as 'good bargain', from OE *seo gode begeate*), *Merewenehaia*, analysed by von Feilitzen as 'Maerwynn's haw', and *Hauok* (von Feilitzen 1976: 158–9; Biddle and Keene 1976a: 237; Biddle and Keene 1976b:, 337, 340; with onomastic contributions by Mattias Löfvenberg).

[10] *OED* hoop, *n.¹*, late Old English, 'circle of wood or flattened metal for binding together the staves of casks, tubs, etc.' 1.b. 'in tavern signs'; *MED* hop (n.) (b) 'a circular band used to support the sign outside a house or inn'.

[11] *Caponhors* (1258–9) excepted, see discussion in Appendix 1. I have placed *le Ernedore* (and *þe lyoun atte Dore*) in the 'visual descriptor' category but *Aerneselde* and *la Lyoun* in the 'heraldic' category. This

Croweonethehop [91]

le Kok [32]

le Meire [97]

la Mariole [98]

le George on the hoƥe [292]

Scotothehop [115]

atte Got [122]

le Bere toumbeth [128]

le Hors atte hope [132]

la Lyoun [139]

la Cardinaleshat [143]

ye Hert on ʒe hoƥ [156]

Aerneselde [148]

le Horssho [149]

Mayden en la Hope [159]

le Lamb atte Hoope [161]

le Bele on the Hoƥ [162]

le Ram onthehope [86]

le Taborer [164]

le Harpe [166]

le Sterre [80]

le Melle atte Hope [168]

Horshed [170]

Saraʒineshed [171]

la Bole [173]

le Catfithele [212]

the Keye of the Hoōp [177]

le Boreshede [190]

la Dragoun [188]

le Helm on ye Hoope [183]

le Thre legges [186]

le Whitehors [180]

le Castel atte hoôp [135]

le Swan othe Hop [85]

le Culuer on the hope [217]

le fflourdelys [291]

le Horn in the Hoƥ [192]

Pye on the hope [126]

le Bal on the hop [199]

le Ship on the Hope [200]

la Rauen [218]

la Worm on the hope [216]

le Harowe on ye houpe [211]

le Irenhope [215]

le Pecok on the houp [230]

le Vernycle [223]

le Mechele [223]

le Hood on the Hoop [229]

le Mayde on the Hoƥ [227]

le Swerd on the hoƥ [231]

Tabard [207]

le Glene on the hoôp [233]

Sadel [238]

Boor [239]

le Cherch on the hoƥ [236]

le Croune [237]

le Tonne [252]

le Herteshed on the hoop [251]

le Bere on the hoop [253]

the Cheker on the hope [254]

le Potte on the hope [255]

leʒ Thre Nonnes [272]

le Vnicorne [264]

le Crane [268]

the Cristofre on ye hope [260]

le Garland on the hoôp [259]

le Walssheman sur le hoôp [267]

le Sonne on the Hoôp [269]

le Griffoñ [270]

le Lampe on the hoôp [273]

le Herteshorne [286]

le Crowneselde [247]

le panyer del hoôp [281]

le Blakehors on the hope [282]

le Holebole [283]

le Katerine on the hope [285]

le Wollesak onthehoôp [289]

---

is because the former pair appear to reference door furniture – hagodays – rather than house signs (see fn. 8). Similarly, *le Walsherente* is in the 'name of householder' category, as referencing the rent belonging to a Welshman, but *le Walssheman sur le hoôp* is in the 'heraldic' category, along with *Scotothehop*.

Personal names constitute further evidence for heraldic house names. The names of Matilda's tenements in 1349 mentioned earlier (p. 13), if they had names, are not recorded, but her name, Matilda atte Vine, her late husband's name, John atte Rose, and the name of her niece's husband, John Ram, all reference house names. There was a London house named *atte Vyne* in 1346–7, a house named *le Ram onthehope* in 1353–4, and a house named *þe Rose* in 1422. Lucie and Rađi *Atecok* 1282–3 predate *le Kok* 1325; *Thom atte Ramme* 1319 predates *le Ram onthehope* 1353–4; *Wiłłs atte Redecok* 1343 predates *atte Rede Cok yn the pultrie* 1418–40; *Henr᷄ atte Swan* 1319 predates *le Swan othe Hop* 1363; *Rico ate Sterre* 1319 predates *le Sterre* 1354–5; *Alicia atte Harpe* 1355 predates *le Harpe* 1384–5. Further surnames presuppose house names that I have not found attested in London before 1400, such as *Wiłłm atte Redehoꝑ* 1343, *Thomas atte Hoke*, butcher, 1349 (Plea & Mem).

Lillywhite (1972: xvi) notes that many of these emblems have remained constant over long periods of time, and overlap domains. Emblems featured in coinage and medallions, royal insignia and heraldic blazonment, seals, watermarks, book and manuscript decorations, stained glass, masonry, tombs and monuments, furniture, jewellery, pilgrim's souvenirs, tapestry, fabric, weaponry, and ships' names as well as house names. What kind of house took a heraldic name in fourteenth-century London? (See Table 1.1)

Fourteenth-century heraldic names pertained to the overall scope of the holding, the block (*domus, tenementum, messuage*), also specifically to the commercial part of the holding (*selda*), and especially also to the brewhouse/alehouse/tavern part of the holding (*bracinum, taberna, hospitium*). These last terms were not interchangeable: the *hospitium* or inn provided refreshment for travellers; the *taberna* or tavern served wine, which was comparatively expensive; the *tenementum bracinum* or brewhouse brewed and sold ale but not wine; and the *domus bracinus* or alehouse was a humbler establishment that sold ale by the jug or cup, often in a shop or cellar (Carlin 2013: 460). Tellingly, heraldic names, and only heraldic names, took the prepositional phrase 'on the hoop': *le Brodedore on the hoop*, *le Stonhus on the hoop* and the like are not attested. Missing from the heraldic column are names for rooms within a house, and I have not noted any pre-fourteenth century halls or houses named [heraldic name + *haw, bury, house, hall*]: *Lionhaw, *Unicornbury, *Worm House, *Dragon Hall* and the like are not attested. These absences may be due a to a paucity of data, but it is more likely that they are significant, given events in the late eighteenth century when the heraldic names dropped out of use on all buildings except for pubs. Heraldic names, then, coupled with commercial premises only.

Barron may hold the explanation as to why houses with signs of the same animals, artifacts and earthly and heavenly bodies of heraldry increased at this point in time:

> In the fourteenth century the London merchants seem to have been a class apart: men who dressed in the long robes of clerics rather than the tunics and armour of knights, and

Table 1.1 Types of heraldic and non-heraldic fourteenth-century London premises

Head noun	Non-heraldic	Heraldic
domus ('house')	*domo vocat' le Tannereselde*	*domū cū shopa & suis ptinent' que vocatur la Mariole*
house	*Stonhus*	–
tenementum ('freehold house')	*teñ meū cū celar' solar' shopis & omībʒ suis ptiñ vocat' Gysors halle*	*vno tenemento vocat' le Lamb atte Hoope*
messuagium ('house + appurtenances')	*mesuagiū meū vocatū la Ryngedehalle*	*mesuagio . . . vocat' le Bere on the hoop̂*
aula ('hall')	*aulam vocatam Dyneshemanhalle*	–
hall	*la Blakehalle*	–
bury ('manor house')	*Paules byri*	–
haw ('enclosure')	*Ceolmundingchaga*	–
mansio ('mansion, house')	*vnâ mansionê . . . in le Walsherente*	*teñ . . . vocat' le lyon on the hope cū aleya shopis & alijs mansionibʒ eidem teñ ptinent'* (indirect evidence)
manerium ('town house')	*ad Mar̃iū de Eybury*	–
rent	*Stonerente*	–
selda ('kiosk')	*selda que vocat͛ Peinteselde*	*seldā meam vocatam le huse*
pistrina ('bakery')	*pistrina vocata la Redebakhous*	–
bracina ('brewhouse')	*domū bracineam vocatam le Burgate*	*domū meam braciñ vocatam le horn in the hop̂*
taberna ('tavern')	*Tab̃na cū ptiñ que vocat͛ le Brokeneselde*	*Tab̃ne vocat' la Cardinaleshat*
tavern	*Cherchegatestaůne*	*Taůne apelle la Bole*
inn	*Blosmeshyn*	–
hospitium ('inn')	*hospitium eoʒ vocat' Camera Diane alŝ Segraue*	*hospiciū vocatū le Katerine on the hope*
camera ('room')	*hospitium eoʒ vocat' Camera Diane alŝ Segraue*	–
cellarium ('cellar')	*Celario vocato le Holceler*	–
garita ('garret')	*vnam de iłł duabʒ garitas videlicet la Westñe Garite*	–
solarium ('upper room')	*magno Solar' vocat͛ le Wynsoler*	–

who eschewed tournaments and did not fight. They were distinguished by their merchant marks and by their seals which displayed mottos and flora and fauna. . . . In the fifteenth century things began to change: the London aldermen seem to have aspired to gentry status: they adopted coats of arms.

(Barron 2000: 411)

Over the century certain merchants who had hitherto not aspired to gentry status prospered and entered the City administration, becoming aldermen. Lending credence to Barron's observation about merchants, their seals and their social status aspirations is the direct correlation between merchants' and craftspeople's seals and house names.[12] Table 1.2 shows the devices that make up the London heraldic house names listed in Appendix 1.

The lower-register artifacts were to burgeon in following centuries as shop names reflected the trade practised within. One name in this group warrants discussion, partly because it was common in the fourteenth and fifteenth centuries in London and elsewhere but dropped out of use thereafter, and partly because it has been misinterpreted. This is *Tabard*, the name of a large inn in Southwark in Chaucer's *Canterbury Tales* where the pilgrims met before setting out on their adventure.[13] There were fourteenth- and fifteenth-century buildings named *Tabard* in Bread Street, Wood Street, Watling Street; in the parishes of Farringdon Without, St Michael Paternoster Royal, St Benet Gracechurch; outside the City in Southwark and Tothill Street Westminster; and there were further nearby *Tabards* in the London environs of Acton and Tottenham.[14] *Tabard* was not a rare tenement

---

[12] McEwan (2016) catalogues early London craftspeople and merchants' seals showing images of birds (*le Ernedore, Croweonethehop, le Kok, Aerneselde, Pye on the hope, la Rauen, le Swan othe hop, le Pecok on the houp*), armed men on horseback (*le George on the hoƥe*), lions (*la Lyoun*), boars' heads (*le Boreshede*), wheatsheaves (*le Glene on the hooƥ*), lambs (*le Lamb atte hoope*), crenellated buildings (*le castel atte hooƥ*), unicorns (*le Vnicorne*), women (*Mayde on the Hoƥ*), lilies (*le fflourdelys*) and ships (*le ship onthehoƥ*). These are McEwan's own categories; a scrutiny of the photographs of seals in McEwan (2016) also reveals suns (466, 513) (*le Sonne on the hooƥ*), legs (530, 531) (*le Huse*), and harts (1016, 1063) (*Hert on ƺe hoƥ*). New (2008: 247) 'the design of personal seals seems to have reached its apex in terms both of quality and diversity in the late-thirteen to early fourteenth centuries'.
[13] For a history and description of the Tabard in Southwark, see Carlin (2013).
[14] Bread Street: 1384 Plea & Mem A27 (i) m 11r '*Bredstret Johes hostiller atte Tabard*'

Wood Street: 1391 Plea & Mem A 30 m 5v '*les quatre jurreƺ mestres des masons & Carpenters ount view la paveye de piere del teneñt q̄ Robt Lynde<seye> tient en Wodestret al Tabard en la poche de seint Alban*'.

Watling Street: 1463 LMA, Dean and Chapter of St Paul's Cathedral MS Press A Box 12 1123 (old ref), CLC/313/L/H/001/MS25121/020 '*totum illud teñtum suum cum shopis solarᵖ supedificatᵉ celarᵖ & omnibƺ alijs suis ptiñ . situat' sup Cornerium vicoᶋ Regioᶋ de Watlyngstrete & ffridaystrete in pochia sci Johannis Euᵃ ngeliste dĉe Ciuitatis put iacet int' vicum Regnum de ffrydaystrete ƥdict' ex parte Occidentli & teñ dict' Decani & Capitli vocat' le Taberd*'.

Farringdon Without: 1371 Plea & Mem A 17 m 2 '*Johs atte Tabard . . . de ffarndoñ extᵃ*', 1384 Plea & Mem A27 (i) m 11v '*ffarindoñ exᵃ Joh lenhmᵃ atte Tabard*'; 1411 HR 150/8 '*Item do & lego Johi Duk filio meo totū tentū meū cum shopis & omībƺ alijs ptiñ suis vocatū le Tabard on the hoop in pochia sĉe Brigide in ffletestret in suburbijs londoñ*'; 1433 HR 162/46 '*tria mesuagia siue tenementa mea in eadem pochia*

Table 1.2 Heraldic devices included in fourteenth-century London house names

Heraldic devices	House names
birds	Croweonethehop, le Kok, le Swan othe hop, Pye on the hope, la Rauen, le Culuer on the hope, le Pecok on the houp, le Crane
mammals	atte Goth, la Lyoun, Hert on ȝe hoƥ, le Lamb atte hoope, le Ram onthehope, Horshed, le Holebole, le Catfithele, le Boreshede, le Whitehors, le Bere on the hooƥ, le Herteshorne, le Blakehors on the hope, le Dolfyn on the hoƥ
plants	la Pirie, le fflourdelys, le Glene on the hooƥ, le Garland on the hooƥ
people and parts thereof	Scotothehop, Mayden en la Hope, le Taborer, Saraȝineshed, le Thre Legges, leȝ Thre Nonnes, Mayde on the Hoƥ, le Walssheman sur le hooƥ
clothing and armour	le Huse, la Cardinaleshat, le Helm on ye Hoope, le Hood on the hoop, le Swerd on the hoƥ
heavenly beings, saints and their symbols	le George on the hoƥe, le Katerine on the hope, le Vernycle, le Mechele, the Cristofre on ye hope, the Keye of the hoōp, le Harpe
the heavens	le Sonne on the hooƥ, le Sterre
fabulous beasts	le Griffoñ, la Dragoun, la Worm on the hope, le Vnicorne
buildings	le castel atte hoop, le Cherch on the hop
occupations	le Harowe on ye houpe, le Horssho, le Melle atte hope, le panyer del hoop, le wollesak onthehop
higher-register artifacts	le Croune, le ship onthehop
lower-register artifacts	le Kok, le Irenhope, le Bele on the hop, le Horn in the hop, le Potte on the hope, le Lampe on the Hoop, Tabard

---

quoꝝ vnū vocat⁰ʳ the Tabard et situat⁰ʳ int' teñ vocat' the Castell ex pte orientli & teñ vocat' le George atte Sholane end cū shopis adiac⁰ ex pte occident'.

St Michael Paternoster Royal: 1396 *Calendar of Patent Rolls* 19 Richard II part II p. 685, m 24; 1424 HR 152/52 '*totū illud hospiciū nrmˡ vocat' le Tabbard on the hooƥ cū ptiñ vna cū quatuor shopis & omĩbȝ suis ptiñ ad p'dcm̃ hospic' ptiñ in pochia scĩ Michis de patnosterchirche in Riola in londoñ*'; 1492 LMA DL/C/A/001/MS09065, fo 104v '*in hospicō ad signū le Tabde in le Ryall in q⁰ d⁰ manet iste jur'*.

St Benet Gracechurch: 1418–40 Lillywhite (1972: 545).

Southwark: late 14th cent. British Library, Harley MS 1758 fo 1 '*In suthwerk . at the Thabard as I laye*'.

Tothill Street Westminster: 1381 WAM 17702 '*vocat' le Cocke vel Tabard in vico de Tothull*'.

Acton: 1377 *Calendar of Close Rolls* 51 Ed III, 17 June 1377, m. 4d.

Tottenham: 1411–12 Robinson (1840: 183).

name in fourteenth- and fifteenth-century London, nor indeed elsewhere.[15] It signified some sort of accoutrement for a barrel or tank, as is apparent in the following accounts entries (see Wright 1992 for further illustration):

> ffor iij *Tabardes for the tonnes atte Crowne ayenst the Briggehous gate*
> ffor *a tabard to a kechyñ Sesterñ atte signe of the iij bonettes vpoñ the Brigge*
> ffor *a tabard of lede to paynes hous Glover atte Standard in chepe*
> ffor ij *tabardͤ to the kechyñ Cesterne in maistͣ gaddͤ hous*
>   1482/3 LMA CLA/007/FN/02/003, fo 370, 370v, 371

In the accounts of London Bridge, tabards occurred in the context of cisterns and tuns used in brewing, kitchens, waterdraughts (privies), window-sills and roofs, signifying either a lid, or some other piece of kit for a tank, cistern or tun. The Anglo-Norman word *tabard* meaning a poor person's overgarment is attested in English from around 1300, and is attested as a tenement name from the 1360s in Winchester and 1370s in London. However, *tabard* meaning 'heraldic surcoat' is not attested until the second half of the fifteenth century, making it unlikely that all these earlier inns and tenements primarily referenced chivalric knighthood.[16] I suggest that the original use of the term was metaphorical, the earliest meaning of *tabard* in English being a sleeveless overgarment worn outdoors by the poor, similar to the present-day metaphor of lagging a cistern with a jacket.[17] Houses named *le Tabard* signalled their commercial function via synecdoche, the use of the part for the whole, as did buildings in Appendix 1 named *atte Basket*, *le Tonne*, *le Potte on the hope*, and further fifteenth-century London house names *the Pewter Potte*, *le Pewter Dyshe*, *the Cup*, *the Platter*.

The other early heraldic name to do something similar was the *Cock*. The holding expressed as '*apᵈ le Kok in vico Tothull*' in a document of 1325 was also recorded as '*vocatᵗ le Cocke vel Tabard in vico de Tothull*' in a document of 1381, and there were tenements called both the *Coke on the Hope* and the *Tabard on the Hope* at Acton in the 1380s. *Cock* signified both a fowl (*OED* cock, *n.1*), and also a tap, as in present-day *stopcock* (*OED* cock, *n.1* IV. 12. a. 'spout or short pipe serving as a

---

[15] There were fifteenth- and sixteenth-century *Tabards* in Oxford, York, Chester, Yarmouth, Bokkyng, Notts. and Stylton, Hunts., but as they do not predate the London ones they are not included here. The *Tabard* of the 1360s in Winchester (Keene 1985a: i 167, ii 501) is earlier, however.

[16] *OED* tabard, *n. 1*, *n. 2.*, *n. 4*, *MED* tabard(e (n.(1)), tabard(e (n.(2)) (illustrated with quotations taken from Wright 1992). Nevertheless Cox (1994: 12) insists on the 'heraldic surcoat' interpretation rather than the 'tank' interpretation for the inn name, although seemingly unaware of the dating implications and basing his objection on propriety: 'a leaden tank seems hardly appropriate in such a visual context. . . . Nor does "the ale-tank" seem an appropriate name for a large up-market hostelry such as Chaucer's Tabard'. Actually, 'receptacle' nouns were particularly apt for hostelry names, as attested by multiple premises named *Panyer, Peauter Pott, Cowpe, Basket, Purs*, in William Porlond's Book of 1418–24 (he was clerk to the Brewers' Livery Company), and the sign of the *Bottle* on London Bridge. Carlin (2013: 470) finds Cox's objection 'unconvincing'.

[17] *Jacket* is not attested in English until 1451 (*MED* jaket (n.)), so it is plausible that cisterns wore tabards before they wore jackets.

channel for passing liquids through', first attested as a noun 1481–90). Thus the inn name referenced the cock in the tun through which the ale or wine was drawn, but the inn sign displayed the cockerel, according to canting rebus interpretation, as was common practice with names and their punning visual representations in the fourteenth century.[18] The *Tabard* inn-name originally referenced the tabard around or above the tank in which the ale was stored, but the sign displayed a heraldic surcoat once that meaning had developed in the later fifteenth century, as a rebus. It is noticeable that early heraldic house names reference birds: once the cockerel was on display as a tenement sign, the way was opened for depiction of all kinds of birds – and from birds, to animals, plants, and onwards to the whole panoply of heraldic devices.

I stated earlier that as heraldry was the preserve of the nobility and they formed a minority, heraldic house names might be expected to have been low-frequency items. My claim about the progress of heraldic house names from noble to non-noble needs to be substantiated. Just before the Norman Conquest, the 'nobiliary knighthood' emerged in France and was brought to England by the Anglo-Norman administration; that is, the chivalric, courtly culture of knighthood for noble-born men, at the expense of practical military prowess (Boulton 1987, 1995). Members adopted the chivalric code of honour, together with the virtues and duties associated with knightliness, which had previously been the province of princes. Boulton says it was virtually a new status: 'partly semantic, partly symbolic, partly ideological, and partly economic' (Boulton 1995: 58). The distinctive symbols of most Latin nobilities – castle, surname, seal, arms – which had codified in the century and a half before 1180, were now expressed outwardly from around 1225 by knights' personal heraldic arms on shield, lance-pennon, and horse-trapper. This was a significant change, because heraldic devices previously conferred by birth and shared by all members of the dynasty now also became symbolic of individual knights – and by association, their heraldic devices became invested with their glamour. Chivalric orders were created in the fourteenth century: the Society of St George, or Order of the Garter (1344/9), the Company of the Star (1344/52), the Order of the Sword (1347/59), the Order of the Ship (1381–6).[19] To be elected to these chivalric orders was a high honour, and it is these same emblems that begin to appear on fourteenth-century London taverns and brewhouses: *le George on the hoþe, le Huse, le Sterre, le Swerd on the hoþ, le Shipp on the hope* – all were to become common and long-lasting house names. Thus there were two routes of adoption for heraldic house names: via synecdochal canting interpretation of trading

---

[18] Other Germanic and Slavonic languages also have a single word meaning *cockerel/tap/penis*, see Cooper (2008) and Immonen (2014) for a discussion. My thanks to Jukka Tuominen for this information.

[19] Information on chivalric orders is taken from Boulton (1987), and it should be said that the Orders of Star, Sword and Ship were European rather than specifically English, as the conventions and symbols of knighthood were common to Latin Christianity.

equipment, acting as an amusing kind of advertisement for the wares within; and via prosperous craftsmen and merchants' borrowing of knightly emblems for reasons of social cachet.

So there was an overlap, as it were, between aspirational names such as *le George*, *le Sterre*, *le Swerd*, and the synecdochal names such as *le Kok* and *le Tabard*. Not surprisingly, given the mercantile and brewing occupations of their bestowers, these heraldic house names remained within the realm of commercial property. There is a parallel here with the Victorian faux-authentic place-name house names such as *Fernlea*, in that *Fernlea* sounded as though it had a long English ancestry although it did not, conferring a soupçon of landed-gentry prestige on the house-holder. In the fourteenth century, houses named *le Hert*, *le Sterre*, *le Swan* did not signify noble ancestry, since dynastic usage remained the preserve of the nobility. Nevertheless such names would have implicitly conveyed an air of social privilege, however inauthentic.

Fifteenth-century commercial premises

One of the most remarkable facts to emerge from this assemblage of early London house names is the speed and consistency with which heraldic names were adopted on commercial premises. London heraldic building names date from the 1320s, appearing a little earlier as part of people's names in tax lists (Lucie and Raði *Atecok* 1282–3, Hugo *ate Cocke* 1319). A hundred years later (1418–40), the Brewers' Livery Company clerk William Porlond kept a memorandum book in which he recorded the names of alehouses. I have culled 136 house names from his book, all of which bar 4 per cent are either synecdochal or heraldic, and these are given in Table 1.3. The numbers in brackets after each name indicate the number of locations bearing that name, e.g. Angel (3) indicates that there were three premises named *atte Aungelł* in William Porlond's Book: in the parish of St Michael Queenhithe, in Fleet Street, and in the parish of St Ethelburga Bishopsgate. As these names have multiple spellings in Porlond's Book I have given their modern equivalents. See Appendix 2 for details.

The borders between the categories are not entirely clear-cut; I have placed the *Cock* under synecdoche but the *White Cock*, *Red Cock* and compound *Cock* names in the heraldic column; similarly the *Ax* and the *Hammer* could equally be placed in the heraldic column along with the *Dagger*. But the weight of distribution at 93 per cent is clear: by the early fifteenth century, heraldic and synecdochal names together had come to dominate the nomenclature of commercial premises selling ale, wine and beer.

I hypothesised above that *Cock* was a synecdochal name for the tap of an ale-tun, with a canting interpretation of a cockerel depicted on the house sign. There were 36 individual London premises named the *Cock* in William Porlond's Book, and a

Table 1.3 London inn names: 378 premises with a name-stock of 136 names, taken from William Porlond's Book

Heraldic	Synecdochal/ Occupational	Appearance	Personal name
Angel (3), Ball (3), Bear (3), Bell (13), Bell Crowned (1), Bell & Dolphin (1), Bell & St Peter (1), Bishop (1), Black Horse (1), Bull (3), Cardinal's Hat (2), Castle (5), Chequer (2), Chequer & Lamb (1), Chough (1), Christopher (9), Cock & Bell (2), Cock & Star (1), Cony (2), Cow Head (1), Crane (2), Cross (1), Crown (5), Culver (1), Dagger (1), Dolphin (4), Dragon (6), Eagle (3), Eagle & Garland (1), Ewe & Lamb (1), Falcon (1), Fleur de Lys (5), Garland (4), George (7), George & Horn (1), Glene (3), Goat (1), Golden Hart (1), Greyhound (3), Hand (1), Harp (6), Hart (3), Hart's Head (1), Hart's Horn (9), Helm (2), Hind (2), Horn (5), Horse (3), Horse Head (6), Horse Shoe (1), Katherine Wheel (3), Key (12), King's Head (1), Lamb (10), Lily (2), Lion (6), Maid (3), Maiden (1), Maiden Head (1), Mermaid (1), Mill (3), Mitre (1), Moon (1), Nun (2), New Lion (1), Paul's Head (1), Peacock (3), Peahen (2), Peter & Paul (1), Pie (5), Popinjay (1), Ram (4), Ram's Head (2), Red Cock (1), Red Lion (2), Rose (1), St Julian (1), Saracen's Head (5), Saracen's Head & One Maid (1), Scot (1), Seven Stars (1), Ship (6), Snipe (1), Squirrel (1), Star (6), Star & Moon (1), Swan (25), Swan & Ship (1), Three Kings (1), Three Legs (1), Three Nuns (1), Trump (1), Two Keys (1), Two Nuns (1), Unicorn (2), Vernacle (3), Welsh Man (1), White Bear (1), White Bull (1), White Cock (1), White Cross (1), White Culver (1), White Hart (2), White Leg (1), White Lion (3), Whole Bull (1)	Ax (4), Basket (3), Black Hoop (1), Bolt & Tun (1), Cock (36), Coop (6), *ad fontem cũ ij bokettę* (1), Hammer (2), Iron (1), Pannier (3), Pewter Pot (2), Purse (1), Round Hoop (1), Scummer (1), Sickle (1), Tabard (1), Tankard (1), Vine (3), Woolsack (2)	Cellar (4), Corner Cellar (1), Green Gate (1), Lamp (4), Lattice (1), Leaden Porch (1), Long Entry (1), Two Stulps (1)	*atte belle voc̉ Savagis Inne* (1), Copedon Hall (1)
N = 291 premises (77%), 107 names (79%)	N = 71 premises (19%), 19 names (14%)	N = 14 premises (3.5%), 8 names (6%)	N = 2 premises (0.5%), 2 names (1%)

Source: Brewers' Livery Company, 1418–40, London Guildhall Library CLC/L/BF/A/021/MS05440.

further two named the *Cock & Bell* and *Cock & Star*, making *Cock* the single most productive alehouse name, followed by *Swan* (25 premises, plus one *Swan & Ship*). Collectively, fowl account for 80 (21 per cent) of the premises in William Porlond's Book: *Chough, Cock, Cock & Bell, Cock & Star, Crane, Crow, Culver, Eagle, Eagle & Garland, Erne, Falcon, Peacock, Peahen, Pie, Popinjay, Raven, Red Cock, Snipe, Swan, Swan & Ship, White Cock, White Culver*. The synecdochal field of 'receptacle for containing or carrying' is also prominent: *Basket, Bolt & Tun, Coop, ad Fontem cũ ij Bokettę, Pannier, Pewter Pot, Pot on the Hoop, Purse, Scummer, Tabard, Tankard, Tun, Woolsack*. The doublet *Bolt & Tun* ('*atte bolt and þe tonne yn ffletestrete*') is a reparsing of the brewer's bolting tun.[20] This could only have happened once two-element names had become commonplace, and William Porlond's Book shows that this had occurred over the course of the fourteenth century. Essentially all the naming developments with regard to heraldic names had been completed well within the century after their introduction, the only exceptions being names to do with legendary characters, and names with *Arms* as a second element.

Here is a list of house names on London Bridge in the 1480s. The only new developments are names of legendary characters (*Robin Hood*), and an increase in occupational terms (*Chapman, Milkwife, Shepherd*) and low-register artifacts (*Three Bonnets, Bottle, Top & Scourge*). McEwan (2016: no. 234) portrays an image of the seal of Bartholomew de Capella, glover, dated 1276x1277, which depicts a glove, and the seal of Robert le Buckle-maker (764), dated 1300x1301, which depicts a buckle, so the linking of occupation and image (the chapman, the shepherd, the milkwife) had been familiar for centuries by the 1480s.

> *atte signe of the Cornysshe Chough vpon the Brigge*
> *at signe of the Crane vpon the Brigge*
> *atte signe of the Chapman vpon the Brigge*
> *a teñt vpon the Brigge atte signe of the goote*
> *a teñt vpon the Brigge at signe of the Castell*
> *atte signe of the dolfyn vpon the brigge*
> 1481–2, London Metropolitan Archives, CLA/007/FN/02/003, fos 350v, 351

> *atte signe of the iij bonettes vpon the Brigge*
> *atte signe of the Rose vpon the Brigge*
> *atte signe of the sarsens hede on the Brigge*
> *the teñt called the Nonhede at london Brigge*
> *atte signe of the Rammes hede vppon the Brigge*
> *atte signe of the ffloure delice on the brigge*
> *atte signe of Robyn hode vpon the brigge*

---

[20] *OED* bolting, *n.1*; c.f. buildings named *gyle house* and *gyling house* in Appendix 1: '*domo vocaƚ ʒylyn-ghous . . . in vico de Bredstreƚ in poch Omĩ Scõ₂ Londoñ*'; "*teñ bracineo exceptis cisterna mea magno plumbo . . . ad Celariũ vocatũ yilhuys*'.

atte signe of the Trinite vpon the brigge
atte Signe of the George vpon the Brigge
atte signe of the iij Shepard vppon the brigge
atte signe of the bottell vpon the brigge
atte signe of the horshede vpon the brigge
atte Signe of the Ravyns hede vpon the brigge
atte signe of the belle vpon the Brigge
atte signe of the Toppe and George vpon the brigge
atte signe of the bore vpon the brigge
atte signe of the Cheker vpon the brigge

    1482–3, London Metropolitan Archives, CLA/007/FN/02/003, fos 370v, 371

at Signe of the trever vppon the Brigge
next the Signe of the Ball vppon the Brigge
the Signe of the Mylk Wife of london Brigge
at Signe of oure lady vppon london Brigge
at Signe of the blac Bull vppon the Brigge
att Signe of the Toppe and the Scourge vppon the Brigge
at the Signe of the Maremaid vppon yᵉ brigge
at the Signe of the Whyle horne vpon the Brygge
at the Signe of the Whyte horse vpon the Brygge

    1483–4, London Metropolitan Archives, CLA/007/FN/02/003, fos 390, 390v[21]

These tenements on London Bridge show that shops bore the same heraldic names as the ale-sellers' premises in William Porlond's Book. Heraldic names therefore signified commerce in general from their first adoption.

Can personal stance or attitude be inferred from any of these early names?[22] The very earliest house names record householder, house usage, and house appearance,

---

[21] The *Toppe and George* of 1482–3 is likely to be an error for the *Toppe and Scourge* of the following year. Suggestions for *trever* and *Whyle horne* are AN *treveure* (*AND* troveure s. 2. 'Invention of the True Cross'); OF trouvere (*OED* trouvère 'troubadour') and 'whorl horn' with omitted <r> graph, or 'white horn' with <l> instead of <t> graph. The Cornish chough featured on the arms of St Thomas a Becket, to whom the chapel on the bridge was dedicated. However it was also the badge of John Trevilian, knight, squire of the Duke of Suffolk and intimate of Henry VI. His was an up and down career, belonging to a group 'hated beyond any others. . . . Their greed and the success with which they engrossed the king's favours explains much of the hatred they incurred.' His heyday was during the 1440s when he was in the king's favour. In 1447 he and another squire of the Duke of Suffolk's forcibly expelled the occupants of the castle of Stone in Kent and held it themselves for the next three years; his ship the Edward of Polruan sacked a Spanish ship. But he was unpopular and named as a traitor in Jack Cade's rebellion, and lampooned in popular verse. In 1450 he was denounced in parliament, yet by March 1452 he had regained power, being reinstated as Yeoman of the Crown and Keeper of the Armoury in the Tower. Further arrests and pardons were to follow. He died in 1494 (Harvey 1988: 49, 51, 123, 241–3). Although the London Bridge chough references St Thomas, John Trevilian's exploits kept the symbol before the public eye.
[22] I thank Rik Vosters for raising this possibility.

all of which are factual. But the heraldic names encoded a social distinction, signalling both an allusion to the new societal class of chivalric knights, and a commercial
function. Those early birds, *Croweonethehop* of 1323 and *le Kok* of 1325, may have
simply been immediately obvious signifiers of a place of business, as distinct from
noblemen's residences. Or they may have been in contradistinction to the more
patrician fauna of lions, dragons, unicorns and eagles. Just as late Victorian *Wee
Neste* poked fun at aspirational names such as *Holkham Hall, Croweonethehop* and
le Kok may have poked fun at aspirational heraldic names. Certainly a stance of
pejorative affection can be posited for the Order of the Garter becoming known as
le Hose and *le Leg,* just as seventeenth-century names in *Horse* shifted to *Nag,* with
a semantic direction of movement from higher register to lower register.[23] Along
with drinking goes an increase in merriment, and *Croweonethehop* and *le Kok* may
have been not just word-play but possibly also sarcasm lobbed by the lower orders
at the higher.

Movement and naming change

William Porlond's Book of 1418–40 shows that certain districts were especially
populated with heraldic and synecdochally-named buildings selling ale, beer and
wine. Table 1.4 shows some of these.

  Table 1.4 gives evidence not only of where Londoners slaked their thirst but also
where they met in order to travel to other parts of the country. Whether travelling by horse and coach or by boat, coachmen needed somewhere to change, feed,
water and stable their horses; boatmen needed somewhere to wait out the tides;
and passengers needed designated places to board and alight. These clusters along
the main roads out of town show that inns were already serving these functions
in the early fifteenth century. Organised travel around the country is not directly
evidenced until the sixteenth, with the *flying posts* of 1548, 'mail travelling across
the country by relays of horses' (*OED* flying, *adj.* 4. b), and the word *stagecoach,*
meaning 'a coach that runs daily or on specified days between two places for the
conveyance of passengers, parcels, etc.', not attested until as late as 1649, although
the ferrying of passengers back and forth is described slightly earlier:

> There is of late such an admirable commodiousness, both for men and women, to travel
> from London to the principal towns of the country that the like hath not been known in
> the world, and that is by stage coaches, wherein anyone may be transported to any place
> sheltered from foul weather and foul ways, free from endamaging one's health and one's
> body by hard jogging or over violent motion on horseback, and this not only at the low

---

[23] As a pub carpark child in the 1960s (children outside whilst adults were in the pub) I was unaware
that the various riverside *Mucky Ducks* frequented by my parents, godparents, aunts and uncles were
known to the Post Office as the *White Swan.*

Table 1.4 London inn names (modern spelling) from three arterial roads and two hithes taken from William Porlond's Book, 1418–40

Aldersgate	Aldgate	Bishopsgate	Billingsgate & Queenhithe
Bear	Ax	Angel	Angel
Bell	Bear	Bell	Basket
Christopher	Bell	Bell & Dolphin	Bell
Cock	Cock	Cardinal's Hat	Bull
Dolphin	George	Castle	Cardinal's Hat
Eagle	Hammer	Cock	Chough
Falcon	Hartshorn	Crown	Christopher
George	Horse	Dragon	Cock
Horn	Horse Head	Garland	Fleur de Lys
Horse	Horseshoe	Hart's Head	Glene
Lion	Key	Helm	Lion
New Lion	Nun	Lamp	Pannier
Peacock	Peacock	Lion	Pie
Rose	Peahen	Moon	Ship
St Julian	Saracen's Head	Peahen	Swan
Swan	Swan	Scott	
	Three Kings	Swan	
	Two Nuns	Two Keys	
	Woolsack	Vine	

Source: London Guildhall Library CLC/L/BF/A/021/MS05440

price of about a shilling for every five miles, but with such velocity and speed in one hour as the foreign post can make but in one day.

1649. Chamberlayne. The Present State of Great Britain[24]

The carriers of St Albans do come every Friday to the sign of the 'Peacock' in Aldersgate Street; on which days also cometh a coach from St Albans, to the 'Bell' in the same street. The like coach is also there for the carriage of passengers every Tuesday.

1637. John Taylor. The Carrier's Cosmography. 229

The *Bell* and the *Peacock* in Aldersgate are both listed in William Porland's early fifteenth-century manuscript, so the carriers of St Albans had been ferrying passengers into London long before the seventeenth century. That these inn names were highly salient to the local population in earlier times is evidenced by the fact that some of them went on to have a considerably wider currency at a later date. The district of Islington known nowadays as the Angel is named after one of the several coaching inns servicing

[24] Antedating *OED* stage-coach, *n.* 1658.

coaches heading northwards out of Aldersgate and Newgate. World's End, the name of the district at the end of the King's Road in Chelsea, is mentioned in Congreve's *Love for Love* of 1695, the inn then being the only building in the vicinity. Nunhead, with a zero genitive marker, was a relatively common shop and inn name and is the name of part of the borough of Southwark. Tally Ho Corner in the Finchley Road is named after the Tally Ho coach which called there. A semantic grouping of coach names reveals the mechanism by which names spread from coach to inn and inn to coach and around the country. Appendix 3 presents 279 stagecoach names taken from directories of the 1830s, the decade when the coaching system was at its height immediately prior to coming of the railways, serving 151 inns countrywide. Many of these coach names advertised speed: the *Rocket* out of Stratford, the *Dart* and the *Express* out of Sutton Coldfield, the *Vivid* out of Oakhampton, the *Celerity* out of Bristol, the *Flycatcher* out of Bolton. A subset of these 'speed' names invoked the alarm of the hunt (see Table 1.5).

'Tally-ho', 'tantivy' and 'hark forward' were hunting cries. The various Tally-ho coaches along with the other hunt-referencing names conveyed not only extreme rapidity but also competition, as carriers on the same route raced each other from stage to stage, from inn to inn. Another frequently attested hunting alarm was *so-ho*. There is evidence of *so-ho* as a cry in texts from every century from 1300 to the mid-1800s in works by popular authors with large readerships, such as Shakespeare, Bunyan, Shelley and Dickens. Soho in London is the area bounded by Charing Cross Road to the east and Wardour Street to the west. It has been known as Soho since at least 1636, where it occurs as a heading in a list of ratepayers indicating that twenty people were living in the vicinity in the parish of St Martin in the Fields. The dwellings in the area are grouped under the headings 'Little Church Lane, Mewes, St Martin's Lane, Millitary Street, Long Acre, Drury Lane, Russell streete, White hart yard, Covent garden, Brick Kills neare Sohoe'.[25]

Table 1.5 Coach names 1828–44

Scheduled stop	Coach
Rose & Crown, Tamworth	the Tally-ho
Packwood's General Coach and Waggon Offices, Coventry	the Patent Safety Tally-ho
Dolphin Inn, Cross Cheaping	the Independent Tally-ho
Chapel House, Chipping Norton	the Tantivy
Jones & Herbert's Office, Chester	the Hark Forward
Bear, Crickhowell	the Monmouth Hunt
Bath	the Beaufort Hunt
Berkeley	the Berkeley Hunt

Sources: directories at http://specialcollections.le.ac.uk, and Corbett (1891: 300–1)

[25] Westminster City Archives, Parish Records Overseers Accounts, St Martin in the Fields. 29 April 1636–26 April 1637. Microfilm F363 item 13, page 30.

In 1641 Anna Clerke was bound over to keep the peace after 'threteninge to burne the houses at So: ho'. These houses stood on the east side of the modern Wardour Street, to the north of Bourchier Street. The word Soho is an ancient hunting call, and there is evidence that hunting took place over the lands to the west of Wardour Street. With the passage of time what had originally been the name of a group of wayside cottages in the open country was extended to denote the streets and squares of the whole parish of St. Anne, which had been formed out of the parish of St. Martin in the Fields in 1686.

(Sheppard 1966: 1)

It is held that Soho took its name from the hunting-call *so-ho*, but the mechanism of transfer from cry to district has not yet been explained. The lands lying west of Wardour Street towards Hyde Park were hunting grounds in earlier centuries, but those to the east were not; that is, there is no evidence that hunting occurred where Soho is situated. None of the locations taxed along with 'Brick Kills neare Sohoe' lie to the west of Wardour Street. Yet there is another Soho, Soho Warren, known from 1757 in Handsworth, Birmingham, with an inn depicted there on a map considerably before its name is on record as 'The Soho' in 1817.[26] The London Stage Coach Directory printed in *Cary's New Itinerary* of 1828 shows that daily London–Birmingham coaches left from London coaching-inns the Saracen's Head at Snow Hill, Bolt in Tun in Fleet Street, and Belle Sauvage at Ludgate Hill: Birmingham also has locations named Snow Hill, Fleet Street and Ludgate Hill, so-called 'from a desire of imitating the metropolis' (Hutton 1835: 92–3). I hypothesise that the mechanism of transfer from London street name to Birmingham street name stems from coaching termini, and I infer that Soho in London and Soho in Birmingham marked the starting and ending inns, named after a London to Birmingham stage-coach *Soho*, which was named as an advertisement for its speed. I can find no direct record of an earlier coach named *Soho* (evidence of coach names prior to the nineteenth century is scarce) but a century later, from about 1823, there were London to Birmingham coaches named *Tally-Ho*, the *Independent Tally-Ho*, the *Eclipse Tally-Ho*, the *Patent Tally-Ho*, the *Safety Tally-Ho*.[27] If John Taylor's *Carrier's Cosmography* of 1637 is taken as the date when the stagecoach system began, then this hypothesis fails because Soho in London was already so-called by that year. But if the clustering of inns along arterial and main roads in William Porlond's Book of 1418–40 is taken as evidence of organised coaching at that date, then coach names are just as likely to have been in use too.

---

[26] Dickinson (1939: 44).

[27] Corbett (1891: 129–30, 172); *OED* tally-ho, *int.* and *n.* 2. a. 'Originally, the proper name given to a fast day-coach between London and Birmingham, started in 1823; subsequently appropriated by other fast coaches on this and other roads, and treated somewhat as a common noun.' Poland Street, Soho, was the terminus for the Green Line fleet of coaches as late as 1933 (www.greenline.co.uk/discover/history1/). I boarded and alighted coaches at Tally Ho Corner in the 1960s.

Golden Tea Kettle and Speaking Trumpet

Shop names were not recorded in medieval deeds and wills, and only become apparent in any number with the advent of trade-cards, but their names were also transferred from place to place. Trade-cards were not quite what they sound: they did indeed advertise the name of the shop and sometimes the wares, but they were far larger than a present-day business card. They were printed on sheets of paper and they often also acted as a receipt, with spaces left blank for the date, the customer's name, and the goods they bought. Trade-cards show that the linking of heraldic names together with synecdochal names had become the norm by the seventeenth century. From a handful of trade-cards, here are the inscriptions that sit underneath the engraving of the shop sign:[28]

> Willm Boyce Coffinmaker at ye Whight Hart & Coffin in ye Grate Ould Bayley Near Newgeat
>
> Thomas Jemmit, Y^e Blackmoors-Head & Golden Sugar-Loaf against Fetter Lane in Fleet Street
>
> Ann Coleman, At the Sign of the Porter and Dwarfe, Hand and Shears and Queen's Head, upon the Common-Shore, in Houndsditch, London
>
> John Brown at the Three Cover'd Chairs & Walnut-Tree, the East Side of St Paul's Church Yard, near the School, London
>
> Willm Browne, Stay-maker & Mercer, At the Golden-Stays and Hoop-Coat, in the Borough, near the Bridge-foot, Southwark, London
>
> Edward Chandler Coffin Maker and Undertaker (from the Corner of Fleet Lane) At the Naked Boy & Coffin, the Corner of Turnagain Lane, by the Fleet Market near Holborn Bridge, London
>
> John Cotterell at the Indian Queen and Tea Cannister against Stocks Markett
>
> Ann Hebert a Coat shop at the Black Moors head & Pine Apple, in Fenchurch Street
>
> Mary & Ann Hogarth from the old Frock-shop the corner of the Long Walk facing the Cloysters, Removed to ye Kings Arms joyning to ye Little Britain-gate, near Long Walk

Doublet names expressed either existing house name + synecdochal trade, or trade + trade:

> Willm. Mendham, at the Wheatsheaf and Boddice, against Gutter Lane, Cheapside
>
> Tompson Davis, at the Cross Guns and Pheasant, High Holborn
>
> Samuel Bevington, at the Golden Tea Kettle and Speaking Trumpet, in Lombard Street
>
> Edward Smith, Jeweller, the Parrott and Pearl, in Foster Lane against the Church

---

[28] Sources for trade-cards cited here are the collections of Sir Ambrose Heal and Sarah Banks at the British Museum; John Johnson at the Bodleian Library, Oxford; the London Guildhall collection now kept at the London Metropolitan Archives; and trade-cards kept in the archive of Hoare's Bank, Fleet Street.

Doublets also expressed continuity from father to child, or master to apprentice:

> Samuel Darkin ye Elder, at the sign of the Bleeder, next door to the Cow and Hare, in Church Lane, Whitechappel

> Samuel Darkin the Younger, at the sign of the Bleeder and Star, the corner of Adam and Eve Alley, White Chapel facing the Church Yard Gate

Doublet names expressed continuity from old premises to new, such as when John Cotterell moved from the *Indian Queen* on the corner of Grocers' Alley in the Poultry to the *Indian Queen and Tea Cannister* opposite the Stocks Market. A convention of trade-signs consolidated: the rainbow to signal a dyer, the frying pan to signal an ironmonger, the civet cat to signal a perfumer, the sugar loaf to signal a confectioner. But the old style of descriptive names also continued: William Salmon (1644–1713) medical empiric (a scientist who relies on observation) and author, was resident and in practice at the Red Balls tavern in Salisbury Court, Fleet Street, in 1679, from whence he moved to George Yard near Broken Wharf, then to the Blue Balcony by the ditch side near Holborn Bridge in 1684, and to the Great House by Black Friars Stairs in 1698.[29] Garrioch (1994: 27–35) reports certain trends: the decrease in saints' names in buildings occupied by booksellers during the sixteenth century, the mid-seventeenth century trend for London buildings bearing the same names as ships in the navy, reflecting the importance of maritime activity, and the rise of the sign of Britannia in the late seventeenth century. But essentially from the 1320s when they began, to the late 1700s when shop names terminated, heraldic commercial names enjoyed a long period of equilibrium.

The end of shop names

When the Royal Exchange opened in 1569 it became the main trading area for international commodities and shipping, with 120 shops on the upper floor, which was known as the Pawn.[30] Shops in the Pawn were more seld than shop – 5 feet wide and 7½ feet deep, with certain trades represented by multiple firms: 55 haberdashers, 25 mercers, 17 merchant taylors, 10 leathersellers.[31] Presumably there was no point hanging out, say, the sign of the Indian Queen (to signal mercery) in so cramped a space when there were 54 others nearby in the same business, and so someone – perhaps Thomas Gresham himself – named all the shops after birds and beasts. Not all are known, but there was the *Squirrel*, the *Bull*, the *Catt and Mouse*, the *Blewe Boare*, the *Broode Henne*, the *Buck*, the *Owle*, the *Unicorne*, the

[29] Salmon, William (1644–1713): Philip K. Wilson, https://doi.org/10.1093/ref:odnb/24559. See also Wright (2006a).
[30] *OED* pawn, *n.*⁴ 'gallery, colonnade', from Dutch *pand* 'cloister'.
[31] Saunders (1997: 89–90).

Camellion, the *Cockatrice*, the *Wolf*, the *Lapwinge*, the *Cony and Phesant*, the *White Bull*, the *Spredd Eagle*, the *fferitt and Nitingale*, the *Marten*, the *Pleasant Lyon*, the *Male Griffin*, the *White Boare*, the *Marmoset*, the *Grasshopper*, the *Black Raven and Green Dragon*, the *Half Moone*, the *Turkey Henne*, the *Lyonesse*, the *Popinjay*, and the *Black Boare*. Some of these were commonly found outside the Royal Exchange; others were more unusual. But the names of both shops in arcades and buildings in streets were signalled by large hanging signs, and by the mid-eighteenth century, London was perceived as being choked. This was an age when plague was thought to be airborne, and such a blockage of signs stultified free passage of air. As a result there was a general tidying up of paving and pavements in which sign-removal was ordered by Act of Parliament in 1762.[32] What took their place was numbering. For a while, both the old heraldic/synecdochal system and the new numbering system were used together, but now that the old names were no longer pictorially visible, they became forgotten. Nor was there any longer the need to refer to local landmarks by means of prepositional phrases. The new numbering had the effect of knocking out *over against* (in the sense of 'opposite'), *under* (in the sense of 'hard by'), *the corner of* (as opposed to 'on the corner of'), *the upper end of*, *next*, *the back side of*. Rather than throw away hundreds of already-printed trade-cards, 'the newly acquired street number (was) spatchcocked into the old design', as twentieth-century trade-card collector Ambrose Heal put it, which helped to prolong the names to the turn of the century.[33] But once the old batches had been used up, the traditional names in all their various two-element juxtapositions were forgotten. Grand houses aside – Spencer House, Somerset House – London property became nameless.

Garrioch (1994: 37–8) however does not accept a cause and effect scenario due to the untidy, non-thorough process of signboard removal, with vestigial signs and numbers coexisting as late as the mid-nineteenth century. He suggests that what ultimately caused the medieval system to fall into abeyance was its irrelevance to modern society; that the family dynasty indicated by the passing of sign from father to son no longer had any function following 'a profound change in family identity and behaviour among the commercial middle classes'. In a study detailing the careers and movements of individual workers within the book trade, Raven (2007) shows that the name of the house in which a family originally worked could symbolise the business over generations: 'the fourteenth-century Peter et Poule house of Paternoster Row continued to support leading booksellers for the next five

---

[32] 2 Geo. III 21 London Streets Act 1762, enhanced by 3 Geo. III 23, 4 Geo. III 39, 5 Geo. III 50, and 6 Geo. III 54, *House of Commons Journal* 29 (15 March 1762: 233–8). The City passed its own comparable act a little later; City of London Commissioners of Sewers and Pavements (1767: 1–69); see Webb and Webb (1922: 276–88). For Westminster street legislation and its effect on paving, lighting and street-name signs, see Ogborn (1998: 91–115).

[33] Heal (1927: 5); *OED* spatchcock, *v.* 'to interpolate', a usage well on the wane by 1927. Heal was aged 55 at the time.

centuries' (Raven 2007: 360). But by the early nineteenth century, the primary audience for such signs, the inhabitants of the local neighbourhood who were fluent in interpreting their symbolism, had largely disappeared from major thoroughfares. Symbols of rank, heraldry, coats of arms, the rituals of dominancy and authority, all began to lose their potency. The coming of the glazed shop window with artfully arranged wares, decorated shopfronts and lit interiors visible from the street also rendered the old eye-catching signs obsolete. A further factor was the rise of advertising in the second half of the eighteenth century, which caused trade signs to predominate, so that the medieval naming system, even when descriptive rather than heraldic or synecdochal (the *Blue Post*, the *Dutch House*), became commensurate with trade rather than residence. Raven (2007: 275–6) discusses the retention of trade signs post-1762 amongst booksellers (he refers to it as booksellers 'waging sign warfare'), in particular the use of a notable writer's head: *Seneca's Head, Cicero's Head, Horace's Head, Homer's Head, Chaucer's Head, Otway's Head, Dryden's Head, Pope's Head, Tully's Head, Shakespeare's Head*. Pub signs also remained, because as a different kind of social space their names were high-frequency items kept alive in local speech. But whereas successful early eighteenth-century shopkeepers lived above the shop, their early nineteenth-century equivalents began the move to the suburbs, with wife and children residing away from the commercial premises. This shift in residential circumstances prompted a shift in house naming, which is the subject of the next chapter.

House name timeline

Before 1300: *Haw, bury, seld, hall* and *house* were the predominant house-naming nouns, but *haw, bury* and *seld* ceased to be productive at the end of the Old English period. Modifiers were limited to householders' name, householders' occupation, and the appearance of the house.

From 1320s: Heraldic names became common for commercial premises, adopting the emblems used by chivalric knights. Commercial premises also used synecdoche (the part standing for the whole) to signal their wares, and double meanings were exploited visually on signage. *Cock* seems to have been the first (literal meaning 'tap', punning meaning 'fowl'), starting a fashion for bird names.

By 1440s: Doublets were in use.

By 1480s: Names of legendary characters were in use for commercial premises. Occupational terms and low-register artefacts were common for shop names.

Continued

Timeline continued

By 1700s: An extensive informal code of trade signs had evolved. Doublets had become the norm, expressing such relationships as house name + trade sign, former premises sign + trade sign, parent/master's sign + trade sign. The doublet or multiple-element sign was a means of expressing continuity across space and time.

From 1762: Numbering replaced urban building signs, with the exception of bookshops and pubs.

2

VICTORIAN VILLAS

The introduction of railways in the 1840s caused another punctuation mark in the equilibrium. This chapter illustrates the effects on house names by comparing mid and late nineteenth-century London house names in the Wandsworth and Finchley Roads, and three further specific developments are detailed. The first, the fashion for shrubberies and ferneries, resulted in still-popular house names containing elements *laurel*, *holly*, and *fern*. The second, *box*, is now almost entirely forgotten although it was a frequent nineteenth-century term. The third, *court*, a second-element marker signifying multiple occupancy, has now become so ubiquitous throughout the English-speaking world as to be almost invisible. But first, some background.

By the first decades of the nineteenth century long roads led out of the metropolis across the fields linking distant villages, bordered with sporadic groups of houses. These arterial roads, not being urban streets, were as yet unnumbered, and houses along them were given the kinds of names found outside the City. In the early nineteenth century, London's middle ring of suburbs still consisted of farming villages – Ealing, Clapham, Merton – with the occasional weekend retreat for wealthy gentlemen, which would take hours to get to by coach and horse. But once railway lines and railway stations were in place, workers could live permanently in such villages as Ealing, Clapham, and Merton, and new houses went up in these emergent suburbs. Supposing you were a rich early Victorian gent (but not aristocratic, because aristocrats inherited their castles, palaces and town houses): you wanted a detached house, close enough to a station to get to the City but far enough away to have some peace and space. A place where you and your wife could bring up a family, with, in time to come, a shrubbery, a rockery, and a fernery. As well as altering the landscape, the coming of the railways also effected a social upheaval. Whereas eighteenth-century gentry had largely been born into their estate, mid-nineteenth-century villa owners in Peckham and Hornsey and Wandsworth were decidedly not noble:

> Tom had already looked at one or two places which he thought might suit him for a four-months' residence in the winter, and give him at least an amphibious position between a landed proprietor and gentleman from town; but he had not yet satisfied himself. One was too much of a place; another had not sufficient stabling; another looked like a citizen's villa at Brixton; and a fourth like a consumptive hospital, or a lunatic asylum with the bars down.
>
> (Charles Clarke, *A Box for the Season: A Sporting Sketch*, 1864: 7)

A citizen's villa at Brixton. Unspeakable in 1864, yet to modern ears it's hard to fathom what could have been so objectionable. The problem lay not so much with Brixton as with the citizen. The word *citizen* was a term of abuse, and had been for at least 200 years. It meant flash, brash, confident Londoners who, though born humble, did not stay put in their lowly station and had no intention of deferring to their betters. With a lack of good taste they built startling raw mansions amongst the groves and meadows. Shortened to *cit*, the term was 'used more or less contemptuously, for example to denote a person from the town as opposed to the country, or a tradesman or shopkeeper as distinguished from a gentleman'.[1] Dr Johnson's *Dictionary of the English Language* of 1755 defines '*Cit*, an inhabitant of a city, in an ill sense. A pert low townsman; a pragmatical trader'. And what was wrong with pragmatical traders? Their speech, for one thing. The grammarian Pegge mocked:

> Citizen: Villiam, I vants my vig.
> Servant: Vitch vig, Sir?
> Citizen: Vy, the vite vig in the vooden vig-box, vitch I
>   vore last vensday at the vestry.

(Pegge 1814: 77–8)

Pert in this context meant 'impertinent', and *pragmatical* meant 'conceited, self-important, pompous' (*OED* pragmatical, *adj.* and *n.* 3.b., as in 'Lacqueys were never so saucy and pragmatical, as they are now-a-days').[2] Pragmatical traders spoke with a London accent, and used London grammar. The interchange of *v* and *w* mocked by Pegge, and familiar from Dickens's *Pickwick Papers*, is likely to have been a merger of syllable-initial /v/ and /w/ to an unrounded bilabial approximant (like pronouncing a [w] but without rounding the lips or raising the back part of the tongue), which must have become indexical of working-class speech by the late eighteenth century. This inference is due to the disapproval it attracted from grammarians such as Pegge, but also because it subsequently demerged: that is, middle-class variants must have retained etymological /v/ and /w/, as the bilabial approximant realisation was abandoned in the nineteenth century and [v] and [w] restored etymologically.[3] (Although not always restored etymologically:

---

[1] *OED* cit, *n.*, first attested before 1644.

[2] 1712, J. Addison, *Spectator* 481, paragraph 4.

[3] See Trudgill (2010: 61–91) (a marvellous piece of detective work in tracking this phoneme), and Trudgill, Schreier, Long and Williams (2004). The unrounded bilabial approximant merger and subsequent demerger to unetymologically-positioned syllable-initial [v] and [w] can still be heard (or was heard until recently) in Anguilla, Bermuda, the Bahamas, St Vincent, the Florida Keys, the Cayman Islands, the Bay Islands off the coast of Honduras in the North Atlantic, Tristan da Cunha and St Helena in the South Atlantic, the Bonin Islands in the North Pacific, and Pitcairn, Norfolk Island and Palmerston in the South Pacific, and although it cannot be ruled out that substrate languages in these places influenced its realisation, the fact that it is a rare phoneme makes it more likely that it is the London v~w merger in each of these widely-dispersed, relatively isolated places. For historical attestations

Whipp's Cross, in the London borough of Waltham Forest, was etymologically *Phypps Cross, Phip* being the short form of *Philip*.[4] However, [f] > [v] in London, a sound-change known as Southern Voicing. Once Phipp's Cross had become *Vipps Cross*, the word-initial [v] was eligible for the v~w merger, becoming pronounced with the unrounded bilabial approximant. When that sound was abandoned, and the underlying [f] pronunciation that caused it having been forgotten, the options were to pronounce it with [v] or [w]. *Vip* not being a word, *whip* won the day.) Pegge's citizen is mocked for wearing his white wig to his vestry meeting because City of London citizens could (and still can) become members of the establishment overnight by joining the governance of the City: they could participate in the vestry of one of the 108 parishes, with responsibility for such matters as sewage, lighting, roads, the poor, the vagrant and the criminal of the parish.[5] To qualify to sit on the vestry, all an ambitious, pert, low, pragmatical townsman had to do was become a householder within the parish, and then be voted in by the neighbours. Money bought the position.

So, then, moneyed townsmen began to buy houses in the environs of London that were reachable by railway. And from the early 1840s, directories were published giving their addresses. Houses of this sort tended to be named, because although numbering had been in force for 80 years, the roads leading out of town to what were fast becoming suburbs were not yet fully built up, and numbering was not yet sequential along them. Terraces of smaller houses went up in piecemeal fashion, so that in the early days house-numbering couldn't be consecutive along the length of the road. Although each terraced house was given a number, the numbering didn't rise much above twenty or so before it would start all over again at the next terrace (by contrast, number 114, St Martin's Lane, by Trafalgar Square, was in existence by 1843). Terraces of adjoining houses were given group-plural names, such as *Victoria Villas, Rose Cottages, Belmont Terrace*, with addresses following the template '5, Warwick Villas, Harrow Road'. Note the new plural term, *villas*, for a series of contiguous houses, not necessarily sharing a party wall.[6] The word *terrace* came to be used for what Americans know as *row houses* because a famous set of adjoining houses, known as 'The Adelphi', was built on a vaulted Thames-side terrace.[7]

---

and discussion of orthoepistic comment, see Jordan (1925 [1974]: § 300), Ellis (1889: 227), Wyld (1956: 292), Poussa (1995) and Wright (2010b: 179–80).

[4] Reaney (1935: 103).

[5] www.londonlives.org/static/CityLocalGovernment.jsp#WardsParishes.

[6] In 1873, *Prospect Villas*, Hornsey Lane, for example, was a row of contiguous detached houses (London Metropolitan Archives, ACC/1395/59–77). OED *villa, n.* 1. d. 'any residence of a superior or handsome type, or of some architectural pretension, in the suburbs of a town or in a residential district; also, any small better-class dwelling-house, usually one which is detached or semi-detached. The word is frequently employed in the names given to particular houses of this type, as *Windsor Villa*'; first attested 1755.

[7] OED *terrace, n.* 5. '... loosely, a row of houses of uniform style ... common in street nomenclature; Adelphi Terrace (formerly Royal Terrace), London, is one of the earliest examples', first attestation 1769:

Here are the houses named in the *Post Office Directory* of 1843 in two such roads, before the coming of the railways: Finchley New Road, a new road built by 1829 leading north out of London,[8] and Wandsworth Road, an older road leading out of town in a south-westerly direction. In 1843, the named houses and their heads of household were:

George Blakeway, Esq., Albert Villa, Finchley New Road
Henry Gilbertson, Esq., Tudor Lodge, Finchley New Road
Charles Guichard, Esq., Vernon Villa, Finchley New Road
Christopher Harrison, Esq., Cintra Villa, Finchley New Road
Francis Heathcote, Esq., Boscombe Lodge, Finchley New Road
William Page Penney, Esq., Westbourn Villa, Finchley Road
John Brownrigg Gore, Esq., solicitor, 89 Chancery Lane and Weller Cottage, Wandsworth Road
Thomas Catlin, Esq., 4 Vimiera, Wandsworth Road
Thomas Grissell, Esq., Lavender Sweeps, Wandsworth Road
James E. Hobson, Esq., Courland, Wandsworth Road[9]
Samuel Seddon, Esq., Springfield Lodge, Wandsworth Road
William Traher, Esq., Gothic Cottage, Wandsworth Road
Thomas Whitehurst, Esq., Hartington Cottage, Wandsworth Road

On the one hand, these names are no different from those found in towns and villages up and down the country, but *lodge* in such contexts was not interpreted in its sixteenth-century sense of 'a house or cottage, occupied by a caretaker, keeper, gardener, etc., and placed at the entrance of a park or at some place in the grounds belonging to a mansion' (*OED* lodge, *n.* 3), but in its new sense, 'a residence . . . freq. as the second element of house . . . names' (*OED* lodge, *n.* 4.b.), first attested *a.* 1817. Nor did *cottage* signify a cottage. In 1845 Weller Cottage was for sale: 'A brick-built Cottage, known as Weller Cottage, nearly opposite the Nag's Head on the Wandsworth-road, occupying considerable frontage, a large garden at the rear, and coach house and stabling'.[10] *Gothic Cottage* indicated a house built in the prevailing gothic fashion, and the name became popular; there was one advertised in Stamford Hill in 1807 and another in Finchley in 1810: 'A Singularly elegant new-built Gothic Cottage situated on Finchley Common, near the seven-mile stone, erected on an uniform plan. In the most substantial manner, and fitted up with the best materials; the rooms are arranged in the most convenient manner, and

---

'Lease 23 June in Mortgage (1782) 20 Aug. A parcel of Ground..[which] adjoineth towards the north on vaults situate under the houses built on The Royal Taras'. By 1850 *terrace* was used of non-grand houses: 1850 C. Kingsley *Alton Locke* I. i. 1 'My earliest recollections are of a suburban street; of its jumble of little shops and little terraces'.

[8] www.british-history.ac.uk/vch/middx/vol9/pp60–63.
[9] Elsewhere Courland House; e.g. *The Times*, 30 September 1825; *The Standard*, 25 October 1836.
[10] *The Morning Chronicle*, 12 September 1845.

comprise five sleeping-rooms, two elegant drawing-rooms, dining and breakfast parlour and study, excellent kitchen, scullery and offices, and good cellaring, a forecourt, and good garden'.[11] Peckham Rye's *Gothic Cottage* of 1813 had 'a portico entrance with stained glass, a drawing-room opening into a conservatory . . . and four bed chambers, elegantly furnished in the Gothic style', with five acres of land.[12] *Vimiera* and *Cintra* refer to the Peninsula War of 1808; the Anglo-Portuguese defeated the French at Vimiero, and an agreement signed at Cintra allowed them to leave Portugal without further conflict. The houses are likely to have been named not so much as to attract patriots as to trumpet the fact that they were brand new and the *dernier cri* in 1808. Similarly *Albert Villa* is likely to have been built in 1840, the year Queen Victoria married Prince Albert of Saxe-Coburg and Gotha. *Hartington* and *Boscombe* are place-names in Derbyshire and Hampshire respectively, and *Westbourne* and *Springfield* are toponyms that occur in various places throughout southern Britain. *Vernon* is a title in the British peerage. *Courland* was the British name for a duchy in what is now Western Latvia; Courland House was *in situ* by 1825. *Lavender Sweep* consisted of five *rus in urbe* villas, situated amongst lavender fields and linked by an approach crescent, a carriage sweep, built in the 1780s by a City cloth merchant, Peter James Bennett.[13]

Who lived in these houses in 1843? I have traced the following:

George Blakeway, gentleman[14]
John Brownrigg Gore, Solicitor
Thomas Catlin (elsewhere Cattley), White Lead and Colour Merchant[15]
Henry Gilbertson, Glass Merchant[16]
Thomas Grissell, Public Works Contractor[17]
(Guillaume) Charles Guichard, French Agent (merchant)[18]

---

[11] *The Times*, 7 March 1807 and *The Times*, 21 July 1810. Subsequent advertisements also mention 'several servants' sleeping rooms'.

[12] *The Times*, 8 March 1813.

[13] www.english-heritage.org.uk/content/imported-docs/a-e/battersea-vol-50-chap-14.pdf.

[14] Occupation on Marriage Certificate is 'gentleman', but at this date and in this context *gentleman* signified someone who had retired from trade. London Metropolitan Archives, Christ Church, St Marylebone, Register of Marriages, P89/CTC, Item 064.

[15] www.thegazette.co.uk/London/issue/20820/page/352/data.pdf: 'Thomas Thompson Cattley, of Cousin's-lane, Upper Thames-street, in the city of London, and of No. 4, Vimiera, Wandsworth-road, in the county of Surrey, Colour Merchant'. In 1837 the house was just 'Vimiera, Wandsworth-road' (*The Gentleman's Magazine*, 1837, vol 7, new series, 554), as it was in *Robson's Directory* for 1842. 1851 census, Class: H0107, Piece: 1573, Folio: 444, Page: 25.

[16] 1841 census, Class: HO107, Piece: 678, Book: 11, Civil Parish: St Marylebone, County: Middlesex, Enumeration District: 15, Folio: 49, Page: 19.

[17] Thomas Grissell won the contract for building the Houses of Parliament and Nelson's Column: Grissell, Thomas (1801–1874): M. H. Port, https://doi.org/10.1093/ref:odnb/49437.

[18] 1843 *Post Office Directory*.

Francis Heathcote, Bank of England, In-Teller's Office[19]
William Page Penney, Varnish Manufacturer[20]
Samuel Seddon, Merchant[21]

Citizens, that is, men who had made their own money rather than inherited it from their ancient Anglo-Norman forebears, were the first to populate the new houses on the Wandsworth and Finchley New roads. Untrammelled by the weight of history, with no ancestral reputation to maintain or titled relatives to offend, they were free to name their houses whatever they pleased. However, they adhered to English house-naming conventions, and their choices did not outlast consecutive numbering; many such house names had become abandoned by the 1880s. By the railway-age, then, these house-naming conventions consisted of:

the transferred place-name: *Boscombe Lodge, Hartington Cottage*
the nostalgically rural: *Westbourn Villa, Lavender Sweeps, Springfield Lodge*
the commemorative: *Vimiera, Cintra Villa, Albert Villa, Weller Cottage, Courland*
the upwardly-mobile: *Tudor Lodge, Vernon Villa*
the latest fad: *Gothic Cottage*

Only two main British house-naming categories are missing from this list: the do-it-yourself pick & mix from British place-name elements (such as *Hurstholme*), and the jocular (such as *Wee Neste*), both of which were to come later.[22] That all these names fit within a set of house-naming conventions can be tested by seeing what does not occur. Within the United Kingdom, certain nouns and descriptors denoting the natural world are common: *Oak Lodge, Hillcrest, The Grove, Ivy Bank*, but not (in Britain) *November Rain, *Green Ice, *Pearl Eye*. The latter are real present-day house names on the Mediterranean island of Malta, where different naming conventions apply, and the parched climate makes desiderata of cold, damp, and green.

The transferred place-name is often a subset of the commemorative type, with houses named after a person (*Adeline Villa*), town or village that was significant to the householder – a birthplace, a honeymoon or holiday venue (to account for all the houses named *Osbourne, Ventnor, Shanklin*, and other Victorian seaside resorts). *Aberdeen Villa*, Maida Hill – Aberdeen in Scotland being nowhere near

---

[19] 1856 *Post Office Directory*.
[20] 1851 census, Class: H0107, Piece: 1491, Folio: 824, Page: 6. 1829 *Post Office Directory*: William Penney, Varnish & Japan-manuf., 251 Tottenham Court Road.
[21] 1841 census, Class: H0107, Piece: 1055, Book: 9, Civil Parish: Lambeth, County: Surrey, Enumeration District: 17, Folio: 26, Page: 7.
[22] I use the term 'pick & mix' in reference to Woolworth's, where it was a term for choosing different types of sweets from separate containers and putting them in a bag to make your own assortment, as opposed to a pre-assembled selection. *OED* pick 'n' mix, *n*. (and *adj*.), first attested 1958: 'Frederick (Maryland) News 26 Nov. 7/4 (advt.) Make Your Own Selection From Our Pick 'n' Mix Candy Asst.'

Maida Hill in London, Maida Hill being nowhere near Maida, Italy, the site of a battle in 1806 during the Napoleonic Wars. (Maida Vale and its neighbour St John's Wood were particularly rich in early villa names, where large mid-nineteenth century citizens' houses extended out from Regent's Park towards Swiss Cottage.) That the transferred place-name was a relatively new invention can be seen by contrast with older, traditional, house names. In Berkshire, for example, the older names of stately homes differ from the post-1830 house names in that stately home place-names are not transferred. Aldermaston Court really is near Aldermaston, Benham Park is at Marsh Benham, Calcot Park is near Calcot, Englefield House is at Englefield, Farley Hall is in the village of Farley Hill, Sunninghill Park is in Sunninghill, Basildon Park is between Upper Basildon and Lower Basildon, and Windsor Castle is situated in the town of Windsor. Stately home names are rarely if ever of the nostalgically rural (*Springfield Palace*), latest fad (*Fern Castle*), or jocular (*Grande Neste*) sort, although they can be commemorative (*Blenheim Palace*).

Because the stately home took its name from the nearby village (with following head noun *Park, Hall, House, Manor, Court, Lodge, Palace, Castle*), the Old English, Old Norse and Anglo-Norman and Celtic components of village names – *ford, ton, ham, glen, aber, bury, worth, avon, thorpe, leigh* – all looked good to upwardly-mobile Victorians when naming their new houses.

The pick & mix place-name house name came after the transferred place-name. Place-name components are not spread evenly over Britain, but cluster wherever speakers of the various languages settled. Old Norse place-name elements only occur in specific sections of the eastern and northern parts of the country. Celtic place-names cluster on the western side, with those in Cornwall differing from those in Cumbria. Here, by way of illustration, are some elements from Old English, Old Norse, Anglo-Norman and Celtic words for landscape features that enjoyed a second airing as house-name elements far removed from their ancestral region:[23]

hurst	Old English *hyrst* 'wooded hill, hillock'
holm	Old Norse *holmr* 'island, inland promontory, raised ground in marsh, river-meadow'
dene	Old English *denu* 'main valley, long open valley'
glen	Scottish Gaelic *gleann*, Celtic *glennos*, Welsh *glyn*, Cornish *glin* 'valley'
dale	Old Norse *dalr* 'main valley, long valley', mainly in northern England

---

[23] Place-name etymologies are taken from Watts (2004) and Gelling and Cole (2003). Medieval Latin descriptors also occur in place-names (*Zeal Monachorum, Ryme Extrinseca, Weston Super Mare*), but such elements are far less frequently transferred to house names.

combe	Old English *cumb* 'bowl', 'short, broad, bowl or trough-shaped valley with three fairly steeply rising sides' south of Yorkshire; and Old Celtic **kumbos* 'valley' in the South West
thorp	Old Norse *thorp*, Old English *thorp*, *throp* 'secondary settlement, outlying farm, hamlet'
wick, wich	Old English *wic* 'buildings used for a specific purpose, specialised farm'
toft	Old Norse *toft* 'building site, deserted site, younger than *by* and *thorp*'
mont	Anglo-Norman 'hill'
thwaite	Old Norse *thveit* 'clearing, meadow, paddock, enclosed pasture', common in the North-West
pen	Celtic *penn* 'place at the end of something', Welsh, Cornish, Cumbrian 'head, headland, end'
by	Old Danish *by* 'yard, farmstead, village'

These landscape features are qualified in place-names with locative adjectives, such as *west, side, under, nether*; with people's names (such as *Bada* + Old English *hyrst* 'wooded hill' in Bathurst, Sussex; *Twicca* + Old English *hamm* 'land in a river meander' in Twickenham, Middlesex), and with all kinds of nouns and descriptors taken from the surroundings, such as:

Old English *lind* 'linden, lime-tree' + Old English *hyrst* 'hill'	Lyndhurst, Hants
Cumbric *penn* 'headland' + Cumbric *rid* 'ford'	Penrith, Cumb
Cornish *lost* 'tail' + Cornish *gwthyel* 'woody place'	Lostwithiel, Cornwall
Old Norse *borg* 'fortress' + Old Norse *dalr* 'valley'	Borrowdale, Cumb
Anglo-Norman *bel* 'beautiful' + Anglo-Norman *mont* 'hill'	Belmont, Lancs

But all this was immaterial to the new house-namers, who just liked the sound of the various components. They uncoupled the place-name elements and recombined them, so that their houses came to bear new, but traditional-sounding, amalgamated names, even though the amalgamation in question had never previously existed and didn't necessarily make etymological sense. Examples of the pick & mix sort are house names *Penthwaite* (Welsh, Cornish and Cumbrian *pen* 'end, head' + Old Norse *thwait* 'dwelling in clearing in woodland'); *Strathmead* (Scots Gaelic *strath* 'wide valley' + Old English *mæd* 'meadow'), *Inverdene* (Scottish Gaelic *inver* 'river confluence' + Old English *denu* 'wood'). Perfectly good traditional-sounding house names, just invented ones.[24] *Thorne Blae* (next door to *Wilhelm Lodge*, which

---

[24] *Hurstholme, Penthwaite, Strathmead, Inverdene*, are present-day British house names in the Royal Mail database.

was next door to *Sunnyside*) in Boston Park Road, Brentford, Middlesex, in Kelly's *Directory for Ealing and Acton* of 1889–90, combines *blae*, a Scots word for 'blue', in keeping with Queen Victoria's (and hence everyone else's) love of all things Scottish, but its unScots postposed position, and the extra -*e* on *Thorne*, speak of historical romance rather than actual Lowlands Scots. Sentiment plays a large part in British house-naming: looking good on the gate trumps etymological legitimacy every time.

So the modern London housing name-stock emerged in what were at the time the new outer suburbs. Early names were bestowed on self-made, well-to-do peoples' houses, and the most popular name-types (then as now) – the transferred place-name and the nostalgically rural place-name – were popular right from the beginning. By the end of the century, commuting daily by train from a greater distance had become the norm. Forty-odd years of suburb-building later, house names in Finchley (to which the Finchley Road leads) and Kingston (the eventual projection of the Wandsworth Road) were as follows, taken from the 1882 *Post Office Directory*. The first address in each case is the central London workplace and the second is the residence from which the householder commuted:

Dale, George, 27 Chancery Lane & Eldersley, Nether Street, Finchley
Elwes, Edward Golding, 8 Furnival's Inn & Etchingham Lodge, Etchingham Park Road, Finchley
Hart, Percival, 16 Devonshire Square & Middleton House, East End, Finchley
Saunders, Albert, 21 Great St. Helen's & Malabar House, Church End, Finchley
Henry, Stevens, 22 Bedford Row & Ferndale Lodge, Finchley
Fox, Edwin, jun., 99 Gresham Street & Ballard's Lodge, North Finchley
Fox, Edwin, 99 Gresham Street & Rosemont, North Finchley
Gole, Russell, 4 Lime Street & The Ferns, 65 Finchley New Road
Kisbey, Henry Edwin, 106 Cheapside & Dunedin Villas, Finchley
Osbaldeston, Matthew Davenport, 36 Lincoln's Inn Fields & Florence Villa, East End, Finchley
Pritchard, Henry, 10 Billiter Square & Clovelly Cottage, Brownlow Road, Finchley
Sayer, Edward, 9 Clifford Street, Bond Street & Oak Lodge, Finchley
West, Charles, Artillery Chambers, 16 City road, & Fernville, Fortis Green, Finchley
Pearson, John Michael, 41 Finsbury Circus & The Grange, Kingston Hill
Russell, Henshaw Skinner, 2 Mitre Court Chambers, Fleet Street & Priory, Surbiton Hill, Kingston
Saunders Edward George, 27 King Street, Cheapside & Warren Lodge, Kingston Hill

These citizens were lawyers (I surveyed that part of the *Post Office Directory* of 1882 which covered the law as it gives both work and residential addresses), and lawyers were as susceptible as anyone else to house-naming conventions:

Transferred place-name:

> *Etchingham Lodge* (a Sussex place-name; a neighouring villa was *Sussex Lodge*);[25]
> *Middleton House, Malabar House, Dunedin Villas* (the Scottish Gaelic name for
> Edinburgh), *Florence Villa, Clovelly Cottage* (an especially picturesque Devonshire
> coastal village)

Nostalgically rural:

> *Oak Lodge, The Grange*

Commemorative:

> *Ballard's Lodge, Priory*

Upwardly-mobile:

> *Warren Lodge* (a name from the peerage)

Latest fad:

> *The Ferns, Eldersley* (although possibly from the Old English words for 'elder-tree' +
> 'meadow', *Eldersley* is uncommon. The house name is more likely to be referencing
> John Donald Carrick's *Life of Sir William Wallace of Elderslie* of 1830, which spawned
> numerous houses named *Elderslie*)

Pick & mix:

> *Rosemont, Ferndale, Fernville*

What were these villas like to live in? A Christian didactic story for children written by 'Aunt Clara' called *Rambles at Sunnyside; or, A Week with my Godchildren*
(1862) gives some idea. The preface tells that Aunt Clara (a pseudonym for Clarissa
Woolloton) wrote her *Rambles* at Clapham Park, Surrey.[26] Her description of
Sunnyside is more generic than specific:

> let us describe Sunnyside, the old-fashioned dwelling, which has been Mrs Clare's home
> for many years. It was a low, red-bricked house, standing on a rising ground with tall trees
> at the back and one side. In front, a large, gently-sloping lawn, fringed with shrubs and
> fine trees, at one end of which stood a lodge. At the opposite side, a small gate admitted
> into the fruit and kitchen gardens, with the poultry-yard adjoining. Beyond was a field,
> in which were two cows; and in one corner was a model pig-sty, with a fat white pig, the
> happy mother of twelve squeaking little ones.
>
> The drawing and dining-rooms opened into a pretty verandah, covered with fresh
> climbing plants, now bursting into leaf and bud. They were both large rooms, pleasantly
> furnished, with pictures on the walls, and bright curtains to the windows. Comfortable
> chairs and sofas were scattered about; on some of the tables were pretty statues, and little
> fine old china; and against the walls at one end was a long, well-filled book-case. Both

---

[25] www.british-history.ac.uk/vch/middx/vol6/pp38-55.
[26] See *The Gazette* (10 March 1865: 1463): Charles Woolloton, Lynton Lodge, Clapham Park, Surrey.

rooms opened into a spacious hall, in which were some family pictures, and a polished side-table, surmounted by some noble antlers. At one end was the massive door, going into a pleasant porch, which led, by a flight of stone steps, into the garden. At the opposite end of the hall was the broad oaken staircase, leading to the four bedrooms first mentioned. Each room was furnished with everything to make it comfortable. The beds had white hangings, with pretty pink trimmings; and from the pleasant windows you could see the lawn, with the road and valley beyond, in which lay the village and church of H–. At the opposite end of the landing was another door which led into the servants' rooms, and, down a back staircase, into the kitchen and out-houses.

    (Aunt Clara, *Rambles at Sunnyside; or, A Week with my Godchildren*, 1862: 3–6)

More country than town at this date, but the red-brick with its porch decoration tells us this is a new-build, as does the verandah. Victorian houses built in the style known as 'Redbrick' (including the subtypes 'Queen Anne' and 'Old English') had a deliberately old-fashioned air, with exteriors sporting shaped brackets and sprocketed eaves, balconies and porches, oriel, sash and mullioned windows, and stained glass. A typical red-brick built on a medieval manor plan might display sixteenth-century style twisted chimney stacks, seventeenth-century style barge-boarding on the gables, and a nineteenth-century conservatory and Macadamed driveway.[27] Modifiers in the text are *pretty* x 3, *pleasant(ly)* x 3, *comfortable* x 2, *fine, well-filled, spacious, polished, noble, massive, broad*. Confident, commodious Victoriana: lawn, shrubs, verandah, porch, and antlers in the hall. It was to be a blueprint for housing throughout the British Empire.

Town and country boxes

> The statesman, lawyer, merchant, man of trade,
> Pants for the refuge of some rural shade . . .
> Suburban villas, highway-side retreats,
> That dread the encroachment of our growing streets.
> Tight boxes neatly sashed, and in a blaze
> With all a July sun's collected rays,
> Delight the citizen, who gasping there,
> Breathes clouds of dust, and calls it country air.
>   (William Cowper, 1781, extract from *Retirement*)

Cowper's phrase 'tight boxes, neatly sashed' is in reference to the late eighteenth-century newly built houses on the roads leading out of town. The *Oxford English Dictionary* (box, *n.2* 14.) defines this usage of the word *box* as a 'small country-house; a residence for temporary use while following a particular sport, as a hunting-box, shooting-box, fishing-box,' with illustrative attestations dating from *a*.1713, although these do not match Cowper's arterial-road, suburban-villa-retreat sense. Turning to advertisements, *box* was used of the most central property:

---

[27] Austin, Dowdy and Miller (1997: 124) 'Redbrick'.

May-fair.– A Bachelor's Box, Furnished, to be LET, or the Lease, held at a low rent, and Furniture to be Sold on reduced terms. For particulars and cards to view apply, if by letter, post paid, to Mr. Nutter, No. 4, Curzon-street, Mayfair.

(*The Morning Post*, 12 May 1835)

Bachelor's Box, or a desirable Residence for a small Family, commanding a view of the Gardens of Buckingham New Palace. – Mr. Wilmot is instructed to Sell, by Private Treaty the Lease, Fixtures, and truly elegant Furniture of a House, consisting of ten rooms, fitted up with great taste, and in substantial repair, with the usual convenient offices. Particulars and cards to view of Mr. Wilmot, Auctioneer, Appraiser, Estate and House Agent, Grosvenor-street West, Easton-square, next the Church.

(*The Morning Post*, 15 September 1835)

And here is a client speaking to his lawyer in a novel of 1854:

'Will you do me the favor to inform me where I reside?'
  'I have obeyed your commands to the letter, and have secured for you a small but convenient bachelor's box in Hertford Street, with a suitable establishment.'
  'No spare bed-room, I trust?'
  'Not one; but excellent stabling, and a good cellar.'
  'I am obliged to you; but am I to infer I could not offer a night's hospitality to a stray cousin, even in the event of a thunderstorm or a tornado?'
  'Not without personal inconvenience certainly.'

(Miss (Julia) Pardoe, *Reginald Lyle*, 1854)

Hertford Street is in Mayfair. Here is a description of a barrister's clerk in a novel of 1861:

Mr. Crabwitz was a genteel-looking man, somewhat over forty years of age, very careful as to his gloves, hat, and umbrella, and not a little particular as to his associates. As he was unmarried, fond of ladies' society, and presumed to be a warm man in money matters, he had his social successes, and looked down from a considerable altitude on some men who from their professional rank might have been considered as his superiors. He had a small bachelor's box down at Barnes, and not unfrequently went abroad in the vacations.

(Anthony Trollope, 'Orley Farm', *Harper's New Monthly Magazine*, 1861, 23: 217)

'Presumed to be a warm man in money matters' meant 'well-to-do'. Mr Crabwitz with his meticulous appearance, his small bachelor's box down at Barnes, his not unfrequent trips abroad in the vacations, and his impression of being a warm man, had a wealthy front, and the bachelor's box at Barnes contributed to that general impression. 'Expensive' was part of the meaning of 'bachelor's box', and 'giving an impression of wealth' fits with estate-agents' advertisements. One advertising the sale of 40, Grove End Road, St John's Wood, was worded: 'bachelor's box, charming cottage ornée'.[28]

---

[28] *The Morning Post*, 10 January 1871. The word 'bachelor' in estate-agent speak did go on to have a life meaning 'without women' and also 'small': Charles Dickens, *Our Mutual Friend* (1865: I.i.xii.109): 'Mr. Mortimer Lightwood and Mr. Eugene Wrayburn ... had taken a bachelor cottage near Hampton'; *Globe & Mail* (Toronto), 17 February 1968: 'Accommodation ... from bachelor apartment to 6-bedroom home ... in some of Ottawa's finest locations'.

What exactly was a 'cottage ornée' at that point in time?

> The term *cottage* has for some time past been in vogue as a particular designation for small country residences and detached suburban houses, adapted to a moderate scale of living, yet with all due attention to comfort and refinement. While, in this sense of it, the name is divested of all associations with poverty, it is convenient, inasmuch as it frees from all pretension and parade and restraint.
>
> (*Penny Cyclopaedia Supplement*, 1845, I. 426)

Here, 'parade and restraint' are presented as undesirable qualities – with a cottage ornée you could do what you wanted with regard to the exterior, which you couldn't with a house on a landed-gentry estate such as that of the Grosvenor or Howard de Walden, as they had (and have) to be maintained in a certain style. 'Parade', in that the stucco had to be painted periodically in a certain specific shade of cream so that the houses all presented a uniform exterior; 'restraint', in that you were not free to choose any other kind of décor. But in the context of St John's Wood, a cottage was a detached villa done up very nicely according to your taste, and a cottage ornée was decorated, in the tint of your choice, possibly with a verandah, French windows, shutters, a balcony, a porch, lattice, or wrought-iron work. You could suit your fancy. The phrases 'bachelor box' and 'cottage ornée' were used somewhat interchangeably to mean picturesque houses which may or may not have been for bachelors; they were both small and large, they were both in and out of town, they were also in the suburbs, and they were both for temporary purposes such as sport and also for permanent purposes such as living in. Fluid in meaning, these vogue phrases hit the target of the self-made rich, who were equally ambiguous in terms of rank, social class, and concomitant cultural behaviour.[29] No need to be constrained by the frigid good taste of the estate-owning classes if commuting from a cottage ornée up the Finchley Road – their reach did not extend that far.

Nevertheless, a freedom from the dictates of tradition did not result in a free-for-all, either in terms of naming, or in terms of presentation. Rather, certain fashions periodically prevailed.

Before there were streets of suburban houses, there were shrubberies – shrubberies had been in vogue in England since the 1740s, but in a rather different sense. The *Oxford English Dictionary* dates the word 'shrubbery' from 1748, but it did not signify laurel, rhododendron or holly lining the fence to screen off the house

---

[29] On 15 March 1864 a play called *Bachelor's Box* by T. W. Robertson opened at the Polygraphic Hall, King-William-street, Charing cross (the street is now called William IV Street and leads eastwards off the Charing Cross Road opposite the National Portrait Gallery). The Polygraphic Hall started life as the Lowther Rooms in 1840, and was taken over in 1855 by William S. Woodin, an entrepreneurial monologuist. He provided 'graphical, Polygraphical and Anthropographical Entertainment', playing all the characters himself, up to 50 of them. A review of *Bachelor's Box* reads: 'the scene is the villa of a testy old gentleman who has retired from London to the suburbs in the hope of finding peace, but who soon discovers that noise and annoyance find their way into the most secluded abodes.' (*The Morning Post*, 23 March 1864). A one-man tour-de-force, clearly the phrase 'bachelor's box' resonated with the audience.

next door.[30] Shrubberies that bordered the lawns of eighteenth-century detached houses consisted of a considerable variety of trees, shrubs, climbing plants and flowers which decorated paths that led to the 'orchard, kitchen-garden, botanical borders, green-house, dairy, ice-house, mushroom-hut, aviary, poultry-yard, or stables'. 'Ornamental plantations are now so universally spread over the face of this country, that our island may be compared to a vase emerging from the ocean', wrote Henry Phillips in 1823.[31] Like their later descendants, eighteenth-century shrubberies were artfully positioned, bulked in dense proximity to screen off the neighbours on the other side, be that *en route* to mushroom-hut and aviary in the eighteenth century, or away from next-door's garage in the twentieth. The many homes with name-elements *Laurel* and *Holly* attest the nineteenth-century fashion for these particular shrubs.

The word 'rockery' is first found in print in 1775, reached a peak of usage in the early 1900s, and declined thereafter.[32] Early rockeries were much the same as modern rockeries, albeit on a grander scale. Joseph Paxton's rockery at Chatsworth, begun in 1842, included towering stacked boulders, crags, chasm and waterfall. Although it was not easy to replicate cliff and ravine in a non-stately garden, you could attempt a miniature version with stones. From the 1840s, suburban garden-ers needed rockeries to participate in the next wave, which was ferneries containing different species of fern.[33] This particular fad was stimulated in 1840 by the pub-lication of Edward Newman's *A History of British Ferns*, and sales of Nathanial Bagshaw Ward's ornamental indoor display-case on a fancy table. Everyone could participate. In 1855, an irritated Charles Kingsley wrote: 'Your daughters, perhaps, have been seized with the prevailing "Pteridomania", and are collecting and buying ferns, with Ward's cases wherein to keep them, (for which you have to pay,) and wrangling over unpronounceable names of species, (which seem to be different in each new Fern-book that they buy), till the Pteridomania seems to you somewhat of a bore', although he rather liked the end product.[34] Ferns were both collected in the wild – stripping Scottish mountainsides in the process – and bought from

[30] *OED* shrubbery, *n.* '"Nature has been so remarkably kind this last October to adorn my Shrubbery with the flowers that usually blow at Whitsuntide", written by Lady Luxborough in a letter of 16 October 1748.
[31] Phillips (1823: 1/32, 1–2). '. . . and between the Bowling-Green, and an Avenue of fine Elms, is a beautiful Serpentine Canal, which, in its Meandering, glides through a Shrubbery of the choicest and gayest Flowers' (a house advertised for sale at Weston Green, Thames Ditton, Surrey, *London Evening Post*, 2 June 1757–4 June 1757).
[32] *Public Advertiser*, 28 August 1775: Villa for sale at Friday Hill, near Woodford, Essex, 'At a suitable Distance a Barn, Farm-yard, Rockery, Fish-pond, &c.', antedating *OED* rockery, *n.* first attestation 1794, *Walker's Hibernian Magazine*, March, 247/1: 'Besides ponds for aquatic plants, artificial rockeries, and mounts for saxatile and alpine plants.' For peaks in usage, enter 'rockery' and tick for British English at https://books.google.com/ngrams/.
[33] *OED* fernery, *n.*, first attested 1840.
[34] *OED* pterido-, *comb. form*, first attested in Kingsley (1855: 4). For details of the fern craze, see Whittingham (2012).

the Fern Department of James Veitch's Royal Exotic Nursery in the King's Road, Chelsea.[35] This particular garden fad was highly productive in terms of nomenclature, giving rise to such house names as *The Ferns, Fernbank, Ferndale, Ferndale lodge, Fernleigh, Fern villa, Fern Villas, Fernville* (all present in *Kelly's Ealing, Acton, Hanwell, Gunnersbury & Chiswick Directory for 1889–90*), among other *Fern-* combinations.

More than one writer sneered at the modest artificial rockwork of domestic gardens, especially rockeries containing shells and broken china.[36] Yet: 'I found a new contentment in working about The Fort with my own hands – planting the herbaceous borders, moving shrubs, mowing the hay in the summer, building a rock garden with cascades supplied by water pumped up from a dam which I had installed below Virginia Water', the Duke of Windsor (ex-King Edward VIII) told *Life* magazine in 1950, referring to his rockery at his house in Windsor Great Park. 'With my guests I cleared away the dank laurels in the Fort's gardens. My brother Bertie often came over to help.'[37]

By 1929 when the Prince of Wales took over the house he named Fort Belvedere, which had been built as a Gothic folly and known previously as Shrubs Hill Tower, shrubberies had fallen out of fashion and so he co-opted his entourage into rooting them out. (Five years earlier, he had been invited to stay with millionaire James Abercrombie Burden and his wife at Woodside, Muttontown Road, Syosset, Long Island. Apparently the Burdens installed a set of garden gnomes, possibly Welsh, especially for his visit, and thus another trend was born.[38] However, it is difficult to be high-minded when confronted with gnomes, Welsh or otherwise, so from around 1927 when they began to take up their toadstool, wishing-well and windmill residences in the front gardens of the lower classes, gnomes too became deplored by persons of taste.) For a brief period, between 1919 and 1928, the Prince of Wales – he who got his guests and brother Bertie to dig up the laurels at Fort Belvedere, he who carefully installed a water-feature, he who was to become Edward VIII in

---

[35] See 'Economic history: Farm-gardening and market gardening', in *A History of the County of Middlesex: Volume 12, Chelsea*, ed. Patricia E. C. Croot (London, 2004), pp. 150–5 (www.british-history.ac.uk/vch/middx/vol12/pp150–155, accessed 17 December 2014); and also Veitch family (per. 1768–1929): Elizabeth Baigent, https://doi.org/10.1093/ref:odnb/61986.

[36] 'A very common error in composing what is called rockwork is, to intermix . . . pieces of scoriae, vitrified bricks, &.; with artistical fragments, such as . . . shells, corals, &c.' (Loudon 1837: 535). 'How absurd are urns made of slag, or flowerbeds bordered with concrete stuck full of coloured glass. An old stump will make a most handsome urn, and a good window-box is much more attractive than all the glass or shell-bordered flowerbeds in the world.' (*Suburban Life, the Countryside Magazine*, 1908: 324).

[37] *Life*, 29 May 1950: 65.

[38] Way (2009: 27–8). Way is the authority on British garden gnomes. The first mention I can find of the word *gnome* in print referring to commercial garden statuary (as opposed to gnomes of legend, or private gnomes) is *The Times*, 16 May 1927: 11 'Garden furniture is being displayed in some [shop] windows and also small figures in the shape of gnomes that would brighten up difficult corners where flowers are reluctant to appear' (antedating *OED* gnome, *n.*[2]1.b. 'garden statue', first attestation 1938).

the following decade – became a hunting enthusiast. 'Putting up at a box' was what he did when he went to Melton Mowbray to hunt with the Quorn (named after a village) and the Fernie (named after Master of the Hunt Mr Charles Fernie of Keythorpe Hall), and it was his repeated going there that made the Leicestershire countryside the fashionable place to be in the 1920s and 30s. For a decade or so, Melton Mowbray in Leicestershire became the centre of the world for the wealthy and leisured, including Americans and Rajahs, and anyone else who had the time and the money and the social connections. Melton Mowbray boxes that the Prince of Wales is known to have stayed at included Newport Lodge, Craven Lodge, and Burrough Court. Craven Lodge became the Craven Lodge Club, and the Prince of Wales liked it so much he had his own private quarters appended. Craven Lodge was owned by the Craven family who also owned a London mansion in Fulham named Craven Cottage (the name was later transferred to the ground of Fulham Football Club). Burrough Court was another stately home nearby, and it was here, at 7.30pm on Saturday 10 January 1931, that the Prince of Wales first met Mrs Wallis Simpson.

Blocks of flats named 'X Court'

When Mrs Simpson (1896–1986) travelled to Burrough Court to meet the Prince of Wales for the first time, she was resident at no. 5, Bryanston Court, Bryanston Square, London.[39] There is nothing unusual about the name (Bryanston being the transferred name of a village in Dorset), but the transfer in meaning of the second-element from *OED* court, *n.[1]* 2. b. 'Often in proper names of English manor-houses, e.g. *Hampton Court*' to urban residential blocks needs explanation. The nineteenth-century terms for blocks of flats, when such edifices began to be built, were *mansions* and *chambers*. Maida Vale is the name of the London end of an arterial road leading northwest out of town containing many early blocks of flats, bearing the names Southwold Mansions, Morshead Mansions, Cleveland Mansions, Carlton Mansions, Delaware Mansions, Leith Mansions, Ashworth Mansions, Elgin Mansions, Lauderdale Mansions, Biddulph Mansions. By the nineteenth century, the word *chambers* often indicated a set of rooms for occupation by a single person – more the equivalent of a one-bedroom flat – whereas flats in mansions-blocks could have as many as ten or twelve rooms. In contradistinction to early purpose-built blocks of flats, London courts were usually tenanted by the poor (until they were largely demolished by the Luftwaffe and town-planners).[40] Courts were the

[39] Bloch (1986: chapter 1) gives the letter that places their first encounter on this date at Burrough Court. Windsor (*née* Warfield; *other married names* Spencer, Simpson), (Bessie) Wallis, duchess of Windsor (1896–1986), wife of Edward, duke of Windsor (doi.org/10.1093/ref:odnb/38277).
[40] *OED* mansion, *n.* I. 1. e. 'a large residential building divided into flats', first attestation 1868; flat *n.[2]*; chamber, *n.* 6. a. 'Rooms forming part of a large house or other building and let out as a suite or

small rectangular yards around which buildings were arranged, and they could be very small and very mean indeed. The slum-cleared areas of St Martin's in the Fields, St Giles and Victoria contained many courts. However the names of stately homes such as Hampton Court have always been well-known, acting as an obvious precedent for property developers to talk up their latest block of flats. But this does not explain why residential blocks named on the template *X Court* were virtually unknown in the nineteenth century yet became so common in the twentieth.

In the property columns of *The Times* newspaper, the earliest blocks of flats in London with *court* as a second element were Kensington Court Mansions just off Kensington High Street (planned 1882, advertisement 12 April 1888) and Whitehall Court Flats on the Embankment (planned 1883, advertisement 27 December 1890). These were both built by the same property developer, Jonathan T. Carr (1845–1915).[41] Kensington Court Mansions was so-named because it was built on a street which was at first named Charles Street, but which by 1881 had been renamed Kensington Court Place.[42] Whitehall Court Flats and the newly-built street on which they stood, named Whitehall Court, took their name from the historic site of the Court of the Palace of Whitehall. Kensington Court Mansions and Whitehall Court Flats were followed by Hyde Park Court, Albert Gate, Knightsbridge (announced as a project 18 July 1887, opened to residents in 1892 when still unfinished) and Bedford-court-mansions, Bloomsbury (advertised 1895). As Carr was about to go bankrupt, he sold Whitehall Court to Jabez Balfour and his associates. As well as Whitehall Court, the Balfour Group were also developers of Hyde Park Court, Albert Gate.[43] Thus the second-element *court* was carried over from Carr's properties to the new project. Here is an advertisement for the super-deluxe, high-end block from 1893, by which time Whitehall Court Flats had become advertised as Whitehall Court:

---

apartment', first attestation 1581; court, *n.*[1] I. 3. 'In a town: A confined yard or more or less quadrangular space opening off a street, and built around with houses . . . usually tenanted by the poor', first attestation given in this sense 1687. Old English *flett* 'floor' developed the meaning 'a storey', and is first attested with its present-day meaning in the Scottish context of Sir Walter Scott's novel *Redgauntlet* of 1824. A celebrity during his lifetime, Sir Walter has probably had more influence than any other single person on British house-naming practices.

[41] Carr, Jonathan Thomas (1845–1915), Andrew Saint (doi.org/10.1093/ref:odnb/49290). *Whitehall Court* is the conspicuous château on the north bank of the Thames looking upstream from Waterloo Bridge.

[42] 'Colby Court, Kensington House and Kensington Court', in *Survey of London: Volume 42, Kensington Square To Earl's Court*, ed. Hermione Hobhouse (London, 1986), pp. 55–76. *British History Online* (www.british-history.ac.uk/survey-london/vol42/pp55-76, accessed 21 February 2018). Bedford-court-mansions, Bloomsbury, advertised *The Morning Post* 16 February 1895.

[43] 'Knightsbridge North Side: Parkside to Albert Gate Court, West of Albert Gate', in *Survey of London: Volume 45, Knightsbridge*, ed. John Greenacombe (London, 2000), pp. 53–63. *British History Online* (www.british-history.ac.uk/survey-london/vol45/pp53-63, accessed 21 February 2018).

Whitehall Court

Facing Thames Embankment, Whitehall-place, S. W. and the new Horse Guards-avenue, S. W.

The building of Whitehall Court occupies one of the finest positions in London, affording extensive views of the river (with the Surrey Hills beyond), and overlooks the Embankment gardens, and is also most conveniently and centrally situated with respect to the Houses of Parliament, principal clubs, theatres, &c. It is fitted throughout with every modern convenience, e.g. hot and cold water, electric light and bells, visitors', tradesmen's and servants' lifts in operation night and day. Everything has been done to render the drainage system perfect. The entire building – walls, floors, partitions, and staircases – is fireproof. The handsome marble corridors and staircases are well lighted and heated by hot air. The rooms are all finished to suit the wishes of incoming tenants. A club for the use of tenants and their friends only has been established on the premises, affording the following accommodation:- Large dining room, private dining rooms, smoking room, billiard rooms, cloak rooms, &c; by this means tenants will be enabled to be served either in their own apartments or in the dining rooms. Arrangements can also be made with the Residential Club for the provision of full or partial service, thus relieving tenants from all the trouble with servants. The rental of each suite includes the use of the rooms of the Residential Club, all rates and taxes, water (hot and cold), lighting and heating of corridors, use of lifts, services of porters, &c., the only extra being for electric light used in tenants' rooms, which is supplied by meter.

(*The Times*, 20 March 1893)

Kensington Court, Whitehall Court, and Hyde Park Court were all expensive central London blocks developed by the same individuals so *court* can be regarded as a form of brand name, signalling 'latest luxurious development'. Manhattan was being filled with skyscrapers at this time, marketed as 'apartments', and 'elevator apartments'. By 1902 the Manhattan norm was to append no second element at all, but of the few that did carry second-elements, *court* predominated. The *New York Tribune* of 1902 advertised 36 buildings, six of which were *courts*:

The Albert Court, The Antoinettes, The Arlington, The Avonmore, The Barnard, The Ben Hur, The Brayman, The Broadway, The Chatilion, The Corinseca, Dorothea, The Dunsbro, The El Dorado, El Nido, The Eleanor Court, The Forres, The Friesland, Graham Court, The Irvington, the Ivy Courts, The Kendrick, The Magnolia, The Manhanset, The Meissonier, The Pamlico, The Rexmere, The Rosemary, The Rudolph, The Saint Hubert, The Saxony, The St. Germaine, The St James Court, The Sweet William, The Versailles, The Von Colon, Watt Court

The earliest use of the word *court* in a Manhattan apartment-block name that I can find is in an advertisement in the *New York Tribune* of 16 September 1900 for 'The St James Court, Southeast Corner Broadway and 92d Street'. A plan is given, showing a 'courtyard' and a 'light court' (a light-well). Other *New York Tribune* advertisements over the following couple of years also feature Manhattan residential buildings Harold Court, Chatham Court ('A court 30 feet square in the centre of the building'), Graham Court ('surrounding a court garden . . . Entrance to the building is through a Romanesque arch in the middle of the avenue front to the interior court'), so one might deduce that New York *courts* were so-named because of the present of a courtyard of some sort.[44] Yet other *court*-named buildings did not mention such a feature, nor did advertisements in *The Times* of the same date for London blocks Wellington-Court, Vale-Court, Albert-Court, Campden-Hill-Court, although their advertisements all puffed other amenities.[45] Rather, it looks as though Kensington Court, Whitehall Court and Hyde Park Court, stemming as they did from a shared portfolio, influenced the naming practices of the new-build apartment buildings in Manhattan too. In the early twentieth century the name-elements *mansions* and *chambers* started to decline but *court* continued to signify upmarket, central, fashionable flats well into the Jazz Age, for example in Chiltern Court, Baker Street (1928–30) and Stafford Court, Kensington High Street (1932). It was not until after the Second World War that *court* became appended to ordinary residential blocks everywhere.

Nineteenth-century timeline

London outer-suburb house-name categories were the transferred place-name, the nostalgically rural, the commemorative, the upwardly-mobile, the latest fad

Post mid-century: the pick & mix

Post 1860s: purpose-built blocks of flats final element -*mansions*

Post 1880s: the jocular

Post 1895: purpose-built blocks of flats final element -*court*

Overall, shifts in naming trends were caused by movements of people, both socially and geographically, but in the main house names have been consistently conservative across time and place. All this lays the background for investigation of the house name that so startled me when I first saw it in a Post Office directory for 1872: Scott, General, Sunnyside, Ealing Green.

---

[44] *New York Tribune*, 28 October 1900, 8 September 1901, 17 August 1902.
[45] *The Times*, 27 January 1900, 15 March 1902.

3

LONDON'S FIRST SUNNYSIDERS

In Chapter 2 I investigated the names of houses in the Finchley New Road and the Wandsworth Road as they began to be built up in the nineteenth century. Forming the southern portion of the Finchley New Road as it leads northwards from Regent's Park is Upper Avenue Road, now known as Avenue Road. The *Post Office Directory* for 1855 shows the following newly-built houses along this stretch:[1]

> Up. Avenue road, *Regent's park.*
> 26 Grahame Alexander, esq
> 27 Wordsworth Henry, esq
> 28 Tuke William Epworth, esq
> 29 Pett Alfred, M. D
> 30 Clode Nathaniel, esq
> 31 Nelson Rev. Edward Hamilton M.A
> 32 Jenkins George Thomas, esq
> ....*here Norfolk road intersects.............*
> 33 Hill Henry, esq. (Norfolk house)
>   Fletcher Thomas Keddy, esq. (Avenue house)
>   Matthew Henry, esq. (York villa)
>   Tatham Mrs. Elizabeth, ladies' school (Walmer lodge)
> ....*here Queen's road intersects.............*
>   Hodges Miss (Gothic lodge)
>   Firmin Philip, esq. (Ufton house)
>   Tompkins Saml. esq. (Hampstead ho)
> 14 Brown Lady Mary
> 16 Orme Charles, esq
> 18 Cockburn James, esq
> 20 Beresford Francis Marcus, esq
> ....*here St. John's wood park intersects......*
>   King Thomas, esq. (Park villa)
>   Frankau Sidney, esq. (Rossmare villa)
>   Jennings John Rd. esq. (Florence villa)
>   Frankau Joseph, esq. (Benario villa)

---

[1] Known as Upper Avenue Road by 1824 (www.british-history.ac.uk/vch/middx/vol9/pp60-63).

Hull Henry William, esq. ⎱ Marley
Hull William Charles, esq. ⎰ villa
Buckingham James Silk, esq. (Stanhope lodge)
Felgate William, esq. (7 Park villas)
Berwick Geo. Jackson, esq. (Park lodge)
London Society's Blind School,
       Rev. J. K. Jennings, M. A. hon. sec
Lattey Robert John, esq. (Erin house)
NEW COLLEGE CHAPEL
......*here Adelaide road north intersects*..........
       Twigg Mrs. Mary, ladies' school (Macclesfield house)
       Liddell Charles, esq. (Berwood house)
33A, Cock Edmund Rand, esq
31 Smith Rev. William, D. D
27 Stevenson Leader Cox, esq
23 Davidson Madgwick Spicer, esq
21 Thompson William, esq
19 Cuming Rev. Joseph, M. A. (Abbey ho)
       Willcock John Wm. Q. C. (Rosenstead)
       Lush Robert, esq. (Balmoral house)
       Freund Madame Louisa (Osborne ho)
          Post Office Directory, 1855, Upper Avenue Road

Transferred place-names account for the majority, there are references to royal estates in *Balmoral House* and *Osborne House*; *Gothic lodge* is a latest fashion name, and *Rosenstead* is a pick & mix name. Sidney Frankau's house name (*Rossmare villa*) is less easy to account for, but neither Frankau had English as a mother-tongue.[2] Note New College Chapel, just south of the London Society's School for the Blind and Erin House. At some point in either 1858 or 1859, New College Chapel changed its name:

UPPER AVENUE ROAD
(N.)

PARK VILLAS	⎰ *London Society for teaching*
Rev. Henry Christopherson 7	⎱ *the Blind to read.*
Stanhope lodge ⎱	Self, John *Sec.*
Thomas S. Watt ⎰	
Samuel Smith Travers 5	AVENUE GARDENS.
William G. Todd 4	4 Crompton, Mrs. *Sunnyside.*
Florence villa. J.R. Jennings 3	3 Bryant, James
Rossmare villa Sid.Frankau 2	2 Tagart, Mrs.
Park villa Thomas King	1 Silver, Hugh Adams

        Royal Blue Book, 1860, Upper Avenue Road

[2] Details of biographical sources are given at the end of this chapter.

By 1860, New College Chapel (which was in fact a large house), Upper Avenue Road, St John's Wood, had become known as Sunnyside. This is the first London house of this name that I have found, and this chapter presents the earliest London Sunnysiders. There is no easy way of finding out historical house names: my method has been to search for *Sunnysides* in Post Office and other directories, newspapers, censuses, societies' membership lists, the various websites devoted to finding one's ancestors, the Mormon IGI website, ancestry.co.uk, familysearch.org, oldbaileyonline.org, Google ... anywhere where someone might have recorded an address. It is never really possible to establish the first usage of a word, so my claim must be that Roger Crompton was the first person that I have been able to discover who used *Sunnyside* as a name for a London house. This is who he was:

Roger Crompton, Paper Manufacturer, Sunnyside, Upper Avenue Road, St John's Wood, 1859

Mrs Crompton of No. 4, Avenue Gardens, Upper Avenue Road, was married to Mr Roger Crompton (1798-1859), whose death was announced in the newspaper: 'On the 2nd instant, at his residence, *Sunnyside*, St. John's Wood, London, Roger Crompton, Esq., paper maker, Kearsly, near Bolton.' (*The Preston Guardian*, 13 August 1859). Roger Crompton was a bleacher's son from Radcliffe, Lancashire, and a member of the New Jerusalem Church (the members of the New Jerusalem Church are known to others as Swedenborgians, although they refer to themselves as New Churchmen and women). Being a Swedenborgian is a way of life, an all-encompassing commitment to Christianity which gives a person their primary sense of identity and informs all actions, including business ones. On his deathbed, Roger Crompton's father requested his two sons not to forsake the New Church. They subsequently inherited the family business, and although his brother died soon after, Roger Crompton turned the bleaching concern into an immensely successful paper manufactory and became a very wealthy man, recorded in the 1851 census as employing 61 men, 16 boys, 25 women and 25 girls. He was a conscientious and life-long member of the New Church, moving from Vestry Warden, to Auditor of Accounts, to Sunday School Superintendent, to Committee Member, to benefactor. In London he met and married a London Swedenborgian, Mary Presland, and together husband and wife were active and philanthropic members of the New Church of Jerusalem – Roger contributing not only on his own behalf, but on that of his dead brother too.

Roger and Mary Crompton lived at *Kearsley Vale House* opposite his Stoneclough Brow paperworks, with, in later life, a house at Upper Avenue Road (variously described as being in Regent's Park, St John's Wood and South Hampstead; the locality is known as Swiss Cottage today), to which Roger Crompton retired. Presland (*c.*1984: 28) reports a family descendant describing *Sunnyside* as 'a house in Regents Park, London, where they kept an almost princely retinue of servants'. However, it

3.1 Label (1861) showing the Stonecloug Paperworks, formerly owned by Roger Crompton; Presland (*c.*1984: 31).

seems that they did not name this London house *Sunnyside* immediately upon purchase. In the 1840s, Roger Crompton's friend Henry Bateman was trying to raise money to build a New Church school for children of London members (this was before the 1870 Education Act provided schooling for all), and in 1845 rules were drawn up for the proposed 'Emmanuel College'. However in 1847 the name was objected to on the grounds that it was 'bringing one of the names of the Lord into common use, and thus leading to a breach of the Commandments' (Bateman 1859: 3). In 1850 a start was made by renting a Sunday School room in Islington, and the Reverend Augustus Clissold and Roger Crompton gave money for a plot of land in Devonshire Street, Islington, to further the project. In 1852 the foundation stone was laid, and the School Room was opened that year, although the building was not entirely finished. In 1854 the name was changed from 'Emmanuel College' to 'New Church College', Devonshire Street. The school was not successful, however, as few children enrolled, although the lecture rooms were put to use. Post Office directories between 1855 and 1858 show that the house owned by Roger Crompton in Upper Avenue Road, listed as *Sunnyside* in 1859, was known during this period as *New Chapel College*. Perhaps he loaned the house to the Devonshire Street college whilst their building works were ongoing? Roger Crompton died in 1859, bequeathing a further £10,000 to the New Church College in Devonshire Street and £17,400 in all to the New Jerusalem Church. His wife, and after her death, his daughter and her husband, continued to live at *Sunnyside*.

George Cargill Leighton, Printer,
Sunnyside, Hornsey Lane, 1863

THE LATE MR. G. C. LEIGHTON.

3.2 George Cargill Leighton, as published in his obituary in the *Illustrated London News*, 18 May 1895, 606. www.britishnewspaperarchive.co.uk/titles/illustrated-london-news.

The second London house named *Sunnyside* that I have found in the London Post Office directories was owned by George Cargill Leighton in Hornsey Lane. George Cargill Leighton (1826–95) was born in Shacklewell, North London, to Stephen Leighton and Helen Blair, who were married in 1822 in Dunkeld, Perthshire. The Leightons were a family of Scottish bookbinders working in London. Like Roger Crompton, George Cargill Leighton belonged to a Nonconformist church.[3] His father, Stephen Leighton, Master Printer, was a Bible Officer and Elder of the Sandemanian Church, of which the Leighton family was a mainstay (George's middle name is likely to be in honour of a founder-member, James Cargill).

In 1849 George Cargill Leighton married Margaret Faraday, the niece of his fellow-worshipper the famous scientist Michael Faraday. Sandemanians did not

---

[3] A note on labels: the eighteenth-century term was *Dissent*, the nineteenth-century term was *Nonconformity* ('*Dissent* is querulous; *refusal to conform* is manly' (Binfield 1977: 7)). I identify people as Sandemanians if they were related to Sandemanian families because I am concerned with establishing social networks. Within the church, 'membership' was a technical term with specific meaning, not invoked here.

proselytise, and new members were rare, so the church was essentially made up of a group of families who intermarried. There were about forty churches during its prime, the greatest concentration of which were in Scotland (with one at Dunkeld), but over the course of George Cargill Leighton's lifetime they were greatly reduced and he would never have had more than a hundred fellow-worshippers in his community at most. He would have known them well. The London Sandemanians met at Paul's Alley, Barbican, until 1862, when they relocated to Barnsbury Grove. George Cargill Leighton's removal from 67, Pentonville Road in 1860 to *Sunnyside,* Hornsey Lane, in 1863 would have been informed by his need to reach the new meeting-house easily, as he spent Sundays and Wednesdays there according to Sandemanian custom.

In 1849 George and his brother Charles set up a successful firm of colour-printing for art books and periodicals, Leighton Brothers, trading first at 19, Lamb's Conduit Street, then from 1852 at 4, Red Lion Square, and later from Stanhope House, Drury Lane. It became quite a sizeable concern; in 1861 Leighton Brothers were employing 80 men and 50 boys. In 1855 George Cargill Leighton became the colour-plate printer for the *Illustrated London News,* and was its printer and publisher between 1857 and 1884. He also had a proprietary interest in the *Daily News.* In 1855 he was elected a member of the Royal Society of Arts, and in 1864 he was elected a member of the Royal Institution. Sandemanians helped each other in business and the Royal Institution's library provided a source of income for the bookbinding Leighton family, facilitated by Superintendent of the Royal Institution Michael Faraday. In 1876 George Cargill Leighton was admitted to the City of London Company of Stationers.

Some 16 documents held by George Cargill Leighton's solicitors Eland, Hare, Patterson detail leases he took out on various houses. In 1858, from his address *Milford House,* Strand, George Cargill Leighton bought building plots in Hornsey and thereafter lived in or let houses named *Treverbyn, Melrose, Fairlight, Sunnyside, Highcroft* and *Springcroft* in Hornsey Lane and Shepherds Hill Road. He is listed in the *Post Office Directory* of 1863 as living in *Sunnyside.* Deeds of 1879 show that *Sunnyside* was next door to *The Cheal* (the name of a hamlet in Lincolnshire), which was next door to *Melrose* (the name of a town in the Scottish borders), which was next door to *Treverbyn* (the name of a Cornish village). I cannot find a description of *Sunnyside* but *Treverbyn,* three doors along (which Leighton let out) had a library, dining room, breakfast room, drawing room, conservatory, wine cellar and larder as well as kitchen, reception, bed, bath and servants' rooms. *Fairlight,* 'most substantially built, of artistic elevation, and within three minutes of Highgate Station' had a handsome entrance hall and staircase, three elegant reception rooms, eight bedrooms, with special attention to the heating and sanitary arrangements, a charming conservatory, a carriage sweep, double coach-house, vinery, greenhouse and an acre of tastefully laid out garden. The two houses George Cargill Leighton actually lived in, *Sunnyside* and *Fairlight,* have names that would have been resonant for his cast of Christianity.

Samuel Straker, Lithographer, Sunnyside, Peckham Rye, 1866

3.3 Samuel Straker, 1868, photograph by the studio of Messrs Maull & Co., London; London Metropolitan Archives, City of London, SC/GL/MAU/004/M0004786CL.

The third owner of a London *Sunnyside*, again first located in the Post Office directories but then found a little earlier in a vestry report, was Samuel Straker of Peckham Rye. Samuel Straker (1806–74), born in Hackney, was a lithographer, printer, press maker, copperplate printer, engraver and etcher. He came from a family of London printers, and established S. Straker and Son at 3, George Yard, Lombard Street in 1834, then at 118, Bishopsgate Within from 1841, and 80, Bishopsgate Within, by 1846, where he pioneered a steam-driven lithographic machine. At the time of the 1851 census he was aged 44 and employed 14 men; by the 1861 census (living at *Rye Cottage*, 49 Peckham Rye with wife Sarah and family) he was aged 54 and employed 50 men and 20 boys; by the 1871 census (living at 22, *Sunnyside*, Peckham Rye) he was aged 64 and employed a hundred hands. *Sunnyside* was described by his daughter Marion as being 'grand in modern style and taste'.

Samuel Straker was engaged in local politics: he was a vestryman at the church of St Giles Camberwell, where he was a Guardian of the Poor, the Tenth Annual Report of the vestry for 1865–6 being the first documentation of his house name.

CONTRACTORS TO HER MAJESTY'S GOVERNMENT.

S. STRAKER & SONS,

STEAM PRINTERS, LITHOGRAPHERS, ENGRAVERS,

ACCOUNT BOOK & ENVELOPE

MANUFACTURERS,
AND

WHOLESALE AND EXPORT STATIONERS.

TRADE CATALOGUES, ILLUSTRATED OR OTHERWISE.

Steam Printing Works & Factories - 80, BISHOPSGATE WITHIN.
Stationery Department - - - - - - 26, LEADENHALL STREET.

S. S. & Sons beg to call the attention of Merchants, Bankers, Brokers, Public Companies, Manufacturers, Shippers, and large consumers to the facilities in the respective Departments of their Establishments, which enable them to execute all orders in the first style, with strict regard to punctuality, and at the most economical rates.

PRINTING & STATIONERY CONTRACTS FOR STATED PERIODS.

Large Consumers contracting with S. S. & Sons for Periodical Supplies will realize a great saving.

3.4 *Strakers' Annual Mercantile, Ship and Insurance Register*, 1863, frontispiece.

Like George Cargill Leighton, Straker was a member of the Stationers' Livery Company and the Royal Society of Arts. In 1861 he became a City of London Common Councilman for Bishopsgate ward, which meant that for the rest of his life he sat on various City committees. Samuel Straker's wife Sarah died in 1865, and he married his second wife, Mary Ann (née Palmer, 1814–74), in 1871 at St Andrew Undershaft. She gave books to the Wesleyan Chapel, Barry Road, some time before 1875, and Samuel Straker bought three loculi in the catacomb of the Nonconformist Chapel at Nunhead Cemetery for himself and his wives (they were three of the only four people ever to be buried there). I wonder whether Samuel and Mary Ann Straker met with some accident, as they died within three days of each other, aged 68 and 59.

Samuel Straker and Roger Crompton had overlapping social networks: on 30 April 1862 Common Councilman Samuel Straker supported the Printers' Pension Society Anniversary Festival, along with Mr Sheriff Twentyman (and also along with Alfred Tennyson, Esq., D.C.L., Poet Laureate). William Holme Twentyman lived next door to Mrs Twigg's Ladies' School in Upper Avenue Road, St John's

Wood (*Post Office Directory* 1853). He was the developer of the most luxurious of the St John's Wood houses, and although he was to leave Upper Avenue Road at much the same time that Roger Crompton moved in, he only went over the road to St John's Wood Park, which stands at an angle to Upper Avenue Road.

Samuel Straker and George Cargill Leighton also had overlapping social networks. Samuel Straker's paternal grandmother, Elizabeth Livermore Straker, married a second husband in 1821, Cornelius Varley (1781–1873), landscape painter, scientist and inventor of optical apparatus, who for a time (1844–1847) was part of the same Sandemanian congregation as George Cargill Leighton and Michael Faraday. At Faraday's invitation, Cornelius Varley became a regular lecturer at the Royal Institution into the 1860s, so relationships were not severed when he left the church to become a Baptist. Cantor (1991a: 50) says of Varley 'both his family and his wife's appear to have had long-term connections with the [Sandemanian] church'. With regard to his wife (Samuel Straker's grandmother Elizabeth Livermore Straker), this may be because she was also a cousin of Michael Faraday's wife, née Sarah Barnard. George Cargill Leighton published an obituary of Cornelius Varley in the *Illustrated London News* (25 October 1873, 389) with an engraving of Varley's portrait. An apprentice of Cornelius Varley was Andrew Pritchard, Sandemanian (he later became a Unitarian), microscopist and optician. In 1829 he married Caroline Isabella Straker, Elizabeth Livermore Straker's sister and Samuel Straker's great-aunt, and in 1854 Samuel Straker took over Pritchard's optician's business.

Theodore Brooke Jones, Accountant and Microscopist, 8 Moorgate Street E. C. & Sunnyside, London Road, Lower Clapton, 1869

The fourth person to own a London house named *Sunnyside* in the London Post Office directories was Theodore Brooke Jones. Theodore Brooke Jones (1828–1920) was born in Kingsland, West Hackney, to father Orlando Jones and mother Anne Eliza. His grandfather, Edward Thomas Jones, had set up an accountancy firm in Poultry, City of London, which his sons Orlando, Theodore and Edwin entered. However, Orlando left the firm and invented a process for extracting starch. He developed the manufactory Orlando Jones & Co. of Osborn Street, Whitechapel, and later of York Street, Battersea. The firm produced rice starch, employed over 200 hands and won International Exhibition silver and gold medals.

Theodore Brooke Jones was thus born into wealth, but he joined not his father's company but his uncle's, becoming an accountant in the City of London at addresses in Coleman Street and Clements Lane. He resided and worked at many addresses over the course of his long life, eventually leaving London to set up further accountancy practices in Harrogate, Leeds and Manchester. Theodore Brooke

3.5 Label: 'Orlando Jones & Co's Original Patent Rice Starch, requires no boiling, prize medal 1851 & 1862'; sciencemuseum.org.uk/objects/co64836/handbill-orlando-jones-co-patent-rice-starch-handbill-printed-ephemera.

Jones received the Freedom of the City of London on 26 October 1858, when he was working as an accountant at 17, Clements Lane, and he was a founder member of the Institute of Accountants and the Institute of Chartered Accountants, a member of the Statistical Society, and an initiator of the YMCA movement.

In 1860 Theodore Brooke Jones married a Scot, Euphemia Turnbull, who was born in 1831 in Abernethy, Perth. She was the daughter of Thomas Turnbull, Sandemanian, and Cecilia Williamson. In his youth Theodore Brooke Jones was a Wesleyan, but he later became a member of the movement known as Plymouth Brethren (they referred to themselves simply as Christian), and he instigated the Harrogate Assembly of the Plymouth Brethren. Whilst still in London, Theodore Brooke Jones took up microscopy, and together with a partner, made microscopic slides, which was also the occupation of Samuel Straker's grandmother's husband Cornelius Varley and his apprentice Andrew Pritchard, who married Samuel Straker's great-aunt Caroline. Theodore Brooke Jones and Andrew Pritchard both exhibited inventions in the same class at the Great Exhibition of 1851, Jones a silent alarum bedstead which tipped sleepers out of bed at a pre-set hour, and Pritchard an achromatic microscope.

3.6 Theodore Brooke Jones; taken from
Pickering (1931: 193).

These are the first four residents of London houses named *Sunnyside* that I have
found, but of course there may have been more. These are all remarkable men
who have left traces of their existence, and there may have been less wealthy, less
lauded Londoners who named their houses *Sunnyside* in the 1850s and 1860s.
Nevertheless, these men all chose the name (or retained it, if it had been so-named
by the developer) rather than another. Why did they do so? What was the appeal of
the name *Sunnyside*, and where did they hear of it? Emergent recurrences common
to these first four pre-1870 London Sunnysiders are the paper and print industries, religious Nonconformism, membership of livery companies and professional
societies, and Scotland. All will turn out to be significant, but first, let's look at the
next 23 Sunnysiders listed in the 1870 *Post Office Directory*, at a time when the
name *Sunnyside* began to boom. I have tracked some of the occupations of these
Sunnysiders in the 1871 census (see Table 3.1).

By 1870, these residents may not have been the original bestowers of the name
– especially those who lived at the terrace of three in Upper Addiscombe Road in
Croydon, and at 3, Sunnyside, Fairfield Road, Croydon, another terrace. Twenty-
one years since Roger Crompton's *Sunnyside* is a long time in terms of people
moving house. But the list shows *Sunnyside*'s continuing outer-suburb, wealthy-
owner, detached-villa affiliation at this point in time, and the growing popularity
of the name. Some of these further 23 Sunnysiders of 1870 are discussed after the
table.

Table 3.1 London *Sunnysides* in the 1870 edition of the *Post Office Directory of the Six Home Counties: Essex, Hertfordshire, Middlesex, Kent, Surrey and Sussex*

Name and address	Occupation	1871 census (or other) reference
Allen, Mrs ?Marsha A., Sunnyside, Balham Hill		RG10, Piece 718, fo 63, p. 5
Bedford, Edward Wilson, Sunnyside, Brockley Road, Forest Hill	City Station Warehouseman	RG10, Piece 772, fo 62, p. 29
Bouch, John, Sunnyside, Bickley Park, Bromley	Merchant Manchester Warehouseman	RG10, Piece 874, fo 72, p. 35
Bovet, Charles, Sunnyside, Spring Grove, Isleworth	Tea Broker	Likely to have been abroad on census night; family from Fleurier, Switzerland
Clayton, James Weston, Sunny Side, Lower Sunbury Road, Hampton	Blacking Manufacturer	RG10, Piece 856, fo 38, p. 18
Elborough, Thomas, Sunnyside, New Road, Shepherd's Bush	Baker Master	RG10, Piece 63, fo 79, p. 4
Eliot, Arthur Henry, Sunny Side, Brockley Hill, Forest Hill	Gentleman	*Wrexham Guardian*, 22 February 1879
Fenerty, Thomas, Sunnyside, Mayow Road, Forest Hill	Retired Merchant	RG10, Piece 773, fo 45, p. 1
Hughes, A., Sunny Side, Oakfield Road, Croydon		
Livingstone, Miss Jane, Sunnyside, Central Hill, Upper Norwood	Lodging House Keeper	RG10, Piece 639, fo 93, p. 17
Morley, William, Sunnyside, Leigham Court Road, Streatham	Manchester Warehouseman	RG10, Piece 719, fo 140, p. 34
Prior, Holland, Sunny Side, North Park, Croydon	Wine Shipper	RG10, Piece 718, fo 91, p. 32
Scott, General Henry Young Darracott, Sunnyside, Ealing Green	Lieut. Col. Royal Engineers, seconded to Civil Service	RG10, Piece 1318, fo 88, p. 29
Seppings, Nicholas L., Sunny Side, 4 Seymour Road, Wandsworth	Senior Clerk Admiralty	RG10, Piece 709, fo 68, p. 16
Skehn, Mrs, Sunnyside, Beulah Hill, Upper Norwood		
Slater, Samuel, Sunnyside, Fairfield Road, Croydon	Member of Stock Exchange	RG10, Piece 843, fo 63, p. 47
Stuart, William Watt Backhouse, Sunnyside, New Road, Chigwell, Buckhurst Hill, Woodford Green	Clerk to East & West India Dock and Landowner	RG10, Piece 1639, fo 54, p. 38

Table 3.1 *continued*

Name and address	Occupation	1871 census (or other) reference
Ward, William Henry S., Sunnyside, London Road, Kingston on Thames	Sale Clerk in a Company	RG10, Piece 858, fo 51, p. 37
Weston, Luke, Sunnyside, Selhurst Road, South Norwood	Solicitor Clerk	RG10, Piece 847, fo 19, p. 32
Woodfall, Hernan Thomas, 3 Sunnyside, Upper Addiscombe Road, Croydon (another two heads of household are listed (Henry Fawcett, fundholder, and Frederick Laxer, Insurance Broker) so this *Sunnyside* was a terrace of three houses	Retired Clerk in HM Exchequer	RG10, Piece 843, fo 50, p. 22
Waldram, John, Sunnyside, Manor Road, Lordship Road, Stoke Newington	Builder & Contractor employing 871 men	RG10, Piece 309, fo 14, p. 17
Wallace, Alexander John, Sunnyside, Wimbledon		
Williams, George, Sunnyside, Teddington	Gentleman	RG10, Piece 866, fo 100, p. 5

EDWARD WILSON BEDFORD, SUNNYSIDE, BROCKLEY ROAD, FOREST HILL, KENT, 1870

In the 1871 census Edward Wilson Bedford's occupation is given as 'City Station Warehouseman'. He was born in the City of London in about 1831, and lived with his wife Anne, six children and two servants. In 1861 he was working as an Oilman at no. 10, Bell Yard, Gracechurch Street, City of London, and in 1869 as Italian Warehouseman, Bell Yard, Gracechurch Street. The London Metropolitan Archives hold a photograph of Edward Wilson Bedford's oil warehouse, no. 10, Bell Yard, Gracechurch Street, as it appeared in 1934. An oilman was 'a dealer in sweet oils and eatables preserved in them'; in practice, oilmen stocked a rather wider range of grocery. An Italian Warehouseman was much the same thing: a dealer in eatables from Italy and elsewhere. By the 1870s, the Royal General Annuity Society, a charity for decayed merchants, was administered from 10, Bell Yard, Gracechurch Street, although I cannot discover that Edward Wilson Bedford subscribed to it and they may simply have shared premises.

A wealthy Manchester Warehouseman (that is, a wholesaler of cloth from Manchester), born in Monument Yard and trading at 7–8, Bread Street, E.C., with partners Alfred Luck and Thomas Coath, John Bouch (1811–95) lived at Sunnyside, Bickley Park Road, which was built around 1868 by developer George Wythes (1811–83). John Bouch junior was son of John Bouch senior (*c.*1770–1830), who started the family firm in Bread Street. John Bouch junior was married firstly to Margaret Lowther (1814–60) of Islington, Middlesex, and subsequently in 1864 to Helen Rose Carey (*c.*1829–1902). He was a member of the Fishmonger's Livery Company and he was charitable, selling tickets for the First Annual Festival of the Free Dispensary for Throat Diseases and Loss of Voice in June 1865, and, like William Morley (see below), contributing to the Albert Orphan Asylum in 1867. William Morley and John Bouch would have known each other, being in the same business on opposite sides of Cheapside. On 3 June 1868, John Bouch attended the Hospital for Diseases of the Throat's biennial festival at the Freemasons' Tavern, as he did on 27 June 1870, 22 May 1872 and 13 May 1874. Other attendees were William Holme Twentyman, Esq., J.P. (the developer of the grand houses in Upper Avenue Road, where Roger Crompton had named his house *Sunnyside* in 1859), and also George Glas Sandeman, Esq. George Glas Sandeman was a descendant of Robert Sandeman (1717–73), who had married one of the daughters of the Sandemanians' founding father, John Glas (they were known as Glasites in Scotland). In 1841, George Glas Sandeman took over his uncle's business, George Sandeman and Co., wine shippers and cotton merchants, specialising in port and sherry.

Charles Henri Bovet (1803–77) was a member of the Swiss watchmaking Bovet family, Bovet Frères et Cie, of Fleurier, Switzerland. He was a merchant who travelled internationally, passing on various occasions through the ports of Dover and Liverpool. He was elected to the Royal Geographical Society in 1855. 'Messrs. Townend Brothers, of 9, Mincing-lane, intimate that Mr. Charles Bovet has been admitted a partner in their firm, which from this date will be conducted under the style of Townend Brothers and Bovet'; 'Messrs. Townend, Brothers, and Bovet, tea brokers, have dissolved partnership'; 'Mr. Charles Bovet has admitted as partner Mr. George F. Sanders, and the business will be carried on under the style of Charles Bovet and Sanders'. By 1877 he had moved away from Spring Grove. The deaths column reported: 'Charles Bovet. – 3d, of Fleurier, Switzerland, at his residence Beau-Sejour, Tufnell-park, N.W.'. Spring Grove was an estate of large villas aimed at the middle classes that had been laid out in the early 1850s to the north of Isleworth. Neighbours on the Spring Grove estate in 1870 lived in *Glen Mohr Villa, Fern Villa, Mont Blanc Villa, Green Bank, Linden Villa, Aylesbury Villa, Burlington House* and *Lampton Lodge.*

JAMES WESTON CLAYTON, BLACKING MANUFACTURER, SUNNY SIDE,
LOWER SUNBURY ROAD, HAMPTON, MIDDLESEX, 1870

James Weston Clayton (*c.*1831–1914) was the grandson of the manager (John Weston) of Day and Martin's blacking firm at 97 Holborn. John Weston was brother-in-law to the owner Mr Day. A Surrey freemason by 1862, James Weston Clayton married his first wife Elizabeth Moy in 1860, divorced her in 1866, and married his second wife Julia Starkie in 1868. He took out a patent for 'improvements in the manufacture of waterproof paper' in 1874, and bought Day and Martin's blacking firm in 1877. Charles Day, James Weston Clayton's grandfather's brother-in-law and co-founder of the firm, died in 1836, leaving a will that was contested through the courts until 1854. It is thought that this is the will that Charles Dickens refers to in the preface of *Bleak House* in defence of the length of *Jarndyce* v. *Jarndyce*. Dickens had a particular interest, as he had been both a court stenographer and a label-paster at Warren's Blacking Factory, Day and Martin's main rival. Dickens cocked a snook at Warren's in *Pickwick Papers*: 'a polish which would have struck envy to the soul of the amiable Mr. Warren, (for they used Day and Martin at the White Hart)'. In 1899 James Clayton Weston was a yachtsman: '(he) was born on the Holborn premises, and brought up in the business, still manages the entire concern, and is an enthusiastic yachtsman' – enthusiastic enough to order his own two-masted 163.5 ft steel screw steamer yacht in 1894, the *Xenia*, which he sold a year later to the Rajah of Sarawak. In 1867 James Weston Clayton gave £15 to the National Society for the Protection of Young Girls, and £15 for the support of one boy from the Refuge for Homeless and Destitute Boys in Queen-street, Holborn on the training ship Chichester for one year.

In 1879 James Clayton Weston started to sell for £8,200 'my freehold House known as Sunnyside Hampton' ('a very good residence'), including outbuildings, boathouse and eight acres, to the Grand Junction Waterworks. The waterworks complex had been growing up around him since 1855, but he wanted to stay on for another seven years, renting Sunnyside back from the waterworks, and through the winter of 1880 he argued with them about moving an iron safe and vase from outside the house. James Weston Clayton retired from Day and Martin in 1899, by which time he was resident both at 8, Tavistock Square and *The Cedars*, Hampton on Thames. Sunnyside Reservoir, Hampton, remains so-named to this day.

THOMAS ELBOROUGH, SUNNYSIDE, NEW ROAD (RENAMED GOLDHAWK ROAD),
SHEPHERD'S BUSH, MIDDLESEX, 1871

Thomas Elborough was a widower living with his son, sister and sister-in-law in the 1871 census. He may or may not have been the apprentice of that name who entered the City of London Tallow Chandlers' Livery Company. In 1831 he was working in Cross Street, Islington. The 1851 census lists him as a Baker Master, and the 1881 census as a Retired Baker.

ARTHUR HENRY ELIOT, SUNNY SIDE, BROCKLEY HILL, FOREST HILL, KENT, 1870

An Arthur Henry Eliot is recorded in *The Times* of 27 October 1919, although whether living or not is not stated – the will of his wife is announced. The address of his wife at death was Curzon Street, Mayfair.

THOMAS FENERTY, SUNNYSIDE, MAYOW ROAD, FOREST HILL, KENT, 1870

In the 1871 census, Thomas Fenerty was aged 64, living with his wife Isabella, aged 52, three children and two servants. His occupation was 'Retired Merchant' and he was born in Canada.

WILLIAM MORLEY, SUNNYSIDE, LEIGHAM COURT ROAD (ONE END OF WHICH KNOWN AS ST JULIAN'S ROAD), STREATHAM, SURREY, 1870

Leigham Court Road was laid out from 1836 by developer Beriah Drew, and the coming of the railway in 1856 resulted in the leasing of numerous grand mansions there to prosperous London businessmen. William Morley junior (1816–83), born in Finchley, was one such. He was a partner in W. & R. Morley, 36, Gutter Lane, Cheapside, a firm of Manchester cloth wholesalers. The 1871 census shows that *Sunnyside* in Leigham Court Road housed William and his wife Elizabeth and their five children, plus two housemaids, two nurses, a cook, a parlourmaid, a kitchen maid and a potman. William Morley was charitable: when the Lord Mayor took oversight of the Albert Orphan Asylum in 1864, William Morley was one of the main donors and canvassers of donations, seconding a motion of thanks to the Lord Mayor. On 15 January 1870 *The Standard* recorded that William Morley, Esq. had given five guineas to the Whitechapel Ragged Schools. His personal estate at death in 1883 was the then-enormous sum of £78,762 3s 1d.

GENERAL HENRY YOUNG DARRACOTT SCOTT, SUNNYSIDE, EALING GREEN, MIDDLESEX, 1870

Henry Young Darracott Scott (1822–83) was born at Plymouth (Darracott is a village in North Devon). His father, Edward Scott, was a quarry owner. Henry Scott entered the Royal Military Academy at Woolwich, took various postings, and whilst at Gibraltar, experimented in making cement. On return, he took up chemistry at King's College, London, and invented 'Scott's Patent Cement', subsequently known as selenitic cement and a rival to Portland Cement. In 1851 he married Ellen Selena Bowes (after whom his cement was named) and they were to have 15 children. After several army promotions he was seconded to the civil service for the commissioners for the Great Exhibition of 1851, and in 1866 he became Director of Works of the new museum complex at South Kensington. In 1867 Scott became design and construction co-ordinator of the Albert Hall, with his selenitic cement used throughout, which had the effect of making terracotta fashionable. In 1871 he was made a Companion of the Bath. Scott published in learned journals on chemistry, he did good works, lecturing on science to convicts at Chatham Prison, he took out 59 patents for cement, lime and kilns, he won prizes and honours. He retired from the army in 1871 as an Honorary Major-General and in 1872, living at *Sunnyside*, Ealing Green, his prospects must indeed have looked sunny. But this came to an abrupt end: in 1882 the government made the Board of Works responsible for the South Kensington museums and Scott's position was terminated. There was no pension. Scott died a year later, having moved from Ealing to *Davenport House*, Silverdale, Sydenham, leaving a personal estate of £775. A memorial fund was set up by his colleagues to prevent his wife and children becoming destitute.

NICHOLAS L. SEPPINGS, SUNNY SIDE, 4 SEYMOUR ROAD, WANDSWORTH, SURREY, 1870

Nicholas Lockyer Seppings (1811–87) was born in Greenwich, Kent. His wife was Harriet Sarah Blogg, and at the time of the 1871 census he was retired from his post of Senior Clerk at the Admiralty, in Somerset House in the Strand. He is recorded in the Navy List of 1864 as Clerk of the First Class (Second Section). His will shows City connections: one executor was Edward Barber, merchant, of No. 32, Fenchurch Street, and his solicitor was of Philpot Lane. His address is given as Sunny-side, Southfields, Wandsworth.

SAMUEL S. SLATER, 3, SUNNYSIDE, FAIRFIELD ROAD, CROYDON, SURREY, 1870

Samuel S. Slater was born *c.*1830 in Lambeth. His wife Margaret was born in Bickington, Devon. In the 1871 census he lived in Fairfield Road, Croydon, with his wife, six children, and three servants. *The Times* of 15 June 1870 mentions a Samuel Slater, Accountant, of 36a, Moorgate Street, City of London.

WILLIAM WATT BACKHOUSE STUART, SUNNYSIDE, NEW ROAD, BUCKHURST HILL, CHIGWELL, WOODFORD GREEN, ESSEX, 1870

William Watt Backhouse Stuart (*c.*1834–1904), Clerk to the East and West India Dock and landowner, was aged 37 in the 1871 census and was born in Birmingham. In 1862 he married Elizabeth Straker in Romford. Elizabeth Straker, aged 32 in the 1871 census, was the daughter of Samuel Straker's cousin Frederick Straker (who like Samuel Straker was a printer) so it is probable that she knew of her father's cousin at *Sunnyside*, Peckham Rye.

JOHN WALDRAM, SUNNYSIDE, MANOR ROAD, LORDSHIP ROAD, STOKE NEWINGTON, 1870

John Waldram, CE, born *c*.1837 in Leicester, was a builder and contractor, and later surveyor, who traded from 7, Kingsland Road, Dalston, Hackney. At the time of the 1871 census he was employing 871 men and living with his wife Louisa Jane, four children and three servants. John Waldram and Co. won the contract for building offices at Paddington Station in 1876. He seems to have moved to 13 Buckingham Street, Adelphi (but as this is from *The Times* of 22 August 1892 it may refer to a son).

ALEXANDER JOHN WALLACE, SUNNYSIDE, WIMBLEDON, SURREY, 1870

By 1870, two streets in London named Sunnyside had been developed. One, in Hornsey, must have been named after George Cargill Leighton's *Sunnyside*, as it is hard by his house. The other was in Wimbledon, leading off the road known as Ridgeway. The 1871 census shows the residents: Edward Holland (barrister), Lourraine Brun (French Professor), Charles Bond (publisher/printer), the Misses Sweet, Mary Ann and Jane, who lived off the interest of investments, Sir Edwin Pearson, FRS, William Mackford, property owner, and Charles Deakins (silkwear mercer employing 40 hands). Alexander John Wallace is not among them, however.

WILLIAM HENRY S. WARD, SUNNYSIDE, LONDON ROAD, KINGSTON ON THAMES, SURREY, 1870

William H. Ward is recorded in the 1871 census as born in around 1829 in Cookham, Berkshire, and married to Elizabeth, born about 1842. He was living in Kingston with his wife, two sons and one servant. His occupation was 'Sale clerk in a company'; in the 1861 census, when he was living with his mother and sister in Brighton, he is listed as a 'holder of houses'. A William Henry Ward was witness to a Freedom of the Drapers' Livery Company in 1859 and again in 1868. He was a member of the Goldsmith's Livery Company.

LUKE WESTON, SUNNYSIDE, SELHURST ROAD, SOUTH NORWOOD, SURREY, 1871

Born in around 1819, Luke Weston, Solicitor's clerk, was recorded at the address in the 1871 census, together with his wife, Sibba, and three children. *The Times* of 29 April 1887 reports the death of Luke Weston, *Balfour Villas*, South Norwood, aged 68.

GEORGE WILLIAMS, SUNNYSIDE, TEDDINGTON, MIDDLESEX, 1871

Living with wife Mary and two servants in the 1871 census, George Williams was born in about 1807 in Lambeth. His stated occupation of 'Gentleman' is likely to indicate that he was retired.

HERNAN THOMAS WOODFALL, 3 SUNNYSIDE, UPPER ADDISCOMBE ROAD,
CROYDON, SURREY, 1870

Listed in the *Post Office Directory* of 1870 as Thomas Woodfall but in the 1871 census as Hernan Thomas Woodfall, a retired Clerk in HM Exchequer. Born around 1808, he was living with two daughters in a terrace of three houses. His neighbours were Henry Fawcett (a Fundholder) and his servant, and Frederick Laxer, an Insurance Broker.

Profile of early London Sunnysiders

The population of London in 1860 was 3,188,485.[4] Yet the first 27 Sunnysiders had overlapping social networks, via their professions (Roger Crompton, George Cargill Leighton and Samuel Straker all worked in the paper and print industries; William Morley and John Bouch were both Manchester Warehousemen); via their livery companies (George Cargill Leighton, Samuel Straker, Theodore Brooke Jones, Thomas Elborough and William Henry Ward belonged to livery companies); via their charitable activities (William Morley and John Bouch both gave to the Albert Orphan Asylum); via their religion (Samuel Straker's great-aunt and grandmother's second husband were part of the same Sandemanian congregation as George Cargill Leighton; Theodore Brooke Jones was married to Euphemia Turnbull, of the Sandemanian Turnbull family; John Bouch and George Glas Sandeman both attended the same charity dinners); and via their family ties (the daughter of Samuel Straker's cousin married William Watt Backhouse Stuart). Most had City of London connections.

The original Victorian *Sunnyside* resident who caused me such surprise, General Scott of Ealing Green, can now be seen to fit the profile of the other early London Sunnysiders. Early London Sunnysiders were a specific class of citizen: hard-working, moneyed, socially-embedded businessmen who lived in grand new suburban houses. Six were merchants (Bedford, Bouch, Bovet, Fenerty, Morley, Prior), five ran companies (Crompton, Leighton, Straker, Clayton, Waldram), three were clerks of a senior sort (Stuart, Ward, Weston), three were civil servants (Seppings, Scott, Woodfall), two were accountants (Brooke Jones, Slater), one was a Master Baker,

---

[4] www.oldbaileyonline.org/static/Population-history-of-london.jsp#a1815-1860.

one was a self-declared gentlemen (probably in the sense of 'retired and well-off'). They were influential in their spheres; none were gentry. There may have been others less notable, but these people were all early adopters of the name and something caused them to choose it, or to retain it, if the house had been named by someone else.

In sum: early London *Sunnysides* were large detached houses with room to house numerous children and servants. They had the kinds of accoutrements that appealed to wealthy Victorians: wine cellar, library, conservatory, breakfast room, vinery, double coach-house, carriage sweep. They were newly built on land freshly available for the purpose in the outer suburbs: green and leafy yet near to railway stations. Early London Sunnysiders were wealthy, successful, respectable businessmen, owning their own companies, employing others, who either commuted from the suburbs or retired to the suburbs; religious dissenters, committed to their interpretation of Christianity as a way of life and involved in their churches, brotherly, charitable and philanthropic; City of London liverymen, members of learned and professional societies, convivial, with overlapping professional networks. They also had a raised likelihood of Scottishness: either of Scottish descent, or with a Scottish connection. Theodore Brooke Jones's wife Euphemia Turnbull was Scottish, George Cargill Leighton's mother was Scottish. Allen, Cargill, Eliot, Livingstone, Scott, Starkie, Stuart, Wallace, Watt, are all surnames that preponderate in Scotland.

* * *

In 1870 the name *Sunnyside* must have connoted modernity as the fashion for the name gathered apace. However, not everybody looked forward when naming their home. Others preferred to use commemorative names. For example, looking at the London suburb of Ealing in the 1874 *Post Office Directory*, speculative builders reached to the British Empire when naming terraces:

Nyanza Villas, Grange Park
Nile Villas, Grange Park
Ceylon Villas, The Grove
Singapore Villas, Uxbridge Road
Alberta Villas, Ranelagh Road

By contrast, moving 15 years later to *Kelly's Directory for Ealing and Acton* for the year 1889–90, a generation had lived out a life in the furthest reaches of the Empire and come home to Ealing and Acton to retire. Their house names record a more personal Empire experience (Table 3.2).

Gaining official recognition for fighting at the Battle of Ghuznee or the Fort of Ali Masjid left its mark over a lifetime, such that these old soldiers made their experience public at the end of their lives. Acts of commemoration narrate life-events, although exactly whose life is not usually recoverable – especially as it is easier to discover historical facts about men than women, although the decision to

Table 3.2 House names of the London suburbs of Ealing and Chiswick commemorating the British Empire

Name in Kelly's Directory, 1889–90	Origins of the house name
Miss White, Nilgiri House, 10, Longfield Road, Ealing Mrs Arthur A. Dawson, Neilgherry, Windsor Road, Ealing	*Nilgiri/Neilgherry*, derived from Sanskrit meaning 'blue hills', is a place-name which repeats across Indian states: 'The Nilgiris (formerly spelt Neilgherries) 'are a mountain block in Southern India, formed by the convergence of the two great systems of mountain ranges which give rise to the Peninsular: the Eastern and Western Ghats' (*Nilgiri Guide and Directory*, 1916: 5), and were frequented by Europeans as a holiday resort.
Miss Barter, Deccan, 3, Freeland Road, Ealing Common	*Deccan*, derived from Sanskrit for 'south', refers to the plateau between the Eastern and Western Ghats south of the Narmada River.
Gordon Hardie, Mawallock Lodge, Florence Road, Ealing	*Mawallock* is a sheep-station in Pyrenees Shire, Victoria, Australia.
Charles Milner, Lallkoti, 71, Barrowgate Road, Chiswick	*Lal Kothi* is the name of the palace house of the Maharaja of Cooch Behar, Darjeeling, India. 'Maharajah Prasad Nath Roy had built it in the likeness of a western villa and was in fact the Maharaja's own private "Taj Mahal" dedicated to his beloved wife. During the British Raj itself, (Lal Kothi) became very popular among the British officers as the king and the queen hosted sumptuous parties.'[5]
John M. Wright, Kurrajong, 9, Freeland Road, Ealing Common	*Kurrajong*, the name for a species of tree from the Dharug language of the Sydney area, is a town in the Blue Mountains, New South Wales, Australia.
Mr Alfred Ames, Avisawella, 26, Disraeli Road, Ealing Green	*Avisawella* is a town in Sri Lanka, where the British set up rubber plantations named *Penrith, Elston, Glenesk* (Wright 1907: 712, 882).
Captain Thomas Brown, Ghuznee Lodge, no. 4, Surrey Road, Chiswick	*Ghazni* is a city in Central Afghanistan. The Battle of Ghuznee, First Afghan War, took place on 23 July 1839. 'Riding Master (Thomas) Brown served with the 16th Lancers during the campaign in Affghanistan under Lord Keane in 1839, including the siege and capture of Ghuznee (Medal).' (Hart 1871).
Major General Robert S. Moseley, Ali Musjid, 34, Mattock Lane, Ealing.	The Fort of Ali Masjid is at the western end of the Khyber Pass in Afghanistan. 'Lieut. General R.S. Moseley served in China and was present in the engagement of the 8th January 1859 when the battery and village of Shek-tsing were captured (Medal). Served in the Afghan war in 1880 on the Khyber Line of Communications (Medal).' (Hart1899). Roderick Fraser Sandeman, Wine Merchant, lived at no. 10, Mattock Lane.

[5] http://darjeeling.gov.in/lal-kothi.html.

name a house may have been more the wife's than the husband's. By contrast, the name *Sunnyside* carried less apparent freight, conveying an ostensibly transparent, optimistic message about the side of the street the house is situated on receiving sunshine, and resonating in a metaphorical way with Christians, who have faith in the light of God.

Biographical sources

Edward Wilson Bedford: see *London Gazette*, 22 October 1861; *The Morning Post*, 21 October 1869; *OED* oilman, *n*. 1.

Colonel Francis Marcus Beresford: Conservative MP, *Wikipedia* Marcus Beresford (1818–90).

John Bouch: *Post Office Directory* 1843: Luck, Bouch & Coath, Warehousemen, 7 & 8 Bread St. Cheapside; Luck left the partnership in 1849 (*London Gazette*, 1849, 3900). See www.ideal-homes.org.uk/bromley/assets/galleries/bickley/lauriston-house and also www.londongardensonline.org.uk/gardens-online-record.asp?ID=BRO067: 'Wythes' estate is a good example of suburban development built for the upper classes after the railway brought greater access to the capital.' For Bouch's charitable giving see e.g. *The Times*, 5 March 1863, *The Morning Post*, 22 June 1865, *The Standard*, 17 January 1867, *The Pall Mall Gazette*, 21 May 1872, *The Standard*, 12 November 1888. He may not always be distinguishable from his son, see *The Times*, 20 June 1865, where both 'John Bouch, Esq.' and 'John Bouch, jun., Esq.' were stewards at the Free Dispensary for Throat Diseases and Loss of Voice First Annual Festival. For John Bouch's death, see *The Standard*, 30 March 1895: 'March 29, at Coombe Lea, Bickley. John Bouch (late of 7 and 8 Bread-street, E.C.), aged 84.' For George Glas Sandeman, see London Metropolitan Archives CLC/B/196, Records of George G. Sandeman, Sons and Company Limited, wine shippers and cotton merchants. John Bouch's will:

> Mr John Bouch, of Coombe Lea, Bickley, and formerly for many years of the firm of Bouch, Couth, and Co., warehousemen, of Bread-street, Cheapside, who died on March 29, appointed as executors his wife, Mrs. Helen Rose Bouch, and his sons, John and Ernest Riethmuller Bouch. He bequeathed to his son John and his daughter Alice, £3,000 each; to his son Charles, £2,000; in trust for his son Alfred and his daughters, Margaret Morell Mackenzie, Frances Carry, Marian Luck, and Jane Peto Betts, £2,000 each; to his son William, £1,000; to his sons Ernest, Herbert, and Frederick, £500 each; and to Mrs. Bouch £300, his furniture and household effects, the income during her widowhood of a sum of £10,000, which may be left on deposit with Bouch, Couth, and Co., and the income during her widowhood of his residuary estate, which, on her death or remarriage, is to be in trust for the children of his first marriage'. *The Morning Post*, 18 May 1895.

Charles Bovet: for details of Charles Bovet's London business relationships see *Daily News*, 4 January 1869; *The Times*, 2 January 1873; *The Times*, 6 January 1876; *The Standard*, 8 January 1877. For his travel see Charles Bovet, merchant, port of Dover, 23 June 1838, Alien Arrivals, Class H02, Piece 42, Certificate 1072. For his election to the Royal Geographical Society see *The Morning Chronicle*, 29 March 1855. For Spring Grove, see 'Heston and Isleworth: Introduction', in *A History of the County of Middlesex*: Volume 3, Shepperton, Staines, Stanwell, Sunbury, Teddington, Heston and Isleworth, Twickenham, Cowley, Cranford, West Drayton, Greenford, Hanwell, Harefield and Harlington, ed. Susan Reynolds (London, 1962), pp. 85–94 (www.british-history.ac.uk/vch/middx/vol3/pp85-94, accessed 8 July 2015).

James Silk Buckingham (1786–1855): author, see Buckingham, James Silk (1786–1855): G. F. R. Barker, revised by Felix Driver, https://doi.org/10.1093/ref:odnb/3855.

James Weston Clayton: in the 1871 census see RG10, Piece 865, fo 38, pg 18. For James Weston Clayton's freemason membership see *The Era*, 19 January 1862. For his divorce, see The National Archives, J 77/67/130. For his second wife, Julia Starkie's baptism, see London Metropolitan Archives, St Marylebone Christchurch, Register of Baptism, p89/ctc, Item 009. For his patent see *The London Gazette*, 17 April 1874, p. 2155. For his charitable giving see *The Morning Post*, 7 January 1867, and *The Standard*, 17 January 1867 (the same article recorded that Mr. John Bouch had given £10 10s. to the Albert Orphan Asylum, the charity supported by William Morley). For an interview with James Clayton Weston see *The Mercury*, 22 April 1895:

> 'Can you,' [the journalist] asked Mr. Clayton, 'tell me exactly what your blacking is made of?' Of course, Mr. Clayton smiled and looked wise. 'If I told you *exactly*,' he replied, 'I should be divulging a secret which has been faithfully kept ever since the firm started. Needless to say many persons have endeavoured to find it out, but they have never succeeded. While the blacking is being prepared the doors of the factory in which it is made are kept locked, and we take such strict precautions that it is absolutely impossible for anyone to solve this problem of the blacking's excellence. When an employee is appointed "maker" – an important post in this firm – he has to deposit £500 by way of caution-money, and is bound down under a penalty of £5,000, never to disclose the nature of the recipe. At his death the £500 which he deposits with us is returned to his family. The amount of caution-money which he pays is of course made up for by an increased salary and interest on the money during the time we hold it. A man once tried to discover our secret by climbing on to the roof of the department in which the "makers" work, and peering through a chink. Before, however, he had time to make any discoveries his presence there was known, and in his hurry to escape he fell off the roof and broke his leg. But I can tell you that among the ingredients of which our blacking is composed are malt vinegar, ivory black, candy, treacle, and the best whale oil that money can buy.

For information on Day and Martin, see www.gracesguide.co.uk/Day_and_Martin. The preface to *Bleak House* reads:

At the present moment (August, 1853) there is a suit before the court which was commenced nearly twenty years ago, in which from thirty to forty counsel have been known to appear at one time, in which costs have been incurred to the amount of seventy thousand pounds, which is A FRIENDLY SUIT, and which is (I am assured) no nearer to its termination now than when it was begun.

(Dickens, *Bleak House*, 1853).

For Day and Martin in *Pickwick Papers*, see Dickens (1837: 92). The authority on Warren's Blacking Factory is Allen (2011). For yachting see *Freeman's Journal and Daily Commercial Advertiser*, 4 February 1899, and for the yacht *Xenia* see www.clydeships.co.uk/view.php?ref=11502. For leases and the Grand Junction Waterworks see London Metropolitan Archives ACC/2558/GJ/01/0475; ACC/2558/GJ/01/0557. For James Clayton Weston's addresses at death see *The Daily News*, 15 February 1899.

Nathaniel Clode: wine merchant, *London Gazette*, 10 September 1846.

Edmund Rand Cock: tea and coffee dealer, *The Morning Post*, 24 November 1848.

Leader Cox Stevenson: merchant, TNA ACC/0942/016.

Roger Crompton: information is taken from *The Monthly Observer & New Church Record* 3/33, 1 Sept 1859, 342, and 7/83, 1 Nov 1863, 387; *The Intellectual Repository, and New Jerusalem Magazine* 6/69, 1 Sept 1859, 431–2; *The New-Church Magazine* 21/245, May 1902, 193–8; Cooke (1908); Bateman (1859); Ashmore (1982: 102); Bayley (1884: ch. 29); and Presland (*c.*1984: 28, which contains information on Robert Fletcher & Son who took over Crompton's Stoneclough Brow papermill). Roger Crompton is present in the 1851 census at Class H0107, Piece 2206, fo 75, pg 17, and his wife's baptism is at Piece 4399, Hatton Garden, Cross Street, (Swedenborgians), 1797–1837. The *Victoria County History* briefly mentions Crompton's *Sunnyside* in St John's Wood: 'A large house, Sunnyside, with a Greek Doric porch . . . built by 1862 and possibly in 1847.' (T. F. T. Baker, Diane K. Bolton and Patricia E. C. Croot, 'Hampstead: St. John's Wood', in *A History of the County of Middlesex*: Volume 9, Hampstead, Paddington, ed. C. R. Elrington (London, 1989), pp. 60–3 (www.british-history. ac.uk/vch/middx/vol9/pp60-63, accessed 5 January 2015). In 1861 the house-number changed from 4, Avenue Gardens, Upper Avenue Road, to 8, Upper Avenue Road, Regent's Park when the terrace-name 'Avenue Gardens' was discontinued, cf. B. W. Gardiner & Son, *Royal Blue Book* (1860: 246, 519); *Boyle's Court Guide* (1861). Roger Crompton's £17,400 bequest was considerable; the Rev. Augustus Clissold left the church £4,000 out of his £34,000 estate – but he is better known because his wife's estate in Stoke Newington was secured for the public in 1889 and was named Clissold Park (Clissold, Augustus (1797–1882): Gordon Goodwin, revised by Timothy C. F. Stunt, https://doi.org/10.1093/ref:odnb/5689). See *The Illustrated London News*, 22 March 1856, for 'the New Church College School, Devonshire-Street, Islington'.

Madgwick Spicer Davidson: lawyer, TNA 610/35.

Thomas Elborough: for his admission to the Tallow Chandler's Livery Company apprenticeship see London Metropolitan Archives COL/CHD/FR/02/1239/073, 1800. *Old Bailey Proceedings Online* (www.oldbaileyonline.org), trial of Charles Robson (t18310217-234): 'Thomas Elborough: I left my sister in care of the shop – on my return she stated this circumstance; I have bought bags of the prisoner, but he had never left any bundle of paper there, and I had not ordered any bags then.'

William Felgate: East India Company merchant, *The Morning Post*, 15 February 1843.

George Jackson Berwick: surgeon, National Archives of India, PR_000002329429, 31st December 1844 p. 999.

Philip Firmin (*c.*1790–1874): button maker with shops at 153 Strand and 13 Conduit St, www.ukdfd.co.uk/pages/button-makers.html.

Thomas Keddy Fletcher: Conservative supporter, *The Standard*, 10 March 1869.

Joseph Frankau (1813–1857): born into a Jewish family in Diespeck, Bavaria (Endelman 1994). He came to London in 1837, not long after cigars had been popularised by British officers returning from the Peninsular War (1807–1814) in Spain and Portugal – by the 1830s sales of cigars had overtaken snuff, and by the 1850s the fashion had spread from the aristocracy to the middle classes. Joseph first lodged with a Jewish cigar merchant before opening his own cigar business, where he prospered sufficiently to be able to move to Benario Villa, Upper Avenue Road in 1854 or 1855 (Benario is a Jewish surname). Less is known of **Sidney**, but he was probably one of Joseph's brothers (Endelman 1994: 118–21). For Sidney Frankau's bankruptcy see the *London Gazette*, 27 Sept 1861, 3886: Sidney Frankau, Importer of Meerschaum Pipes, Dealer and Chapman, No. 79, Bishopsgate-street-Within and No. 12, Bridge-street, Westminster.

George Thomas Jenkins: barrister, Foster (1885: 242).

Theodore Brooke Jones: his addresses are listed in the London *Post Office Directory* of 1869 as 8, Moorgate Street and Sunnyside, London Road, Clapton. For Theodore Brooke Jones's birth on 20 August 1828 see London Metropolitan Archives, Hackney, Register of Baptism, p79/wh, Item 001. For his marriage, see *The Morning Post*, 15 February 1860 'On the 9th inst., at 8, Great Kelvin-terrace, Glasgow, by the Rev. Andrew Bonar, Theodore Brooke Jones, Esq., of "Kirk Dale", Sydenham, Kent, to Euphemia, eldest daughter of Thomas Turnbull, Esq., of Auckland.' For Sandemanian Thomas Turnbull, Euphemia Turnbull's father, see Sandeman and Peat (1895). Accountants Theodore and Theodore Brooke Jones are briefly mentioned in Matthews, Anderson and Edwards (1998: 19). In the 1871 census he is at RG10, Piece 1033, fo 41, p. 7, with his wife, six children and three servants.For his probable invention of microscope slides, see Stevenson and Warren (2013). For charitable giving, the *Local Preachers' Magazine and Christian Family Record* (1854: 320) records Theodore Brooke Jones as subscribing a guinea. For his Freedom of the City of London Admission Papers see London Metropolitan Archives, COL/CHD/FR/02/1929–1931. For mention in connection with the Brethren's Clapton Hall, Alkham Road, and Theodore Jones's baptism at Tottenham, see C. Russell Hurditch (1896: 83). For election to the Statistical Society, 20 February 1877, see *The Journal of the Statistical Society* 40, 1877. For an obituary and the Harrogate Assembly see www.gospelhall.org/ index.php/bible-teaching/138-history/brethren-biographies/3061-biography-86-theodore-brooke-jones. For the Great Exhibition of 1851 catalogue see –www. gracesguide.co.uk/1851_Great_Exhibition:_Official_Catalogue:_Class_X.

Orlando Jones: for his manufactures at Whitechapel and Battersea see Ramsey (1913: 84), and for some prizes see advertisements in *The Leeds Mercury*, 10 August 1871.

Robert John Lattey: lawyer, www.landedestates.ie/LandedEstates/jsp/family-show. jsp?id=816.

George Cargill Leighton: the first mention of his *Sunnyside* (that I can find) is in the *Post Office Directory* of 1863. For a biography see Leighton, Charles Blair (1823–1855): Lucy Peltz, https://doi.org/10.1093/ref:odnb/16397. For George Cargill Leighton's parent's marriage, see 'Scotland, Marriages, 1561–1910,' index, FamilySearch (familysearch.org/pal:/MM9.1.1/XY3Q-LMV, accessed 5 January 2015), Stephen Leighton and Helen Blair, 24 May 1822; citing Dunkeld, Perth, Scotland, reference; FHL microfilm 1,040,066. For the Scottish Leighton printing family in London see Laurence Worms (https://ashrarebooks.word-press.com/2012/11/22/a-blocking-of-leightons, accessed 4 January 2015). For **Stephen** and George Cargill's participation in the Sandemanian Church see Cantor (1991a and 1991b) and James (2008: 174). For house leases see London Metropolitan Archives, ACC/1395/059-77. For the description of *Fairlight* see *The Morning Post*, 6 July 1895. George Cargill Leighton's election to member-ship of the Royal Institution was published in the *Notices of the Proceedings at the Meetings of the Members of the Royal Institution of Great Britain* 4, 1862–6, 17, and his membership of the Royal Society of Arts from 1855 in *Journal of the Society of Arts* 13/677, 10 Nov 1865, 18. His admittance to the Company of Stationers is in the Freedom of the City Admission Papers (1681–1925), 25 April 1876. For George Cargill Leighton in the England & Wales Non-Conformist & Non-Parochial Registers, see Piece 0139, Cert. No. 77004, Vol 15 (1837 Feb 24 – Mar 2). For an obituary see *The Penny Illustrated Paper and Illustrated Times*, 18 May 1895, 307.

Robert Lush: lawyer, *Monthly Law Magazine*, 1841: 227.

William Morley: for his charitable giving see *The Morning Post*, 6 August 1864, *Daily News*, 15 December 1864, *The Times*, 5 January 1865. For his will see England & Wales, National Probate Calendar (Index of Wills and Administrations), 1858–1966, Morley William Esq, 21 July. 'The Will with seven Codicils of William Morley the Younger late of Gutter-lane in the City of London and of Streatham in the County of Surrey Esquire who died 10 April 1883 at Sunnyside

Leigham-Court-road Streatham was proved at the Principal Registry by Edward Bailey and Edward Horsman Bailey both of 5 Berners-street Oxford-street in the County of Middlesex Esquires and Elizabeth Harriott Morley of Sunnyside Widow the Relict the Executors.' See *Colonist* 27/3826, 5 May 1884, 3, on the death of his father: 'The death is announced of Mr William Morley, who is supposed to be the founder and "Father" of the wholesale Manchester trade in the City of London, having established the first wholesale warehouse under the title of W. and J. Morley, at 36, Gutter Lane, Cheapside, in the year 1806, a business which is still carried on under the name of W. Morley & Gray. In the early days of railway enterprise Mr Morley became chairman of several companies, and was one of the promoters of the Union Bank of London. He was born on January 1, 1787.'

Charles Orme: distiller, see his daughter Orme, Eliza (1848–1937): Leslie Howsam, https://doi.org/10.1093/ref:odnb/37825.

Andrew Pritchard: see Pritchard, Andrew (1804–1882): B. B. Woodward, revised by Brian Bracegirdle, https://doi.org/10.1093/ref:odnb/22818.

Nicholas L. Seppings: *The Navy List, Corrected to 20th December, 1864*; *London Gazette*, 5 July 1887, 3648.

Henry Young Darracott Scott: Scott, Henry Young Darracott (1822–1883): John Weiler, https://doi.org/10.1093/ref:odnb/24876. 'England, Devon, Parish Registers, 1538–1912,' index and images, FamilySearch (https://familysearch.org/pal:/MM9.1.1/KCSM-PBB, accessed 5 January 2015), Henry Young Darracott Scott, 1822, Baptism; from 'Church of England parish registers 1538–1911', index and images, findmypast (www.findmypast.com); citing Devon, archive reference 167/9, images provided by FamilySearch International.

Elizabeth Straker: born in 1839, the daughter of Frederick Straker (b.1812). In 1861 Frederick Straker was a printer, employing nine compositors, two printmen and six boys. Frederick Straker's parents were William Straker (b.1778) and Elizabeth Shackleton. William Straker (b.1778) was the son of William Straker (b.*c.* 1744) and Elizabeth Livermore Straker, who also bore Ezra (b.1772, d. *c.*1821), the father of Samuel Straker.

Samuel Straker: for his baptism and parents, Ezra and Mary Straker, see London Metropolitan Archives, St John of Hackney Register of Baptisms, Jan 1770–Dec 1812, P79/JN1/027. For **Mary Straker**, see Cantor (1991a: 6, 67, 273); James (1996: 69); GRO Death Certificate 1842/S/vol 03/p. 63. (Another member of George Cargill Leighton's Sandemanian congregation was called Mary Straker. She died poor, a spinster at 23, Green Terrace, Clerkenwell, 30 June 1842, aged 65. I have been unable to discover her relationship to Samuel Straker.) For his first marriage to Sarah Isabella Wright, see London Metropolitan Archives, St James Clerkenwell, Register of Banns of Marriage, P76/JS, Item 064. For his second marriage to Mary Ann Palmer, see Guildhall, St Andrew Undershaft, Register of Marriages, 1837-1970, P69/AND4/A/01/MS 4111/2. For Mary Ann

Palmer's donation of books to the Wesleyan Chapel, Barry Road, see Blanch (1875: 228).

For Samuel Straker's City of London committees as a Common Councilman see London Metropolitan Archives COL/CC/11/02/042 (1863: Library; 1865: Commissioners of Sewers, Markets; 1866: Commissioners of Sewers, Coal and Corn and Finance, Markets, Cattle Plague; 1867: Coal and Corn and Finance; 1868: Coal and Corn and Finance, Special Reception; 1870: Police, Officers & Clerks', Gas; 1871: Police, Officers & Clerks', Gas; 1872: General Purposes, Officers & Clerks', Gas; 1873: General Purposes, Law Parliamentary & City Courts; Gas & Water; 1874 (his death): Commissioners of Sewers, General Purposes, City of London School). For his vestry commitments see *St Giles Tenth Annual Report of the Vestry* (1865–6: 122–3) and subsequent reports. He was a Guardian of the Poor until his death. For membership of the Royal Society of Arts see *Journal of the Society of Arts* 9/444, 24 May 1861, 496. For the Printers' Pension Society Anniversary Festival see *The Era*, 27 April 1862. On 31 January 1848 Samuel Straker appeared in court as a witness and his direct speech is recorded:

> SAMUEL STRAKER. I am a lithographer, at 80, Bishopsgate-street Within, and sell lithographic materials. On 17th Sept. last Friedeburg and Kauffman came to my shop and purchased two lithographic stones for 3s. 6d.—this is the bill of parcels I gave to Friedeburg (produced)—he said he had no money to pay for them, that he had come out without his money, and he would step and get the 3s. 6d., which he did—Kauffman could articulate a few words in French, by which I understood that he had come from Paris, and that he was a poor artist, and he was about to do some lithographic work, and having no press, he asked me whether I would allow him to bring his work to prove—that is the technical term for taking an impression—I said he might do it—he did not come to do so—he came again on 29th Sept., with Aaronson, and purchased another lithographic stone, which was cut in three pieces—these produced are two of those pieces—I think Aaronson was the only person that could speak English, therefore he must have given the instructions to have it cut into three—he said his press was nine inches wide—that is an unusual size, and there was no alternative but to cut the stone—this is my bill for them (produced.).
>
> *Old Bailey Proceedings Online* (www.oldbaileyonline.org) trial of Leybe Aaronson, Jacob Friedeburg, Raphael Kauffman, Solomon Muscovitz (t18480131-598)

More of his direct speech is reported in a court case in *The Daily News*, 6 September 1858. For information on his interment see Woollacott (2006: 8). The Nunhead Cemetery Nonconformist mortuary-chapel was bombed in the Second World War, and in 1951 the four lead coffins in its catacombs were removed to the floor of the crypt of the Anglican chapel, where they were subsequently vandalized. For the quotation from Straker's daughter see Woollacott and Burford (2014: 110–11). For Elizabeth Livermore Straker and Cornelius Varley see Varley, Cornelius (1781–1873): Charlotte Klonk, https://doi.org/10.1093/ref:odnb/28113.

William Watt Backhouse Stuart: for his marriage see July Quarter 1862 Romford vol 4a p131. William Watt Backhouse Stuart died 10 February 1904 in Christchurch, Hampshire, with probate to Elizabeth Stuart, widow and Herbert William Stuart, bank clerk; effects £4,286 14s 3d.

William Epworth Tuke: wine broker, *The Spectator,* 12 October 1861.

Cornelius Varley (1781–1873): doi:10.1093/ref:odnb/28113. Varley's obituary is in the *Illustrated London News,* 25 October 1873, 389, and see also Cantor (1991a: 301, 314 fn 28).

John Waldram: for his business address see *The London Gazette,* 20 July 1875. For his contract at Paddington Station see Thompson and Matthews (2013: 16).

Henry Wordsworth: may have been the Threadneedle Street solicitor of that name, see *The Illustrated London Almanac of 1851,* 59.

4

RELIGION, FAME AND SUNNYSIDE

The first three London homes named *Sunnyside* (1859–69) were the residences of Swedenborgian Roger Crompton, Sandemanian George Cargill Leighton, Plymouth Brother Theodore Brooke Jones, and Samuel Straker, who had a Sandemanian grandmother and great-aunt, and who was married briefly at the end of his life to Wesleyan Methodist Mary Ann Straker. These people were interconnected in several ways: Crompton and Leighton and Straker worked in the print industry; Leighton, Straker and Jones were City of London liverymen; Jones and Andrew Pritchard (Samuel Straker's Sandemanian great-uncle who was also his grandmother's husband's apprentice) both made microscope slides, of which there were few practitioners in the early nineteenth century. Leighton was a Sandemanian, Straker's grandmother was married to a Sandemanian, and Jones's wife was a Sandemanian. Crompton, Leighton, Straker and Jones were all Nonconformists.

Did the house name *Sunnyside* correlate particularly with Nonconformists and especially appeal to them for some reason, or was their religious denomination just coincidence? I needed to find out who the Nonconformists were, what it was that they did not conform to, how it influenced their life-choices, and which denomination was the first to use the name *Sunnyside*. The majority of Nonconformist sects were small but there were lots of them, having proliferated since the Puritan reform movement within the Established Church began in the 1630s. It turned out that there was a correlation between Nonconformism and the name *Sunnyside* – but in relation to a sect I had not yet encountered.

What Dissenters were dissenting from was the religion of the state, the Church of England (particularly high-church Anglicanism) and from the Established Church of Scotland. Theologically they objected to (amongst other things) the notion of a national church and to hierarchy, priestly or secular, for neither of which is there Biblical authority. But there were also material benefits in dissent: in particular, the Church of England was tied to the feudal class system, from which financially-successful commoners could not benefit, as rank was fixed by birth. Nobility would always take precedence in church, no matter how wealthy or influential a person might become. Perhaps it is not so surprising, therefore, that dissenting churches enjoyed a heyday during the nineteenth century. An authority on Victorian Nonconformism, Bebbington, says 'Up to about 1840 they had been growing faster than the population; from then until the 1880s their membership was increasing at roughly the same rate as the population'. And in particular:

> Nonconformists had therefore tended to have chapels in places that had escaped from the dominance of the gentry – places that were new, large, on boundaries, scattered in their populations and/or marked by a range of commercial and industrial occupations. . . . In the suburbs that sprawled outwards in the final decades of the century, the more affluent Nonconformists felt entirely at home. . . . Nonconformity was fostering a new urban – or rather, suburban – civilisation.
>
> (Bebbington 2011 [1992]: 19–23)

The upper echelons of Nonconformity were 'merchants and manufacturers, typical entrepreneurs of their age', who liked to carve out an individual path in religion as they did in business. And '(a)lthough workpeople readily found a place in Nonconformity, it attracted them partly because it could act as a vehicle for embourgeoisement' (Bebbington 2011: 19–23). As Nonconformists, top dogs in business could sit in the front pews (benches, chairs, depending on the denomination) and attain positions of authority – Deacon, Elder, Presbyter. If you were used to being the boss in your own paperworks, printworks, lithography works or accountancy practice during the week, you didn't have to shift social polarity on Sunday and defer to people of higher social rank. Most dissenting churches preached an egalitarian message of all men being equal in the sight of the Lord, although how that played out must have varied in practice because these first four Sunnysiders were truly wealthy, unlike most of their fellow worshippers.

The name *Sunnyside* has an obvious appeal for those of religious bent, in a general kind of way. This earthly vale of sorrows contrasts with the heavenly blessings to come, the metaphorical light in which Christians walk. And, as I set about researching Dissent and Sunnyside, I discovered that Nonconformist churches in the English-speaking world outside Britain still have an affinity with the name. The name-stock of British Nonconformist churches draws on names of streets and towns (such as *Dunstable Baptist Church*, which is in the Bedfordshire town of Dunstable), as well as from the scripture of Christianity. British Nonconformist church names include *Emmanuel* (a Hebrew name, applied to the Messiah); *Ebenezer* (a Hebrew name, applied to a stone); *Cephas* (name of an Apostle, Aramaic for 'rock'); *Jireh* (part of one of the Hebrew names for God); *Adullam, Berachah, Bethany, Bethel, Bethlehem, Bethesda, Calvary, Carmel, Eden, Elim, Enon, Hebron, Hermon, Rehoboth, Salem, Zion, Zoar* (Hebrew place-names taken from the Bible); words taken from the King James Bible (*Ark, Grace, Hope, Pilgrim, Providence, Tabernacle*); words taken from the liturgy (*Apostolic, Trinity*); and the type of sect (*Community, Evangelical, Free, Independent, Presbyterian, Puritan, Reformed, Strict and Particular*). Words from the wider metaphorical Christian realm do occur, but in far lower numbers (*Harbour Mission, Lighthouse Church, Rock Chapel, The*

Sailors Chapel).[1] The word *Sunnyside* has no Biblical authority, it is not Hebrew or Aramaic, it does not figure in the language of the liturgy, it is not a type of sect and it does not fit the seafaring metaphor. Yet as I researched the history of Sunnyside and Nonconformity, I kept coming across present-day Sunnysides, so I started to take note. These Sunnyside churches are situated in English-speaking countries, particularly in America. A handful are listed in Table 4.1.

Table 4.1 New World *Sunnyside* churches with websites operative in 2017

USA	
Sunnyside Adventist Church	Portland, Oregon, OR 97216
Sunnyside Seventh Day Adventist Church	Fresno, California, CA 93704
Sunnyside Adventist Church	E. Lincoln Ave, Sunnyside, Washington, WA 98944
Decatur Sunnyside Seventh Day Adventist Church	530, N. Sunnyside Rd, Decatur, IL 62522
Sunnyside Spanish Adventist Church	Scoon Rd, Sunnyside, Washington, WA 98944
Sunnyside Alliance Church	East New Market, Maryland, MD 21631
Sunnyside Assembly of God	Van Buren, Arkansas, AR 72956
Sunnyside Assembly of God	Jeffersonville, Indiana, IN 47130
Sunnyside Baptist Church	Douglas, Arizona, AZ 85607
Sunnyside Baptist Church	Flagstaff, Arizona, AZ 86004
Sunnyside Baptist Church	Tucson, Arizona, AZ 85706
Sunnyside Baptist Church	Rogers, Arkansas, AR 72756
Sunnyside Baptist Church	Fresno, California, CA 93727
Sunnyside Baptist Church	Los Angeles, California, CA 90044
Sunnyside Baptist Church	Wichita, Kansas, KS 67211
First Baptist Church of Sunnyside	Sunnyside, Georgia, GA 30284
Sunnyside Baptist Church	LaFayette, Georgia, GA 30728
Sunnyside Baptist Church	Albany, Georgia, GA 31705
Sunnyside Baptist Church	Greenville, Georgia, GA 30222
Sunnyside Baptist Church	Lagrange, Georgia, GA 30241
Sunnyside Baptist Church	Newnan, Georgia, GA 30263
Sunnyside Baptist Church	Rome, Georgia, GA 30161
Sunnyside Baptist Church	Toccoa, Georgia, GA 30577
Sunnyside Baptist Church	Waycross, Georgia, GA 31501
Sunnyside Baptist Church	Burlington, Iowa, IA 52601
Sunnyside Baptist Church	Shepherdsville, Kentucky, KY 40165
Sunnyside Baptist Church	Somerset, Kentucky, KY 42503
Sunnyside Baptist Church	Cadillac, Michigan, MI 49601

[1] Names taken from www.grace.org.uk/churches/chdir.php.

Table 4.1 *continued*

USA	
Sunnyside Baptist Church	High Point, North Carolina, NC 27260
Sunnyside Baptist Church	Oklahoma City, Oklahoma, OK 73109
Sunnyside Baptist Church	Broken Arrow, Oklahoma, OK 74014
Sunnyside Baptist Church	Cheyenne, Wyoming, WY 82003
Sunnyside Baptist Church	Greeneville, Tennessee, TN 37743
Sunnyside Baptist Church	Wichita Falls, Texas, TX 76301
Sunnyside Baptist Church	North Rose, New York, NY 14516
Sunnyside Baptist Church	Kingsport, Tennessee, TN 37664
The New Sunnyside Baptist Church	Atlanta, Georgia, GA 30310
Sunnyside Road Baptist Church	Oaklandon, Indiana, IN 46236
Sunnyside Baptist Theological Seminary	Opelousas, Louisiana, LA 70570
Sunnyside Bible Chapel	Atlantic, Iowa, IA 50022
Sunnyside Chapel	Minter City, Mississippi, MS 38944
Sunnyside Christian Church	Colorado Springs, Colorado, CO 80915
Sunnyside Church of the Nazarene	Happy Valley, Oregon, OR 97086
Sunnyside Kinnear Church of the Nazarene	Kinnear, Wyoming, WY 82516
Sunnyside Church	Clackamas, Oregon, OR 97015
Sunnyside Church	Clayton, Louisiana, LA 71326
Sunnyside Church of God	Tuscumbia, Alabama, AL 35674
Sunnyside Church of God	Woodstock, Georgia, GA 30188
Sunnyside Church of God	Canton, Georgia, GA 30114
Sunnyside Church of God	New Castle, Indiana, IN 47362
Sunnyside Church of God	Great Falls, Montana, MT 59405
East Sunnyside Church of God of Prophecy	Houston, Texas, TX 77051
Sunnyside Church of the Brethren	New Creek, West Virginia, WV 26743
Sunnyside Church of the Brethren	Keyser, West Virginia, WV 26726
Sunnyside Grace Brethren Church	Franklin Avenue, Sunnyside, Washington, WA 98944
Sunnyside Free Lutheran Church	Stacy, Minnesota, MN 55079
Sunnyside Conservative Mennonite Church	Kalona, Iowa, IA 52247
Sunnyside Mennonite Church	Sarasota, Florida, FL 34232
Sunnyside Mennonite Church	Arthur, Illinois, IL 61911
Sunnyside Mennonite Church	Elkhart, Indiana, IN 46516
Sunnyside Mennonite Church	Lancaster, Pennsylvania, PA 17605
Sunnyside Mennonite Church	Conneaut Lake, Pennsylvania, PA 16316
Sunnyside Centenary United Methodist Church	Portland, Oregon, OR 97214
Sunnyside United Methodist Church	Kalamazoo, Michigan, MI 49048

Sunnyside United Methodist Church	Frederick, Maryland, MD 21703
Sunnyside United Methodist Church	906, E. Edison Ave, Sunnyside, Washington, WA 98944
Sunnyside Ministry, Moravian Church	Winston-Salem, North Carolina, NC 27127
Sunnyside Pentecostal Holiness Church	Blacksburg, Virginia, VA 24060
Sunnyside Presbyterian Church	South Bend, Indiana, IN 46617
Sunnyside Presbyterian Church	Fayetteville, North Carolina, NC 28312
Sunnyside Presbyterian Church	16th St, Sunnyside, Washington, WA 98944
Sunnyside Presbyterian Church	Winchester, Virginia, VA 22603
Sunnyside Reformed Church	Sunnyside, New York, NY 11104
The United Reformed Church of Sunnyside	Sheller Road, Sunnyside, Washington, WA 98944
Sunnyside Christian Reformed Church	700 North 16th Street, Sunnyside, WA 98944
Sunnyside Road Church of Christ	821, N. Sunnyside Rd, Decatur, Illinois, IL 62522
Sunnyside Church of Christ	Hillsboro, Ohio, OH, 45133
Sunnyside Church of Christ	1313, E. Edison Ave, Sunnyside, WA 98944
West Sunnyside Congregational Holiness Church	Griffin, Georgia, GA 30223

Canada

Sunnyside Wesleyan Church	Ottawa, Ontario, ON K1S 4S4
Sunnyside United Church	Surrey, British Columbia, BC V4A 2J6
Sunnyside Christian Retreat Centre	Sylvan Lake, Alberta, AB T4S 1R6
Sunnyside Hutterite Colony	Newton Siding, Manitoba, MB R0H 0X0
Sunnyside Hutterite Colony	Warner, Alberta, AB T0K 2L0

South Africa

Sunnyside Methodist Church of Southern Africa	Sunnyside, Pretoria
Sunnyside Seventh Day Adventist Church	Sunnyside, Pretoria
United Apostolic Faith Church Sunnyside Victory Centre	Sunnyside, Pretoria
Sunnyside Church of the Nazarene	Athlone, Cape Town

None of these New World *Sunnyside* churches are particularly old. Most date from the late nineteenth century or were built during the twentieth. Many take their names from locations named *Sunnyside*, which in turn were named after houses named *Sunnyside*. Nor am I trying to bludgeon with numbers here – the United States is a populous country with a lot of churches. My point is that *Sunnyside* belongs to the name-stock of Nonconformist churches in the New World yet does not belong to the name-stock of other churches, nor to Nonconformist churches in Britain. There are far fewer, if any, Anglican or American Episcopal (the American equivalent of the Established churches, from which Nonconformists dissent), Roman Catholic churches, Jewish synagogues, Muslim mosques or Buddhist temples named *Sunnyside*, either in the New World or in the Old. One reason for this is simply that, as new churches, Dissenting churches needed naming. Nonconformism only officially came into being in 1689 after the Act of Toleration was passed in England, whereas older Christian churches already had names, usually that of the patronal saint. A naming distinction between Dissenting churches and older ones might therefore be expected. But it does not explain why the name *Sunnyside* came to feel right to the congregations of widely disparate religious communities, from the Hutterites in Alberta to the Baptists in Georgia. Therefore I needed to put Nonconformist Sunnysides in date order, to find out which was the first. This led me back to England, where the 1851 census pointed me to Sunnysides in the northern counties of Lancashire, Durham, and Northumberland.

Sunnyside, Crawshawbooth, Rossendale, Lancashire, 1706, SD 80933 25113

The oldest Nonconformist *Sunnyside* church that I have been able to identify still exists, in the part of the village of Crawshawbooth, Rossendale, Lancashire, named Sunnyside. (Crawshawbooth is less than 20 miles north of Stoneclough Brow, Kearsley, Lancashire, where Roger Crompton's paperworks was situated.) The southwestern part of the village is marked Sunnyside on Greenwood's map of Lancashire of 1818 (Figure 4.1).

The Quaker Burial Register, Crawshawbooth Meeting, of 27 November 1706 records the death of 'Margaret Raine, Sunnyside'.[2] Pevsner says that the Sunnyside Quaker Meeting House was built by 1716, and that prior to that, Rossendale Quakers had met in the open air.[3] Thus by 1706, residents of Sunnyside, Crawshawbooth, are known to have been Quakers, and by 1716 there was a Nonconformist church in Sunnyside: the Friends' Meeting House (Quakers refer to themselves as Friends). By 1828 the market town in the vicinity, Haslingden, had a Swedenborgian and a Sandemanian church, as well as churches for Independents, Methodists and Baptists.[4] Nonconformism, proselytised in 'highways and hedges' by the lower

---

[2] Transcript of the Quaker Burial Register, Crawshawbooth Meeting, Rawtenstall Library. My thanks to Fiona McIntyre of Lancashire County Council's Libraries, Museums, Culture and Registrars. The Rain (Rayne, Raine, Rains) family continued in the area: Joseph Wood, a Yorkshire Quaker, kept a notebook in which he wrote in 1774 'we went by Haslingden to Margaret Rains of Sunnyside in Rossendale, got there at 5 o Clock were we lodg'd, but drunk Tea and Supp'd at Henry Mariots.' (Cooksey 2011: 17).

[3] For the Friends' Meeting House at Sunnyside see Pevsner (1969: 26).

[4] Pigot & Co. (1828: 255).

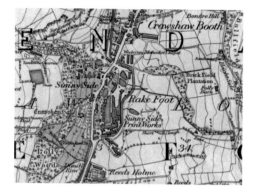

4.1 Ordnance Survey Map LXXII, 6-inch, Crawshawbooth, Lancashire, surveyed: 1844–7, published: 1849; www.maps.nls.uk/geo.

social classes (including women) was popular amongst industrial and agricultural workers, finding a foothold amongst the workforce of the Lancashire mills and going on to become the predominant denomination there for most of the nineteenth century.

The next recorded Nonconformist group in the Sunnyside area of Crawshawbooth was the Sunnyside Primitive Methodist Church, mentioned in its 1832 Quarterly Meeting Report.[5] In the late 1820s, John Brooks, owner of the Sunnyside Print Works, gave room to Catholic Irish immigrant workers until their church could be built in 1836. Baptists then took over their old quarters in 1845–7.[6] Sunnyside, Crawshawbooth, Lancashire, is thus known to have been home to Quakers from 1706, to Primitive Methodists from the 1830s, and to Baptists from the 1840s (the Catholic church became known as St James the Less, the others were known as 'Sunnyside Primitive Methodists', 'Sunnyside Baptists'). Lancashire, then, provided a precursor for most, if not all, the New World Nonconformist Sunnysides.

But why did this rather remote Lancashire valley became home to Nonconformist sects? The answer lies partly in industrialisation, and in particular in the series of protectionist Acts of Parliament from 1666 onwards which were designed to protect home cloth manufacturers against East India Company imports. Acts passed between 1700 and 1720 went so far as to outlaw the wearing of East India silks and cottons, which had been so successful as to threaten British weavers' livelihoods. A compromise of sorts was reached whereby the East India Company was allowed to sell raw material from Asia, which was then to be finished off in Britain. The Lancashire mill industry thus came into being, powered by the many small rivers streaming off the peaks and moors, finishing the cottons and silks that arrived at the Liverpool docks. The Sunnyside Print Works, sited alongside the River Limy and printing calico, was one such factory.[7]

---

[5] Riley (1979). The Primitive Methodists seceded from the Wesleyan Methodists in 1807.
[6] Newbigging (1893: 198).
[7] O'Brien, Griffiths and Hunt (1991: 398); Lee-Whitman (1982: 39); Nevell (2008: 33).

Perhaps now is the moment to tackle the common-sense objection that the name *Sunnyside* merely meant 'the side that gets the sun', and that there is nothing more of interest to discover. There are several objections. Firstly, 'the side that gets the sun' in a north–south river valley like that of Crawshawbooth is not obvious. The western side of the valley (where Sunnyside sits) gets the rising sun, and the Eastern side opposite gets the setting sun. Both receive sunlight at different times of day. From a crop-raising point of view, facing the rising sun might be better, but from a residential point of view, facing west is more sheltered. If Sunnyside really meant 'the side that gets the sun', then no historical *Sunnyside* ought to be north-facing (some are). Historical *Sunnysides* ought only to occur on the sides of features such as hills, mountains, rivers and lakes, not in the middle of featureless plains where sunshine reaches from sunrise to sunset (some do). There would be no reason for a regional distribution (which there was), other than that the south of the country, being closer to the equator, receives more sun in general and might be expected to have a higher proportion of historic *Sunnysides* (it did not). And the reason why the name *Sunnyside* should have boomed so dramatically in the late nineteenth century would remain unexplained.

Quakers, or the Religious Society of Friends, had been meeting in Lancashire since the 1650s, one of the radical sects born out of the Civil War. Their roots were in the lower social classes of the north of England, and they deliberately chose quiet, out of the way places in which to build their Friends' Meeting Houses in order to avoid persecution – the Quaker Act of 1662, repealed in 1687, made their refusal to swear allegiance to the Crown illegal, and their pacifist refusal to fight for their country rendered them unpopular at various points in time, both in Britain and in America. So Sunnyside, Crawshawbooth, met the Quakers' need for discretion, and provided a factory site which in turn provided a workforce ripe for conversion.

But why was the west side of Crawshawbooth called Sunnyside? Sunnyside House is not named on these maps of 1818 and 1849, but it stands in the area marked 'Sunny Side'. Pevsner says *Sunnyside House* is Elizabethan or Jacobean, with much subsequent modernisation.[8] *Sunnyside House* has a date-stone marked 1757 and the initials IRM, marking the tenure of John Raynes Marriott. He was a Quaker who ran up debt, causing his creditors to seek the deeds to the house in order to sell it. Apparently his creditors were unable to find them, so its anterior history remains unknown, neither is the person who named it known, nor which came first: the name of the area, or the name of the house.[9]

In the main, Quakers were industrious, sober and principled. They made sound business judgements – John Raynes Marriott excepting – and were as a result dispro-portionately wealthy, meaning that they were potential house-namers. They looked

---

[8] Pevsner (1969: 206); see also Trippier (2007: 4, 8; 2008: 4).
[9] My thanks to Fiona McIntyre of Lancashire County Council's Libraries, Museums, Culture and Registrars for this information, taken from Slater (1986).

ahead to the world to come, and were unfettered by allegiance to the feudal system: the only lord they recognised was the Almighty. Today we tend to characterise Puritans as dour, reclusive and censorious people, unlikely to have an affinity with what seems a cheerful, even frivolous name with its seaside, holiday air. But religious Dissenters were actually highly social beings, the antithesis of hermits. They spent long, regular hours, week in, week out, interpreting scripture together. They knew their fellows well and they looked after them, with relationships maintained for life. Quakers in particular travelled the country on foot, on horseback, with both men and women journeying to monthly, quarterly and yearly meetings – and providing means by which the name *Sunnyside* spread. And this is where they spread it:

Sunnyside, Sunderland, County Durham, 1734, NZ 39977 57192

Rachell Maude, widow, of Sunniside in the parish of Bishop Wearmouth and County of Durham

(extract from registered copy of will 2 February 1734)[10]

Sunnyside in Sunderland was a mansion on the High Street between Sunderland and Bishopswearmouth built in 1730 by Quaker Ebenezer Wardell, although it is not known if he named it. In April 1730 wealthy coal fitter and fellow Quaker Samuel Maude died, leaving a wife, Rachel, and thirteen children. The Maudes

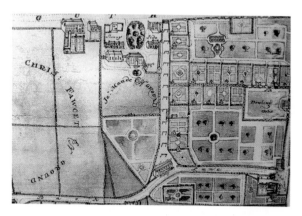

4.2 Detail of John Rain's *An Eye Plan of Sunderland and Bishop Wearmouth from the South*, 1785, Sunderland Antiquarian Society, showing Sunny Side top centre; reproduced by permission of the Sunderland Antiquarian Society.

[10] Durham University Library, Archives and Special Collections, Durham Probate Records pre-1858 will register 14B, GB-0033-DPRI/2/14B, pp. 126–30.

were a prominent Quaker family. Rachel Maude moved into Sunnyside but she died four years later, and in 1739 Ebenezer Wardell sold Sunnyside to one of the children, Warren Maude.[11]

Sunnyside, Coalbrookdale, Shropshire, 1751, SJ 66401 04646

this evening we went and Supt at Abiah Darbys of Sunnyside, taking a turn in her Gardens which are very large and beautiful, adorn'd with Harbours and Summerhouses
(Joseph Wood, Quaker, 25 April 1773, diary extract taken from Cooksey (ed.) 2011)

Sunnyside, Coalbrookdale, was home to Warren Maude's younger sister, Abiah Darby née Maude, a Quaker minister. On her second marriage (to Quaker Abraham Darby of Coalbrookdale) she moved to Coalbrookdale and in 1751 moved into a new house, which they named *Sunnyside*. Joseph Wood (1750–1821), a Yorkshire Quaker and diarist who visited the Quaker community of Sunnyside in Rossendale and lodged there with Margaret Rains in 1774 (recall the Margaret Raine who had been buried there in 1706), visited Abiah Darby at *Sunnyside* in Coalbrookdale.[12]

Sunnyside House and Sunnyside Mills, Ordsall Lane, Salford, Lancashire, 1808, SJ 82256 97575 and SJ 82526 97554

got to Manchester about 1 o Clock were the young Women took up their Quarters at John Cooks, and me and my companion at his Brother James Halls
(Joseph Wood, Quaker, 16 April 1774, diary extract taken from Cooksey (ed.) 2011: vol 3, 4.14)[13]

23 February 1795: Thomas Hall, birth, Sunny Side, Salford, Lancaster. Father: James Hall, mother: Ann.[14]

Jas. and Jas. Hall, Dyers, Sunnyside, Salford
(Pigot & Dean's *New Directory of Manchester and Salford*, 1821–1822)

---

[11] Town (2006: v, 11, 12); Smith (1843: 136). Samuel Maude (1665–1730), Rachel Maude née Warren, (1667–1734), Warren Maude (1710–79).

[12] Abiah Darby née Maude (1716–94); Cooksey (2011: vol 3, 4.2, 4.5, 4.17); Darby [née Maude; other married name Sinclair], Abiah (1716–1794): Nancy Cox, https://doi.org/10.1093/ref:odnb/55521. (Abiah and Abraham Darby's son, also named Abraham, built the famous Iron Bridge at Coalbrookdale.) There is a correlation between Dissenters and Old Testament names ending in –*ah*.

[13] For *Sunnyside House*, Salford see https://services.salford.gov.uk/forum/forumposts.asp?forum=22&id=118081.

[14] 'England Births and Christenings, 1538–1975', database, FamilySearch (https://familysearch.org/ark:/61903/1:1:N1KF-86T, accessed 4 December 2015), Thomas Hall, 23 Feb 1795; citing Sunny Side, Salford, Lancaster, England, reference R.G.6/934 p 5; FHL microfilm 583,996.

4.3 Detail of Lancashire CIV (includes: Manchester; Salford), surveyed: 1845, published: 1848; http://maps.nls.uk/ view/102344087.

Another Quaker family, the Halls, had been dyeing in Manchester since 1763. The firm employed 40 people, with another 4,000 men, women and children employed as outworkers in cloth production by 1784.[15] Sunnyside House and Sunnyside Mills, Lower Seddon Street, Ordsall Lane, Salford, were built by James Hall (1749–1843) between 1805 and 1808.

Sunniside, Hartlepool, County Durham, a.1816, NZ 52607 33816

Their first place of worship at Hartlepool was a room in the yard of Ralph Taylor, Sunniside, which was fitted up with a gallery at one end. The second was the house which stands right across the main street, leading to the dock, and is now in the occupation of George Souter, Cooper; this also had a gallery across the end. The third was a chapel on the Town Wall, built about fifty-eight years ago

(Sharp 1851 [1816]: 93).

Sunniside 1816 Sharp, Sunny Side 1828 Pigot, 1841 Plan

(Watts 2007: 110).

Sir Cuthbert Sharp's undated reference above to the room in the yard in Sunniside in his 1816 *History of Hartlepool* refers to Wesleyan Methodists. Watts (2007) is an English Place-Name Society volume dealing with County Durham, and on page 110 the evidence for Sunnyside, Hartlepool is given in date order: Sharp first, then Pigot's Directory of 1828, then a plan of 1841 showing the place-name. The earliest evidence that Watts could find for the name Sunniside in Hartlepool was the

---

[15] Seed (2014 [1992]: 118).

4.4 Sunniside, Hartlepool, County Durham, detail from Ordnance Survey 6-inch Durham XXXVII (includes Elwick, Hart, Hartlepool, West Hartlepool), revised: 1914, published: 1923; http://maps.nls.uk/view/102341659 (Sunniside is written north–south, middle right)

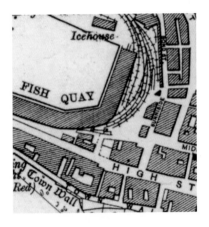

publication of Sharp's *History of Hartlepool* in 1816, but the name may have been in use before that. The date of the third Wesleyan Methodist meeting-place, the chapel on the Town Wall, 58 years before 1816, must have been about 1758, and presumably the first and second meeting-places were a little earlier, although after July 1757 when Wesley first visited Hartlepool.[16]

By the 1860s and 1870s there were further Quaker and Nonconformist *Sunnysides*:

Sunnyside, Box, Wiltshire, named in or before 1860 by tenant Struan E. Robertson.[17] Struan E. Robertson was brother of clergyman Frederick W. Robertson (1816–53) and together they published *Sermons Preached at Trinity Chapel, Brighton* in 1856. Trinity Chapel was a dissenting chapel.[18]

Sunnyside, 20 Fonnereau Road, Ipswich, Suffolk, IP1 3JP, TM 16204 45088, built in 1867. James Edward Ransome (1839–1905) is recorded living there in the 1869 *Post Office Directory for Cambridgeshire, Norfolk and Suffolk*. He was an agricultural engineer of the firm Ransomes, Sims and Jeffries founded by his Quaker grandfather Robert Ransome (1753–1830). 'Members of the family retained their Quaker affiliation, and were active civic and philanthropic figures in Ipswich.'[19] *Sunnyside* is a grand Victorian residence in a street of grand Victorian residences and is now a Grade II listed building.[20]

Sunnyside, Upper Mayfield, Staffordshire, built in 1872 and owned by Joseph Simpson (1835–1901), Quaker, cotton mill owner, brewery owner, JP and antislavery campaigner.[21]

[16] Sharp 1851 [1816]: 92.
[17] *Cheltenham Looker On*, 28 January 1860; for a discussion of the house and the several names it has borne see www.boxpeopleandplaces.co.uk/bybrook-house.html.
[18] Faulkenburg (2001); Frederick William Robertson (1816–53): doi:10.1093/ref:odnb/23792.
[19] Robert Charles Ransome (1830–86): doi:10.1093/ref:odnb/48140. James Edward Ransome (1839–1905): doi:10.1093/ref:odnb/48139. Robert Ransome (1753–1830): doi:10.1093/ref:odnb/23139.
[20] www.britishlistedbuildings.co.uk/101247680-sunnyside-ipswich#.WNe7Vo61tcB.
[21] www.wolfson.ox.ac.uk/~ben/FamilyHistory/SimpsonHeritage.html#JS_1835-1901 and www.bbc.co.uk/history/domesday/dblock/GB-412000-345000/page/6.

Sunnyside, Falkland Grove, Dorking, Surrey, bought in 1872 by Quaker William Allen (1808–97) of Jeffrey, Allen & Co., wallpaper manufacturer and numismatist.[22]

Sunnyside, Conyngham Road, Manchester, designed by Quaker architect Richard Lane (1795–1880), who also designed the Friends Meeting House, Manchester.[23]

To sum up: the earliest English *Sunnyside* associated with a Nonconformist group that I can find was that of Sunnyside, Crawshawbooth, Rossendale, Lancashire, where Quaker Margaret Raine was buried in 1706 and a Friends' Meeting House was erected in 1716, and where Quaker John Raynes Mariott resided at *Sunnyside House* in the 1750s. Quaker and diarist Joseph Wood lodged with the Rains family in Sunnyside, Rossendale in 1774. Joseph Wood also visited Quaker Abiah Darby (sister to Quaker Warren Maude of Sunnyside, Sunderland) at *Sunnyside* in Coalbrookdale in 1773, and Joseph Wood also visited Quaker James Hall of *Sunnyside*, Salford, in 1774. Joseph Wood's diary is full of long journeys made in the company of other Quaker Friends to distant meetings, lodging with Friends as he went.

The next usage in a religious context is that of Wesleyan Methodists in Hartlepool some time between 1757 and 1816, with Primitive Methodists at Sunnyside, Crawshawbooth, Lancashire, from the 1830s, and Baptists at Sunnyside in Crawshawbooth from the 1840s. Clearly the name *Sunnyside* circulated within the Dissenting community, and as mill-owners were often Nonconformists, the name came to be used of mills too, starting with the Brooks's Sunnyside Print Works in Crawshawbooth in 1809, James Hall's Sunnyside Silk and Cotton Mill at Salford from some time before 1821, Tootal Broadhurst and Lee's Sunnyside Mills, Daubhill, Bolton, Lancashire of 1868 (Ashmore 1982: 83). There were further *Sunnyside* residences owned by Quakers in the 1860s and 1870s. Quakers took the name to North America: the Quaker Lewis family of West Vincent, Pennsylvania, were helping fugitive slaves at their farm named Sunnyside from 1847 to the 1860s.[24]

* * *

Someone who is now known for his upper-middle-class high-church Anglicanism but who actually found the whole business of lower-class Nonconformism equally enthralling (especially the arguments), and who was also an authority on British houses, was Sir John Betjeman (1906–84). Sir John's lifelong companions were Archie and Jumbo, his teddy bear and toy elephant, who went with him to university at Oxford and who were in his arms when he died, aged 78. In the 1940s Sir John wrote a story for children about Archie, *Archie and the Strict Baptists*. In

---

[22] Hobbs *et al.*(2011: 300).
[23] Glinert (2008).
[24] Bonta (1985: 30), Young (2014: 36), Papson and Calarco (2015: 142).

letters to girlfriends Sir John would talk about Archie. Apparently Archie liked to preach himself; '(h)e went on for eight or nine hours until the chapel was empty'. In another letter, Archie had 'accepted a call to the Congregational Church on Wanstead Flats where he has been doing the duty of lay reader for some years'; in another he 'is very interested in Temperance Work at Clacton-on-Sea'; and in another 'Archibald has accepted the Incumbency of Raum's Episcopal Chapel, Homerton, E17 ... He will distribute Holy Supper at the Lord's Table after the seven o'clock evening service every fourth Sunday in the month. I hope, as do we all in Homerton, Clapton, Walthamstow and Hackney Marshes that his ministry will be successful and fruitful.'[25]

Sir John is using the language of Nonconformism: 'He will distribute Holy Supper at the Lord's Table', not 'he will give communion at the altar'. Here are some extracts from his short story called *Lord Mount Prospect*, first published in 1929 when he was 23 years old. It is fiction, but fiction informed by reality, about a sect the narrator is trying to track down called the Ember Day Bryanites. You will recognise some of the locations from early Sunnysiders' places of worship:

> That spirit of research and curiosity which made possible the forthcoming adventure prompted me to visit a deserted part of north London during the autumn of last year. Could it be that Ember Day Bryanites were still prophesying away up the Caledonian Road? Could it be that even now tired charwomen and weary tailors dressed themselves in sackcloth to listen? Under 'Places of Worship' in the *London Directory* I wondered at the hopeful signs I found. Last and almost least, beneath 'Other Denominations', below the Particular Baptists, and the Peculiar People, below the Sandemanians and Independent Calvinistics, came the glorious words, 'Ember Day Bryanite', and the address, 'Hungerford Green, Barnsbury, N.1.'

(The narrator sets out on his quest one twilit Sunday evening):

> Hungerford Green was attractive enough. It was a relic of successful Regency commerce. Two-storeyed houses, once 'tight boxes, neatly sashed', surrounded an oblong space of burnt grass with a curious pavilion in the middle, some conceit of a former merchant aping the gazebos of the great and good. The railings round the grass were sadly bent to make loop-holes for dogs and children, the noble urns of ironwork were battered: from all over Hungerford Green came the whooping of hymns loud enough to stream through ventilating spaces in the pointed windows of Baptist and Wesleyan chapel. The worn grass was

[25] Betjeman (1994: 77, 79, 87). Quoted from Gardner (2014: 242–3, 254 fn 25). Lombard Street banker Stephen Ram (*c.*1671–1746) quarrelled with the churchwardens of Hackney Parish Church who would not rent him an exclusive pew, and so he built a chapel in his garden in Homerton, with glass from Rouen, marble from Italy, Cornwall and Ireland, and a pulpit carved by Grinling Gibbons. Ram's Episcopal Chapel remained in use from 1723 until 1932 ('Hackney: The Parish Church', in *A History of the County of Middlesex: Volume 10, Hackney*, ed. T. F. T. Baker (London, 1995), pp. 115–22. *British History Online* (www.british-history.ac.uk/vch/middx/vol10/pp115-122, accessed 28 February 2018); *Look and Learn*, 7 April 1934). The London districts listed by Sir John are outer, poorer, eastern suburbs populated by Nonconformists. Clacton-on-Sea is in the county of Essex, especial home to eighteenth-century Nonconformist sects.

bright with the rays of gas-light from the places of worship, with an additional brightness from the outside lamp of a more prosperous chapel where electric light had been installed.

Joyous opening strains of a hearty Nonconformist service! How anxious was I to know under what gas or electric light Ember Day Bryanites, possibly in sackcloth, were even now praising the Lord!

(The narrator then asks some locals which is the Ember Day Bryanites' chapel, but no one knows):

With no faint heart I walked round the green, yet fearful of breaking silence with irreligious feet, and I scanned the names on the black and gilded notice-boards. 'Congregational', 'Primitive Methodist', 'United Methodist', 'New Jerusalem', 'Presbyterian Church of England', and the last was the last of the lighted chapels which made glorious Hungerford Green.

(The narrator finally succeeds in locating the chapel of the Ember Day Bryanites):

I could just discern a printed notice about an electoral roll, years old and clinging limply to its inefficient paste. The double rows of windows were bolted and boarded up. The great doors were shut. But beside them was a wooden notice-board with the remains of lettering still upon it. I struck a match and read:

THOSE WHO ARE CHOSEN FOR HIS COURTS ABOVE WILL MEET HERE (GOD WILLING) ON THE LORD'S DAY AT 11 A.M. AND AT 6.30.

Holy Supper by Arrangement.

The Lord had received His Ember Day Bryanites.

(Sir John Betjeman, extracts from *Lord Mount Prospect*, 1929, taken from Guest (ed.) 2006 [1978]: 124-6; first published in the December issue of *London Mercury*)

Now this is entertainment, but Sir John knew about church-going and he knew about north London, and all of these sects were real.[26] Taking them in turn:

Particular Baptist: founded in 1633, and immersed in water as a profession of their faith, Particular, as opposed to General, Baptists believed that Christ died only for an elect. The name 'Particular' comes from a heading in the Doctrines of Grace, the Calvinistic doctrine of 'particular redemption' (Blunt 1874: 65).

Peculiar People: founded by John Banyard, son of a farm labourer, in 1838 in Rochford, Essex. Wesleyan Methodist, the name comes from Deuteronomy 14:2 ('For thou art an holy people unto the Lord thy God, and the Lord hath chosen thee to be a peculiar people unto himself') and 1 Peter 2:9 ('But ye are a chosen

---

[26] Gardner (2014: 225–6): 'An index of British Nonconformity in Betjeman's writings would include General Baptists, Strict and Particular Baptists, Seventh Day Baptists, Wesleyan Methodists, Primitive Methodists, Bible Christians, Plymouth Brethren, Moravians, Lutherans, Independents and Congregationalists, Presbyterians and Unitarians, Quakers, Christian Scientists, Swedenborgians, Sandemanians and Glasites, the Peculiar People, Countess of Huntingdonites, Fifth Monarchists, Covenanters, Millenarians, Muggletonians, Agapemonites, Irvingites, Bryanites, and nondenominationals.'

generation, a royal priesthood, an holy nation, a peculiar people'). *Peculiar* here means 'distinct', 'unlike others'. Blunt (who lived up to his name) says: 'Peculiar People. A quite recent sect of very ignorant people, found chiefly in Kent, whose principles are very similar to those of the American Tunkers. The characteristic which has been most prominently brought forward is their refusal to adopt any material means for recovery from sickness; their dependence being placed entirely on prayer.' (Blunt 1874: 416).

Sandemanian: the name in England for those who in Scotland were known as Glasites. Robert Sandeman (1718–71), son-in-law to John Glas, opposed Calvinistic views by professing that faith is a simple assent to divine testimony concerning Christ (i.e. that the Kingdom of Christ is not of this world, and men's feelings, acts of faith, etc., are irrelevant).

> The sect never attracted any large number of followers; but it still exists as an insignificant body, possessing at the census of 1851 six places of worship in England (of which one is in London), with an aggregate attendance of about 750 worshippers, and the same number in Scotland, with an aggregate attendance of about 1000. . . . They observe various primitive practices with great strictness: *e.g.* weekly administration of the Lord's Supper, with a weekly offertory; love-feasts, *i.e.* the dining together between morning and afternoon services; the kiss of charity at the admission of a new member, and at other times; washing each other's feet as an occasional work of mercy; abstinence from things strangled and from blood; . . . Perfect unanimity is secured in all proceedings by the simple expedient of expelling any one who obstinately differs in opinion from the majority.
> (Blunt 1874: 517)

> (T)hey are strongly disposed to unchurch all the Christian world but themselves
> (Wilson 1810: 267).

Independent Calvinistic: Founded by reformer John Calvin (Cauvin, Chauvin) (1509–64) from Picardy, who opposed the Catholic church and developed his own theology, based on Holy Scripture, notably that God will save an elect but condemn the non-elect to damnation. 'A full statement of these dreadful opinions may be found in the Confession of Faith set forth by the Westminster Assembly of Divines (A.D. 1643), which is still the authoritative Confession of the Kirk of Scotland, and is recognised as more or less authoritative by all Calvinistic sects.' (Blunt 1874: 97).

Congregational: 'A sect so called from its fundamental principle that every particular congregation of Christians is an independent body . . . their object in holding assemblies apart from the Church was to escape from the liturgical and doctrinal system of the latter, and to have such preaching and praying as suited their tastes.' (Blunt 1874: 222).

Primitive Methodist: Anti-Calvinist, pro-Wesleyan; some proponents of camp meetings (which were considered highly improper), who had been expelled from the main body of the Methodists, set up the Primitive Methodist sect in 1810. Primitive Methodists were popular, with 150,169 members in 1870 and a further 12,000 elsewhere worshipping in 6,397 chapels (Blunt 1874: 325).

United Methodist: Begun in 1857, with 62,898 adherents and 1,460 chapels in 1870, the 'United' part refers to the coming together of two separate disputes which had caused secession from the main body. The first sect to secede was the Wesleyan Methodist Association, and the second was the Wesleyan Methodist Reformers. The disputes were over the establishment of the Wesleyan Theological Institution (Dr Warren, the prime mover, was expelled), and criticisms of the Methodist Conference President (three members were expelled) (Blunt 1874: 326).

New Jerusalem: This is the Swedenborgians, not actually directly initiated by Emmanuel Swedborg (1689–1772) himself but by a Methodist Clerkenwell printer named Robert Hindmarsh about ten years after Swedenborg's death, who gathered fellow enthusiasts together at St Paul's Coffee House, St Paul's Churchyard, to study Swedenborg's works. The first two ministers he appointed had seceded from Wesley's Society. 'In the year 1818 the Eleventh General Conference of the sect settled some doubts which had been raised as to the competency of Robert Hindmarsh to ordain others, seeing he had not himself been ordained, by determining unanimously "that Mr. Robert Hindmarsh was virtually ordained by the Divine Auspices of Heaven," a decision more convenient than logical.' In 1871 there were 58 societies, seven of which were in London with 752 members, and the rest mostly in Yorkshire and Lancashire, with 4,098 adult members (Blunt 1874: 581).

Presbyterian Church of England: Founded by Calvin, who established the general system at Geneva in 1541. The ministry consists of one order, the Presbyters or Elders, gathered in Synods, as opposed to individual persons in the Episcopal system, or individual congregations in the Independent system. Descended ideologically from the Lollards and the Puritans, the first separation from the Church of England took place at Wandsworth in 1572. However, in 1719, most Presbyterians became Unitarians. The 1800s saw a small resurgence of interest, and in 1844 the title 'The Presbyterian Church of England' became official, with seven Presbyteries and about seventy congregations (Blunt 1874: 443).

Bryanite: Bryanite Methodists or Bible Christians were led by a preacher named O'Bryan in Cornwall, who separated from the main body of the Methodists in 1815, and then returned to it in 1829. 'There are no substantial differences whatever between their doctrines and customs and those of the sect from which they seceded, except that they permit women to preach' and 'there is a chapel to every 33 members of the sect' – there were 18,466 members in 1870, plus about 7,000 further Bryanites in Canada and Australia, and 544 chapels, mostly in Cornwall and Devonshire (Blunt 1874: 326). Bryanites came to an end altogether in 1907, when they reunited with other Methodists. They believed that all liturgy should be taken directly from the Bible, but:

Ember days: specific days of fasting and prayer in the Anglican liturgy codified at the Council of Placentia in 1095, which are likely to have predated Christianity in Britain; that is, ember days are not specified in the Bible. Ember-Day Bryanites would therefore be contradictory. This is Sir John Betjeman's theologically-informed joke.

All these sects commemorate quarrels, firstly with the Church of England or Scotland, and subsequently with each other.[27] Sir John Betjeman's *Lord Mount Prospect* was written over 50 years after the publication of Blunt's *Dictionary of Sects and Heresies* in 1874, and as Sir John was neither sectarian (at least, not for long) nor heretic, his enjoyment of these quarrels would have been fulsome and without qualm.[28] His description of the Ember Day Bryanites' chapel at the fictitious location of 'Hungerford Green, Barnsbury, N.1.' is a conflation of the Sandemanians' meeting-house in Barnsbury Grove and the Swedenborgians' New Jerusalem Church at Argyll Square.[29] From 1862 the London Sandemanians met in a hall in Barnsbury Grove, London, N1 (it is now truncated by a housing estate), but because they did not proselytise, they did not outlast the century. James Ewing Ritchie, in *The Religious Life of London* of 1870, says:

> it is a neat, simple structure, of white brick, with no architectural pretensions of any kind. It only differs from other places of worship in having no board up announcing to what denomination it belongs, nor the name of the preacher, nor the hours of assembly, nor where applications for sittings are to be made, nor to whom subscriptions are to be paid. Indeed, the only reference at all to an outside world seems to consist in the putting up a caution intimating that the building is under the guardianship of the police, and persons evilly disposed had better mind what they are about.[30]

So I had learnt that conventicle had played a part in the spread of the house name Sunnyside, 'conventicle' meaning not only religious sectarianism but also secrecy, sedition and unlawfulness. Network analysis, used for things like pinpointing terrorists from email traffic, scores individuals on such criteria as *centrality* (being in

---

[27] Not limited to Nonconformism. Novelist Barbara Pym sorted the circumstances of those who had left the Anglican congregation of St Laurence's, Queen's Park, into 'Rome', 'death', and 'umbrage'. 'Umbrage of course removed the greatest number' (Holt 1990: 152).

[28] '(H)e spent several of his early adult years in the Quaker faith and even flirted briefly with the Countess of Huntingdon's Connexion. Perhaps there was a familial disposition for Protestant Nonconformity and its various branches. Members of his father's family were Congregationalists; his mother dabbled in Christian Science, and his son Paul was briefly converted to Mormonism. At some point in his youth or early adulthood, Betjeman discovered that his teddy bear, a lifelong companion whom he had named Archibald Ormsby-Gore, was a fervent Nonconformist of a stern and censorious conventicle; his lone children's book, *Archie and the Strict Baptists*, is a loving tribute to his bear and to this obscure denomination.' (Gardner 2014: 228).

[29] Sir John Betjeman wrote a poem titled *The Sandemanian Meeting-House in Highbury Quadrant* (*Mount Zion*, 1932, London: The James Press), although the location in Highbury Quadrant is fictitious. Sandemanians did not meet there; Congregationalists did.

[30] Ritchie (1870: 315). 'The morning service . . . begins at eleven, and is never over till half-past one. No wonder the Sandemanians are not a vigorous sect.' 'I should say nothing was ever more uninteresting, nothing ever more calculated to alienate from religion intelligent young people, than the services conducted by the Sandemanians. The elders and deacons, excellent men undoubtedly, are singularly deficient in oratorical ability. I think the worst sermon I ever heard in my life was preached by one of them. . . . There is a relation between the Bible and modern thought of which the good people who preach dull sermons and make dull prayers up in Barnsbury have no idea.' (Ritchie 1870: 316, 319–20).

the thick of things, how influential a person is), *betweenness* (the ways in which an individual interacts with other people), and *degree* (the number of individuals interacting).[31] Nonconformists would have scored highly on betweenness, spending their Sundays in the company of their fellows, and they would have scored highly on degree, because although each sect was small in comparison with the Established Church, each congregation consisted of several families, so that most base units consisted of fifty-odd persons who would have talked to each other, unlike, for example, a work situation where one can coexist with many but converse with few. But they would not have scored highly on centrality, as there was no single influential religious leader who initiated the name *Sunnyside*. Centrality did not figure at all in relation to why Dissenters liked *Sunnyside*, but it did in relation to another powerful motive for naming houses: famous individuals sparking a craze – the latest fad or fashion.

Paper, print and illustration

The first London Sunnysider was papermill owner Roger Crompton, living at Sunnyside in Upper Avenue Road, Regent's Park, London. George Cargill Leighton, the next London *Sunnyside* owner, came from a bookbinding family and was a colour-printer and printer and publisher of the *Illustrated London News*. Samuel Straker, the third London Sunnyside owner, also came from a bookbinding family and owned a lithography, engraving and etching print works. I turned to the *Illustrated London News* and looked for the word 'Sunnyside' in the issues preceding 31 December 1859. I found five uses:

The first Sunnyside was a pseudonymous chess-player:

> Solutions by 'Sigma,' 'G. A. H.,' Leeds; 'M. P.,' 'Ambulator,' 'T. R. C.,' 'Sunnyside,' 'H. P. L.,' 'A. L. M.,' 'S. P. Q. R.,' 'E. G. D.,' 'F. R. S.,' 'A. D. A.,' 'E. P. K.,' 'T. R. S.,' 'J. H. H.,' are correct. Those by 'Bagshot,', 'A. Z.,' 'F. T. V.,' 'F. G.,' 'Woodstockiensis,' are wrong.
>
> (*Illustrated London News*, 8 January 1848)

The second Sunnyside was a racehorse:

> THURSDAY. – A very busy afternoon, particularly on the Two Thousand Guineas Stakes, for which, owing to a liberal outlay on Glendower and Sunnyside, and the prospect of a good field, the two cracks went back to 5 to 2 each. Magnet, Keleshe, and Sunnyside were in great favour for the Chester Cup, and Glendower and Besborough for the Derby; Springy Jack is still peppered in two or three quarters; he will require constant support to keep him in the market.
>
> (*Illustrated London News*, 22 April 1848)

---

[31] As initiated by Freeman (1978).

The third Sunnyside was an invented Scottish house-name in a novel:

> MERKLAND: A Story of Scottish Life. By the Author of "Passages in the Life of Mrs. Margaret Maitland, of Sunnyside." 3 vols.
>
> (*Illustrated London News*, 21 December 1850)

The fourth Sunnyside was a pseudonymous comic-song writer:

> I, TOO, AM SEVENTEEN, MAMMA!, Fifth Edition. Enlarged issue. Price 2s. 6d. Words and Music by NECTARINE SUNNYSIDE, Esq. 'The author of the words, who is also the composer of the music, has approved himself not only an elegant writer of light verses, but likewise a facile and graceful writer of light music. It is the plea of a young girl to be married, as was the Queen's daughter; and, put as it is in pleasant rhyme and cheerful melody, it is well-nigh irresistible' – Observer. CRAMER, BEALE, AND CO., 201, Regent-street.
>
> (*Illustrated London News*, 6 March 1858)

The fifth Sunnyside was the real house name of an American author:

> SUNNYSIDE, ON THE HUDSON. The latter years of Washington Irving's life were spent at his charming retreat, Sunnyside, on the banks of the Hudson, about twenty-five miles from the city of New York.
>
> (*Illustrated London News*, 24 December 1859)

And turning to *The Times*, I found nine more Sunnysides. The first was *Sunnyside*, Crawshawbooth, Lancashire:

> We mentioned a few days ago the turn-out of the apprentices employed by Messrs. Butterworth and Brooks, of Sunnyside, near Haslingden, in consequence of their refusal to work a certain description of blocks called five-overs.
>
> (*The Times*, 18 January 1831)

The second was a ship:

> LIVERPOOL, Sept. 3 – Arrived the Gondolier, from Buenos Ayres; Nightingale, from Paraiba; Euphemia, from Nassau; Dalhousie Castle, from New Orleans; Silas, from Bursley; and Marengo, from New York; Birkby, from Montreal; Adelaide, from St. John's, New Brunswick; Robert Kerr, from St. Andrew's, New Brunswick; Sunnyside, from Archangel
>
> (*The Times*, 6 September 1833)

The third was a house name from Prestonkirk, Lothian, Scotland:

> Mr. Slate, of Sunnyside, in the parish of Prestonkirk, observed the *inexpressibles* of one of his Irish bandsters in rather a bad state, so that he presented him with a cast-off pair of his own.
>
> (*The Times*, 10 November 1843)

The fourth was a house name from Lanarkshire, Scotland:

> MARRIED. At Sunnyside-lodge, Lanarkshire, on the 9th inst., by the Rev. William Menzies, Joseph Stainton, Esq. of Biggarshiells, to Grace, second daughter of Alexander Gillespie, Esq., of Sunnyside.
>
> (*The Times*, 17 January 1845)

The fifth was Sunnyside Silk and Cotton Mill at Salford:

PARTNERSHIPS DISSOLVED. . . . W. McKenna and R. Turner, Sunnyside, Salford, manufacturers

(*The Times*, 12 May 1852)

The sixth was a character in the play *A Capital Match!* by J. M. Morton:

Mrs. Singleton (Mrs. Leigh Murray), a fascinating widow, is bound by one of those legal difficulties, so convenient in farces, not to enter wedlock a second time till her niece Rosamond (Miss R. Bonnett) has accepted a husband. It is therefore the obvious interest of Mr. Sunnyside (Mr. Keeley), who aspires to the widow's hand, to seek a husband for the niece.

(*The Times*, 5 November 1852)

The seventh was in the title of a song:

NEW SONG, 'So Dear art Thou to Me.' Composed by E. L. HIME, Author of 'Look always on the Sunny Side,' 'We yet may Meet again.' Price 2s., sent postage free. This charming song, composed expressly for Mr. Sims Reeves, who is singing it at the principal concerts, where it is universally encored, is one of Mr. Hime's most successful compositions. London, Duff and Hodgson, 65, Oxford-street.

(*The Times*, 28 April 1853)

The eighth was the name of a street:

Bryntirion, a capital detached residence, located amidst lovely scenery, in Sunnyside-road, on the summit of the hill, and near to the Wimbledon Station

(*The Times*, 26 October 1857)

The ninth was the title of a novel:

With Illustration by Absolon, price 1s. cloth. THE ANGEL OVER the RIGHT SHOULDER; or, the Beginning of a New Year. By the Author of 'Sunnyside.' Sampson Low, Son, and Co., 47, Ludgate-hill.

(*The Times*, 14 December 1858)

So by the 1850s, one did not have to be a Nonconformist to come across the name Sunnyside. It had had press exposure in 1830–60 as the name of places, mills, houses (fictitious and real), a suburban road, people (fictitious), a racehorse, a ship, a song-writer and a song-title. Horseracing, novels, plays and songs constituted the popular culture of the day. The song 'Look Always On The Sunny Side' was written by lyricist Stuart Farquharson and composer Edward Laurence Hime. Hime was a prolific popular song composer and singer at Evans's Music and Supper Rooms, 43, King Street, Covent Garden, which was the most popular venue of its sort in nineteenth-century London.[32] I have been unable to discover the true name of Nectarine Sunnyside, but his advertised song went into five editions. The three

---

[32] Scott and Howard (1891: 370).

authors who used the name in their novels, Margaret Oliphant Wilson, Elizabeth Wooster Stuart Phelps and Washington Irving, were all highly successful, selling hundreds of thousands of copies of their works both in Britain and America. All three had Nonconformist and Scottish ancestry.

Margaret Oliphant Wilson (1828–97) was born of Scottish Nonconformist parents in Wallyford and spent her early childhood in nearby Lasswade, Midlothian, moving to England aged 10. She wrote more than 120 works, sustaining her children after the death of her husband – all six of whom were to predecease her. *Passages in the Life of Mrs. Margaret Maitland, of Sunnyside* was her first novel in 1849, dealing with the Free Church of Scotland. Her novels were highly successful, her first going into several editions and being noticed by Charles Dickens and Charlotte Brontë. A later one (*A Beleaguered City*, 1879) moved Robert Louis Stephenson to tears, and Tennyson, Gladstone and Darwin praised her work. She conversed with Queen Victoria, Henry James wrote her obituary, and J. M. Barrie unveiled her monument.[33] Very few people read her nowadays, but in a pre-radio, TV, cinema and internet world, her books were widely known.

Elizabeth Wooster Stuart Phelps (1815–52) was descended from a line of American preachers, and both her father (Moses Stuart) and her husband (Austin Phelps) were American Nonconformist Congregationalist theologians and ministers. Her fiction *The Sunny Side; or, a Country Minister's Wife* (1851), sold a hundred thousand copies in its first year, and was followed by a sequel, *The Last Leaf from Sunnyside* (1853). The *New Englander and Yale Review* of 1854 noted that Phelps's books had prompted a small industry of fictionalised accounts of ministers and their wives.[34]

Washington Irving (1783–1859) is the only one of the three still read today; his most famous stories are *Rip Van Winkle* and *The Legend of Sleepy Hollow*. He too had a Scottish minister father. Washington Irving was born in New York, the eleventh child of an English mother from Falmouth, Sarah Sanders (1738–1817), and Scottish merchant-seaman William Irving (1731–1807), who was born in the isolated farmhouse of Quholm, Shapinsay, Orkney. William Irving was a Presbyterian deacon and Sarah Sanders was an Episcopalian. Their son Washington was to become America's most famous author during his lifetime, and he named his house at Tarrytown, New York, *Sunnyside*. To discover why he did this, I return to the start of his career.

In August 1816, the then unknown Washington Irving travelled to meet Sir Walter Scott – 'the mighty minstrel of the north' as he termed him in his memoir – at his residence Abbotsford near Melrose, Roxburghshire. Irving had a letter of

---

[33] Oliphant, Margaret Oliphant Wilson (1828–1897): Elisabeth Jay, https://doi.org/10.1093/ref:odnb/20712.
[34] Beebe (2003: 297), including *The Shady Side; or, Life in a Country Parsonage* (1853, by a Pastor's Wife), *The Prairie Missionary* (1853, Anonymous), and *A South-Side view of Slavery; or, Three Months at the South in 1854* (Nehemiah Adams, 1855).

4.5 Abbotsford House, Melrose, Roxburghshire, Scotland, remodelled home of Sir Walter Scott; © Christian Bickel, https://creativecommons.org/licenses/by-sa/2.0.

introduction to Sir Walter Scott from Thomas Campbell the poet, and had already been in correspondence. The impact of Sir Walter Scott's novels on house-naming practices, and the impact of Abbotsford on domestic architecture, cannot be overstated (see Figure 4.5).

Of his arrival at Abbotsford, Washington Irving wrote:

> While the postillion was on his errand I had time to survey the mansion. It stood some short distance below the road, on the side of a hill sweeping down to the Tweed, and was as yet but a snug gentleman's cottage; with something rural and picturesque in its appearance. The whole front was over run with evergreens, and immediately above the portal was a great pair of elk horns, branching out from beneath the foliage, and giving the cottage the look of a hunting lodge. The huge baronial pile, to which this modest mansion in a manner gave birth, was just emerging into existence: part of the walls, surrounded by scaffolding, already had risen to the height of the cottage, and the court yard in front was encumbered by masses of hewn stone.
>
> (Washington Irving, *Abbotsford*, 1835)

Sir Walter Scott's house set the pattern for the architectural style known subsequently as Scottish Baronial. He embroidered Border castle architecture, which was actually rather more austere (Figure 4.6).

Unconstrained by history, Sir Walter crenellated and crowstepped, turretted and battlemented, machicolated, mullioned and quoined. Where he could corbel he corbelled, where he could bartizan he did so, and Victorians liked the effect. In particular, Victoria liked it – so much so that she had Balmoral knocked down, and a new castle put up (Figure 4.7).[35]

---

[35] Hitchcock 1958 [1977]: 146.

4.6 Newark Castle, Selkirkshire; © Walter Baxter; https:// creativecommons.org/licenses/by-sa/2.0.

4.7 Victoria's Balmoral: crenellations, crowsteps, turrets, battlements, machicolations, mullions, quoins, corbels, and bartizans; © Colin Smith, https://creativecommons.org/licenses/by-sa/2.0.

Washington Irving liked it too. By the time Irving returned home from Europe in 1832, he had become America's most famous author. In 1835 he bought an old farmhouse near Tarrytown in New York state. Known as the Van Tassel cottage, Irving renamed it *Sunnyside* some time before 1842.[36] Surrounded by trees in landscaped grounds and overlooking a lake, Irving's *Sunnyside* was given hanging eaves, dormer windows, a crowstepped gable, Dutch-style weathervanes, and walls covered with stucco scored to look like old stone. It sported a foundation plaque ('1656'), ivy and a 'piazza', then in 1847 Irving added a 'Spanish Tower'.[37] Images of *Sunnyside* began to circulate, and the craze took hold – in 1850 an image of Irving's house decorated the cover of the sheet music of *Sunnyside Waltz*. *Sunnyside* had become top of the pops (Figure 4.8).

Sunnyside was reported at the time to reflect Washington Irving's desire for repose, retirement and seclusion, but this was not to be. Around the middle of the century Irving's popularity as a writer was declining but his house was a hit. By 1853

4.8 Currier and Ives's lithograph of Irving's Sunnyside, *c.*1860. https://upload. wikimedia.org/wikipedia/commons/e/e8/Sunnyside_Tarrytown_Currier_and_ Ives_crop.jpeg.

---

[36] United States Department of the Interior National Register of Historic Places Inventory Nomination Form: http://focus.nps.gov/pdfhost/docs/NHLS/Text/66000583.pdf. Irving addressed a letter of 1842 from 'Sunnyside (Tarrytown)': *The New-England Weekly Review* (Hartford, Connecticut), Saturday, February 12, 1842; Issue 7.

[37] A fanciful replica stands by Cinderella Castle in Walt Disney's Magic Kingdom, Florida. (http:// en.wikipedia.org/wiki/Sunnyside_(Tarrytown,_New_York)).

engravings of Sunnyside had become popular and the house so much of a visitor attraction that the following year a neighbouring entrepreneur arranged trips by carriage for sightseers, who would peer in the windows and trample the lawn and strip the ivy off the walls as souvenirs. By 1859, it was claimed that Sunnyside had become 'next to Mount Vernon, the best known and most cherished of all the dwellings in America'.[38]

Washington Irving's *Sunnyside* was known about in Britain. The January 1868 issue of *The Connoisseur* magazine featured 'Washington Irving and Sunnyside', 'a picturesque house on the banks of the Hudson'; and there were articles in *The Times*.[39] Thus, that London should have experienced a vogue for naming houses *Sunnyside* directly after Irving's death can be explained by Irving's model. The cumulative effect of Nonconformist millionaires' grand suburban villas bearing the name, press coverage of Irving's glamorous American *Sunnyside*, plus its inherent semantic optimism, meant that the name *Sunnyside* connoted modernity, spiritual beneficence, and extreme material success.

But it does not explain why Irving chose the name *Sunnyside* in the first place. As I looked over maps of Abbotsford, the answer to this question became apparent. In 1816, Washington Irving had spent several days on his summer visit rambling with Sir Walter Scott and his dogs around the neighbourhood.[40] About a mile away from Abbotsford, along a lane with views out over the landscape, there still lies a traditional stone-built farm which has been named *Sunnyside* since at least 1590 (see Figure 4.9).[41] Here, surely, is Washington Irving's source of inspiration.

* * *

The *Oxford English Dictionary* suggests that Sir Walter Scott invented the word *bartizan*, meaning 'over-hanging battlemented turret projecting from an angle at the top of a tower', apparently in mistake for *bratticing* (a *brattice* was a temporary wooden parapet, erected on the battlements during times of siege, see *OED* bartizan, *n.* and brattice, *n.*). The *Oxford English Dictionary* entry for *bartizan* is

---

[38] Kime (1977: 149–155); Faherty (2007: 102, 108); Oliver Wendell Holmes quoted in Faherty (2007: 100). For pictorial representations of Irving's *Sunnyside* see Eagen Johnson and Steinhoff (1997); Westover (2008: 155–8).

[39] British readers could have learnt about Irving's *Sunnyside* from, e.g.: 'Autumn On The Hudson', *The Times*, 30 April 1860: 12; 'America In The Stereoscope', *The Times*, 3 May 1860: 12; 'Washington Irving', *The Times*, 17 May 1883: 4.

[40] 'On passing the bounds of Abbotsford we came upon a bleak looking farm, with a forlorn crazy old manse, or farmhouse standing in naked desolation . . . One of my pleasantest rambles with Scott about the neighborhood of Abbotsford, was taken in company with Mr William Laidlaw the steward of his estate. . . . In the course of our mornings walk we stopped at a small house belonging to one of the laborers on the estate. . . . During several days that I passed there, Scott was in admirable vein. From early morn until dinner time, he was rambling about, shewing me the neighborhood' (Washington Irving, 1835, *Abbotsford*).

[41] Gazetteer no. 105. Sonnyesyde, Melrose, Roxburghshire, NT 52055 34052.

4.9 Sunnyside Farm, Melrose, Roxburghshire TD6 9BE; Google Maps Streetview.

unusually subjective: 'Apparently first used by Sir Walter Scott, and due to a misconception of a 17th cent. illiterate Scots spelling, *bertisene*, for *bertising*, i.e. *bretising*, bratticing *n.* < *bretasce* (brattice *n.*), < Old French *breteshe*, "battlemented parapet, originally of wood and temporary"'; and under *bratticing, n.*: 'From the Scots spelling *bertisene* . . . Sir Walter Scott appears to have evolved the grandiose *bartizan n.*, vaguely used by him for *bretising* or *bratticing*, and accepted by later writers as a genuine historical term.'

However, there is nothing especially illiterate or Scottish about the spelling *bertisene*. The sequence of letter-graphs <-ene> for –*ing* (pronounced /ɪn, ən/) is not particularly remarkable, and metathesis of /er/ is regular (compare Old English *gærs*, *gers* 'grass'; Old English *cerse* 'cress'). Spellings of words with both <ar> and <er> are not uncommon, as in *Derby/Darby*, *clerk/Clark*. Nevertheless, the *OED* commentary reads '*Bartizan* is thus merely a spurious "modern antique", which had no existence in the times to which it is attributed.' The lexicographer who made this entry had clearly grown exasperated with his frustrating search for *bartizan* antecedents. This lexicographer was the Chief Editor himself, Sir James Murray, as evidenced not only by his handwriting on the original printers' copy, but also by a testy letter he wrote to the journal *Notes and Queries* (29 August 1885: 177), berating readers for responding to his earlier request for *bartizan* examples not with genuine attestations but with references to mere dictionary entries ('I must express my disappointment . . . the counterfeit word . . . Scott has palmed off even upon professed writers of architecture. . . . Can it be found before its appearance in *Marmion*? Yes or No?'). Sir James Murray was another Roxburghshire Scot; of a stern Nonconformist conventicle, a meticulously conscientious scholar and entirely unsympathetic to, as he thought, Sir Walter's over-egged reconstruction in -*zan*. Had Sir Walter called his overhanging pointed conical tower a *bartising*, Sir James might have let it go, but that –*zan* was a step too far. Yet *bartizan* was genuine. Here is a passage from John Stoddart's *Remarks on Local Scenery and Manners in Scotland* of 1801, which Sir Walter is likely to have read:

> About a mile south of Duddingston, is the ruined castle of Craigmillar. . . . This stately pile, at one time the favourite residence, and at another honourable prison of Queen Mary, is now an appendage to a farm-house, whose inhabitants are unwilling to take any trouble, and unable to give any information about the castle. They could not even furnish us with a breakfast, of which, after our walk, we stood in much need; and it was not without difficulty, that we prevailed on an old man to conduct us over the ruins. . . . The Scotch castles, in general, are not large; but many, like the one before us, are not only invested with the obscure grandeur of antiquity, but strikingly varied, and picturesque in their forms. The pointed gabels contrast with the circular towers; the windows are seldom under each other; the upper part of the building is diversified by the battlements, the bartizan (or outer gallery), and the projecting turret; whilst, perhaps, below, as in the present instance, appears the rock on which the castle is founded.
>
> (Stoddart 1801: 1, 86)[42]

Why might Sir James have become so exasperated with his countryman? Sir James Murray (1837–1915) was born in the village of Denholm, Hawick, in the Scottish Borders, of Puritan stock. His father was an Elder and Precentor of the Congregationalist Church, and in later life, when Sir James moved to Oxford to become Chief Editor of the *Oxford English Dictionary*, Sir James joined the Congregationalist Church there, becoming a Deacon. His Nonconformity was such that it came as a considerable blow to him when his eldest son married the daughter of a Church of England minister, and another blow when a second son took up Holy Orders in the Church of England.[43]

In 1870, Sir James took up a position as schoolmaster at Mill Hill School for the sons of Protestant Dissenters in London. He and his family moved into a nearby house in Hammer's Lane, Mill Hill, which he named *Sunnyside*. Sunnyside is the name of the North West side of Denholm's central village green. In 1885 Sir James Murray and his family moved to Oxford in order for him to take up the post of Chief Editor of the *Oxford English Dictionary*. His new address was 78, Banbury Road, Oxford, which he also named *Sunnyside* (and in the twentieth century, Sir James Murray's eldest daughter Hilda, linguist and literary scholar, who became vice-mistress of Girton College, University of Cambridge, retired with her mother and younger sister to *Sunnyside*, Kingsley Green, Haslemere, Surrey). So Sir James was just as nostalgically romantic about his Borders heritage as Sir Walter – and also marking his Nonconformity. The difference between them lay in their attitude to historical accuracy: Sir James, the painstaking Congregationalist scholar; Sir Walter, the fanciful Church of Scotland storyteller.

---

[42] I am grateful to Peter Gilliver of the *Oxford English Dictionary* for checking the original printers' copy and alerting me to Sir James' enquiries in *Notes and Queries*, and for finding earlier *bartizan* tokens in *Eighteenth Century Collections Online*.

[43] Information on Sir James Murray is taken from Murray (1977).

Sir James Murray was not the only Sunnysiding lexicographer. Henry Watson Fowler (1858–1933), son of the Reverend Robert Fowler, author of *A Dictionary of Modern English Usage,* was born in Tonbridge, Kent, became a schoolmaster at Fettes College in Edinburgh, and then moved with his brother to Guernsey, where together they translated classics and edited dictionaries for the Clarendon Press. In 1925 Henry Watson Fowler settled with his wife Jessie at *Sunnyside,* Hinton St George, Somerset. 1925 is, of course, a long time from the 1850s, when news and views of Washington Irving's *Sunnyside* in Tarrytown were being published, and Fowler may not have named his house himself.[44] But just as prosperous lawyers up the Finchley New Road had named their houses after the latest craze (*The Ferns, Eldersley*), so academic lexicographers were similarly susceptible. House-naming had been a solidly middle-class pursuit, but by 1925, that was about to change.

---

[44] Fowler, Henry Watson (1858–1933): R. W. Burchfield, https://doi.org/10.1093/ref:odnb/33225.

5

SUNNYSIDE AND THE NORTH

Sunnyside farm near Sir Walter Scott's Abbotsford in Roxburghshire is so-named in a manuscript dated 1590. I have suggested that it was this particular *Sunnyside* which inspired Washington Irving to name his remodelled house at Tarrytown in New York State.[1] But why was this Roxburghshire steading called *Sunnyside*? In order to try to answer this question I searched for historical evidence of other farms named *Sunnyside* in the Scottish border area. I had to pay attention to both sides of the border, because national boundaries are not necessarily divisive linguistically. The Sunnyside Gazetteer (p. 198) presents the historical northern *Sunnysides* that I found. Their distribution is shown in Figure 5.1.

5.1 Distribution of British steadings historically named *Sunnyside*, plotted from the Sunnyside Gazetteer (uncertain locations not included). Map produced in ArcGis.

---

[1] There are *Sunnysides* in Orkney (see Sunnyside Gazetteer), but I have been unable to establish whether they were so-named in the eighteenth century before Washington Irving's father left Shapinsay.

Once plotted on a map, these historic *Sunnysides* are revealed to form three main groups: the first in the north-east of Scotland bounded inland by the Grampian mountain range; the second in the Central Lowlands south of the Grampians and north of the Southern Uplands; and the third to the south of the Southern Uplands in the eastern lowlands of Scotland and north-eastern part of England, divided by the Cheviots. My next question was then: why were there so many *Sunnysides* clustering in certain parts of Scotland and northern England?

In order to answer this I am now going to focus on 'Sunnyside' not as the name of a building, but as part of a process – 'on the sunny side' – because the sunny part of a landholding was a concept in Scottish land law. The sunny side was demonstrably not as defined in the *Oxford English Dictionary*:

> OED sunny, *adj.* 2. b. 'sunny half, sunny quarter: that side of a piece of land which faces the south (opposed to *shadow half*). Sc(ottish). Ob(solete)'.

'The sunny side' cannot have meant 'that side of a piece of land which faces the south', as the land divisions in the *Records of the Sheriff Court of Aberdeenshire* from the sixteenth and first half of the seventeenth century show (see Table 5.1).[2]

Table 5.1 Sunny portions of land excerpted from the first two printed volumes of the *Records of the Sheriff Court of Aberdeenshire*

1508	The landis of Auchinschogill . . . fvye marks wortht of the sonny sid of the said landis liand narrest the said ferd part
1509	ane part of the landis of the sonny third of Mydmar
1559	Third part sunnylands of Wodderburne in the Barony of Drumblait
1559	the Sunny half landis of Collane witht the myln outseitt
1559	the Sunny Quarter part Lands of Balmalie
1560	Sunny third part lands of Reidhill in Barony of Auchterless
1560	the sunny third part lands of Tulledesk in the Barony of Kelly
1560	the sunny side of her late husband's lands of Cultir
1574	The third part of the sunny half of the shadow town and lands of Cremound in the Barony of Johnstoun
1574	The sone four oxingang of the sone pleuch lands of the Kirktoun of Balheluy
1574	the sone third pleuch of the toun and landis of Wodlands in the Barony of Monycabok
1574	The sone pleuch of Sauchinlone in the Barony of Wranghayme
1574	The sone half of the Mill Millands &c. of Boquhendauchie
1574	The Eister sonne half landis of Nether Formestoune in the Parish of Aboyne
1574–5	Sunny third part of the Mains of Dumbreck in Ellon

[2] Littlejohn, ed. (2 vols, 1904 and 1906) is a digest of court cases decided by the Aberdeenshire Sheriff's Court, and some summaries give the original spellings and some do not. As spelling is not the point at issue here I have simply followed Littlejohn.

Table 5.1 *continued*

1575	Sunny half of Lowesk in the Parish of Rayne
1575	Sunny half Lands of Moreisseit
1575	Shadow half of the Sunny half of Hairmoss in Kingedward
1575	Sunny half of Outseat of Rothynormound in Barony of Bambreicht
1575	Four oxingang of the sunny plough of Milhill in the Barony of Kynmoundy
1575–6	The Sunny half of the Lands of Tulliquhorty
1576	the shadow and sunny four oxingangs of the shadow plough third part lands of Harlaw
1576	The haill sonne third of the toun and landis of Petmonie
1576	the sonne third of the toun and landis of the Mains of Abirdour
1576	Four oxingang of the Sonne pleucht of Kynminity
1584	The sonne tua oxingangs of the schadow half of the toun and lands of Gilcomestoun
1584	The sunny half lands of Westfield, Balgowny
1584	Parts of the sunny plough of Touchis
1584	Sunny half toune of Ardmakorne in the Parish of Rathene and Barony of Phillorth
1595	The sunny half of the Mill and Mill Lands of Bairnis
1595–6	Sunny half lands of Ruthrestoune in the Barony of Bairnis
1595–6	The sone half landis of Setoun
1597	Sunnysyd in Drumneok and Barony of Drum
1602	The sunny half of Mill of Carneculie, Burnend of Carneculie, in Cushnie
1602	Sunny third part of Mains of Petmedden with houses, buildings, &c. in the parish of Ellon
1604	the sunny half of Auchlok
1606	ane sone pleuche . . . the said sone aucht oxingait of Easter Echt
1606	All and Haill the [blank] half of the sone half lands of Logyruiff
1606	the Sone pleuche of Barriewallis (one of two pleuchis of the Lands of the Mayneis of Drumbrek)
1607	sunny half of Condland and shadow third of the same in the Barony of Frendraucht
1607	the sunny half lands of Wester Fowlis in Lochell
1608	The sunny plough of Balfour in the parish of Forbes
1608	the sone thrie pairt lands of Mekill Fynerseis, in the parish of Echt
1608	the sunny half lands of Bruklis
1609	The sunny plough of Ullaw in the Barony of Essilmont
1610	the sunny eight oxengait of Little Drumquhendill
1611	two sunny ploughs of North Colpnay
1611	sone pleuche of the toune and lands of Auchereis in the barony of Addan
1612	Sunny half of town and lands of Craigtoun of Lumphannand, &c., in the barony of Lumphannand

1612	Sunny half of Fichlie and Sonnaboth
1612	The sunny half of the town and lands of Scattertie in Kinnedwart
1612	the sunny plough of the shadow half of Aucheireis in Raithen
1613	The sunny half of the town and lands of Invernocht, in the Barony of Phillorth
1613	toune and landis of the Sone pleuche of the toune and landis of Fechill
1613	the sone or eist half of all and haill the toune and landis of New Rain half landis of Barrelldyikis
1616	Sunny half lands of Ruddrestoune, with fishings, in the parish of Saint Machar
1616	The sunny third part of Knokleyth, in the Barony of Auchterles-Dempster
1617	the sunny half of Ferrihill
1617	sone pleuche of Nathair Altrie
1617	the sunny half of Ailhous of Dumbrek, in the parish of Udny
1617	sone pleuche of the Mains of Ardmacher in the parish of Deer
1618	The sunny third part of Meikill Finnersie, Littill Finnersie and Monecht
1619	Two oxgait of the two sunny ploughs of Percock. One oxgait of the sunny plough of the shadow half thereof. Also one-seventh part of three oxgait of all three ploughs thereof
1620	Necnon in totis et integris quatuor solaribus lie dealls cum dimidietate alterius lie daill solaris parties terrarum de lie bank una com umbrali parte lie rige de Sandeland vulgo sa maikle of the shadow rige as the said four sone daills and shadow halff daill wyneis upone
1621	eight oxengait of the sunny half of Scottistoune
1621	The lands of Ower Cremongorthe in the parish of Cremonperk. the sunny third part of said lands. . . . the shadow fourth part thereof . . . the sunny fourth of the shadow half thereof
1623	the sunne halff of Porterstoune in the parish of Monkeigie
1624	sunny third part of Memsie
1626	the sunny fourth part of the lands of Chappeltoun of Essilmonth
1628	the two ploughs of the sunny half of the Kirktoun of Fyvie
1633	the sunny and shadow halves of Blairtoun in Belhelvie
1634	the sone half lands of Newbigging in Drumblet
1631	the sunny plough of Carnehill in the parish of Ellone
1637	the sunny third plough of Reidhill
1641	the sunny half lands of Belscamphie
1643	the half of the sunny half of Lentushe in the Parish of Rayne
1643	two ploughs of the sunny half of Balhaggartie . . . in the parish of Logiedurno
1643	the sunny plough of the Maynes of Udny

Source: Littlejohn 1904, 1906.

I have excerpted a hundred or so years' worth of entries from the *Records of the Sheriff Court of Aberdeenshire* in order to demonstrate that splitting land into sunny and shady parts was a common process in this part of Scotland in the sixteenth and seventeenth centuries, and that such halves were also split into ploughs and oxgangs/gaits. I have not detailed equivalent citations of shadow sides because they are apparent from context (e.g. '1584: The sonne tua oxingangs of the schadow half of the toun and lands of Gilcomestoun').

Before considering the realities behind the concepts of sunny and shadow halves, ploughlands and oxgaits, I provide Latin extracts from the *Register of the Great Seal of Scotland* where *solarem dimidietatem* equates to 'sunny half' and *umbralem* to 'shadow', showing similar land division in Forfarshire, Perthshire and Fife as well as Aberdeenshire (see Table 5.2).

Table 5.2 Sunny portions of land taken from *The Register of the Great Seal of Scotland* AD *1620–1633*

1620	solarem dimidietatem terrarum de Greinnes
1621	solarem dimidietatem tertie parties terrarum de Cubakie, in parochial de Leucharis, vic. Fyiff
1621	solarem tertiam partem ville et terrarum de Knokleith . . . villam et terras de Halsiewallis tam solarem tertiam partem quam binam partem earunden, solarem tertiam partem ville et terrarum de Lenschaw et Lenschawbray
1621	villam et terras de Month tam solarem quam umbralem dimidietatem ejusdem
1622	solarem suam tertiam partem ville et terrarum de Logyaltoun . . . in baronia de Auchterles, vic. de Abirdene
1622	terras de Kirktoun de Kinfawnis tam solarem quam umbralem earum dimidietatem . . . vic. de Pearth
1623	solarem dimidietatem terrarum de Boighoill
1623	terras de Balhelweill, tam solarem quam umbralem earundem dimidietatem
1623	necnon dimid. molendini de Kinloch, ejus terrarum &c., cum dimid. de Brewlandis et Smiddilandis de Kinloch, astringendo dict. solarem dimid. ad dict. Molendinum
1627	villam et terras de Aulderaig, tam umbralem quam solarem earum dimidietatem
1628	villas et terras de Pitforkie, solarem et umbralem earum dimidietates
1628	solarem dimidiam partem terrarum de Cornabo, in dominio de Monimusk, vic. de Abirdeine
1628	solarem dimidietatem ville et terrarum de Auldtoun de Creimond cum pendiculis, viz. solarem dimid. de Newmylne de Cremond, terrarum molendinariarum &c., solarem dimid. de Auldmylne, solarem dimidietatem ville et terrarum de West et Eist Hillis de Cremond
1629	solarem dimidietatem terrarum et terrarum dominicalium de Wodwraith, cum manerierum locis et petinentiis, presertim solarem dimid. de Corstoun, tres solares quarterias terrarum de Hoill

1629	solarem suam dimidietatem terrarum et ville de Sillietoun-Eister . . . in parochial et regalitate de Dunfermling, vic. Fyiff
1630	solarem dimidietatem suarum terrarum et ville de Ardownie, in parochia de Monyfuith, vic. de Forfar
1630	solarem dimidietatem terrarum et ville de Fingask
1630	solarem dimid. earundem (lie Waird de Reidie, vic. Fyff)
1630	solarem dimid. terrarum de Balgreigies. . . in dominio de Lochorschyre, - vic. Fyff
1631	necnon dimid. solarem quarte partis ville et terrarum de Newgrange
1632	solarem dimidietatem terrarum arabilium et campestrium lie Chappellandis de Caldhame
1632	solarem dimidietatem terrarum de Pitkany . . . vic. de Fyif; solarem dimid. terrarum de Muirtoune, in dominio de Lochorschyre, vic. Fyif
1633	solarem dimidietatem terrarum de Seatoun
1633	solarem dimidietatem terrarum de Ovir Balbrogie, in dominio de Cowpar, vic. Pearth
1633	terrarum de Eister Gellettis . . . umbralem et solarem dimidietates alterius tertie partis earundem . . . in parochia et regalitate de Dunfermeling, vic. Fyiff

Whether written in Latin (*umbralem/solarem*), or Older Scots, the descriptions are the same. The dictionary definition 'side of a piece of land which faces the south' cannot be right as it is far too general – the whole point of these deeds is to specify who gets which portion. Historical Scottish farms named *Sunnyside* preserve the memory of this division of lands into sunny and shady parts, and these deeds refer to the practice of *solskifte*, 'sun-shift' or sun-division, a Nordic method of dividing lands on open or common-field systems, identified and discussed in Scotland by historical geographer Robert A. Dodgshon.[3] Whether recorded in Older Scots or Latin, the process of identifying strips of land according to a sun/shadow partition was a traditional and legal procedure.[4]

---

[3] Dodgshon (1975, 1987, 1988).

[4] 'If sixteenth- and seventeenth-century charters for the north-east of Scotland are examined, one sometimes finds landholders possessing the sunny or shadow portions of a particular farm or township. Early legal texts, such as Sir Thomas Craig's *Jus Feudale*, make it abundantly clear that shares so designated were meant to be divided after the fashion of a sun-division, with the person holding the sunny share being given the strips which lay in the east or south of each furlong or sequence of allocation and the person holding the shadow share being given those which lay to the west or north' (Dodgshon 1987: 8). There are many extracts from printed records further illustrating sunny and shadow sides in the *Dictionary of the Older Scottish Tongue*, spread under the headwords Son(n)y, Sun(n)y, *adj.*; Son(e, *n.*1 4 b.; Sun, *n.* 26. (Sunnyside 'land having a southern exposure'); S(c)had(d)ow, *n.* 9. a.; S(c)had, *n.* 3.; Cavill, *v.*1. I am not the first to conclude that steadings named *Sunnyside* mark sun/shadow land division: 'The frequent name Sunnyside can signify a former division of land into Sun side and shadow side. Its dialect pronunciation was like Sin Side (Alexander)' (Watson 2013: 144); 'Alexander' refers to Alexander (1952: 385), who says: 'Sunnyside. A frequent name for a farm. It is derived from the former practice of dividing lands into a sunny side and a shadow side'. See also Taylor with Márkus on the place-names of Fife (2012: 508) who discuss *sunny* as a place-name element.

What are the land divisions and why was finding the sunny side necessary? Donnelly (2000) explains what ploughlands and oxgaits were in the context of medieval Auchencrow in Berwickshire.[5] The macro unit of the manor or *demesne* was known as the *town* or *township*, and it included uncultivatable land such as moor, bog and mountainside. The next subdivsion down from the township was the *land*. Lands were made up of cultivatable *ploughlands* or *ploughgaits*, which were in turn subdivided into (in the case of Auchincrow) *husbandlands*, and then into *oxgaits* (also known as *oxgangs* and *bovates*), and then into *acres*.[6] The fields were ploughed into a series of high-backed ridges, as high as six feet, running parallel to each other in strips, which were in practice more or less long, thin, or sinuous, and with considerable variation as to size.[7] Donnelly suggests a typical 220 yard strip with a width of 22 yards, bearing in mind that any one example would probably deviate from this.[8] This system, known as the open field system, was the way in which farming rights were distributed before the privatisation of land – that is, before individuals owned land privately, to be passed on to their heirs or sold as they saw fit. Under the open field system, demesnes of land were bestowed upon chosen favourites – lords of the manor – by kings, not as theirs to own or sell, but as theirs to live on and farm. On receipt of the rights to such unhedged (hence 'open') land, the said lords of the manor owed fealty to the king, and in turn, rather than farm it personally, they bestowed the rights to chosen underlords, also in return for fealty. This fealty was paid in kind, such as goods and labour, as well as money. The underlords (who might, for example, be younger brothers) in turn bestowed the right to farm to commoners, who in turn bestowed it to tenants under them,

---

[5] Cf. Sunnyside Gazetteer no. 64, *Sunnyside*, Auchencrow, Berwickshire, first attested in the 18th cent., NT 85262 61380. Hooper (2002: 242) suggests that *solskifte* was practised in parts of the Highlands too.
[6] *Dictionary of the Older Scottish Tongue*: 'Oxgang, *n.* 15th cent. north midland Middle English. Before the mid-16th cent. the localised quotations for *oxgang* all refer to southern or south central Scotland. "A measure of land equal to one eighth of a ploughgate and reckoned as (more or less) equivalent to 13 acres. The extent of land calculated as the share of one ox in the land ploughed by the standard eight-ox team of a single plough in the course of a year, thus one-eighth of a ploughgate."' Note that the nomenclature here for farming divisions pertains to Auchincrow; there were numerous other terms in use for field divisions elsewhere in Scotland. '(T)he medieval kingdom of the Scots was created out of at least three earlier kingdoms, each of which probably had their own systems of land division and assessment. Accordingly, Scottish historical records list a wide number of different terms in relation to land division and assessment, depending on which part of the country is being researched. These include terms like *merkland, unciate/ounceland, pennyland, husbandland, carucarate, (Scottish) ploughgate, soum, oxgang, arachor* and *davoch*. This maze of different terms continues to baffle modern scholars looking for order in the landscape. In marked contrast, kings of Scots and their governments never seem to have had a problem in dealing with all these different systems in practical terms since, as far as we know, no attempt was ever made to standardize them and introduce a truly common "Scottish" system of land division and assessment before the union of the crowns in 1707.' (Ross 2008: 23).
[7] Whittington (1973: 537).
[8] Donnelly (2000: 757); Sheppard (1973: 173). Sheppard suggests oxgaits elsewhere ranged from about 6 to 30 acres, bearing in mind that an acre also varied in size from locale to locale. Auchincrow's oxgait in 1298 consisted of 13 acres, with 8 oxgaits to the ploughgate.

in a sequence not too dissimilar to subletting chains today. However, unlike today's subletting chains, nobody other than the king actually owned land outright. The lord of the manor ruled the demesne but the lowest-status cultivators had rights of *usufruct*; that is, to use it for such things as drawing water, chopping wood, grazing stock, and growing crops. And for growing crops they needed fields. Fields had to be ploughed, and as heavy clay soil required a team of eight weighty oxen to pull the plough, making for a cumbersome turn-around, long thin slightly S-shaped strips became the norm. Sequences of these strips were allocated to the cultivators, and this is where sun/shadow division comes into play, as a means of identifying who had the right to farm which strips.[9]

Individual cultivators' holdings of these ridged strips were not grouped together but dispersed in fragmented form around the township: some in the sunny two oxgangs of the shadow half of the town, some more in the sunny four oxgangs of the shadow plough third part lands. The strips would periodically be reallocated, although it is not known how often – whether annually, triennially, or just at the beginning of a permanent tenancy. It is likely to have differed from place to place. Farming these high ridges, together with their periodic reallocation, is known as the *runrig* system.[10] The open field system of runrig was a feature of flatter ground, and the map showing the distribution of historical Sunnysides reflects this. The name 'Sunnyside' clusters on low-lying, relatively level farmland. Despite the common-sense assumption that it proclaims the sunny side of a hill, sides of hills were not where Sunnysides were typically situated.

Distinguishing the sunny from the shadow side was a process to which local interested parties bore witness. *Vesying* ('scrutinising, inspecting, surveying') was the Older Scots verb for collectively watching, observing, recording, memorising and thus making legal:

> 2 June 1509. The said day the Shreff ordanit precepts to be direct to summond certane famous personis to be chosin be him with consent and assent of Georg Gordone of Mydmar and Beatrix Hay his modir to be suorne to devyd and part the landis of the sonny and schaddow sidis of Mydmar debatable betuix Thomas Patirsone and Robert Doddis quhilks personis sal be of the four quarters about the said landis of Mydmar.
> (*Records of the Sheriff Court of Aberdeenshire*. Littlejohn, (ed.), 1904)

> 6 May 1555. Vesying of the Sonysyde. The inqueist ordanis the nychtbouris to pas efter the rising of court and vesy the feildis of Sonyside, quhilk is ane part and pertinentis of thair commonte of Glentres, quhilk pertenis to the liberte and fredome of thair burgh of Peblis instantlie, and to vse thair possessioun thairof vsit and wont, and ordanis all nychtbouris that takis part thairintill to be chargit be the officiaris to pas with thair baillies counsale and communite to vesy the samin, vnder the pane of forfalting of thair fredome.
> (*Charters and Documents relating to the Burgh of Peebles*. Chambers 1872)

---

[9] Whyte (2001 [2007]: 206).
[10] Whittington (1973: 537–45).

29 March 1572. that ane of the bailჳeis of the said burgh with four circumspect burgessis of the samyn pas to the landis ... and thair cawill and diwyd the sone syd of tham fra the schaddow syd thairof that the said William ჳoung may knaw and intromet with the ane auchten part thairof of quhilk lyis on the sune syd thairof be resson the said William ჳoung hes gottin assignatioun thairof be the haill burgessis of the said burgh

(*Records of Elgin.* Cramond 1903: I, 130)

Vesying, dividing and parting the sunny side of the land in a township required two constants: firstly, the time of day, and secondly, the time of year. The fixed point in the time of day is most likely to have been sunrise, as this is an unmistakeable event the eye can stand to look at for a second or so, but noon or sunset would have functioned equally well, so long as the same time of day was used on subsequent occasions. The fixed point in the year is likely to have been a solstice or equinox, but any day would do, so long as the same day was chosen the next time the land needed reallocating. Keeping the time of day and the day of the year the same from reallocation to reallocation was crucial, because *solskifte* worked by means of the interested parties and their witnesses moving in the same direction (today we know it as clockwise, but of course that is anachronistic, clockfaces only having been invented in the late fourteenth century). Making a sunwise division is easy to do: stand at your selected spot on your territory on your given day at your given time, start moving in a sunwise (clockwise) direction, and as you proceed, see where your shadow lies. Where it falls is the shadow side, and the other side is the sunny side. It will always be the same. As you walk around the township, or land, or ploughland, or oxgait, or acre in a sunwise (clockwise) direction your shadow will shift, and so long as you and all your witnesses take note of the place, time of day, and time of year, this exercise when repeated will always cast shadows in the same direction, into perpetuity. Only when there is an absolute storm or blizzard will it not be possible to see a shadow, and if so, being a few days late won't make much difference. Many people seem to feel the need at this juncture to point out that *solskifte* can't have worked in Scotland, the sun not being known to bless that benighted country, but wherever you are reading this, if there is daylight, observe your surroundings: perfectly visible shadows are cast on cloudy days. There is no need for a high pressure system overhead and a celestial blue sky to see shadows.

So, now those divisions such as 'the sonne tua oxingangs of the schadow half of the toun and lands of Gilcomestoun' (1584) can be made sense of. First, the town and lands of Gilcomestoun would have been split into sunny and shadow halves, by collectively picking a specific point whilst walking sunwise around the strips at which to observe where the shadows fall. In some parts of Scotland a 'cavill' was cast in order to determine who received which half.[11] Then, the shadow half would be

---

[11] *DOST* cavil n.[1], S(c)had(d)ow, n., adj. A. noun. I. 1. 'The "dark" or west side, or end, of a piece of land, as opposed to the "sunny" or east end or side. *Cavilling be sone and schadow*, drawing lots to decide whether, when dividing land, to begin the division at the east ('sone') or west ('schadow') end of the land."

walked around in the same fashion, and also split into sunny and shadow halves. The two oxgangs which lay in the sunny side would thus be identified. 'The sone four oxingang of the sone pleuch lands of the Kirktoun of Balheluy' (1574) required the villagers to go to the ploughlands subdivision of the Lands of Kirktoun of Balheluy, and to firstly split it into sunny and shadow halves. Then, they would walk round the sunny half, and split it into half again, so that it consisted of four sunny and four shadow oxgangs. 'Ane part of the landis of the sonny third of Mydmar' (1509) required the villagers to split the Lands of Mydmar into sunny and shadow halves. The sunny side was then divided into three, and one of these thirds is specified.

Notice that there is no need to understand the points of the compass, or even to own a compass or know what one was in order to put *solskifte* into practice, but there is a cardinal direction implication: as the sun rises in the east and sets in the west, sunlight at sunrise hits objects from the east, casting a shadow on the west side. However this is only so at equinoxes. Depending on the latitude and the time of year, Scottish sunrises are northeast in summer and southeast in winter, casting shadows correspondingly to the southwest and northwest, so the sunny/ shadow division does not correlate exactly with the cardinal points of east and west. However it does have a tendency that way, because the equinoxes appear to have been a common time for reallocating land. Certainly Lady Day, within a day or two of the March equinox, was the day when tenancy agreements were entered into in more recent times. Movement of sunrise from the northeast quadrant to the southeast quadrant over the course of the year is why even the dictionary definitions that do refer to *solskifte* are not quite right: the *Dictionary of the Older Scottish Tongue* under headword 'S(c)had(d)ow, n., adj. A. noun. I. 1.' defines 'The "dark" or west side, or end, of a piece of land, as opposed to the "sunny" or east end or side' – this equation of east and west with sunny/shadow is static. Dodgshon (1988: 74, 78) emphasises how *solskifte* was a process of relation and movement: the people round the landholding, the landholding in relation to the rest of the township, the sun across the sky as the procession wound around back to the starting point. 'In a world of recurrent scarcities and famine, such practices acted out a concept of how these vagaries of farm output could be countered. Fertility and abundance were to do with observing a proper order of things, both in the laying out of the township and when performing the regular tasks of husbandry'.[12]

Evidence for this invocation of blessing by moving sunwise can be found more recently, as in this eighteenth-century account of a well on the Isle of Skye:

> Several of the common people oblige themselves by a vow to come to this well, and make the ordinary tour about it, called dessil [deiseil in modern Gaelic – Murray] which is performed thus: they move thrice round the well, proceeding sunwise from East to West.
> (Martin (1716: 93), taken from Murray (2014: 91)).

---

[12] Dodgshon (1988: 78).

And here's Edward Dwelly's account from his *Illustrated Gaelic-English Dictionary*, written between 1901 and 1911:

> *Deiseal*: Prosperous course, turning from East to West in the direction taken by the sun. *Deiseal air gach ni*, the sunward course (is the best) for everything. This is descriptive of the ceremony observed by the Druids, of walking round their temples, by the South, in the course of their divinations, keeping the temple always on their right. This course was deemed prosperous, the contrary (*tuathal*) fatal, or at least, unpropitious. From this ancient superstition are derived several customs which are still retained amongst us, as drinking over the left thumb, as Toland expresses it, or according to the course of the sun. Martin says, 'some of the poorer sort of people in the Western Isles retain the custom of performing these circles sunwise about the persons of their benefactors three times, when they bless them and wish good success to all their enterprises. Some are very careful, when they set out to sea, that the boat be first rowed sunwise and if this be neglected, they are afraid their voyage may prove unfortunate'. I had this ceremony paid me when in Islay by a poor woman, after I had given her an alms. I desired her to let alone that compliment, for that I did not care for it; but she insisted to make these three ordinary turns and then prayed that God and MacCarmaig, the patron saint of that island, might bless and prosper me in all my affairs. When a Gael goes to drink out of a consecrated fountain, he approaches it by going round the place from East to West and at funerals, the procession observes the same direction in drawing near the grave. Hence also is derived the old custom of describing sunwise a circle, with a burning brand, about houses, cattle, corn and cornfields, to prevent their being burnt, or in any way injured by evil spirits or by witchcraft. This fiery circle was also made around women, as soon as possible after parturition, and also around newly born babes. (*Dwelly-d*, deiseal, -eala, a)

The Register of the Great Seal of Scotland contains transcriptions of charters from 1306 to 1668.[13] Here's an extract from one in Latin and Older Scots in which we can follow part of a boundary course as it snakes north across the landscape:

> Apud Edinburgh, 11 Feb (1585) Rex confirmavit cartam Jacobi Dempstar portionarii de Petforkie, ed Davidis D. ejus filii et heredis apparentis feoditarii earundem,-[qua, -pro impletione contractus de data apud Brichinen, 12 Sept. 1584, -eum consensus Jonete Fentoun et Eliz. Ramsay sponsarum suarum, vendiderunt Thome Collace portionario de Petforkie, heredibus ejus et assignatis pluribus aut uni quibuscunque,- partem solaris dimidietatis terrarum suarum de Petforkie quam de rege tenuerunt (that is to say sa mekill of our foirsaid sony halff landis haldin be ws as said is, as lyis outwith the propper designit boundis heirefter following, viz. beginnand at the south side of the Lausched-burne quhair it enteris in the burne of Petbaidlie, passing direct north as the burne rinnes quhill it cum to the kingis gait that passis betwixt Petpullokis and the new place of Carraldstoun, and quhill it cum to Erne-burne anent Robert Fyffis quhair Johne Dailkeris sumtyme duelt, and sua passand direct north as the burne rynnis quhill it cum to the north end of Kowhill, and thair-fra passand eist as the stripe rynnis quhilk devidis the Kowhill and Clausnaboige, and fra that north as the west syde of the cairt gait passis to the commoun mure of Brechin fra Cragi, and quhill it cum to the Arne-burne

---

[13] Paul and Thomson (1882–94).

agane, and fra that direct north as the burne discendis fra the mure quhill it enter in the said commoun mure, the lone of Quhitesyde as it is meithit and proppit acceptit), in dominio de Brechin, vic. Forfar;- in excambio pro tanto illius dimid. umbralis dicti Tho. terrarum de Petforkie quantum jacuit infra dictos limites:- Reddend. Regi servitium warde &c.:- cum precepto sasine:- Test. M. Tho. Ramsay commissario Brechinen., Jac. R. ejus filio et herede apparente, Ric. Gairdin burgen, de Montrois, Davide Lindesay ballivo Brichinen., And. Balfour, Jac. Dempstar juniore:- Apud Brichinen et Petforkie, 14 et 15 Mar. 1585]:- Test. ut in aliis cartis &c.

(*Registrum Magni Sigilli Regum Scotorum* 695/2–696/1)

James Dempster and David his son and their wives Jonete Fentoun and Elizabeth Ramsey are conveying to Thomas Collace a piece of their sunny half land which lay outside the 'proper designated bounds'.[14] 'Beginning at the south side of the Lausched-burne where it enters in the burn of Petbaidlie, passing direct north as the burn runs, until it comes to the king's road that passes between Petpullokis and the new place of Carraldstoun, and until it comes to Erne-burne alongside Robert Fyff's where Johne Dailkeris used to dwell, and so passing direct north as the burn runs, until it comes to the north end of Kowhill, and therefrom passing east, as the strip runs which divides the Kowhill and Clausnaboige, and from that, north, as the west side of the cart track passes to the common moor of Brechin from Cragi, and until it comes to the Arne-burn again, and from that, direct north as the burn descends from the moor, until it enters the said common moor, the cattle track of Quhitesyde as it is marked out with boundary markers.' Boundary lines wiggled as they followed meandering streams and detoured round obstacles, zig-zagging and backtracking up hill and down dale. Only the burns, the hill and the moor are natural features here; what entered the collective memory as distinctive landmarks were the modifications made by farming humans: road, steading, house, strip, cart track, cattle track and boundary markers.

As well as movement, Dodgshon stresses the aspect of relation implicit in a sunny/shadow division, that the divided land was once part of a single whole. This parent farm is often signalled by the name *Mains*, from the *demesne* or domain of the local estate. The sunny and the shadow sides are by no means the only name-signalling relationships. Dodgshon (1975: 7–9) counted names premodified in the location index to the *Register of the Great Seal of Scotland* by the cardinal points west (*wast, westir, vestir, occideantalis*) (316), east (*eist, eister, eistir, orientalis*) (287), south (*suther, sowth, australi*) (38), and north (*norther, boreales*) (35); making the point that an east–west relationship in Scottish place-names prevails over a north–south one, presupposing an underlying *solskifte*. Dodgshon (1975: 10–11) relates *nether/over* and *fore/back* to the time taken to process around a landholding and the simultaneous movement of the sun across the sky, recording a relation to the noonday,

---

[14] Detached portions were occasionally necessary because they contained access to resources not provided by a landholder's other holdings, such as fishing or woodland (Ross 2008: 24).

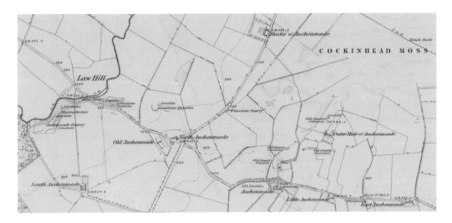

5.2 Ayrshire, Sheet XII (includes: Stewarton; Kilwinning), survey date: 1856, publication date: 1858; showing subdivisions of the agrarian unit at Auchenmade in Ayrshire: *Auchenmade, Old Auchenmade, Little Auchenmade, East Auchenmade* (also known as *Sunnyside of Auchenmade*), *North Auchenmade, South Auchenmade, Hacks of Auchenmade, Outer Muir of Auchenmade.*

overhead sun. He postulates (1988: 79) a correlation of the modifier-set *sunny/easter/ upper/fore* (and the Scottish Gaelic *mor*, meaning 'big') as being in contradistinction to the modifier-set *shadow/wester/nether/back* (and Scottish Gaelic *beg*, meaning 'little'). Scottish place-name scholar Simon Taylor (2014) adds to this list of name-premodifiers expressing a relation *hither/yonder, mid, middle, high/low, meikle/little, wee*. For instance, illustrating subdivision nomenclature, the Ordnance Survey map for Ayrshire, Sheet XII (includes: Stewarton; Kilwinning, survey date: 1856, publication date: 1858) shows subdivisions of the agrarian unit at Auchenmade in Ayrshire: Auchenmade, Old Auchenmade, Little Auchenmade, East Auchenmade (also known as Sunnyside of Auchenmade), North Auchenmade, South Auchenmade, Hacks of Auchenmade, Outer Muir of Auchenmade (Figure 5.2).

Taylor (2014) discusses a further set of relationships in Scottish Gaelic: *s(h)ios* 'down' and *s(h)uas* 'up'. Edward Dwelly observed in *The Illustrated Gaelic-English Dictionary* under *sìos*:

> In W. of Ross *shìos* and *sìos* naturally mean west and westward respectively, that is, down the course of the streams and valleys and *shuas* and *suas*, east and eastward. Yet, *shìos rathad Chataibh*, down the way of Sutherland, is the usual way of speaking of the part of Sutherland on the Moray Firth. These meanings of *sìos* and *suas* are now perpetuated in a curious way in the east of Ross-shire when speaking English; e.g. 'go east to the kitchen,' 'go west to the byre,' &c, expressions that strike anyone as very comical till he understands how they originated and that they have no connection with *ear* [east] and *iar* [west]. This does not apply exclusively to Ross-shire. In Gairloch *shìos* and *shuas* mean practically north and south . . . . In all parts the use of *sìos* and *suas* is regulated by the direction in which the water flows.

As Murray (2014: 203) puts it: 'In some dialects of Gaelic you go up south, *suas gu deas*, and *sìos gu tuath*, down north.' Taylor also reports Victor Gaffney's observation 'how in Banffshire *wester* could mean "upstream" and *easter* "downstream" based on the fact that in this part of Scotland the rivers flow into the eastern seaboard whereas, for example, water courses on the West Coast flow in the opposite direction so that *easter* and *wester* have the opposite meaning there.'[15] Direction of river-flow upstream of the tidal reach, and positioning of shadows, were observational constants in a landscape that shifted as both nature and humans altered it, season by season, year by year. They required no technology, no theoretical knowledge, no calculations, just the ability to see.

Moving to dating, *solskifte* was practised before the first Scottish manuscript evidence, which is late, not much predating 1400 (the *Liber Sancte Marie de Melros* mentions a sunny/shadow division of the West Mains at Hassington in Berwickshire in 1428).[16] Göransson (1961) reports evidence for *solskifte* in central and eastern England in the twelfth and thirteenth centuries, and Britnell reports evidence for *solskifte* in County Durham between 1188 and 1321.[17] The date of manuscript evidence does not mean that *solskifte* originated then – Britnell says 'the origins of subdivision in this part of Durham are mostly earlier than our documentation' – but these charters explicitly refer to *solskifte* at the southernmost limits of the Sunnyside steading area, with manuscript evidence starting around 1200. But if there is evidence for *solskifte* in land charters describing more southerly parts of England, why weren't farms named Sunnyside there with a similar density? The answer lies in the demise of the open field system, which happened in England long before it happened in Scotland. A statute of 1290 known as *Quia Emptores* ended the open field system in England, and its replacement by enclosure of fields led to an entirely new field pattern. The Scottish parliament passed two Acts ending

[15] Gaffney (1960: 35, 318).

[16] Innes, ed. (1837: 519–21), discussed in Dodgshon (1975: 4) and Britnell (2004: 31): 'the said Abbote & the said lorde of Haliburtoun tuke twa kabillis & brocht me thaim & I kest thaim th⸋ tane to th⸋ soun . th⸋ tothir to th⸋ schadow & thus it wes departit' (I have italicised expansions of the abbreviation symbols). Hassington West Mains farm (NT 73739 40420) lies directly south of Hassington (NT 73726 41404), which lies directly south of Hassington East Mains farm (NT 73792 41677), confirming a *solskifte* division rather than one by compass point.

[17] Göransson (1961: 80–104); Britnell (2004: 28–37) reports *solskifte* in a land charter written some time between 1188 and 1212 apportioning land in Hulam and Hutton, and in Fallowfield, Haswell before 1316, and at Great Haswell in 1321, all in County Durham (see Gazetteer no. 2). Goransson expounds a more specific meaning for *solskifte* as it applied in parts of medieval Sweden, Denmark, Estonia and Finland (but not Norway). In these places 'the toft was the mother of the strip', meaning that the strips reflected the width and position of the geometrically laid-out cultivators' housing plots. The strips were reallocated annually and *solskifte* identified who got what to farm each year: 'a simple method of distributing the strips of the village fields so that each holding participated proportionately in the good and bad locations'. However, 'it is not easily inferred from the documentary evidence whether, in the English "sun-division", there was that strong connection with the toft as "the mother of the acre" so characteristic of the Danish and Swedish system' (Goransson 1961: 84).

runrig as late as 1695, but even then, they did not have immediate effect. Indeed, in some parts of Scotland runrig was still the norm into the eighteenth century.[18]

To sum up so far, rather than being a name *per se*, historical Sunnysides are a record of a land division. Sunnyside is just one of a group of steading-name modifiers which express agrarian unit relationships, either in a mother–daughter relationship, or an upstream–downstream one, or with reference to the cardinal points, or altitude, or referencing *solskifte*. Manuscript evidence for *solskifte* dates from 1200 but was practised earlier.

Murray (2014) surveyed Scottish Gaelic place-name components and categorised their frequency according to meaning, classifying them into landform (mountains and hills; hollows, valleys and passes); waterscape; climate, season, sound and time; landcover and ecology; flora and fauna; agriculture and crops; domestic and farm animals; buildings and settlements; church and chapel; cultural artefacts; people and occupations; events and legend and the supernatural. He also included colour, pattern and texture; form, size and position; and the Gaelic anatomy. He found that:

> This is a vocabulary developed to describe a landscape which has been intensely named and differentiated to reflect its human activities and associated land practices. In the highly modified environment of the Highlands, ecology and landcover have the least influence in naming distinctions. . . . The dominance of the cultural toponymic layer counters the romantic perception of the wild Highlander as a kind of noble savage at one with the wild landscape and its grandeur. The realities of subsistence farming in a difficult climate, the gathering of fuel and the continual tending of stock in an unenclosed landscape paints a more pragmatic picture.
>
> (Murray 2014: 210)

Sunnyside, then, is quite in keeping with other Scottish toponyms in recording the effect of humans on the landscape. Taylor and Murray have raised an issue I have not dealt with so far, which is that Scotland was not a monolingual country. Historically, spoken over the territory were p-Celtic languages Pictish and Cumbric; q-Celtic Scottish Gaelic; Older Scots, Old Norse, Anglo-Norman French, and Medieval Latin as a language of written record.[19] There is scant writing

---

[18] Unlike the drastic upheaval which occurred with enclosure south of the border, in Scotland the appearance of the landscape changed more slowly. 'There was nothing in Scotland to match the flood of Parliamentary Enclosure Acts witnessed in England' (Whittington 1973: 538, 566–7). However, there is a possibility that my perception of historic Sunnyside as a northern distribution will be tempered by the forthcoming GB1900 Gazetteer, not yet completed at the time of writing but to which I have been given access (my thanks to Chris Fleet, Map Curator, National Library of Scotland). GB1900 is a Gazetteer of the place names of the second Ordnance Survey revision, 1890–1914, and it shows further Sunnysides in Scotland and all over England (263 hits for 'Sunnyside', 17 hits for 'sunnyside', 2 hits for 'sunny side', and 1 hit for 'Sunny side'). This is to be expected, as the fashion for the name was increasing over this period, but there is no reason in principle why it should not also reveal the location of older Sunnysides.

[19] Cumbric and Pictish may have been on a dialect continuum and were possibly mutually intelligible. P-Celtic and q-Celtic are so named because cognate words pronounced with a /p/ in the one were

surviving from the early period and so Scotland's complex linguistic history has to be deduced from place-name and archaeological evidence.[20] Pictish is thought to have been a p-Celtic language spoken prior to the tenth century north of the Forth and Clyde but with an older, non-related substrate – there is too little data to know for certain. Cumbric, another p-Celtic language more closely related to Pictish and Welsh than Gaelic, was spoken prior to the twelfth century from Strathclyde to the North Riding of Yorkshire. Gaelic, a q-Celtic language, was introduced from Ireland into neighbouring parts of Scotland in the fourth century, expanding out from there to most of the country, but becoming displaced by Anglo-Norman French and Older Scots, the northern variety of English as spoken in Scotland. From the ninth century, Old Norse was spoken in the Northern and Western Islands and the far North.[21] Over time, English so came to dominate that as Gaelic speakers abandoned their language they largely replaced it with Standard English rather than Scots. However, all this is a crude depiction. It elides the fact that at different places at different points in time people were multilingual in two or more of these languages, and could translate from one to the other. There is an implication in this multilingualism for Sunnyside.

The great Scottish place-name scholar W. F. H. Nicolaisen hypothesised that the 'of' found in such Scottish placenames as *Burn of Bogendolich, Water of Leith, Mains of Auchindachy, Bridge of Oich, Boat of Kemnay*, is a translation of an underlying Scottish Gaelic genitive construction, such as *Allt na Muic* '[the] burn of the pig' (Nicolaisen 1976: 56–67). This is relevant, because the Gazetteer shows that there are Scottish steadings named, for example, 'Sunnyside of Badentoy', 'Sunnyside of Gight', 'Sunnyside of Auchmunziell'. Nicolaisen investigated the distribution of placenames *Burn of . . ., Water of . . ., Mains of . . ., Bridge of . . .*, which he collectively referred to as the 'Burn of X' type. Roy's Military Map of 1747–55 shows that plenty 'Burn of X' names were in existence by the mid-eighteenth century, although they were not evenly distributed throughout Scotland: *Burn of Crombie, Water of Deskery, Mains of Tullyfour, Bridge of Dee, Boat of Inchbure*, and others too: *Mill of Blackymuir, Kirk of Pert, House of Fetterkarne, Cotts of Newton, River of North Esk, Castle of Aboyn, Firrs of Drumgask, Muir of Tulloch, Style of Tulloch, Wood of Claritt, Town of Davon, Manse of Cluny, Pow of Erroll, Pass of Leny, Haw of Edinglassea, Lews of Fyvie, Craig of Garnistone, Moss of Boyndie, Birks of Benechie, Braes of Crigie, Hall of Bead, Arns of Cally, Hill of Cally, Meikle Sheloch of Cally, Leg of*

---

pronounced with a /k/ in the other, such as p-Celtic *map* 'son', q-Celtic *mac* 'son'. The two are thought to have become differentiated towards the end of the first millennium BC (James nd: 8).

[20] The synopsis given here is based on Caroline Macafee and A. J. Aitken (2002: xxix–clvii): and is a simplification; in particular ignoring multilingual situations between Gaelic and Danish and Norwegian settlers; ignoring the two inputs to Scots (the Old English of south-eastern and southern Scotland, and the Scandinavianised Anglo-Danish of settlers from England who came with the Norman lords), and ignoring Flemish immigrants into the Scottish Lowlands.

[21] For Scandinavian settlement see Crawford (1987, 1995).

Coplandie, Backside of Ady, Bents of Bandirran, Hole of Scoon, Bogs of North. Contrast *Lochbroom Burn, Markie Water, Niddrie Mains, Queensferry, Gimmenbiecleuch Bridge,* where the word-order is English, with a specific naming element preceding the generic one.

Nicolaisen hypothesised that the earliest of these place-names came into being in a period of bilingualism between Scottish Gaelic and English. He shows that 'Water of X' and 'Burn of X' cluster in the north-east, and that 'Mains of X' names are also largely to be found in the north-east, with a smaller group in the south-west.[22] Figure 5.3 shows a map of the 24 'Sunnyside of X' names that I have located.

This map of 'Sunnyside of X' matches Nicolaisen's observation that the 'Burn of X' phenomenon is largely found in the north-east of Scotland, with a lesser distribution in the south-west. As I was searching for 'Sunnysides of X', I repeatedly noticed another 'Burn of X' construction: 'Greens of X' (see Figure 5.4)

I started to pay attention. Just as Sunnyside in Scotland usually denotes a small steading but occasionally a hillside or piece of moorland, Greens of X

5.3 Distribution of 24 occurrences of 'Sunnyside of X'. Map produced in ArcGis.

---

[22] Nicolaisen (1976: 62) says that the 'Mains of X' construction probably developed around the middle of the fifteenth century as this is when the term *mains* is first on record as a clipping of *desmesne*, but actually there are attestations of the clipped form from manuscripts written around 1200: *MED* maine (n.), first attested in compounded form in 1200 (*mainesfeud*).

5.4 Sunnyside and Greens of Cook. Aberdeenshire 006.13 (includes: King Edward), revised: 1901, published: 1902; http://maps.nls.uk/view/82860549.

usually denotes a small steading but occasionally a swath of hill or moor. Just as Sunnyside seems to self-evidently mean 'side in the sun', Greens of X would seem to be self-evidently referring to a bright green patch of grass, standing out against surrounding dark heather, gorse or bracken. However, there is another possibility. The Scottish Gaelic word *grian* /griən/ means 'sun, sunlight'. Edward Dwelly's *Illustrated Gaelic-English Dictionary* (Dwelly 1901–11/Dwelly-d) translates 'sunny side' as *taobh deisearach* (literally, 'countryside southerly' or 'countryside with a southern exposure); *deisear-gréine* is 'southern exposure', literally, 'southwards of sun'. Under the headword *grianan*, 14 meanings are given, as the word became used metaphorically:

> grianan, -ain, -an, *sm* Sunny spot. 2 Summer-house. 3 Peak of a mountain. 4 Palace, any royal seat. 5 Green. 6 Place where peats are dried. 7** Court. 8 Hall, tent. 9 Round turret. 10 Sunny eminence. 11 Exposure. 12‡‡ Arched walk on a hill commanding an extensive prospect. 13 Any place suited for exposing to the heat of the sun. 14(AH) Felicity, delight.

Note meaning no. 5, 'green', as well as meaning no. 1, 'sunny spot'. However, although *grian*, genitive *gréine* 'sun' appears in place-name elements as 'green', there was also an Old Norse word, *grein*, meaning 'a river-fork or bifurcation of valleys or ravines'.[23] Thus, Scottish farm names in *green* may contain English 'green', Scottish

---

[23] Sedgefield (1915: 149), although as most Scottish 'Green(s of X' and 'Green(s' do not appear to be sited at bifurcations I rule this out. 'Drying green' is also a possibility, but laundry needs airing at all latitudes whereas Scottish Green(s have a specific regional distribution (I thank Richard A.V. Cox for discussion of potential meanings). I have not surveyed England, but Watts has, and provides a map

Gaelic *grian* 'sun', Old Norse *grein* 'fork, bifurcation' – not to mention the name of
a farmer named Green, all potentially spelt <green> on maps. Dwelly's informants
would have been supplying him with information on Scottish Gaelic in the first
decade of the twentieth century and presumably they knew what, in context, they
meant by no. 5, 'green' as a translation for *grianan*, but whatever their understanding was, it is not self-evident now. Therefore, in surveying Scottish place-names
in *green*, I included only 'Green(s of X' and steadings named simplex Green(s, on
analogy with 'Sunnyside of X' and Sunnyside (the form *Greens* has what Watson
(2013) calls 'the Scottish –*s*', frequently appended to Gaelic place-names). I ignored
all other complex and compound forms.[24] I found 47 'Greens of X' (Figure 5.5, and
14 Green(s (Figure 5.6). Figure 5.7 shows the combined distribution.

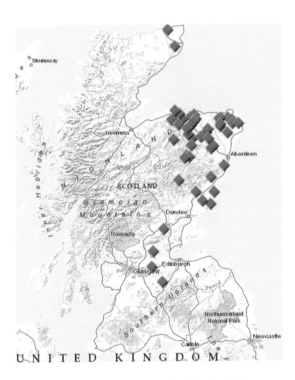

5.5 Distribution of 47
examples of 'Greens of X'.
Map produced in ArcGis.

(2004 [2010]: lix), which shows that *green* is extremely sparse in the north of England. *Green* as an
English place-name, or part of a place-name, predominates in two distinct areas: the counties bordering
Wales, and also in East Anglia and the southeastern counties.
[24] Excluding e.g. *Greenside, Greenhill, Green Field, Greenhaw, Green Know, Green Bank, Green Moss,
Green Law, Green Cott, Greenrig, Green Knap*, and excluding complex forms such as *Greenoch, Greenid*.
I also ignored names with -*green* as a second element. Names have been culled from ScotlandsPlaces,
the Scottish Place Name Society's list of resources, maps, and Google. What Watson calls the 'Scottish'
–*s* phenomenon of adding -*s* to place-names (as in 'we're going round to Stephen's', resulting in place-
name *Stephens*) is actually found all over England too, see Padel (2014: 19–20), and Reaney and Wilson
(1991 [1995]: xxxiii–xxxvi) for a similar phenomenon in surnames.

5.6 Distribution of 14 occurrences of Green(s. Map produced in ArcGis.

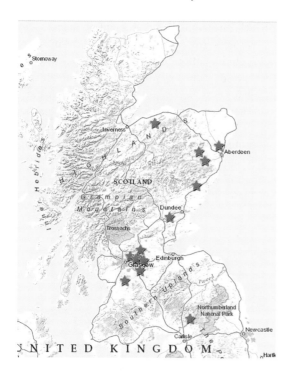

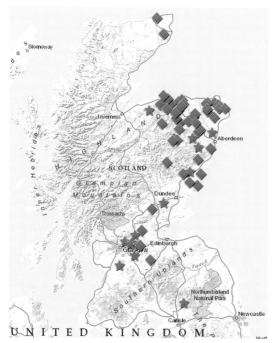

5.7 Combined distribution of Scottish steadings named Green(s (14 stars) and 'Greens of X' (47 diamonds). Map produced in ArcGis.

5.8 Combined distribution
of Sunnyside (orange stars),
'Sunnyside of X' (orange
diamonds), Green(s (green
stars), and 'Greens of X' (green
diamonds). Map produced in
ArcGis.

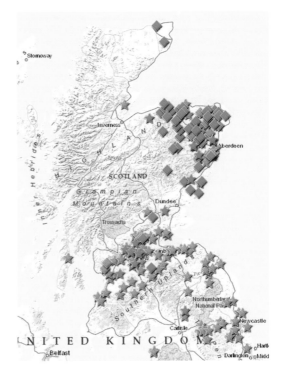

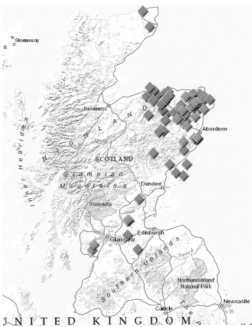

5.9 Combined distribution
of 'Sunnyside of X' (orange
diamonds) and 'Green(s of X'
(green diamonds). Map produced
in ArcGis.

If 'Greens of X' and Green(s are indeed related to 'Sunnyside of X' and Sunnyside, being the Scottish Gaelic expression thereof, then the distribution ought to be similar. Figure 5.8 combines the distribution of Sunnyside, 'Sunnyside of X', Green(s and 'Greens of X'. 'Greens of X' and Green(s are distributed over a sub-set of the Sunnyside area, making it indeed plausible that there is a relationship between the two. Figure 5.9 confirms that the 'X of Y' construction in 'Sunnyside of X' and 'Green(s of X' matches Nicolaisen's observation of the 'Burn of X' distribution.

Further support for the identification of 'Green(s' with 'Sunnyside' comes from Roy's Military Survey of Scotland map of 1747–55. No. 68 in the Sunnyside Gazetteer is Sunnyside, Airth, Clackmannanshire, identified by John Reid in his *Material for a place-name survey of East Stirlingshire* as located at NS 88800 88439. This location is labelled on Roy's map not 'Sunnyside' but 'Greenside'.

Nicolaisen examined the 'Burn of X' construction, finding 261 Scottish streams named 'Burn of X', of which 97, the largest group, contained names of human settlement, and only 1.15 per cent referred to characteristics of the water or water-course. He deduced that the 'Burn of X' construction must therefore be a relatively recent innovation, post-dating the names of the settlements contained in the 'X' element (he suggested post thirteenth century). The distribution is mainly in the north-east, but also in Orkney and Shetland. 'The north-eastern names of the *Burn of X* class did not come into being by spontaneous genesis, but as the result of a bilingual contact situation between outgoing Gaelic and incoming Lowland Scots' (Nicolaisen 1976: 56–64, 59). Nicolaisen found that 'Water of X' also clusters in the north-east, and is absent everywhere else except for the south-west. 'Bridge of X' also occurs mainly in the north-east, but penetrates further into Central Scotland, along with the watercourses they span. 'Mains of X' only occurs in the north-east and to a lesser extent in the south-west. Nicolaisen placed 'Mains of X' later in the sequence, after the hydronyms had been coined, because the concept of the mains, that is, a home farm on a landed estate, belonged to the post-Gaelic way of life. He suggested that the reason the 'Burn of X' names are absent elsewhere in Scotland is due to their comparatively recent formation. That is, 'Burn of X' is missing from areas where streams had already been named 'X Burn' by speakers of English arriv-ing early in the eastern lowlands of Scotland, and the construction is also missing from western and central Scottish Gaelic-speaking areas, which shifted to English too late to join the 'Burn of X' pattern.

One problem here is that the substrate Gaelic pattern began in the west of Scotland, in the land closest to Ireland whence it came, whereas the 'Burn of X' type overwhelmingly preponderates in the north-east, both in Nicolaisen's surveys and my own plotting of 'Sunnyside of X' and 'Green(s of X' in Figure 5.8. Nicolaisen overcame this objection by pointing out that as Gaelic was still alive in the western regions until recently, it was replaced there by Standard English, not Scots. However Standard English allows both 'X Burn' ('Liza's book') and 'Burn of X' ('(the) book of Liza'), so the word order could have been preserved, and Scots outwith the north-east and south-west groupings also has 'X Burn', so there is no need to posit Standard English rather than Scots.

Berit Sandnes (1997) has another explanation. She suggests that the underlying language provoking translation is not Gaelic but French. She adduces 'Isle of X' (Man, Wight, etc.) where *isle* is French, and points out the close ties between the Scottish ruling class and France which persisted until the eighteenth century. Her focus of discussion is Orkney, which was never Gaelic-speaking but which seems to have had an underlying Pictish substrate overlain by Viking settlers speaking Old Norse, before incomers from Fife and Kinross imported Scots to the islands.[25] Orkney has a good many 'Burn of X' names, some of which are traceable back to the first Orkney rentals of 1492. As is customary in British land-management documents of the fifteenth century, these rentals used the medieval mixed-language system, which has an Anglo-Norman French grammatical component (as in the article *le* and preposition *de* in 'le bordland de Snartmal'). Sandnes offers this as evidence that the construction underlying 'Burn of X' is French.

The problem here is that the 'le bordland de Snartmall' construction was default in British documents which kept track of finance from the Norman Conquest in 1066 to about 1500 – that is, 500 years' worth of written usage.[26] 'Le bordland de Snartmall' is how names were expressed in manorial documents all over England, but 'Burn of X' place-names are not found there. Further, the ruling French-speaking classes have always been a small percentage of the Scottish population, whereas everything we know about language change indicates that it occurs in the groundswell of the masses, rather than is dictated by a small elite. And French cannot account for the regional distribution: the Scottish nobles did not all gang up together in castles in Aberdeenshire with a subsidiary set of ganglords around Glasgow.

Cox (2007) may have the answer to these objections. He shows that there is 'plentiful evidence which suggests that there was indeed a perfectly adequate Scandinavian model for the development of X *of* Y type names' (Cox 2007: 24), presenting generic-initial place-names with underlying Old Norse etymologies from the Isles of Lewis, St Kilda, the Faroes, the Northern Isles and Caithness. Cox's Old Norse explanation for the X *of* Y type name and therefore the 'Sunnyside of X' and 'Green(s of X' construction chimes well with the Nordic practice of *solskifte*.

[25] 'In 1468/9, Orkney and Shetland were pledged to Scotland for a dowry that was never paid, and thereafter the Northern Isles were dominated by Lowland rulers, administrators and clergy, with Scots as the sociolinguistically "high" language of the islands from the 16th century or earlier' Macafee (2002).
[26] See, for example, Wright (2012, 2013). A further objection raised and dealt with by Nicolaisen (1976: 60) is that 'Burn of X' is simply a cartographer's standardisation. However, 'Burn of X' constructions such as the fifteenth-century Orkney rentals referred to by Sandnes show that it was older.

Summary

The farm name *Sunnyside* is part of the concept of the open-field system with its numerous ridges that were allocated to tenants, as shown in *The Register of the Great Seal of Scotland*. Runrig, the distribution of strips of cultivatable ground around the township, occurred only in relatively flat areas and was absent from upland areas (Butlin 1964). Vesying the sunnyside (or *solskifte* as it is known in Scandinavia) was a means of identifying cultivatable strips, so that everybody knew who farmed what – and in the case of disputes, who argued over what. The steading name 'Sunnyside' came about under the later ownership system when a splinter farm was set up on land that had previously been designated a sunny portion of a larger unit. 'Sunnyside of X' and its Scottish Gaelic translation 'Greens of X' cluster in the north-east, with a smaller distribution in the south-west, and the construction reflects an underlying Old Norse syntax. In North Britain, farms named 'Sunnyside' and 'Green(s' occurred where there were demesnes split up into smaller units, and Aberdeenshire is particularly rich in them because there is much productive farmland in its coastal plains and the lower slopes and bottoms of its river valleys.

6

SUNNYSIDE TIMELINE

Pre-medieval

Sunnyside was a technical North British legal concept to do with land tenure, evidenced in manuscripts since the twelfth century and already fully established by then, presupposing an earlier origin. It has well-known counterparts in medieval Scandinavia. Vesying the sunnyside was the process of local inhabitants collectively moving in a clockwise direction around the agricultural unit in an open field system, taking note of where shadows lay, in order to allocate strips in an agreed and indisputable manner.

Medieval

North British steadings historically known as Sunnyside and Sunnyside of X embody a memory of vesying the sunnyside (with Sunnyside of X expressing an Old Norse word order). When the older, open-field system was abandoned, the modern practice of field-enclosure and individual farm-ownership replaced it. Steadings that were built on land that had formerly been designated 'on the sunny side' took the name Sunnyside, and farms that were built on land that had been formerly designated 'on the shadow side' took the name Shadowside. I have noted far fewer of those, however, since the name Shadowside has not persisted to the same degree.

Late medieval

In formerly Scottish Gaelic-speaking areas, 'Green(s' and 'Greens of X' was the bilingual Scottish Gaelic–Older Scots expression of Sunnyside, being a rendition of the Gaelic word for 'sun'.

Seventeenth to eighteenth century

The steading name Sunnyside largely stayed within North Britain until the religious Nonconformist movements of the 1600s began to spread it around the country in a north to south direction via networks of travelling Quakers. Quakers in particular were instrumental in its early dissemination and took it to America. There is a legacy of this Nonconformist distribution in New World churches named Sunnyside.

Early nineteenth century

In 1816 Sir Walter Scott entertained the young Washington Irving at his Scottish Baronial house named Abbotsford. Irving subsequently remodelled his old farmhouse along similar lines in Tarrytown, New York, and named it *Sunnyside*. *Sunnyside* was the name of a picturesque old stone steading close to Abbotsford that I presume Irving saw on his rambles with Sir Walter and from which I presume he lifted the name. From 1850 onwards, pictures and descriptions of Irving's *Sunnyside* in Tarrytown were published in both the American and British press, and Irving's *Sunnyside* became extremely influential, both in name and style.

Mid to late nineteenth century

Washington Irving died in 1859, and the *Illustrated London News* printed his obituary, complete with an illustration of his *Sunnyside* at Tarrytown. The first four London Sunnysiders named their houses shortly afterwards, being involved one way or another with Nonconformism, the paper, print and publishing industries, Scottishness, and social and philanthropic socialising. They had overlapping religious, work, family and social networks. Their *Sunnysides* were grand, impressive mansion-like houses with plenty of room for family and servants in what were then the rural outer London suburbs. Non-traditional and architecturally fashionable, they embodied what modern, non-noble, socially-aspirant Victorians aspired to. Other outer-suburb houses were named after transferred place-names; nostalgia for a rural way of life; commemorations of various sorts including named individuals; what I have called the pick & mix uncoupling and recoupling of place-name elements to create traditional-sounding but hitherto unattested names; names linked to the nobility; crazes, fads and fashions; and jocularity (*Wee Neste* 1889, *Kosikot* 1899). The Sunnysiders of the 1870s continued to be non-aristocratic, wealthy, sociable, locally important and influential, living in desirable, large, outer-suburb villas.

Twentieth century

The trickle down the social scale to ever smaller houses occurred in the twentieth century, so that by the sun-worshipping decade of the 1930s, *Sunnyside* sparked a plethora of Sunnyholme, Sunnylea, Sunnywood and the like compounds. Gould (2011) provides figures for this expansion: over 4 million houses were built between 1918 and 1939, constituting one-third of the British housing stock, of which about three-quarters were for sale, and one-quarter council housing. Very few were flats, most were terraced, semi-detached, or detached.[1] Thus about 3 million new houses were potentially ripe for naming in the 1920s and 30s, resulting in the present-day perception that the name *Sunnyside* fits this sort of house.

The cheapest rural housing of the twentieth century could not be numbered because such houses were put up on plots of land before there were streets and services of water, gas, electricity, streetlighting and sewerage to serve them. Here are the names of some such plotland bungalows on the Laindon Rise Estate, Essex, in 1949 (plotlands are socially divisive, being derided as 'rural slums' and 'bungaloid rash' by those who don't live in them):[2]

Tyler Avenue: Adaville, Claremont, Evenley, Fairwinds, Glencroft, Hawley, Heronbrook, Lilian, Mantis, Oakhurst, Roberta, Shirleydene, Sunneyside, Sunneyview, The Token, Treetops, Windemere, Windsor, Wingfield
Albert Drive: Kendrith, Milborne, Norton Lodge, Palawa
Basil Drive: Allwood, Austin, Beechcroft, Cranford, Crowthorne, Eastview, Ellendale, Emberley, Finchampstead, Glenwood, Irene, Kia Ora, Manderley, Maryville, Rose Cottage, Springfield, St Hillier, The Ridges, Verica, Walkern, West View
Cecil Drive: Fairview, Glen Ochil, Jeanette, Willett

There is nothing here to distinguish plotlands housing from other British housing namestock: transferred place-names (Windemere, Palawa, Crowthorne), nostalgically rural (Springfield, West View, Fairview), upwardly mobile (Windsor, Claremont, Norton Lodge), commemorative (Adaville, Lilian, Ellendale), pick & mix (Glencroft, Glenwood), literary (Manderley, Cranford, Verica). When it comes to house-naming, this study has shown that Britons of all social classes have made remarkably similar choices.

* * *

[1] Gould (2011: 54).
[2] Hardy and Ward (1984). Laindon names taken from Bathurst, John, 1999/2000. 'Laindon Memories'. Laindon and District Community Archive. www.laindonhistory.org.uk/page_id__714_path__0p29p21p37p59p24p.aspx.

The story of northern Sunnyside does not end here. As well as the distribution of Gaelic *grian* names across Scotland and Ireland, the 1865 Norwegian census contains 95 farms named *Solem* (*sol* 'sun', *hjeim* 'home'), situated in Buskerud, Telemark, Aust-Agder, Rogaland, Hordaland, Sogn og Fjordane, Møre og Romsdal, Sør-Trøndelag and Nord-Trøndelag.[3] Oluf Rygh's historical Norwegian Farm Names database yields 148 hits for Norwegian farms named *Sol-*; the Swedish *Ortnamnsregistret* returns over 10,650 names beginning with *Sol-* and 28 hits for *Solsidan*; and *Solsida* is also found in Finland.[4] This investigation, starting from one Victorian suburban house name in Ealing Green, leads to a sunray of house names fanning out across northern latitudes.

Such an outcome fits well with Victorian housenamers' sensitivities – the factory owners, the accountants, the wine and tobacco merchants, the civil servants, the shopkeepers, all the lawyers seeking respite from workaday concerns up the Finchley Road – who proclaimed with their transferred place-names, their commemorations, their nostalgia for the countryside, and their pick & mix faux-traditional innovations, a permanency that has resonated for speakers across different languages and from all walks of life across time and space: this house is home.

[3] Norway Heritage: http://www.norwayheritage.com/norwegian-names.htm.
[4] Norwegian farm names: http://www.dokpro.uio.no/rygh_ng/rygh_form.html; Sweden: http://www.sprakochfolkminnen.se/sprak/namn/ortnamn/ortnamnsregistret/sok-i-registret.html; Finland: https://asiointi.maanmittauslaitos.fi/karttapaikka/.

APPENDIX 1

PRE-1400 HOUSE NAMES FROM THE CITY OF LONDON, WESTMINSTER, AND THE IMMEDIATE ENVIRONS

This is a list of pre-1400 London house names assembled in date order that I have transcribed from manuscript, or from microfilm of manuscript (excluding religious houses, abbeys, churches, monasteries, spitals, convents, hospices, almshouses, leperhouses and the like). I have only included names occurring in manuscripts which I have inspected (with the exception of a few available in scholarly transcriptions, in which case the edition is indicated). Entries are given in the order of house name, followed by date and reference of source manuscript, and one or two brief contexts. Usually only one or two sources are given although many names appear in multiple sources and with multiple spelling variations. Abbreviations are unresolved; I have not made editorial guesses but presented the evidence as it is. Empty angled brackets < . . . > signal illegible letter-graphs and square brackets [. . .] indicate that a name is attested as a personal surname prior to attestation as a house name. *Le/la/lez* precede building names from the Norman Conquest to long after 1400 as records were written in a mixture of Anglo-Norman French and Medieval Latin, and continued to be so until the end of the fifteenth century (Wright 2010a). Even when records switched to English, *le/la/lez* continued in the context of house names for long after.

1. Ceolmundingchaga 857 (11th cent.) ESawyer S 208 BL Cotton MS Tiberius A XIII, f. 19r-v '*Ego autē <...> tentissimo deo concedente rex me<...> trado alhuno episcopo meo premedio anime meæ aliquā paruā portionē libertatis cum consensu consiliatoꝗ meoꝗ gaziferi agelluli in uico lundonioe . hoc . ē . ubi nominat^σ ceolmundingchaga qui . ē . non longe from þestgetum positus*'. Viewable at www.bl.uk/manuscripts/Viewer.aspx?ref=cotton_ms_tiberius_a_xiii_fs001r

2. Hpætmundes stan 889 (11th cent.) ESawyer S 346 BL Cotton MS Tiberius A XIII, f. 18v '*in lundonia unam curtem que uerbotenus ad ad antiquum petrosū ædificium id . ē . aet hpætmundes stane a ciuibȝ apellat^σ*'. Viewable at www.bl.uk/manuscripts/Viewer.aspx?ref=cotton_ms_tiberius_a_xiii_fs001r

3. Paules byri (10th cent.) ESawyer S 1483 BL Adds MS 14847 f. 16v (modern foliation) '*And ic an þat lond at Tidweldingtoñ Alfwold ouer mine day . þe he formige ilke
ihere þen hird at paules byri for vre aldre saule*'; ESawyer 1494 Cambridge, University
Library, Ff.2.33 f 46 '*And ic an þat lond at Haddam Berthnoðe Alderman 7 mine
sust(er) hire day . and after hire day .' into Paules biri at lundon(e) to biscope hame*'.
For dating see Kelly 2004: 144–5. Transcription from www.lel.ed.ac.uk/ihd/laeme2/
tagged_data/buryFft.html.

4. Wermanecher 1044 (13th cent.) ESawyer S 1002 Ghent, Rijksarchief, Archives
de l'Etat a Gand, Abbaye de Saint-Pierre a Gand, 1st ser., no. 7 ff 11-12 '*Praeterea
addidi loco illi praelibato infra Londoniam, partem terrae de terra illa, uidelicet,
quae Wermanecher Anglice nuncupatur, cum hueruo eidem terrae pertinenti, et cum
omnibus rectitudinibus et consuetudinibus, quae ad illam pertinent*' (taken from
Anglo-Saxons.net).

5. Stæninga haga 1051–56 ESawyer S 1142, WAM XVI '*mid þam lande stæninga
haga ƿið innon lundone*'

6. Aldermanesƀia, Aldremanesberi, Aldresmaneberi *c.*1130 St Paul's Cathedral MS
Liber L CLC/313/B/001/MS25504 fo 47 '*Baldewin⁹ de aldermanesƀia*'; fo 52 '*Socce
Aldremanesberi . . . In aldresmaneberi. Terra wluredi reddit .iij. soł in feuḋ. & .iij. oƀ
socce. In fronte longitudinis .cxxxiij. pedum. latitudinis. xlj. pedum.*'

7. Bassingeshage 1160–81 LMA St Paul's Cathedral CLC/313/L/H/001/MS25121
deed no. 232 '*ego hugo decan⁹ . . . concessim⁹ . . . terram . . . in parrochia de
bassingeshage*'

8. Blanckesapeltunā, la Blauncheapelton 1168–75 BL Cotton MS Galba E ii fo 73v
'*in ciuitate londonaᶍ . . . terra iacet iuxᵃ Blanckesapeltunā*'; 1336–7 TNA C 135/48
m.27 '*vnū tenement vocato la Blauncheapelton . . . in proch sͨi Olaui v̄sus Turͬ Londoñ*'

9. Musterlingebur 1183–4 WAM Book 11 fo 493r '*pro terra et domo de feudo eccle-
sie Westmonasterii scilicet Musterlingebur quas Ricardus prior de Ruislep de uxore
Stephani sanitarii et heredibus eius in London per assensum eorum comperavit*'
(transcript from M). *Mouster* is a placename in Brittany (I am grateful to Richard
Coates for this information) and is the Breton reflex of Latin *monasterium* (Flatrès
1977: 67), so *Musterlingebur* is 'the bury of the person from the little monastery
in Brittany'.

10. Lodebure 1181–1203 LMA St Paul's Cathedral CLC/313/L/H/001/MS25121
deed no. 1265 '*totā t̄ram qᵃ̄m Margareta filia Rog' i de Abenilla tenuit de noƀ iuxta
eccłiam scē Margarete de lodebure*'

11. Prestebure *c.* 1190–1200 WAM Book 11 fo 369v '*ego concessi Roberto filio
Edwardi terram illam que jacet juxta Prestebure in London in parochia Sancti Martini
de Otteswich*' (transcript from M).

12. Achiesburia, Alfrichebur̄, Alkichesbri 12th cent. (15th cent.) BL Harley MS
3656 fo 19v '*Alia eiusɖ de terra in lonɖ que vocaᵃ Achiesburia . . . de terra sua qᵃm
tenebat de me in lonɖ que nōiata est Achiesbiria*'; 1240 LMA CLC/313/L/H/001/
MS25121 St Paul's Cathedral deed no. 608 '*sup quadā terra que uocatur alfrichebur̄
quam Idam magr̄ Rogꝰus ad p̃bendā suam de Portepol p̃tinere dicebaᵗ*'; 1252 LMA
CLC/313/B/001/MS25504 St Paul's Cathedral MS Liber L fo 118 v '*Iī sūt in poɕ .
xxxvj . mesuagꝰexᵗⁱˢ messuagꝰ de Tothale Ruggeníe . & Northbī. & Alkichesbri .*'

13. Diane, Deane 1220–2 LMA St Paul's Cathedral CLC/313/L/H/001/MS25121
deed no. 693 '*p terra que fuit Ric̄ Rufi que scᵈt extendit se ab aula usqꝫ ad murū qui
est inᵗ ip̄m terram et Domū que fuit Diane*'; 1407 CLC/313/L/H/001/MS25121
deed no. 729 '*c̃ta edificia . . . in venella vulgariter vocata knyghtryderstrete in pochia
sc̄i Benedicti iuxᵃ Pouleswharf londoñ inᵗ hospiciū . . . vocatum hospiciū Deane*'; 10
June 1452 CLC/313/L/H/001/MS25121 deed no. 111 '*hospitium eoꝛ vocaᵗ Camera
Diane alŝ Segraue, situaᵗ in paroch̃ Sancti Benedicti versus Povvles warff Londoñ*'

14. la Blakehalle 1222–46 WAM 17083 '*de toto tenemento meo qɖ habeo In Westm̄
qɖ uocatᵒ la Blakehalle qɖ Iacet Inᵗ t̃ram Langoñ Goldale uersꝰ orientem & t̃ram
Ioh̃is de la Blakehalle uersus occidentem*'; 1357–8 HR 85/41 '*totū illud teñ vocatū le
Blakehalle . . . in pochia sc̃i Andree de Cornhulle londoñ*'

15. Grangia c.1233 LMA CLA/007/EM/02/A/041 Bridge House Deed '*quoddam
mesuagio quod uocatur grangia in parochia < > suwerk*'

16. Northbī 1252 LMA CLC/313/B/001/MS25504 St Paul's Cathedral MS Liber L fo
118 v '*Iī sūt in poɕ . xxxvj . mesuagꝰexᵗⁱˢ messuagꝰ de Tothale Ruggeníe . & Northbī .
& Alkichesbri .*'

17. la Bordhawe 1257 LMA St Paul's Cathedral CLC/313/L/H/001/MS25121 deed
no. 1233 '*tenemento meo cᵘ ptiñ qɖ teneo . . . in La Bordhawe in poɕ scᵉ Marie de
Coleschirch̃*'; 1258-9 LMA CLA/024/01/02/025 Plea & Mem A 24 m. 7 '*De terra &
teñ que Serlo de la Bordhawe teneᵗ*'

18. Sabelinesbir̃ 1258–9 LMA CLA/024/01/02/025 Plea & Mem A 24 m. 7 '*De terre
& teñ que Cresse iudeus fiᵗ magistri mossei tenet in pochia sc̄i laurencij de Iudaisimo
inᵗ t̃ram que vocatᵒ Sabelinesbir̃ ṽsus austrū & terram Witt le Sauser ṽsus aquilonem*'

19. Caponeshors, Capounes Hors, Litelcaponhors 1258–9 HR 2/44 '*Iᵗ legauit
Caponeshors apɖ ñtone*'; 1291 Letter-Book A fo 60v '*Rogꝰ cissor mañ apɖ caponeshors*'; 1324–5 HR 53/76 '*teñ quod vocatᵒ Capounes hors in vico de Candelwykstᵉte*';
1327–8 HR 55/48 '*tenemento vocato Litelcaponhors in vico de Candelwikstrete in
Cornerio de Abecherchelane in pochia b̃te Marᵉ de Abecherche Londoñ*'; 1331–2 HR
59/94 '*quodam tenemento vocato Caponeshors quod Matilɖ de Caxtoñ h̃et & tenet in
poɕ b̃e Marie de Abchirch Londoñ*'; 1337 HR 64/137 '*de quadam t̃ra & dom̃ supedifi-
catꝰquam quon< > Kaxtoñ tenuit in pochia b̃e Marie de Abchurche Londoñ . . . in loco*

vocat̄ Caponeshors'; 1368–9 HR 96/215 '*quoddam teñ meū vocat̄ Capilhors in pochia ƀe Marie de appechirche*'; 1399–1400 HR 128/14 '*teñ bracineo vocat̄ le Welhous . . . teñ vocat̄ le Caponhors situat̄ in pochia p̃dc̄a*'. OED capon, *n*. 'castrated cock', *c*. 1000; OED caple, capul, *n*. 'horse', *c*. 1290. Ekwall (1954: 152–3): 'Caponeshors appears to mean "the horse with a capon" and might designate a sign which showed a horse with a capon on its back'. The first token (in Hustings Roll CLA/023/DW/01/002/44 of 1258–9) is certainly <Caponeshors>, with a 2-shaped <r>, but this is the name of a tenement at Merton, Surrey, owned by Felicia la Colnere of London, who also owned property near le Caponeshors in Cannon Street. As Ekwall (1954: 152) says: 'It would be an odd coincidence if this curious name had arisen independently in London and in a Surrey village as the name of a house belonging to a lady who was evidently resident near Caponhors in London. If this is right, the name must have been in existence about 1250, probably earlier.' However see also Ekwall (1954: 199–200), where he discusses *r* looking like a *v* in the return for Queenhithe in the London Subsidy Roll of 1319, allowing an interpretation of *Bevis* as a misreading of *Beris*, the genitive of *Bury*, in messuage-name *Bewesmarkes* (1405, 'Bevis Marks', i.e., 'Abbot of Bury's Marks'). Adducing the same argument, *caponeshors* could be a misreading of earlier *caponeshous* 'capons' house'. That there were subsequent tokens of *le Caponhors* would be no more objection to this explanation than the perdurance of *Bevis Marks*. 1258–9 would be a very early date for jocular animal signs; other heraldic sign names are not found until the 1320s, and compound signs are not attested until *le Catfithele* of 1358. There certainly were capon houses in the City; William Porlond's Book (1418–22) details bargeboarding the eaves of the Brewers' Company capon house (fos 143v, 144, 145v). The question remains open, however.

20. la Wytecruche 1259–60 HR 2/102 '*domoꝛ suaꝛ cū ptinenî de la Wytecruche*'

21. Barndehaw 1260–1 TNA E 40/1668 '*p̃senti carta confirmauunt̄ Ricardo de Hauering̃ totū Gardinū illum qui vocat̄ᵒ Barndehawe edificatum*'

22. Castrum de Baynard, Chastel Baynard 1265 TNA C 66/83 m. 4 '*domibȝ . . . sup Tamisiam ꝓpe Castrum de Baynard̃*'; 1276 TNA C 66/95 m. 19 '*duas venellas contiguas placee sue Castri Baynard & Ƭris de monfychet obstruend̃*'; 1279 (13th cent.) BL Cotton MS Cleopatra A VI fo 60v '*le fondement de lour nouel eglise a chastel baynard̃*'

23. Wyuelastone, Wyuelatestone 1271–2 TNA E 40/1783 '*in pochia sc̄i Dunstani in London̄ in vico ũsus Turrim cont̃ᵃ wyuelastone de quadam domo cū furno & sopis adiacentibȝ*'; dorse '*Carta Willī de la Cornere de octo solid̃ de furno & sopis in vico ũsus Turrim London̄ côtra wyuelatestone*'; 1283–4 HR 15/48 '*totam domū cum edificiis suis & al̄ ptiñ . . . vocatur Wyuelattestone . . . in poch sc̄i Dunstani vers̄ Turrī Lond̃*'; 1389–90 HR 117/129 '*Et quodam teñ ptiñet̄ dc̄o Ponti londoñ vocato Wyuel atte Stone*'. Presumably owned by a person from Woollaston, Staffordshire, 'Wulflaf's farmstead', cf. Horovitz (2003: ii 644).

24. T*ᵒ*ris de Monfychet, Turr* de Mont Fychet 1276 TNA C 66/95 m. 19 '*duas venellas contiguas placee sue Castri Baynard & Tᵒris de monfychet obstruend*'; 1300 Letter-Book C fo xlviii '*Robto Cantuar* archiepō et assigñ suis duas venellas ᵍtiguas placie sue Castri Baynard & turr* de mont fychet*'

25. Nouus Redditus, la Newerente 1277 HR 8/25 '*totū teñ suū in Tamesestrete . . . vocat*ᵒ*nouus redditus*'; 1316–17 HR 45/225 '*toto illo tenemento cū suis ptinent* vocato la newerente sito in vico de Thamysestree in poch scī Michis de Candelwikstrete*'; 1385–6 HR 113/113 '*de quodam teñ cū ptiñ antiquit*ᵍ *vocat* le Newren<t> . . . in vico de thamise stret in pochia scī Michis in Croked lane iuxta Candilwykstret londoñ*'

26. Bokerelesberi 1277–8 HR 9/1 '*totū teneñ illud cū ptiñ in poch scī Stephi sup Walebroc p vocatur Bokerelesberi*'. The Bukerel family is recorded in London from 1100 (Ekwall 1954: 196).

27. Seldā de Andouer*, Andoureselde 1277–8 HR 9/3 '*domū . . . cū totā seldā de Andouer* & seldā suā in Westchep*'; 1277–8 HR 9/4 '*totā seldā de andouer & seldā suā in Westchep*'; 1312-13 HR 41/45 '*totam seldam meam cū ptineñt suis que vocatur Andoureselde in poch scī Johis de Walebrok*'

28. la Corner<schoppe>, Corn<>shoppe, the Cornersshoppes 1278–9 HR 10/3 '*vnam schoppam que vocat La Corner<schoppe &> aliam schoppam qᵃm tenet de Priorissa de keleburne*'; 1383–4 HR 111/66 '*in poch scī Edī in lumbardestret londoñ in langebournewarde . . . totū teñ suū voc* le sarisinesheued vnam shopam cū solar* supedific* voc* Corn<>shoppe*'; 1385 WAM 17706 '*duas shopas cū solar* supedificatẹ cū suis ptiñ vocat* the Cornersshoppes situat* in vill Westmῑ p̃dict* iuxta mesuag* siue tabernā vocat* Colchestrestau*ne*'

29. Saueye 1279 (13th cent.) BL Cotton MS Cleopatra A. VI fo 60 '*qest apelle Saueye hors de la barre au temple nouell*'

30. Selda Tannator*, Tanñselde, le Tannereselde 1279–80 HR 11/31 '*de selda Tannator* in p̃dcā Ciuitat* scil in Westchepe*';1308–9 HR 37/90 '*in selda vocata Tanñselde . . . in Westchep*'; 1341–2 HR 68/53 '*in quadam domo vocat* le Tannereselde Londoñ in pochia be Marie de Arcubȝ*'

31. Blemondisberi 1280 TNA C 146/765 '*tota Crofta illa cum ptinentiis que vocat*ᵒ *Smithicroft in prebenda de Totenhale que iacet inter terram dnῑ de Totenhale ex parte aquilonar* & terram vocatam Blemondisberi ex parte australi*'

32. le Kok [ate Cok 1282–3 HR 14/43 '*Lucie vxor* quond Radi atecok*'; 1319 TNA E 179 144/3 m 8 '*Warda de Langebourne . . . De Hugone ate Cocke*']; 1325 WAM 17588 '*ap*ᵈ le kok in Tothull*'; [1339 LMA CLA/024/01/02/004 Plea & Mem A 3 m. 10 '*Crepulg* ext*ᵃ . . . hugo atte Cokke*'; 1340 LMA CLA/024/01/02/004 Plea & Mem A 3 m. 14 '*Hug* atte Kocke . . . Thoñ consanguini*ᵍ *Litelwatte*']; 1357–8 HR 85/139

'*de quodam tenemento in pochia sc̄i Egidij ext͞ᵃ Crepelgate in le fforstret & dicit͡ᵒ atte Cok othe houp*'; 1381 WAM 17702 '*vocat͡ le Cocke vel Tabard in vico de Tothull*'

33. Stapledehalle 1285–6 HR 16/56 '*Totum illud tenem̄ cū omībȝ ptiñ suis quod vocat͡ᵒ Stapledehalle . . . in pochia omñ scōꝛ de Berkingesherch quo i͡ᵃ t u͡ sus Turrim Lonꝺ*'; 1292 HR 15/47 '*Wills Atte Stapeldhall*'; 1294–5 HR 24/38 '*Robto le Maderman . . . totū teñ suū cū ptiñ quod vocat͡ᵒ le Stapeledhall in poch om̄ni scōꝛ de Berkynggechirche*'. *OED* staple, *n.*¹ 1. a. 'post, pillar, column'; *MED* stāpel (n.) (d).

34. Redehalle 1288–9 Letter-Book A fo 49v '*dom̄ que vocat͡ Redehalle*'; 1364–5 HR 91/34 '*totū illud mesuagiū cū ptiñ situatū in poch omī scōꝛ de Bredestret & sc̄i Mildrede londoñ vocatū la Redehalle*'

35. la Burgate 1289–90 HR 19/51 '*de quoꝺ tenem̄ vocato la Burgate . . . in poch sc̄i Marie de Colcherch*'; 1358–9 HR 86/17 '*totam illam domū bracineam vocatam le Burgate in pochia b̄te Margarete de ffridaystrete londoñ*'. 1235 *atteburgate*, *Burgate*, Surrey (http://placenames.org.uk/).

36. Peinteselde 1290–1 HR 20/5 '*selda que vocat͡ᵒ Peinteselde in pochi sc̄i ppanc͡ᵃcii*'. Known by the early 14th cent. as *la Graunt Seude*, and during the first half of the 14th cent. as *la Brodeselde* (Keene 2006: 135).

37. le Seelde 1292 [TNA E 179/144/2 m 3 col. 1 '*Warꝺ de Duuegate . . . Joh atte selde*']; 1384 TNA C 145/232 '*totū illud teñ suū vocatū le seelde cum domibȝ supedificat͡ & omībȝ suis ptiñ situatū in pochia b̄e marie de arcubȝ Londoñ*'

38. del Coppedhalle 1292 HR 15/47 '*sex sol annui & quieti redditus del Coppedhalle ad vendenꝺ*'. *OED* copped, *adj.* 2.a. 'peaked'. There was a *Cop(p)idhalle* in Winchester (Keene 1985a: ii 1424).

39. Wyncestre Selde 1293 Letter-Book C fo vii v (xxxi v) '*vnam seldam que vocat͡ᵒ Wyncestre selde in qua m̄catores de Andoue͡ & alij m̄catores ex͞ᵃ nei venrūt ad negociandum*'

40. Helle 1294–5 HR 24/101 '*magnā aulam meā lapideā & puā aulam & dua celaria que vocant͡ᵃ Helle una cum kayo & omībȝ ptiñ suis in pochia sc̄i Jacobi in vineta in venella que vocat͡ᵃ ffatteslane*'; 1309–10 HR 38/111 '*domū meam & quatuor schopas meas vocate̜ helle in dc̄o vico de ffletestrete*'; 1343–4 HR 70/130 '*quandam domū sup solariū cum quodam Celario subtus dc̄m solariū edificato quod vocat͡ puū Helle . . . in venella vocata ffatteslane in pochia sc̄i Jacobi in Garlekhith Londoñ . . . ad Celar͡ . . . vocatum magnū Helle cum domibȝ supedificat͡*'. *OED* hell, *n.* and *int.* 4. 'part of a building . . . resembling hell' (1310). Helle as a name was not uncommon (Kingsford 1916: 135); see also Ekwall (1947: 186–7). There was a messuage and seld called *Helle* in Oxford in 1355/6 (Salter 1929: 530, 551, 554, 557, 1092)), and a *Helle* in Winchester in 1426, probably a cellar tavern (Keene 1985a: ii 501, ii 1426).

41. le Hoppindehalle, la Hoppynghaƚƚ 1293 (1330) WAM 17476 '*illud tenementum cum . . . suis ptinētiis in villa Westmonasterū⁰ quod vocatur le hoppindehalle*'; 1330 TNA C 66/173 m. 18 '*domos suas iuxa Westmonastm̄ vocatas la Hoppynghaƚƚ*'

42. Depeselde 1294–5 HR 24/74 '*in quadam selda que dicit⁰ Depeselde in foro*'

43. Wolhous 1294–5 HR 24/100 '*mee aulā illā cū Cam̄is & domo q̂ vocat⁰ Wolhous cū quid pte gardini mei & omībȝ ptiñ in Sporieres lane in eaɗ poch omñi sc̄oȝ*'

44. le Brodedore 1295–6 HR 25/41 '*quod tenemento qɗ vocat' le brodedore cum ptiñ suis in poch sc̄i sepulc'*'

45. la Ledenehalle 1295–6 HR 25/84; '*quod tenem̄to quod fuit Raɗi atte Horsmelle iuxta La Ledenehalle in vico de Garscherchs'*'; 1357–8 HR 85/101 '*vnū messuagiū vocatū Ledenhalle Londoñ*'

46. atte Horsmelle, le Horsemelne 1295–6 HR 25/84 '*quod tenem̄to quod fuit Raɗi atte Horsmelle iuxta La Ledenehalle in vico de Garscherchs'*'; 1353 HR 81/112 '*tenementis . . . mee vocat' le hors melne in pochia sc̄i Pet'*'

47. Brantefeld Selde 1297–8 HR 27/64 '*totā illa selda cū suis ptiñ q̂ vocat' Brantefeld selde in foro de westchepe in pochia ƀte Marie de Arcubȝ lonɗ*'; 1332–3 HR 60/46 '*totam illam seldam cū quatuor schopis . . . & cū domo integ⁰ . . . q⁰m ƀeo in poch ƀe Marie de Arcubȝ Londoñ . . . que quidm̄ selda vocat⁰ Brantefeldseld'*'. Occupied by William de Brantefeld 1247–8 (Keene and Harding 1987 [1994]).

48. le Taninghus 1297–8 HR 27/68 '*de domo vocato le Taninghus ext⁰ Crepelg'*'

49. Beaurepair 1297–8 HR 27/82 '*in pochia omīum sc̄oȝ ad ffenū Londoñ . . . totum teñ illɗ cum omībȝ ptiñ suis quod vocat⁰ Beaurepair in parochia p̂dcā*'. There was a *Beaureper* (1317) in Winchester (Keene 1985a: i 157; ii 1422).

50. Stonhus 1297–8 HR 27/130 '*illud teñ qɗ vo⁰ stonhus c̑ omībȝ suis ptiñ in vico vocat⁰ Oughenelane in poch sc̄i Michis de <Brede>st⁰ te vocati hoggene cherche londoñ*'; 1358 HR 89/77 '*quodam teñ in Paťnosťrowe Londoñ p̂dict' vocat' le stonhous in pochia sc̄i Michis ad bladu'*'. A relatively common name, 1317 Walbrook; 1322 without Bishopsgate.

51. le Halles 1298 Letter-Book B fo 95 (xl) '*domo q̂ vo⁰ le Halles'*'. See Keene (2006) for the suggestion that this name may have been borrowed from the Parisian market of the same name.

52. Parys 1298–9 Letter-Book C fo xxvii v '*vnū teñ . . . in pochia sc̄i marti<ni> bermancherch vna cum domo illa que appellat⁰ Parys*'

53. Selda sc̄i Martini, Seyntemartynseld 1304–5 WAM 13993 '*in duabȝ platiis duaȝ Cistaȝ in magna selda sc̄i Martini*'; 1322–3 HR 51/128 '*qd shope site sunt in latitudīe inť eanɗ venellā ex pte orientali & seldā vocatam Seyntemartynseld'*'. Also known as

la Streyteseld 'narrow seld' (mean width 5m) and as *Gerdleresselde* 'girdlers' seld' (Keene 2006: 133).

54. Mutis, Mewes, le Mewehous 1306 TNA C 47/4/4 fo 48v '*vni⁹ girfalconis quem traxit ad mutis London... j girfalcoñ quem libauit Georgino ... ad mutas Londoñ ...p pictura & Lumine girfalconis sui quem tᵃ xit de mutis p̃dc̄is*'; 1397–8 TNA E 101/502/14 m. 33 '*faceʒ couenablement repailler & amender si auant come necessairement busoignera toutes les mesons & lieux deinʒ noʒ mewes ioust Charyng*'; 1460 TNA C 66/489 m. 11 '*Quoddam mesuagiũ domũ siue mansionem vocat' le Mewehous apud Charryng iuxta Westm̄ in Com̄ Midđ cum omı̄bʒ domibʒ gardinis t'ris teñ*'

55. Audeleeshalle 1307 TNA C 134/5 m.6 '*warda de Aldergate ... vnũ mesuagiũ quod vocatur Audeleeshalle*'. Nicholas de Aldithelegh K.

56. le Coldha<bber>, le Coldherbegh, le Coldherberuy, le Choldherberwe 1307 LMA CLA/024/01/01/009 Early Mayors Court Roll I m. 5v 1307 '*apud le Coldha<bber> in pochia Om̄i scōꝛ ad fenũ*'; 1317–18 HR 46/6 '*totum capitale tenementũ suũ qd vocatur le Coldherbegh in pochia omı̄ Scōꝛ ad fenũ Londoñ*'; 1348 HR 77/180 '*toto teñ meũ cũ ptiñ vocato le Coldherberuy ... totũ p̃dc̄m teñ meũ vocat' le choldherberwe*'. See K and Coates (1984) for a discussion of *Coldharbour*.

57. Werckhus 1307 HR 36/76 '*domũ meã opariam que vocatᵒ werckhus*'

58. Herlewyne, Harlewyne 1308 (record of a 1308 deed in a deed written 1411) LMA CLC/313/L/H/001/MS25121 St Paul's Cathedral deed no. 1770 '*totum illud teñ cum omı̄bʒ suis ptiñ extra Crepelgate Londoñ in pochia scı̄ Egidij quod vocatᵒ teñ Herlewyne*'; 1389–90 HR 117/97 '*totũ teñ meũ ... vocat' teñtum harlewyne situat' in Redecrouchestrete in pochia sancti Egidij exᵃ Crepulgate in suburbio Londoñ*'. *Herlewyne* was a surname, cf. *Balduinus filius Herluini* 1066, *Roger Herlewyn* 1230 (Reaney and Wilson 1991 [1995]: 245).

59. Rosemunde, Rosamond 1309 LMA CLC/313/L/H/001/MS25121 St Paul's Cathedral deed no. 1772 '*domũ qᵃm idem magister Ricus̃ inhitabat & p̃cipue ad Cam̄am que Rosemunde nũcupatur ... vsqʒ ad murum cimiterij scı̄ Benedc̄t*'; 1333 WAM 17610 '*ad man̄ı̄m quod vocatᵒ Rosamond*'; 1361 WAM 17665 '*de man̄io de Rosemond iuxᵃ Westm̄*'

60. la Monetere House 1309–10 HR 38/111 '*redditum heo in vico dc̄o de ffletestrate de domo vocata La Monetere house*'

61. Bonsieshous or Bousieshous 1309–10 HR 38/111 '*domũ ... vocatam Bonsieshous apud Garlekheth Londoñ*'

62. le Portehawe 1309–10 HR 38/87 '*illud teñ quod heo in le Portehawe in poch sc̄e Marie de Colcherche*'

63. la Wesŕne Garite 130910 HR 38/111 '*duas garitas meas apud la Queneheth Londoñ . . . vnam de iŧ duabʒ garitas videlicet la Wesŕne Garite*'; 1349 HR 77/173 '*illos domos . . . meã que vocatᵒ le Garite*'

64. Fridayselde 1310–11 HR 39/12 '*vnam seldam vbi coriũ ponitᵒ & venditᵒ & qᵃ md domũ in qua ĉingia vendi consueŭat una cũ antiqᶦs ᵒsuetudinibʒ & oĩbʒ suis ptinent' in poch sĉi Maŧhi in ffridaistret' Londoñ que vocantᵒ fridayselde*'

65. atte Stoples, le Stoupeles, le Stulpes 1310–11 HR 39/66 '*et vnũ teñ vocatũ atte stoples cum ptinenŧ in poch sĉi Miĉhis sup Cornhuŧ Londoñ*'; [1319 TNA E 179 144/3 m. 6 '*Warda de Cornhuŧ . . . De Steρho atte Stoples*']; 1357–8 HR 85/5 '*totũ teñ vocatũ le Stoples in poch sĉi Miĉhis sup Cornhulle*'; 1369–70 HR 96/53 '*totũ illud tenementũ meũ vocatũ le Stoupeles cũ domibʒ solariis Celariis & oĩmibʒ alijs suis ptiñ in pochia ƀe Marie de Abbecherche in Candelwykestrete London*'; 1397 HR 126/23 '*totũ teñ meũ cũ oĩmibʒ suis ptiñ situat' in Watlyngstret in pochia ƀe Marie de Aldermarichirche londoñ . . . vocat' le Stulpes*'. MED stulp(e, n. (c)) 'stake, post'.

66. la fflint Halle 1311–12 HR 40/6 '*totũ illam domũ nostram vocatam la fflint halle . . . in vico de Seluerstrate in parochial sĉi Olaui iuxᵃ Muŕ Londoñ*'

67. la Blakelofte 1311–12 HR 40/26 '*illud tenementũ meum cum ptinent' quos dicitᵒ la Blakelofte situm in occidentali laŕe vici de Martelane ad Turrim Lonɗ*'; 1349 HR 77/213 '*redɗ pcipienɗ annuatũ del blakelofte in poch de stanyngĉhche iuxᵃ martelane in Ciuit' Londoñ*'

68. la Taŭnehous 1311–12 HR 40/29 '*domo mea que dicitᵒ la Taŭnehous . . . dcãm domû le Taŭnehous & vnam shopam cũ ptinenĪ suũ inŕ portam dĉe domus & domum meam ad bracinam*'

69. Kote 1311–12 HR 40/60 '*totam illam schopam vocatam kote que est subtus solaŕ . . . in poch ƀe Margaŕ Patyns*'

70. Heyroneshalle 1311–12 HR 40/118 '*illis tenem̃tis cum suis ptinent' . . . in Syuethelane quod vocabatur heyroneshalle in pochia omĪ sĉoჳ de Berkyngcherche iuxta Turrim Londoñ*'

71. le Stokkes 1311–12 Letter-Book D fo cxlv '*totam illam domũ q̃ vocatᵒ le Stokkes*'

72. Loge 1312–13 Letter-Book C fo cxlvii '*Joħes le Wallere tenet vnam ρuam placeam exᵃ Alegate iuxta fossatũ in quadam ρua domo que dicitᵒ Loge longitudina .xij. pedũ & latitudinis .vij. pedũ*'

73. le Isnendore, le Irendore 1312–13 HR 41/94 '*teñ vocatũ le Isnendore in venella sĉi Swithini . . . Itm̃ in illo cum ptinent' qɗ situm est in venella sĉi Swithini quod vocatur le Irendore cum omĪbʒ schopis*'. OED iron, *n.1* OE isern.

74. Dyneshemanhalle 1313–14 HR 42/112 '*in pochia Omī Sc̄oꝝ ad fenum . . . aulam vocatam Dyneshemanhalle*'

75. Bordenhous 1315–16 HR 44/47 '*tenementū meū vocatū Bordenhous vna cū shopa . . . in poch de Aldermaricherche*'

76. Cokedonhalle 1316–17 HR 45/14 '*mesuagium meum vocatum Cokedonhalle cum omībȝ suis pertinentijs in pochia sc̄i Dunstani Londoñ versus Turr̄*'

77. le Webbeloft 1316–17 HR 46/60 '*quoddam tenementū vocatum le Webbeloft . . . in poch sc̄i Laurencij*'

78. la Brodeselde 1318 HR 46/83 '*in quodam loco qui vocatur la Brodeselde in poch sc̄i Pancracij Londoñ*'

79. atte Basket [1319 TNA E 179 144/3 m 6 '*Warda de Cornhull̄ . . . De Margía atte Bascat̄*']; 1418–40 Guildhall Library CLC/L/BF/A/021/MS05440 fo 10 '*atte Basket in ffanchyrch strete en la poch de toutȝ seyntȝ de Stanyng*'

80. le Sterre [1319 TNA E 179 144/3 m. 8 '*Warda de Langebourne . . . De Rico ate Sterre*']; 1354-5 HR 82/39 '*totū illud Capitale teñ meū vocat̄ le Sterre . . . in pochia omī sc̄oꝝ de Bredstrete*'; 1354–5 HR 82/39 '*totū illud Capitale teñ meū vocat̄ le Sterre . . . in pochia omī sc̄oꝝ de Bredstrete*'

81. atte Vine [1319 TNA E 179 144/3 m 14 '*Cordewanerestr̄ . . . De Roḡo ate Vyne*', m 22 '*Warda Ripe Regine . . . De Rīco atte vyne*', m 23 '*Warda Castri Baynard̄ . . . De Cristiana atte Vigne . . . De Joha atte Vigne*'; 1329 LMA CLA/024/01/02/002 Plea & Mem A 1b m. 33d '*Johnes atte Vine*'; 1339 LMA CLA/024/01/02/004 Plea & Mem A 3 m. 21 '*Turr̄ . . . Thom atte vigne & soc̄ suo . . . Nicho atte Boure & soc̄ suo*']; 1346–7 HR 73/136 '*in tota illa domo bracinea dc̄a atte Vine . . . Que quidem dom⁹ sita est infra Bisshopesgate Londoñ*'. There was a *la Vyne* in Winchester in 1401 (Keene 1985a: ii 501).

82. Bruggehous, le Breggehous [1319 TNA E 179 144/3 m. 16v '*Crepelgate ext̄ᵃ . . . De Robto atte Briggehou<>*']; 1323–4 HR 52/118 '*teñ meum quod vocat̄ Bruggehous in poch sc̄i Botolphi ext̄ᵃ Bisshopesgate Londoñ*'; 1340 LMA CLA/024/01/02/004 Plea & Mem A 3 m. 14v '*in redd̄ Iacobi le Sherman vocato le Breggehous*'; 1358 Letter-Book G fo xcv '*teñ Corneriū vocatū le Briggehous*'

83. Topfeldes In [1319 TNA E 179 144/3 m 19d '*Warda de ffarndoñ ext̄ᵃ . . . Will̄o de Toppeffeld̄*']; 1380 HR 109/73 '*totū teñ meū voc̄ Topfeldes In in ffletestrete in pochia sc̄e Brigide londoñ*'

84. Piggesflessch [1319 TNA Exchequer K R Subsidy Rolls E 179/144/3 m 22 '*Warda Ripe Regine . . . De Reynero Piggesfles*']; 1338–9 LMA CLC/313/L/H/001/MS25121 St Paul's Cathedral deed no. 1519 '*Que quedam bracina p̄dc̄a cum omībus vtensilibus & suis p̄tinēt̄ dc̄us dñs Robtus de Mundēn hēt in pochia sc̄i Michis ad bladum in pater nr̄ Rowe Londoñ vocat̄ Piggesflessch*'

85. le Swan [1319 TNA E 179 144/3 m. 23 '*Warda Castri Baynarđ . . . De Henr̄ atte Swan*'; 1339 LMA CLA/024/01/02/004 Plea & Mem A 3 m. 23 v '*Bisshopesgate . . . Godefridus atte Swan*']; 1363 HR 91/125 '*teñ meū vocat̄ le Swan othe hop cū duabʒ shopis annexis situat̄ in vico de Wodestrete in p̄dcā poch sc̄i Michis de hoggenelane*'; 1375–6 HR 103/233 '*de teñ meo bracineo cū ptiñ quondā vocato le Culuer on the hope & modo le swan on þe hope nuncupato in Thamistrete in poch sc̄i Dunsta< > in Est londoñ*'; 1397 HR 126/23 '*totū illud teñ meū cū ptiñ vocat̄ le Swan on the hōp . . . situat̄ ad Macellas sc̄i Nichi londoñ*'. There was a *le Swan* in Winchester in 1395 (Keene 1985a: i 167, ii 501).

86. le Ram [1319 TNA E 179 144/3 m. 23 '*Warda Castri Baynarđ . . . De Thom atte Ramme*'; 1338 LMA CLA/024/01/02/006 Plea & Mem A 5 m. 3 '*Egidius atte Ramme*']; 1353–4 HR 81/101 '*totum tenementū meū Bracineū vocatū le Ram onthe-hope . . . in venella vocata Distaflane in pochia sc̄i Augustini ad portam iuxta eccliam sc̄i Pauli Londoñ*'

87. þe Rose [1319 TNA E 179/144/3 m 24 '*Warda Turr̄ . . . De Thom atte Rose*']; 1422 LMA CLA/024/01/02/051 Plea & Mem A 50 m 7 '*John Stone Bruer̄ be cause of lettyng of the côe wey thoroweoute þe Rose in to Conyhopeslane defectif Item þe hous cleped þe Aungeɫɫ atte Soperslane ende in Chepe be cause þat it is olde and in poynt to faɫɫ to grete pil of þe poeple defectif*'

88. le Ernedore 1321 TNA C 66/154 m. 4 '*sc̄i sepulchri extra Neugate . . . vno mesuagio cū ptiñ quod vocat̄° le Ernedore*'. Either OE ærn, *ern* 'house', which usually occurs as a second-element, or OE *earn* 'eagle'; *OED* earn, *n.¹*; erne, *n.*; *MED* ern (n.(1)) and (n.2.)).

89. le Rouge Sale 1321–2 HR 50/133 '*tenementū vocatur le Rouge Sale q̄ situ est int̄ tenementū Hugonis*'

90. la Hole 1322 HR 51/13 '*quodam teñ vocato la Hole in pochia sc̄i Owyni ex oppoĩto ffratrū dc̄e Ciuitatis*'; 1332–3 HR 60/138 '*quodam teñ vocato atte Hole infra Neugate Londoñ ex oppoĩto ecclie fratr̄ Minoʒ Londoñ*'; 1338 LMA CLA/024/01/02/004 Plea & Mem A 5 m. 11 '*Agnes relicta Robti atte hole conducit q̄ᵃ ndam domû in Sholane*'

91. Croweonethehop 1323 LMA CLC/313/L/H/001/MS25121 deed no. 680 '*Et illa duo teñ vocat̄ Croweonethehop cum domibʒ scopis celariis et solariis supedificato . . . in pochia sc̄i vedasti in venella que vocat̄ Goderounelane Londoñ*'

92. Viene 1323 TNA C 66/159 m. 16 '*domoʒ que vocant̄° domus de viene in Ciuitate Rₑ Londoñ*'. [TNA C 47/4/4 fo 16v (1306) *Johi de Vienna*, fo 18v *Johanni de Viene/Vyene*.]

93. ʒylynghous 1324 Letter-Book E fo clvi '*tot̄ illam dc̄m bracineā cū quađ shopa eidem adiacente & cū quađ domo vocat̄ ʒylynghous . . . in vico de Bredstret̄ in poch Omī Scōʒ Londoñ*'. *OED* gyling, *n.* 'fermenting'.

94. Hauerilleselde 1324–5 HR 53/10 '*quodam Celario q̄d est directe subtus quandā seldā dc̄oᵖ Religiosoᵖ vocat' hauerilleselde in foro Londoñ in poch̄ sc̄i Pet' de Wodest'ᵃ te*'

95. le Stufhous 1324–5 HR 53/27 '*totū ill̄d teñ quod vocat' le Stufhous . . . in venella q̄ vocat' Woderouelane in poch̄ Sc̄i Olaui iux'ᵃ Turrym Londoñ*'

96. Eybury 1327 WAM 26999 '*Eybury*'; 1382-30 WAM 26938 '*ad Mar̄iū de Eybury*'

97. le Meire 1327–8 HR 55/96 '*teñ . . . que vocat'ᵒ le meire in pochia de Staningcherche*'. OED mayor, *n.*, AN, 'chief officer of municipal government'; meirre, *n.* and *adj.* Middle French *meire* 'kind of garment used in heraldry'.

98. la Mariole 1328–9 HR 56/38 '*totam illa domū cū shopa & suis ptinent' que vocatur la Mariole . . . in pochia omniū sc̄oᵖ de Honilane London*'. AND mariole[1] 'image of the Virgin Mary'.

99. Drinkewat̄estauerne 1328 HR 56/119 '*ad illud teñ iux'ᵃ pontem Londoñ vocatū Drinkewat̄estauerne*'

100. Gladewyneshouse 1328 HR 56/121 '*tenementū meū vocatū Gladewyneshouse in Thamysestret̄ Londoñ*'

101. Whitawyeresselde 1328 HR 56/125 '*totam illam Seldam vocatam Whitawyeresselde cum duab₃ shoppis . . . quam heo in poch̄ sc̄e Marie de Colchirch Londoñ*'. OED whittawyer, *n.* 'person who makes whitleather'.

102. la Redebakhous 1329–30 HR 57/34 '*de tota illa pistrina vocata la Redebakhous cū domib₃ & suis ptiñ quā heo in pochia sc̄i Clementis iux'ᵃ Candelwykstrete Londoñ*'

103. de Bethlehem 1330 Letter-Book E fo ccvii v '*ffr' Will̄ms de Banh'ᵃ m ordinis Bethlehemit̄ . . . totum illud teñ vocatu'ᵒ de Bethlehem cū domib₃ & shop supedific̄ cū gardinis / stagnis*'

104. la Bas Court 1331 TNA C 66/175 m.12 '*domos illas cum gardinis & aliis ptiñ suis . . . vocât'ᵒ la Bas Court iuxta Crypelgate in Ciuitate nr̄a' Londoñ*'

105. le Tawynghous 1331–2 HR 59/110 '*toto illo teñ cū suis ptinent' vocato le Tawynghous in pochia sc̄i Egidij ex'ᵃ Crupulg' v̄sus la more in suburb̄ Ciuitatis Londoñ*'

106. ffynesbury 1332 LMA CLC/313/N/006/MS25345 '*Curia de ffynesbury*'

107. le Brokeneselde 1332–3 HR 60/46 '*de domo illa & Tab̄na cū ptiñ que vocat'ᵃ le Brokeneselde in foro de Westch̄p in pochia b̄e Marie Magdalene de Melkstrate Londoñ*'

108. le Post̄nehawe 1332–3 HR 60/60 '*totū teñ nr̄m cū domib₃ supedificat' gardino adiacent' & omīb₃ alijs suis ptiñ q̄d habimu⁹ in vico vocato Lymstrete vna cū q'ᵃ dam p̄ua domo que constructa est in gardino nr̄o vocato le Post̄nehawe . . . tenementi vocati le Ledenehall̄ v̄sus Occident̄*'

109. Gerdleresselde 1333–4 HR 61/24 '*domo illa que vocat͛ Gerdleresselde in poch scī Panc͛ cij Londoñ*'

110. la Ryngedehalle 1334–5 HR 62/56 '*totū illud mesuagiū meū vocatū la Ryngedehalle cum domibȝ supedificatis gardino adiacente vnā cū shopis dc̄i Mesuagij ext͛ portam eiusdem situatis . . . in pochia sc̄i Thome Apłi in warda Vinet͛e in Civitatē Londoñ*'

111. le Holceler 1334–5 HR 62/97 '*quodā Celario vocato le Holceler cū domibȝ & shopis supedificat͛ ex oppoīto eccłie sc̄e Margarete v͛gīs in Briggestrete Londoñ*'; [*Symon atte Holeweceler* 1351 HR 82/3]; 1371-2 HR 98/51 '*totam illam tab̄nam cum omībȝ suis ptiñ vocatā le Holceler in pochia sc̄e Margarete de Breggestrete Londoñ*'

112. le Bretasse, le Bretask 1334–5 HR 62/102 '*le teñ appele le Bretasse en la Rue de Thamyse*'; c. 1340 Letter-Book F fly leaf, '*in domo vocatǫ le Bretask iuxta Turr͛ Londoñ*'. *AND* bretache, s.; *OED* brattice, *n.* 'wooden parapet', 'boarding'.

113. le Crokedhous 1335 HR 63/43 '*totum illud teñ cum oībȝ suis ptiñ vocatū le Crokedhous . . . in pochia eccłie beate Marie de Som̄sete Londoñ*'

114. Eldehalle 1335 HR 63/80 '*totū tenementū nr̄m cū oībȝ suis ptinent͛ quod vocat͛ Eldehalle cum tribȝ shopis in pte occidentali dc̄i tenementi et q͛tuor solaria cū duobȝ Celarijs cū ptinentijs que vocant͛ le Scot in pochia sc̄i Michīs ad Ripâ Regine London*'

115. le Scot, Scotothehop 1335 HR 63/80 '*totū tenementū nr̄m cū oībȝ suis ptinent͛ quod vocat͛ Eldehalle cum tribȝ shopis in pte occidentali dc̄i tenementi et q͛tuor solaria cū duobȝ Celarijs cū ptinentijs que vocant͛ le Scot in pochia sc̄i Michīs ad Ripâ Regine London*'; 1344 HR 74/173 '*totû illud tenementû meû cû quidâ solidat͛ ânui reddit͛ cû suis ptiñ vocat͛ Scotothehop in pochia b̄e Marie de ffancherche*'; 1358–9 HR 86/106 '*totū illud teñ meū vocatū le Scot on the hope . . . in poch sc̄i Sepulcri ext͛ Neugate londoñ*'. Cf. also *le Scut on the Hoope* 1407–8 HR 135/22 '*totum tenementū meū bracineū cū omībȝ suis ptiñ quondā vocatū le Scut on the hoop & iā nōiat͛ le leoñ in Graschurchstrete in pochia Omī Sc̄oᴓ de Graschirche londoñ*'. *OED* scut *n.¹* 'tail, esp. that of a hare, rabbit or deer'.

116. le Wellehous 1335–6 HR 63/205 '*totū illud tenementū cū suis ptinentijs vocatū le Wellehous sitū in pochia sc̄i Michīs sup Cornhułł London*'; 1399-1400 HR 128/14 '*teñ bracineo vocat͛ le Welhous . . . teñ vocat͛ le Caponhors situat͛ in pochia p̄dc̄a*'

117. le Herbeir, Lerber 1335–6 HR 63/209 '*quoddam Mesuag͛ cū suis ptinentijs cū quodam curtilag͛ annexo vocato le Herbeir . . . in pochia sc̄e Marie Atte Helle iuxta Billyngesgate Londoñ*'; 1368 HR 96/215 '*Dat͛ Londoñ iux͛ Lerber in doma mea*'. *OED* arbour, *n.* 'lawn', 'flower-bed', 'orchard', 'vine', 'bower'.

118. la Goutere 1336–7 TNA C 135/48 m.27 '*vnū tenement vocato la Blauncheapelton . . . in proch sc̄i Olaui v͛sus Turr͛ Londoñ et . . . teñ vocat͛ la Goutere in eadem proch*'

119. Berneselde 1337–8 HR 64/153 '*toto illo teneṁto cū ptiñ vocato Berneselde in pochia sc̄i Petri de Wodestrete Londoñ*'

120. atte Celer [1338 LMA CLA/024/01/02/004 Plea & Mem A 5 m. 11 '*Agnes relicta Roḃti atte hole conducit qᵃndam domû in Sholane . . . Iuliana atte Celer . . . in Cokkeslane*'; 1384 LMA CLA/024/01/02/028 Plea & Mem A 27 (i) m. 11v '*fletstret . . . Joh atte Seler*']

121. la Pirie [1338 LMA CLA/024/01/02/004 Plea & Mem A 3 m. cedula (ie first membrane) '*Pons . . . . Iacobus atte Pirye*'; 1349 TNA C 145/163 no. 4/70 '*in poch sc̄e Agnetᵉ . . . in vno muro lapideo desup Gutter' ad reddit' de la Pirie & fundament' alioꝛ domoꝛ ibdm'. MED* piri(e (n.) 'pear tree'.

122. atte Goth, atte Goot, le Gote [1339 LMA CLA/024/01/02/004 Plea & Mem A 3 m. 4v '*Chepe . . . Walt'o atte Got'*']; 1346 HR 73/64 '*tenementū meū vocatū Taḃna atte Goth cum domibȝ supedificat' & cum quadam shopa in pte anteriori & alijs suis ptinencijs. Quod quidem tenementū sitū est in pochia omī scōꝛ de Honylane in warda fori Londoñ*'; 1348 HR 75/20 '*tenementū vocatū Taḃna atte Goot . . . in poch omī scōꝛ . . . de honylane*'; 1373–4 HR 101/164 '*totam illam taḃnam nōiat' le Gote on the hope cū schopis & cū omīḃȝ alijs ptiñ suis in pochia omī Scōꝛ de Honylane in West chepe Londoñ*'

123. atte Crouchehous [1339 LMA CLA/024/01/02/004 Plea & Mem A 3 m. 10 '*Portsokene . . . Johēs atte Crouchehous*']

124. le Rededore [1339 LMA CLA/024/01/02/004 Plea & Mem A 3 m. 23 v '*Bradestrete . . . Thom atte Rededore*']; 1366–7 HR 94/172 '*totum tenementū meû vocat' le Rededore cum domibȝ edificijs gardino adiacent' & omīḃȝ alijs suis ptiñ situat' in pochia sancti Dionisij de Bakcherche Londoñ*'; 1377 HR 106/142 '*in venella & pochia sc̄i Laurencij in Iudaismo Londoñ . videlt de teñ cum suis ptiñ quod p aliquos vocatᵒ la Redebrewehous & p aliquos vocatᵒ la Rededore*'

125. Prestenerente 1339–40 HR 66/100 '*totū illud tenementū vocatū Prestenerente . . . in pochia sc̄e kat'ine Trinitatis iuxta Alegate Londoñ*'

126. Pye on the hope 1340 LMA CLA/024/01/02/004 Plea & Mem A 3 m. 14 '*dom⁹ in Apecherche Lane atte Pye on the hope*'; 1368–9 HR 96/211 '*toto illud teñ meū cum ptiñ vocat' le Peye sup le hoop*';1385–6 HR 114/141 *totū illud teñ vocatū the pye on the hope cum domibȝ supedific' gardino adiacente & omīḃȝ alijs suis ptiñ situat' in vico vocato le barbican in pochia sc̄i Egidij exᵃ Crepulgate londoñ'. OED* pie, *n.¹* 'magpie'

127. le Hyde 1341 WAM 16232 '*quodam mesuagio meo vocato le Hyde iuxᵃ kniȝtebrigg*'

128. le Bere Toumbeth, le Beretombeth 1341? HR 68/37 '*totā illā taḃnam vbi le Bere toumbeth in Westcheṗ in pochia sc̄i Pancracij Londoñ*'; 1344–5 HR 71/151 '*illa Taḃna*

vocata le Beretombeth in Westchepe in pochia Sc̄i Pancracij Londoñ'. Either, tavern 'where the bear dances' (*OED* tumb, *v.*, *MED* tumben (v.) (b) 'to dance'), or, 'where the barley or beer (both *ber(e* in ME) is entombed: the beer-vault' (*MED* tomben (v.) (b) 'to be entombed').

129. ye Ledenpentitʒ 1341–2 HR 68/53 '*domô meâ bracineâ que vocatᵃ ye Ledenpentitʒ in vico de Holebourñ*'

130. la Newewodehous 1341–2 HR 68/110 '*vnam domû infra tenementû meû bracineû que vocatᵒ la Newewodehous cū toto acre , solarᵖ & cū garite supedificato*'

131. atte Rede Cok [1343 LMA CLA/024/01/02/006 Plea & Mem A 5 m. 17b '*Wiƚƚs atte Redecok . . . Willm atte Redehoᵽ* ']; 1418–40 William Porlond's Book, Guildhall Library CLC/L/BF/A/021/MS05440 fo 84v '*atte Rede Cok yn the pultrie*'

132. le Hors atte hope 1343–4 HR 70/152 '*illius tenementi cum p̱tinentijs . . . in pochia sc̄i Michis de Cornhuƚƚ vocat' le hors atte hope*'

133. Arraces Selde 1343–4 HR 70/152 '*illius shope cum p̱tiñ . . . in selda vocata Arraces selde*'. Owned by Robert de Arras before 1283 (Keene and Harding 1987 [1994]).

134. Roustenēmt 1344 WAM 17634 '*teneꝫ vocᵈ Roustenēmt*'. William le Rous held land in Westminster in 1333 (WAM 17610).

135. le Castel atte hooᵽ [1344 LMA CLA/024/01/02/006 Plea & Mem A 5 m. 24 '*Johis atte Casteƚƚ*']; 1363 HR 91/125 '*totū teñ meū vocᵈ le castel atte hooᵽ cū oibʒ suis p̱tiñ situat' in p̱dcā poch sc̄i Michis*'; [1384 LMA CLA/024/01/02/028 Plea & Mem A 27 (i) m. 11v '*ffletstret . . . Wiƚƚ atte Casteƚƚ*']

136. Pecokkesrente 1344–5 TNA E 40/1935 A. '*constructōis quarumdam domoꝗ infra Alegate Londoñ vocatę Pecokkesrente*'

137. Eltammismes 1345 WAM 17640 '*vnū tenementū quod vocatᵒ Eltammismes quod Alicia le Saucer quondam tenuit in villa de Westm̄ Et totū illud tenementū quod vocatᵒ Giffardeshalle*'; 1347 WAM 17644 '*in villa Westmoñ quoꝗ vnī teñ vocatę Elthᵃmmesmes . . . Aliud teñ vocat' Gyffardeshaƚƚ*'

138. Giffardeshalle 1345 WAM 17640 '*vnū tenementū quod vocatᵒ Eltammismes quod Alicia le Saucer quondam tenuit in villa de Westm̄ Et totū illud tenementū quod vocatᵒ Giffardeshalle*'; 1347 WAM 17644 '*in villa Westmoñ quoꝗ vnī teñ vocatę Elthᵃmmesmes . . . Aliud teñ vocat' Gyffardeshaƚƚ*'

139. la Lyoun 1345–6 HR 72/38 '*in tota illa Taḃna vnu vocata la Lyoun cū oi̅bʒ shopis ante situatę solarijs celarijs ac ceƚis suis p̱tinentijs . . . in pochia sc̄i Pancracij in warda de Westchepe Londoñ*'; 1382 HR 117/100 '*teñ meū in Wodestrete in pochia sancti Alphegi vocat' le lyon on the hope cū aleya shopis & alijs mansionibʒ eidem teñ p̱tinent*'

140. Yilhuys 1345 HR 72/55 '*teñ bracineo exceptis cisterna mea magno plumbo . . . ad Celariũ vocatũ yilhuys*'. OED *gyle, n.* 'wort in process of fermentation'.

141. la Longehous 1347–8 Letter-Book F fo cxlix '*totũ illud tenementũ quod vocat[ur] la Longehous in Bisshopesgatestrete . . . cũ alijs duabʒ pecijs gardinaʒ adiacentiũ sciłt illam peciam que vocat[or] le Northlond et illam peciam que vocat[or] fforparadys*'

142. Wodehawe 1348–9 HR 75/17 '*de toto illo tenemento bracini cũ domibʒ supedificat[ur] & cũ quadam placea t' re vocata Wodehawe cũ gardino adiacente . . . in pochijs Stepħi de Colemanstrete*'. It is not clear whether the brewhouse was also called Wodhawe.

143. la Cardinaleshat 1348–9 HR 75/49 '*Taħne vocat' la Cardinaleshat in pochia sc̄i Vedasti in foro de Westcheṕ Londoñ*'; 1350 WAM 13431 '*alio tenemêto tuo apud Grascherche quod Cardinaleshat vulgarit' nũcupat[ur]*'. Cf *le/la Red(e)hatte* in Winchester in 1366 (Keene 1985a: ii 501).

144. le Blakegate 1348 HR 76/28 '*totũ tenementũ meũ apud le Blakegate cum oĩbʒ shopis eidem adiacentibʒ & suis ptiñ in eadē pochia sc̄i Micħis de Hoggenelane*'

145. le Colebrewou*s*' 1348 HR 76/72 '*Oĩa dc̄a teñ cũ placĩa vacua adiacent' vocat' le Colebrewous' . . . in pocħ sc̄i Bartħi pui in Bradstreṭ Londoñ*'

146. le Ledeneporche 1349 HR 76/138 '*toto illo teñ vocato le ledeneporche cũ domibʒ supedificat' . . . in pocħ sc̄i Augustini iuxta portam sc̄i Pauli londoñ*'

147. le Yuyhalle 1349 HR 76/178 '*toto illo teñ cũ suis ptiñ . . . in poch sc̄e Trinitaṭ pue londoñ*' . '*quod quidē teñ vocat[ur] le yuyhalle*'

148. Aerneselde 1349 HR 76/221 '*toto illo teñ cũ ptiñ vocato Aerneselde in pocħ sc̄i Petri de Wodestrete Londoñ & in foro de Westchepe*'. Either OE *ærn, ern* 'house', or OE *earn* 'eagle'; *OED* earn, *n.*[1]; erne, *n.*; *MED* ern (*n.*(1)).

149. le Horssho 1349 HR 76/262 '*totũ illud teñ meũ bracineũ cũ ptiñ vocat' le Horssho . . . in pocħ sc̄i Albani de Wodestrete*'; 1386–7 HR 114/160 '*in pochia sc̄i Albani in Wodestrete londoñ int' teñ vocat' le horssho ex pte boriali*'

150. Tymbirhous 1349 HR 76/311 '*totum illud tenementũ vocatũ Tymbirhous cũ oĩbʒ edificijs & alijs suis ptiñ . . . in Wodestrete in pochia sc̄i Micħis in Hoggenelane*'

151. la Scholdynghous, le Skaldynghous 1349 HR 77/6 '*totam illam domũ meam vocat' la Scholdynghous in pochia sc̄i Georgij de Estchepe in warda de Billynggesgate London*'; 1362 (transcript of 1330 deed), WAM 13764 '*illo teñto cũ omĩbʒ suis ptiñ . . . in pocħ sc̄i Georgij de Estchepe london quod vocat[or] le skaldynghous*'

152. le Brodegate 1349 HR 77/6 '*totũ illud teñ vocat' le Brodegate cũ kayo adiacente & oĩbʒ alijs suis ptiñ quod ħeo in pocħ sc̄i Botħi in warda de Billynggesgate London*'; 'a common name for houses' K: St Michael Cornhill; 1371 St Lawrence Old Jewry;

1372 St Christopher by the Stocks; 1381 St Margaret Bridge Street; 1385 Barbican Street.

153. Bancoꝛ̓ Inne 1349 HR 77/13 'in toto illo mesuagᵒ vocato Bancoꝛ̓ Inne'

154. Seint Nicholas Halle 1349 HR 77/189 'totū illud teñ cū ptiñ vocaꞇ seint Nicholas halle in poch sc̄i Nichi Hacun'

155. le Brewehous 1349 HR 77/219 'poch sc̄i Egidij extᵃ Crepulgate . . . quidā teñ vocatᵒ le Brewehous'; 1380–1 LMA CLC/313/L/H/001/MS25121 St Paul's Cathedral deed no. 113 'le tenem̄t apelle le Brewhous oue la Wodehawe & lalee deủs Temese oue les autꝛ̓s appᵒ tenances en Londꝛ̓s'

156. ye Hert on ȝe hoꝑ 1350–1 HR 78/93 'totum illud teñ . . . in vico vocata le fforstrete quod vocatᵃ ye hert on ȝe hoꝑ'

157. Pauedehalle 1350–1 HR 78/238 'totū illud teñ meū vocatᵖ Pauedehalle . . . sitū est in pochia sc̄i Barthi ꝑui Londoñ'

158. le Wachouce c. 1350 LMA CLA/007/EM/02/B/029 Bridge House Deed 'totū illud mesuagᵒ quod ħeo in poch Sc̄ Nichi ad Maceꞇꞇ Londoñ vocᵖ le wachouce'

159. Mayden en la hope 1350 Letter-Book F fo ccxxxvii 'Itm̄ de Rogerᵖ Brewere atte Mayden en la Hope'

160. Gysors Halle 1350 HR 78/248 'totū illud teñ meū cū celarᵖ solarᵖ shopis & omībȝ suis ptiñ vocatᵖ Gysors halle quod ħeo in poch sc̄e Mildrede virḡis de Bredestꝛ̓ Londoñ'. Owned by John Gisors, K.

161. le Lamƀ atte hoope 1351–2 HR 79/2 'vno tenemento vocatᵖ le Lamƀ atte Hoope situatᵖ in vico de Tamysestꝛ̓ iuxᵃ Oystregate Londoñ'

162. le Bele on the hoꝑ 1353–4 HR 81/19 'de omībȝ teñ cum omībȝ suis ptiñ vocatis le Bele on the hoꝑ . . . in pochia sc̄i Leonardi de Estchepe Londoñ'; 'in poch sc̄i Edī in lumbardestret londoñ in langebournewarde vnū teñ vocatᵖ le Taūne atte Belle'; 1380 HR 109/73 'totum illud teñ meū qd inħito in pochia sc̄i Edmundi in lumbardestrete londoñ in langeburnewarde & vnū teñ vocᵖ le Tauerne atte Belle & septem shopas adiacentes tenemento meo quod inħito in pochia ꝑ̓dcā'

163. Beuereshous or Benereshous 1354 LMA CLA/007/EM/02/G/045 'vno mesuagio cū suis ptiñ in Suthewerk vocatᵖ Beuereshous'

164. le Taborer 1354 TNA C 66/243 m 7 'vnū mesuagiū cum ptiñ in pochia sc̄i Botulphi extᵃ Aldrichesgate in suburbio Londoñ quod quondam fuit Wiꞇꞇi de Gaytoñ dc̄i le Taborer'

165. atte None 1355 LMA CLA/024/01/02/008 Plea & Mem A 7 m. 3b 'Joħes le Brewere atte None'

166. le Harpe [1355 LMA CLA/024/01/02/008 Plea & Mem A 7 m. 6b '*Margeria atte Cocke Alicia atte Harpe*']; 1383–4 HR 112/62 '*toto illo teñ cum ptiñ . . . in vico de Cornhułł in pochia sc̄i xp̄ofori londoñ situat'ppe teñ vocatū le Harpe*'

167. le Depeceler 1355–6 HR 83/58 '*totū illud teñ meū vocatū le Depeceler siue le Melle atte hope . . . in vico vocat'Tamysestret'in pochia sc̄i Michis apud Ripam Regine*'

168. le Melle atte hope, le Mulne on the hope 1355–6 HR 83/58 '*totū illud teñ meū vocatū le Depeceler siue le Melle atte hope . . . in vico vocat'Tamysestret' in pochia sc̄i Michis apud Ripam Regine*'; HR 98/78 1371–2 '*de quodam teñ cum suis ptiñ situat' in pochia sc̄i Bothi ext^a Bisshopesgate Londoñ vocat' le Mulne on the hope*'

169. Anketynesselde 1355–6 HR 83/89 '*illius selde vocat'Anketynesselde in Westchepe in pochia b̄te Marie de arcubʒ London*'. Held by Anketin le Mercer in 1269, also known as Anketil de Auverne (Keene 2006: 133; see *Long Seld*). Old Norse *Arnketil* + diminutive suffix.

170. Horshed 1356 Letter-Book G fo l (ie 50) '*in poch sc̄i vedast in warda de ffarndoñ londoñ quod quidem teñ vocatū est horshed & saraʒineshed*'; 1369–70 HR 96/54 '*toto illo teñ cū ptiñ vocato le horsheued situat'in pochia sc̄i Martini infra Ludgate London*'

171. Saraʒineshed, le Sareʒynesheued 1356 Letter-Book G fo l (ie 50) '*in poch sc̄i vedast in warda de ffarndoñ londoñ quod quidem teñ vocatū est horshed & saraʒineshed*'; 1380 HR 109/73 '*totū teñ meū vocatū le Sareʒynesheued & vnam shopam cū solar' sup̄edific'vocat'Cornershoppe dc̄o teñ adiacent'ad finem venelle sc̄i Clement̨e*'; 1385–6 HR 114/118 '*in vico de ffridaystrete in pochia sc̄i Mathei Ap̄łi londoñ . . . quamdam tab̄nam vocatam le Saraʒyneshed ex pte occidentłi*'

172. Bakkewellehalle 1356 Letter-Book G fo l (ie 50) '*int̨ dictam capella Gyhalle contiguam v̨sus aquilonē & Bakkewellehalle v̨sus austrū*'

173. la Bole 1356–7 HR 84/64 '*tote la Tauˀne apelle la Bole en Westchepe en la poch des toutʒ seintʒ de honylane en Loundr̨s . . . la quele mansioñ est assis enlautre entre la dite eglise des toutʒ seintʒ v̨s le West & la Tauˀne appellee atte Goot v̨s lest̨*'; 1390 LMA CLA/024/01/02/31 Plea & Mem A 30 m. 3v '*in pochia Om̄i Sc̄oǫ de honylane . . . vnâ domū vocat' le Caban . . . dicit qđ p̄dict' Caban est p̄cella p̄dicte domus vocate Bole on the hope*'

174. ffeytishalle 1357–8 HR 85/40 '*in poch sc̄i Andr̨ sup Cornhułł londoñ videlicet in longitudine int' teñ quondam vocatū ffeytishalle ex pte occidentali . . . & teñ . . . ex pte orientali vocatū la Blakehalle*'

175. la fforge 1357 HR 85/95 '*totū illud teñ meū vocatū la fforge cū ptiñ . . . in poch Om̄i sc̄oǫ de Grascherche*'; 1384–5 HR 112/7 1384–5 '*vnū tenementū voc' le fforge . . . situat'in vico de Bassynglane in pochia sc̄e Mildrede de Brede street Londoñ*'; 1405–6 HR 133/76 '*hospicij dc̄i Alani & Iuliane vocat' le Tabbard on the hoop̄ ex pte Austr̨ & vnam shopam eoǫdem Alani & Iuliane voc' le fforge*'

176. la Weyhous 1358 Letter-Book G fo lxxii v '*q̄ᵭ quedam domus infra Algate vocata la Weyhous iam ad terram est p̄strata*'

177. the Keye of the hoōp 1358–9 HR 86/36 '*appele the Keye of the hoōp en holboᵒne en la subur\<b\> de loundres*'; 1391–2 WAM 24567 '*teñti qᵃnd Joħis Shordich militis voc' le keyeonthehoop in Wodestreet londoñ*'

178. le Tanhous 1358–9 HR 86/115 '*totū illud teñ meū braciñ . . . cū qᵃdam domo vocat' le Tanhous . . . in la \<Meℓℓ\> in poch sc̄i Egidij extᵃ Crepelg' londoñ . . . le Tanhous cū Algijs & omībʒ vasis eidē*'

179. le Whiteselde 1362–3 HR 89/26 '*vnam seldam . . . vocantᵒ le Whiteselde*'

180. le Whitehors 1362–3 HR 89/50 '*totū p̄dc̄m tenementū nūc vocatum le Whitehors cū gardino p̄dicto cū omībʒ suis p̄tine\<\>*'

181. le Heghehous 1362–3 HR 89/65 '*teñ p̄d\<\> Joħis de Essex vocat' le heghehous. . . in p̄dictis vico & poch sc̄i Olaui*'

182. Longeentre 1361 HR 89/114 '*teñ meē quod vocataᵃ longeentre quod sit' est in garda de Bredstrete*'

183. le Helm on ye hoope 1361 HR 89/114* '*in pochia sc̄i Petri de Cornhuℓℓ & principale teñ vocatᵃ le Helm on ye Hoope*'

184. le Wynsoler 1361–2 HR 89/115 '*totū illud teñ Cū Camᵖis Coquina & latrina ita integro . . . cū magno Solarᵖ vocatᵒ le Wynsoler ac & cū vna p̄ua shopa sup dc̄m solarᵖ edificat'*'

185. la Peynt house 1361–2 HR 89/115 '*totū illud teñ sup dcām portam edificat' vocat' la Peynt house*'

186. le Thre legges 1361–2 HR 89/137 '*tota illa selda vocata le Thre legges cū domibʒ sit' edificatis & cū omībʒ alijs suis p̄tiñ . . . in Westchepe in pochia b̄e Marie de Arcubʒ in Ciuitate Londoñ*'; 1377–8 HR 106/20 '*toto illo teñ nr̄o vocat' le Threlegges in pochia b̄e Marie de Arcubʒ in Westchêp Londoñ*'

187. le Coldabbeye 1361–2 HR 89/164 '*toto illo teñ cū p̄tiñ quo ħeo . . . in Wendageyneslane vocat' le Coldabbeye*'

188. la Dragoun 1361–2 HR 89/192 '*totū illud teñ bracineū vacatū la Dragoun quod ħeo in vico de Douuegate in poch b̄te Marie de Bothawe Londoñ & totū illud teñ meū vocatū le Catfetheℓℓ in poch sc̄i Benedc̄i shorhogg Londoñ*'; 1384–5 HR 112/33 '*teñ . . . situat' iuxta le Dragoñ in Warda de Douegate in poch sc̄i Michis de Paternosterchirche in Riola london*'

189. þe Lyoun atte Dore 1362 Letter-Book G fo cviii v '*domū suam vocatam vulgarit' þe lyoun atte Dore situatam in Watlyngstret in poch omī scōᴗ de Bredstrete*'; 1366

Letter-Book G fo cxcv '*totam illam domū suam vocatam wlgarit' ye Lyoñ atte Dore situat' in Watlyngstrete in poch Oмi scōₐ in Bredestrete londoñ*'

190. le Boreshede 1362–3 HR 90/159 '*totum illud teñ cū suis ptiñ qd ħeo in Bredstret Londoñ in poch omī scōₐ vocatum le Boreshede*'; 1389–90 HR 117/136 *in toto tenemento vocat' le Boreshed . . . in vico de Grascherchestret in pochia de Omī Scōₐ de Graschurch londoñ*'

191. le Newetauerne 1364–5 HR 92/52 '*totum tenementū meū cum domibȝ suþ edificatᶒ & omībȝ ac singles juribȝ & ptiñ suis quod vocatum est le Newetauerne situatum in pochia scī Petri in Westchepe Londoñ*'

192. le Horn in the hoþ 1365–6 HR 93/139 '*domū meam braciñ vocatam le horn in the hoþ cum tribȝ schopis adiacentibȝ & solar' supedificatᶒ ac eciam duo teñ mea situata in venella vocat' Wolcylane dict' domui braciñ & shopis annexa in poch omī scōₐ Magni & omī scōₐ parui in Ropia londoñ*'

193. Bekenhᵃm 1366–7 HR 94/142 '*totū illud teñ quod dicitᵒ Bekenhᵃm in Ciuitate London cū domibȝ reddiť shopis & alijs ptiñ suis*'

194. Pulteneys In 1367–8 HR 95/99 '*oĩa tenementa mea cū reůcionibȝ & redditibȝ in Grescherchestrete & in venella scī Laurencij iuxta Pulteneys in*'

195. Suruetistour 1367–8 HR 95/99 '*Dat' londoñ in manso meo vocat' Suruetistour xvj die Augusti Anno dм Miłło Tricentesimo sexagesimo quinto*'. See McEwan (2016: no. 1074) for William Servat's seal dated 1303x1304.

196. le Cage 1367–8 HR 95/176 '*totū illud teñ vocatū le Cage cū domibȝ supedificat' et cū gardino adiacente . . . in pochia scī Miċhis de Bassyngeshawe londoñ*'

197. Littel Watte 1368 TNA C 66/278 m. 30 '*teñ situata sunt inť Cokkeslane et unū teñ vocat' teñ de Littel Watte*'; 1340 LMA CLA/024/01/02/004 Plea & Mem A 3 m. 14 '*Hugʾ atte Kocke . . . Thoм consanguiniᵒ Litelwatte*'

198. le Newin 1368–9 HR 96/218 '*vnū mesuagiū meū quod dicitᵒ le Newin in Chauncellerelane & viginti & duo cotagia eidem mesuagio iniūcta & decem cotagia in Holebourne que dicuntᵒ Ratonnesrowe*'

199. le Bal on the hop 1369–70 LMA CLC/313/L/H/001/MS25121 St Paul's Cathedral deed no. 962 '*totam domū meam bracineā cū ptinencijs vocat' le Bal on the hop in ffletstrete in pochia scī Dunstani*'

200. le Ship on the hope 1369–70 HR 97/144 '*vnū tenementū suū cum vna aula dispensatorʾ & Celarʾ sub illa aula & cum duabȝ Cameris vna garita supᵃ dīcam aula atqȝ latrina Stabulis & coquina adiacentibȝ & ptiñ suis vocat' le Ship on the Hope situat' in pochia omī Scōₐ de Bredstret in Bredstret Londoñ*'

201. le ffishous 1369–70 HR 97/173 '*in teñ cum ptiñ vocato , le ffishous situato in Bocherlane in Londoñ*'

202. Cherchegatestaůne 1369–70 HR 97/173 '*in teñ vocat' Drynkwařeswharf cum shopis celar', solar' & omībȝ suis ptiñ situat' in pochia sc̄i Magni Martiris de Briggestret Londoñ & in vno teñ cum shopis , celar' solar' & suis ptiñ vocato Cherchegatestaůne situato in pochia sc̄i Leonardi de Estchep Londoñ*'

203. Drynkwařeswharf 1369–70 HR 97/173 '*in teñ vocat' Drynkwařeswharf cum shopis celar', solar' & omībȝ suis ptiñ situat' in pochia sc̄i Magni Martiris de Briggestret Londoñ*'

204. La Holwone or Helwone 1370 WAM 26924B '*Et in Carpentr' de La Holwone Grang' feni de la Neyt faciend ad tasc' viijs'*. It is not clear if the first element of La Holwone is <Hol-> or <Hel->; the second element is *MED* won(e (n.(2)) 1.(a) 'building or structure for human residence, a house, dwelling, an abode'. I interpret this accounts entry as 'in carpentry for La Holwone haybarn of La Neyt manor' where the haybarn belongs to La Holwone, and Holwone is part of the manor of Neyt, but it may be that La Holwone and the haybarn were one and the same.

205. La Neyth 1370 WAM 26924 '*In C teguł emp̂ p g᷃ ng' feni infʳ mařiū de La Neyth iiijs'*

206. Powlesbrewerne 1370 LMA CLC/313/L/H/001/MS25121 St Paul's Cathedral deed no. 1074 '*p᷃ abatr' vne mur de pere iesq̄s a vne pe desus la terre quele mur estet a Powlesbrewerne*' (dorse, later hand '*In paroch sc̄i Gregorij*')

207. Tabard [1371 LMA CLA/024/01/02/018 Plea & Mem A 17 m. 2 '*Johs atte Tabard*']; 1381 WAM 17702 '*vocat' le Cocke vel Tabard in vico de Tothull*'; 1384 LMA CLA/024/01/02/028 Plea & Mem A 27 (i) m. 11 '*Bredstret . . . Johes hostiller atte Tabard*', m. 11v '*ffletstret . . . Joh lenhm᷃ atte Tabard*'; 1391 LMA CLA/024/01/02/031 Plea & Mem A 30 m. 5v '*la paveye de piere del tenem̂t q̂ Roƀt lyndeseye tient en Wodestret al Tabard en la poche de sient Alban*'; 1463 LMA CLC/313/L/H/001/ MS25121 St Paul's Cathedral deed no. 1123 '*totum illud teñtum suum cum shopis solar' supedificate celar' & omnibȝ alijs suis ptiñ situat' sup Cornerium vicoꝗ Regioꝗ de Watlyngstrete & ffridaystrete in pochia sc̄i Johannis Euᵃ ngeliste . . . & teñ . . . vocat' le Taberd . . . ex parte Orientł*'. There was a *Tabard* in the 1360s in Winchester (Keene 1985a: i 167, ii 501).

208. Litellonden 1371–2 HR 99/126 '*totū illud tenementū meū vocat' Litellonden cum domibȝ supedificatis gardinis adiacent' & omībȝ alijs suis ptiñ . . . in poch Om̄i Sc̄oꝗ dict' atte Walle in Warda de Bradstrete Londoñ*'; 1388 HR 116/123 '*totum teñ meū vocatū litellondoñ cum domibȝ supedificatte gardinis ad iacentibȝ . . . in pochia om̄i Sc̄oꝗ dict' atte walle in warda de Bradstret londoñ*'; 1391 Letter-Book H fo cclxiii '*lego Rič fīlio meo seniori .xl. łī st'ling' et balenc' meas cum le bem et cū omībȝ ponderibȝ dc̄e balancie ptinentibȝ cum vno auncer apud litel londoñ*'

209. le Longeporche 1373 HR 101/102 '*viam regiam de Goderomlane ex pte orientł Et extendit se a vico regio de West chepe v̆sus austrū vsqȝ ad teñ vocat' le Longeporche*'

210. Paṭnosṭrent 1374 TNA C 54/212 m. 24d '*mesuag^r m & decem shopas cum ptiñ vocaṭ paṭnosṭrent in pochia sċi Andree de holbo$^\sigma$ ne ext^a barram vetis templi londoñ*'

211. le Harowe on ye houpe 1374–5 HR 102/16 '*de teñ nr^d vocaṭ le harowe on ye houpe in ffletstret in suburbio Londoñ*'

212. le Catfithele 1374–5 HR 102/55 '*in shopa cont^a le Catfithele*' (location unspecified); 1366–7 Letter-Book G fo cxcii v '*hospiciū vocatū la Sterre on the hoope cum domibʒ supedificaṭ in pocḣ Oṁi Sċõʒ de Bredstrete londoñ . . . iuxta le Catfithele*'. MED fithele (n.)).

213. Blosmeshyn 1374–5 HR 102/120 '*totū illud tenementū meū cum domibʒ supedificaṭ ac cum libʒ introitibʒ & exitibʒ eidm̄ teñ spectantibʒ p magnam portam teñ annexi vocaṭ Blosmeshyn & cum omībʒ alijs suis ptiñ quod hm̄ in venella & pochia sċi Laurencij in Judaismo Londoñ*'

214. le Huse 1375–6 HR 103/72 '*totam illam seldā meam vocatam le huse cum shopis solarijs stallis cistis & armoriolis cū omībʒ suis ptiñ in pochia ḃte Marie de arcubʒ in Westcheṗ londoñ*'; 1375–6 HR 103/76 '*in tota illa selda vocata le huse cum shopis solar^j staḻl cistis & armorioḻ cum omībʒ suis ptiñ in pochia ḃe Marie de Arcubʒ Westcheṗ londoñ*'. Known as *le Leeg* 1389 (Keene and Harding 1987 [1994]).

215. le Irenhope 1375–6 HR 103/136 '*in toto illo teñ vocato le Irenhope cum omībʒ suis ptiñ . . . in pocḣ Sċe Marie Magdalene iux^a Oldefisshstrete londoñ*'

216. la Worm on the hope 1375 HR 103/175 '*in pocḣ sċi Barthi ꝓui ꝑdicṭ in warda de Bradestrete ꝑdicṭ Que quidm̄ duo teñ ꝑdicta vnī videḻt teñ est vocaṭ la Worm on the hope*'. MED worm (n.) 1. (a) (b)) 'dragon'.

217. le Culuer on the hope 1375–6 HR 103/233 '*de teñ meo bracineo cū ptiñ quondā vocato le Culuer on the hope & modo le swan on ꝑe hope nuncupato in Thamistrete in pocḣ sċi Dunsta< > in Est londoñ*'. OED culver, *n.^{1}* 'dove'.

218. la Rauen 1375–6 HR 103/249 '*qd̄ omēs ꝑd̄ce shope cū suis ptiñ vna cū r̊u̇sione taḃne vocate la Rauen . . . in eadm̄ pocḣ ḃte Marie*'; 1394–5 HR 123/58 '*et totū teñ meū cum shopis celar^j solar^j & suis ptiñ vocatū le Rauen in pochia ḃte Marie Magdalene in Milkstret londoñ*'

219. Crachemille 1375–6 TNA E 40/2559 '*in Estsmythfeld suṗ le To$^\sigma$ hill in Côm midḋ & in pocḣ sċi Bothi ex^a Algate Londoñ & eccḻie dċe le whit chapeḻt iḃm . . . In duobʒ molendinis . . . vocaṭ Crachemille & in heremitag̉ cum ptiñ suis vocaṭ Swannes nesṭ*'. OED cratch *n.^{1}* 4. 'hurdle, wooden grating'.

220. Swannes Nest 1375–6 TNA E 40/2559 '*in Estsmythfeld suṗ le To$^\sigma$ hill in Côm midḋ & in pocḣ sċi Bothi ex^a Algate Londoñ & eccḻie dċe le whit chapeḻt iḃm . . . In duobʒ molendinis . . . vocaṭ Crachemille & in heremitag̉ cum ptiñ suis vocaṭ Swannes nesṭ*'

221. Eueshammesyn 1376 LMA CLA/040/02/2 (old ref Miscellaneous Roll FF) m. 37 *'vnū teñ vocat' Eueshammesyn cū gardinis & alijs p tiñ suis . . . in pochia sc̄i Dunstani in ffletestret in suburbio Londoñ in vico vocato ffaytereslane'*

222. Bacūnysyn 1377–8 HR 106/67 *'totū illud teñ . . . situatū in poch sc̄i Sepulcri ex^r Neugate vocat' Bacūnysyn'*

223. le Vernycle 1377–8 HR 106/76 *'vn tenement b^ur cine apelle le vernycle oue vne schope & vne soler aioignantʒ & toutʒ lo^ur app^ur tenantʒ assis en Bradstrete en la poche de Seynt Bartilmew le petite en Loundres'.* MED vernicle (n.)) 'face of Christ', from the sudarium of St Veronica.

224. le Thoroughous 1377–8 HR 106/108 *'quidm̄ teñ cum p tiñ vocant^ur le Thoroughous v̊sus Shetb^ur one lane apud le lamb on the hop'.* Cf. Salzman (1952: 104) 1420 '[Carriage of 6 stones called] thurghes'; *OED* through, *n.1* 3. *a*1350 'large slab of stone'. There was an earlier meaning in Old English of 'throughpipe, gutter, channel' (*OED* through, *n.1.* 1.) which *OED* warns 'only in Old English', although it might be the operative sense here.

225. la Redebrewehous 1377–8 HR 106/142 *'in venella & pochia sc̄i Laurencij in Iudaismo Londoñ . videlt de teñ cum suis p tiñ quod p aliquos vocat^ur la Redebrewehous & p aliquos vocat^ur la Rededore'*

226. le Dolfyn on the hop̂ 1377–8 HR 106/145 *'in teñ cum p tiñ . . . voc' le Dolfyn on the hop̂ in pochia sc̄i Magni de Briggestret londoñ'*

227. Mayde on the hop̂ 1378–9 HR 107/110 *'tres shopas cum domibʒ supedifica- tis vna cum alijs domibʒ edificatis sup introitum tenementi vocati Mayde on the Hop̂ . . . in pochia ƀte Marie de Colchurche londoñ'*

228. le Mechele 1379 HR 108/13 *'totū teñ meū cum domibʒ supedificatis & om̄ibʒ suis p tiñ . . . situm in pochia Oīm sc̄oᴘ vocat' le Mechele Londoñ'*

229. le Hood on the hoop 1379 HR 108/13 *'teñ vocatū le hood on the hoop ex p te orientɫi & vicum regm̄ de la Roperye Londoñ ex p te australi; 1384 TNA C 145/232 'j peir' Garnettᴘ pur un plum en le Brewhous a le hood sur le hoop poisantʒ xvj ℔ de fier'*

230. le Pecok on the houp 1380–1 HR 109/65 *'totū illud teñ bracineū vocatū Le Pecok on the houp cum domibʒ supedific' & suis p tiñ . . . in pochia sc̄i Bothi ex^ur Aldrichesgate in suburbio londoñ'*

231. le Swerd on the hop̂ 1380 LMA CLA/024/01/02/024 Plea & Mem A 23 m. 2v *'Thomas hostiller morans in ffletestret apud le swerd on the hop̂';* 1382 LMA CLA/024/01/02/026 Plea & Mem A 25 m. 6 *'ad domū Thome Taillour hostiller manent' apud le Swerd on the hoop̂ in ffletstret'*

232. Lyncolnesynne 1380 BL Cotton MS Faustina B VIII fo 192 *'totū hospiciū nr̄m vocat' lyncolnesynne in poch̄ sc̄i Andree in holbo°ne in suburb london̄ situat' cū oīb3 messuagiis schopis gardinis & curtilagiis eidē hospicio adiacentib3 '*

233. le Glene on the hoop̄ 1381 HR 110/1 *'totū ten̄ meū bracineū vocatū le Glene on the hoop̄ quod h̄eo in poch̄ia sc̄i Magni apud Pontem London̄'*; 1394–5 HR 123/58 *'totū ten̄ meū bracineū vocat' le Glene on the hoop̄ cum duab3 shopis & suis ptiñ situat' in poch̄ sc̄i Mich̄is apud Quenhethe london̄ '*. MED glene (n.) 'sheaf'.

234. Lawestenemēt 1381 WAM 17702 *'lawestenemēt cū ptiñ in vico de Tothull'*

235. le Barge 1382 LMA CLA/040/02/3 m. 2 *'no°̄ p le barge in bokelesbury'*. Chew & Kellaway (1973: 165) say that this marginal note is in a later hand, but it does not look very much later to me.

236. le Cherch̄ on the hoop̄ 1383–4 HR 112/4 *'totius ten̄ sui voc̃' le Cherch̄ on the hoop̄ in poch̄ia sc̄i Mich̄is ad bladū in Chepe London̄'*

237. le Croune 1383–4 HR 112/37 *'totū tenementū meū vocatū le Croune cum domib3 solariis Celariis & omīb3 suis ptiñ . . . in poch̄ia Omī Scōa꞉ sup solar̃' London'*

238. atte Sadel 1384 LMA CLA/024/01/02/028 Plea & Mem A 27 (i) m. 11v *'fflet-stret . . . Joh̄ Cok҆e atte Sadel'*

239. atte Boor 1384 LMA CLA/024/01/02/028 Plea & Mem A 27 (i) m. 11v *'fflet-stret . . . Thom̄ kirton̄ atte Boor'*

240. Place del Estling҆e 1384 TNA C 145/232 *'place del Estling҆e a le stielwharf'*

241. la Olderente 1384 TNA C 145/232 *'j stoklok҆e en la Olderente de la stielwharf p°̄ j maison de j frowe illeᵃ̂s'*

242. Lostiel del Gascoign 1384 TNA C 145/232 *'lostiel del Gascoign encontre Stielwharfgate'*, *'lostiel de les Gascoignes'*

243. Lostiel Toryn 1384 TNA C 145/232 *'ij cliketlokkes p°̄ lostiel Toryn oue le h̄neys'*

244. del Tylhous 1384 TNA C 145/232 *'j veil cerur̃' p°̄ le hoeux del Tylhous a le stylwharf'*

245. le maison Halstede 1384 TNA C 145/232 *'le maison halstede en Oldefisshstrete'*

246. le maison̄ apele Deyhous 1384 TNA C 145/232 *'le maison̄ apele deyhous q̄ fuit a Ric̃' lyons en le Ropie'*

247. la Selde Coronata, le Crowneselde 1384–5 HR 113/1 *'ten̄ mea in foro de Westchepe london̄ vocata la Selde coronata'*; 1394–5 HR 123/101 *'totam illam seldam cum omīb3 suis domib3 shopis solarijs & edificijs . . . vocatam le Crowneselde situat' in le Mercerie in Westchepe in poch̄ia beate Marie de Arcub3 london̄'*

248. Colchestrestauˀne 1385 WAM 17706 '*duas shopas cū solarˀ supedificatᶒ cū suis ptiñ vocatˀ the Cornersshoppes situatˀ in villꞏ Westmˀ pˀdictˀ iuxta mesuagˀ siue tabernā vocatˀ Colchestrestauˀne*'

249. le Steelyerde 1385 TNA C 54/225 m. 27 '*apud le Steelyerde in pochia oᵐi scōⱥ magna iuxta le heywharf & warda de douuegate*'

250. Estlandia 1385 TNA C 66/319 m. 2 '*quoddam teñ situatum supˀ Cornelio cuius-dam venelle < > Wyndegooslane intˀ eandem venellam et magnam aulam de Estlandia quod quidem teñ fuit Johis Norhamptoñ de londoñ*'

251. le Herteshed on the hoop 1385–6 HR 114/74 '*in toto illo teñ bracineo vocato le herteshed on the hoop cum shopa ante situatˀ cum solariis supedificatˀ & suis ptiñ situatˀ in lumbardestrete in pochia scī Edmundi Regis londoñ*'

252. le Tonne 1385-6 HR 114/112 '*del Tauerne ore appelle le Tonne & iadis appelle atte Gote oue les maisons desusedifies les shopes oue touȝ les autres appurtinantȝ en la poche de Touȝ seyntȝ de honylane en Westchepe de loundres*'

253. le Bere on the hoop̂ 1385–6 HR 114/118 '*in toto illo mesuagio cum shopa eidem annexa & cū solarˀ & Celarˀ ac cum oībȝ suis ptiñ vocatˀ le Bere on the hoop̂ . . . situantᵃ in vico de ffridaystrete in pochia scī Mathei Apłi londoñ . . . & quamdam tabnam vocatam le Saraȝyneshed ex pte occidentłiˀ*'

254. the Cheker on the hope 1385–6 HR 114/161 '*totū illud teñ meu vulgaritˀ modo vocatū the Cheker on the hope cum domibȝ supedificatis & omïbȝ alijs suis ptiñ . . . in pochia scī Dionisij Bakchirche londoñ*'. There was a *la Cheker* in Winchester in 1367 (Keene 1985a: ii 501).

255. le Potte on the hope 1386–7 HR 115/7 '*toto tenemento nrð bracineo modo vocato le Potte on the hope . . . situatˀ in Algatestret in pochia scī Andrˀ supˀ Cornhułl londoñ*'

256. le Cornerhalle 1386–7 HR 115/43 '*vnū teñ angularˀ vocatū le Cornerhalle in pochia scē Trinitatis pue in Warda Vinetrie londoñ . . . intˀ teñ . . . antiquitus vocatū le Ryngedhałl ex pte orientłiˀ*'

257. le Walsherente 1387–8 HR 116/73 '*vnā mansionê . . . simul cum vna cloaca in le Walsherente in pochia sancti Petri de Westchepe londoñ*'

258. le Caban 1390 LMA CLA/024/01/02/31 Plea & Mem A 30 m. 3v '*in pochia Oᵐi Scōⱥ de honylane . . . vnâ domū vocatˀ le Caban . . . dicit qd pˀdictˀ Caban est pcella pˀdicte domus vocate Bole on the hope*'

259. le Garland on the hoop̂ 1390–1 HR 118/60 '*quoddᵃm teñ bracineū vocatū le Garland on the hoop̂ cum gardino & omïbȝ suis ptiñ siue vasis & vtensilibȝ situatˀ in pochia sancti Andree de Estchep londoñ*'

260. the Cristofre on ye hope 1390–1 HR 118/65 'totū illud teñ suū bracineū modo uulgarit' vocat' the Cristofre on ye hope . . . in pochia sancti Michis ad bladum londoñ'

261. le Voute 1390–1 HR 118/71 'vnū teñ cū domibȝ supedificatis & suis ptiñ vocat' le Voute in poch sc̄i sepulcͬ in Westsmythefeld in suburbio londoñ'

262. Trumpouresynne 1390–1 HR 118/86 'totum illud teñ nr̄m vocatū Trompouresynne cum duabȝ shopis & vna mansione eidem contiguis & annexis . . . in pochia sc̄e Trinitatę parū londoñ'; 1396–7 HR 123/113 'in toto illo tenemento meo vocato Trumpouresynne cum duabȝ shopis & vna mansione eidem contiguis & annexis'

263. Godschepsceld 1390–1 HR 119/30 'om̄ia t̄ras teñta siue seldas cū solarͬ & sub-celarijs qui hent ex legato p̄dicti Johis Mangutt in le vnicorne in Westchepe in londoñ quod quondam appellabatͬ Godschepsceld in pochia ƀe Marie de Arcubȝ'

264. le Vnicorne 13901 HR 119/30 'om̄ia t̄ras teñta siue seldas cū solarͬ & subcelarijs qui hent ex legato p̄dicti Johis Mangutt in le vnicorne in Westchepe in londoñ quod quondam appellabatͬ Godschepsceld in pochia ƀe Marie de Arcubȝ'

265. ffermory 1391 LMA CLA/024/01/02/031 Plea & Mem A 30 m. 5v 'domū vocat' ffermory apud ffreAustyns londoñ . . . deux gable crestes del ffermorye des ditȝ ffreres'

266. Montieofysyn 1391 TNA C 66/332 m. 11 'vnū hospiciū vocat' Montieofysyn cum ptiñ in Ciuitate londoñ infra portam de Algate'

267. le Walssheman sur le hooꝓ 1391 Letter-Book H fo cclviii 'ad hospiciū vocatum le Walssheman sur le hooꝓ in ffletestrete in pochia sañcti martini exͬ ludgate in sub-urbio londoñ'

268. le Crane 1390–1 HR 119/74 'teñ vocat' le Crane in pochia Sc̄i Nichi ad macel-las londoñ'; 1393 LMA CLC/313/L/H/001/MS25121 St Paul's Cathedral deed no. 941 'totam illam domū nram̀ bracineam vocat' le Crane on the hooꝓ in ffletestrete in pochia sc̄i Dunstani'

269. le Sonne on the hooꝓ 1390–1 HR 119/90 'vnam shopam cum domibȝ supedi-ficatis vnam Taƀnam vocatam le Sonne on the hooꝓ q̄ vocabatͬ le horn on the hooꝓ . . . sita sunt in Westchepe in pochia sancti Vedasti londoñ'

270. le Griffoñ 1391–2 HR 120/49 'quoddam tenementū vocat' le Griffoñ . . . situat' in pochia sc̄i Vedasti in Westchepe in Warda de ffarndoñ londoñ'

271. Leggesaleye 1391–2 HR 120/69 'om̄ia teñta mea vocata leggesaleye situata in pochia sc̄i Barthi pui londoñ'

272. leȝ Thre Nonnes 1391–2 HR 120/69 'totū teñ meū bracineū vocatū leȝ thre Nonnes situatū in dicta pochia sc̄i x̄pofori'

273. le Lampe on the hoop̄ 1391–2 HR 120/91 '*totum teñ meū bracineū vocatum le lampe on the hoop̄ cum omībȝ domibȝ celař solař eidem adiacenť . . . in pochia Sĉe Ethelburge infra Bisshopesgate londoñ*'

274. le Stuwehous 1391–2 HR 120/130 '*vnū teñ vocať the Brewehous atte Cok on the hoop̄ et aliud teñ vocať le Stuwehous que simul iacent in pochia omī sĉoᴣ pua in le Ropie in Warda de Dowgate londoñ*'

275. le Blakerente 1392–3 HR 121/200 '*omīa teñ mea cum omībȝ suis ptiñ vocať le Blakerente situať iuxta & anneẍ Distaflane in pochia sĉi Augustini iuxta Portam sĉi Pauli londoñ*'

276. Grymmesbiestenement 1393–4 HR 122/19 '*totam teñ meū cum shopis & omībȝ alijs suis ptiñ vocať Grymmesbiestenement in Tourstret in pochia Omī Sĉoᴣ de Berkyngchirche londoñ*'

277. le Mot 1394 TNA 136/85 m.39 (old foliation) m.5/10 (modern foliation) '*vnū mesuagiū cū ptiñ vocať le mot in villa de Westñı̃ cū tribȝ cotagiis*'

278. le Kyngesaleye 1394–5 HR 123/40 '*de teñ meis cum omībȝ suis ptiñ vocať le kyngesaleye que ħeo in p̓dĉa pochia sĉi Stepħi*'

279. Topclyuesyn 1394–5 HR 123/58 '*et illas tres shopas quas ħeo in ffletstret . . . situať ex pte orientali de Topclyuesyn*'

280. la Stoorhous̓ 1395 LMA CLC/313/L/D/001/MS25125/032 '*Iť in vna sera ad ostiñ de la stoorhous̓ iuxˣ Powleswharf*'

281. le Panyer del hoop̄ 1395–6 HR 123/115 '*dun Brewhous en Graschirchestrete qest appelle le panyer del hoop̄*'

282. le Blakehors on the hope 1395–6 LMA CLC/313/L/H/001/MS25121 St Paul's Cathedral deed no. 852 '*totum teñ vocatum le Blakehors on the hope in ffletestrete in suburbia londoñ cum shopis domibȝ & omībȝ alijs suis ptiñ*'

283. le Holebole 1396 LMA DL/C/B/004/MS09171/001 fo 379 '*in Taƀna vocať le holebole in chepe*'

284. Greysyn 1396 TNA C 136/88 m.8 '*de mařio suo de Portpole in holburne vocať Greysyn*'

285. le Katerine on the hope 1396–7 HR 125/31 '*totum illud capitale teñ nsm̃ seu hospiciū vocatū le Katerine on the hope cū omībȝ suis Canřis domibȝ & solarijs . . . in Wodestrete in pochia sĉi Albani Londoñ simul situať inť teñ Rog̓ i Elys quondam vocatū le Horssho*'

286. le Herteshorne 1396–7 HR 125/70 '*illud teñ Bracineū cōiť vocať le Herteshorne situate in poch sĉi Petri sup Cornnhuťt londoñ*'

287. le Lampettes 1397 TNA C 145/261 no. 22 / 107 'shopa Cam̃a Solar̃ & gardinû vocat' le lampettes . . . situat' in pochia sc̄i Botḥi ext˄ algate in suburbio londoñ'

288. le Ship onthehop̃ 1397 TNA C 145/261 no. 22 / 107 'vnū teñ vocat' le ship onthe-hop̃ . . . situat' in pochia sc̄i Botḥi ext˄ algate in suburbio londoñ'

289. le Wollesak onthehop̃ 1397 TNA C 145/261 no. 22 / 107 'vnū al̃ teñ voc' le wollesak onthehop̃ . . . situat' in pochia sc̄i Botḥi ext˄ algate in suburbio londoñ'

290. Stonerente 1397 TNA C 145/259 no.109 / 16 'quoddam teñ vocatum Stonerente in pochia sc̄i Laurencij in Iudaismo infra Ciuitatem'

291. le fflourdelys 1397-8 HR 126/93 'teñti mei vocati le fflourdelys in dc̄a pochia sc̄i Vedasti'

292. le George on the hop̃e 1397–8 HR 126/62 'vno alio teñ . . . vocat' le George on the hop̃e situat' in pochia sc̄i dunstani iuxta Turrim londoñ'; 14012 LMA CLC/313/ L/H/001/MS25121 St Paul's Cathedral deed no. 184 'vnū tenementū cum suis ptiñ vocatum le George sup le hoop̃ situat' in pochia sancti Dionisij de Bakchirche londoñ in warda de langeborñ'

293. Spaldyngporche 13978 HR 126/93 'illis tribȝ shopis cū solar̃ sup edificat' & omĩbȝ suis ptiñ quas ḥeo infra Spaldyngporche in Vet' i Escambio in eadm̃ pochia sc̄i Augustini'

294. le Grenegate 1398 (1407–8) HR 135/71 'vni⁹ tēnti voc' le Grenegate situat' in poch Sc̄i Andree sup Cornhull londoñ'

APPENDIX 2

HOUSE NAMES FROM WILLIAM PORLOND'S BOOK, 1418–40

Names of buildings taken from William Porlond's Book, 1418–40, London Guildhall Library CLC/L/BF/A/021/MS05440

Headword	House name	Parish	Folio
Angel	atte aungett	in pochia sc̄i michis Qwenhithe	37v
	atte Aungett in ffleestrete		38
	atte Aungett	in poch sc̄e Ethelburge iux^ᵃ bisshopisgate	66
Ax	ex^ᵃ Algate . . . atte Ax iḃm		29v
	atte ax yn Aldermannebury		149
	atte ax yn seynt John strete		149
	atte Ax yn holbo^ᵒne		160
Ball	atte Ball ad macett		31
	atte Batt in the olde Cheaunge		50v
	le Batt	in poch sc̄i Andr̄ in holbo^ᵒne	65v
Basket	atte Basket in ffanchyrch strete ap^d le Crosse in Chepe att	en la poch de toutʒ seyntʒ de Stanyng	10
	Baskett		28v
	ap^d Baskett atte Byllyngysgate		29v
Bear	atte Bere in seint Clementislane		37v
	atte bere yn Aldrisshgatestrete		200
	atte Bere w^t owte Algate		253
Bell	atte Belle iux^ᵃ Aldrisshgate		1
	le Belle en Redecrouchestrete	en la poche de seint Gyles	10
	iux^ᵃ le Bett apud Qwenehythe		30v
	atte Bett in Margaretepatyns lane		37v
	atte Belle extra Bisshoppisgate		37v

Headword	House name	Parish	Folio
	atte Bell in poch Scī Andree holboᵘ ne		31
	atte Belle in vico Scī Johannis		44
	atte Bell	*in pochia sĉi Dionisʼ in ffanchirchestrete*	65
	atte Belle wᵗ outen Algate		86
	atte Belle yn philipotlane		149v
	atte Belle yn Colmonstrete		150
	atte Belle ny baynardescastell		160
	atte Belle atte Toᵘ hill		265
Bell called Savage's Inn	*atte belle vocᵒ Savagis Inne in ffletestrete*		44v
Bell Crowned	*atte Belle croûned*	*yn þe pessh of seynt andrew yn Estchepe*	187
Bell & Dolphin	*atte Belle & dolphyn exᵃ Bysshopysgate*		30
Bell & St Peter	*atte Belle & Seynt Petʼ atte Toᵘ hill*		233v
Bishop/Bishop's Head	*atte Bisshopp̄ or els þe Bisshopeshede wᵗ outen þe barres yn holboᵘ ne*		150
Black Hoop	*atte Blake hopp̄ yn Cornhīll*		162
Black Horse	*atte blake hors yn ffletestrete*		150v
Bolt & Tun	*atte bolt and þe tonne yn ffletestrete*		150
Bull	*le Bole apud Byllyngysgate*		29
	atte Bole yn holboᵘ ne		161
	atte Bole on þe Toᵘ hill		187
Cardinal's Hat	*atte Cardenalyshatte apud Byllyngysgate iuxᵃ Cristofre*		29v
	atte Cardenalishatt iuxᵃ hospitʼ sancte Marie exᵃ Bischopgate		44v
Castle	*in ffletestrete . . . apud Castell ibđm*		28v
	apud Castrû in bysshopysgate strete		30

Headword	House name	Parish	Folio
	iux Castrû ap^d Seynt Mary somcete		30
	atte Castell in Woodstrete		51
	yn Sholane ageyns þ^e Castell		114
Cellar	*a le Celer apud finem de Bredstrete*		28
	apud le Celler' iux Reuderesgate atte Horspole in Smethefeld		50v
	apud le Celler' in paťnosťrowe		50v
	atte celer yn seynt laurence lane		121
Chequer	*in domo henr' Grene atte Shekyr in Estechepe*		36v
	atte Cheker	*in poch Oṁi Scôҩ Stanyng in ffanchirchestrete*	72v
Chequer & Lamb	*atte Cheker w^t þe lambe yn ffancherchestrete*		224
Chough	*atte Chowgh < > Storhoues atte Byllyngesgate iux signū Cristofori*		50
Christopher	*atte Cristophr' in Goldynglane*	*in poch Scī Egidij apud Crepulgate*	44
	atte Byllyngesgate iux signū Cristofori		
	apud le Cristofr' apud Baynardyscastell		50v
	atte Xp̄ofre	*in pochia scī Gregorij*	65
	atte Xp̄ofr'	*in poch scī michis ad bladum*	65v
	atte Cristophore yn ffancherche strete		85v
	atte Cristophore ny seynt martyns þe g und		120v
	atte Cristophore w^t outen tempelbarr'		150v
	atte Cristophore yn aldrisshgatestrete		233
Cock	*atte Cok*	*en poche de seynte Margaret Pateyns*	1
	atte Cok iux Dowgate	*in poch oṁi scôҩ mag^s*	1v
	atte Cok	*in poch scī Andree Cornhull*	1v

Headword	House name	Parish	Folio
	atte Cok	in pocħ sĉi Micħis Qwenhithe	1v
	apud Cok in Wodestrete		28v
	apᵈ le Cok iuxᵃ sĉm magnū		29
	atte Cok apud lymestretende		29v
	atte Cok in ffynkyslane iuxᵃ seynt antonys		30v
	atte Cok infra Ludgate		30v
	atte Cok exᵃ Bischopgate		31v
	atte Cok	in pocħ sĉi Joħis ʒakarie	31v
	apud le Cok in Cornhyłł	in pochia sĉi xᵽofori	36v
	apud le Cok exᵗᵃ ledenhalle		36v
	atte Cok iuxᵃ frēs augustiñ		36v
	atte Cok in holboᵒ́ne		38
	domo atte Cok ad finem yvylane		40
	atte Cok	in pocħ sĉi Nicħi ad Macellas	50v
	atte Cok ad finem Goterlane		51
	le Cok in Estchepe		65v
	atte Cok	in pocħ sĉi Dionis' in ffanchirchestrete	65v
	atte Cok in Colmanstrete		65v
	atte Cok	in pochia sĉe Mildrede in Pultria	65v
	atte Cok	in pocħ sĉe Marie Wolchirche	72v
	atte Cok in Trillemillestrete		72v
	atte Cok in Goldynglane		73
	atte Cok ageyns ffrerˀ menoᵒ́s		86
	atte Cok wᵗ Inne Algate		86
	atte Cok ny crouchedffreres		114v
	atte Cok ny holbornecrosse		149
	atte Cok yn crokedlane		149
	atte Cok ny þe ende of Cecolane wᵗ outen Newgate		150v
	atte Cok yn Toᵒ́ strete		160
	atte Cok yn Bassyngehawe		161
	atte Cok yn Tempstrete		161v
	atte Cok yn Brechonelane		187
	atte Cok yn aldrissħgatestrete		224
Cock & Bell	atte Cok & le Belle iuxᵃ holboᵒ́necrosse		31v

Headword	House name	Parish	Folio
	atte Cok & belle yn philipotteslane		162
Cock & Star	atte Cok & sterr' yn Cornhill		84
Coop	atte Cowpe in Crokedlane		31v
	atte Coupe	in poch Scī Nichi ad macellas	44v
	atte Coupe	in poch de Shordissh	45
	atte Coupe wᵗ outen ludgate		84v
	atte coupe beside wolkeye		113v
	atte Cowpe besyde londoñ wall		161v
Cony	atte Cony yn Conyhooplane		114
	atte Cony yn Cornhell		265
Copedon Hall	atte Copedoñ hall	in poch scī Dunstani in oriente infra Tourstrete	65v
Corner Cellar	atte Cornerceler' de Bredestrete		51
Cow Head	apud Cowhede in Chepe		28v
Crane	atte Crane in le fflesshamles		43v
	atte Crane yn ffletstrete		233
Cross	atte Crosse yn Tourstrete		113v
Crown	atte Crowne exᵗᵃ ffratres minores		1v
	atte Croune iuxᵗ le horspooll in Smethefeld		1v
	atte Crowne exᵗ Byschopesgate		30
	atte Croune	in poch sc̄i Dionis'	52
	atte Croune	in poch sc̄i Egidij extra Crepulgate	65v
Culver	atte Colver' yn ffancherch strete		85v
Dagger	atte dagger in Chepe		28v
Dolphin	le Dolphyn ad eccliam sc̄i magni		28,
	atte Dolphyñ ny londoñ Bregge		233
	atte dolphyn	in poch sc̄e Mᵉ Magḍ Oldefysch strete	30v
	atte dolphyn ny seynt Annes		86
	atte dolffyn ny Aldrisshgate		162
Dragon	atte dragoñ saunʒ Bisshopgate		1
	atte Dragoñ in Colmanstrete		44

Headword	House name	Parish	Folio
	atte Dragoñ	*in poch sĉi Gregorij*	65
	atte dragoñ wᵗ owten Newgate		187
	atte dragon ny Baynerdescastełł		187
	atte Dragouñ yn holboᵒʳne		319v
Eagle	*atte Egle in maltmarket*		37v,
	atte Egle in Grasschyrchstrete		44
	atte Egle extra Aldrisshgate		65v
	atte Egle ny seynt Bertilmewe		86
Eagle & Garland	*atte Egle & le Garlande*	*in pochia Sĉi Bendicti Graschirch*	50
Ewe & Lamb	*atte Ewe & lamb in Temsestrete*	*in pochia sĉi Martini Orgar*	44, 50
Falcon	*atte ffakoñ yn Aldrisshgatestrete*		84v
Fleur de Lys	*atte ffloᵒʳdelys in Goldynglane*		31
	in domo Thome atte Wode apᵈ ffloᵒʳdelyßß iuxᵃ qwenehyth		36v
	atte ffloᵒʳdelys	*in pochia Sĉi Dunstani in occidente in fletestrete*	43v
	atte fflourdelys	*in pochia sĉe Marie Somersete*	66
	atte floudelys yn fancherchestrete		149v
Font with Two Buckets	*ad fontem cũ ij bokettο*	*in pochia sĉi martini*	30
Garland	*atte Gerlond saunʒ Bisshopesgate*		1
	apud le Gerland	*in pochia sĉi Andrʳ Estchepe*	65
	atte Gerlonde yn wodstrete		85
	atte Gerlond yn Colmanstrete		187
George	*atte George in ffancherche strete*	*in poch sĉi dionisʳ*	1v
	atte George in ffletestrete	*in poch Sĉi Dunstani*	28v
	atte George ad finê Sholane		31v
	atte George	*in poch Sĉi Botulphi foris Algate Aldrysshgatestrete*	43v
	apud le George in Smethefeld		50v
	apud le George in Colmanstrete		65
	atte Jeorge yn seynt Johnesstrete		253
George & Horn	*atte George and horn*	*yn þe pessh of seynt Nich fflesshameles*	224

Headword	House name	Parish	Folio
Glene	*atte Glene iux^{a} le quenehyþ*		36v
	apud le Glene in Colmanstrete		43v
	atte Glene yn Bredestrete		161
Goat	*atte Gote ex opposito eccƚie sĉe Elene*		28v
Golden Hart	*atte Golden hert*	*in poᴄħ sĉi Egidij extra Crepulgate*	66
Greyhound	*atte Grehounde in bechenlane*		44v
	ap^{d} le Grehounde yn Estchepe		56
	atte Grehound w^{t} oute Crepulgate		303
Green Gate	*atte grene gate yn poodynglane*		114
Hammer	*foris Algate atte haɱ*		43
	atte Hamer' yn þe pessħ of þe whitechapeƚƚ		120v
Hand	*atte hande yn ffleetstrete ny Tempulbarr'*		84v
Harp	*atte harpe*	*en poᴄħ de seynt Giles saunʒ Crepulgate*	1
	atte harꝑ in seint Clementeslane		37v
	atte Harpe iux^{a} holborne brygge		50v
	atte Harꝑꝑ in Temstrete		72v
	atte harpe yn Tourestrete		85v
	atte harpe yn ffleetstrete		86v
Hart	*atte Herte ex^{a} hostis eccƚie de Grasschirche*		50
	atte herte yn seynt Joħn strete		84v
	atte hert yn holbo^{a} ne		253v
Hart's Head	*apud le hertysheɋ ex^{a} Byschopesgate*		29v
Hart's Horn	*atte hertishorne*	*poᴄħ de seynt Sepulcr'*	1,
	atte hertishorn	*ex^{a} Newgate*	45v
	apud hertyshorne	*in poᴄħ sĉe kaťine Crychyrch*	29v
	atte hertishorn	*in poᴄħ sĉe Brigide in ffleetstrete*	31v
	atte ħtishorne in Suthwerk		37v

Headword	House name	Parish	Folio
	atte hertishorn in vico scī Joħis exᵃ liḃtaꞇ		44v
	atte hertishorn yn pety wales		84
	atte hertishorn	*yn þe pessħ of alle halwen þe liteꞇ yn Tempstrete*	150
	atte hertishorne wᵗ outen Algate		150v
	atte hertis horn yn smythfeld		253v
Helm	*apud le helme*	*in poċħ sĉi Petri Cornhuꞇ*	65
	atte helme wᵗouten Bisshopesgate		199
Hind	*atte Hynde*	*in pochia Ōmj Scōꝝ de stanyng iuxᵃ eccliam pochialem de ffancħirċħ*	50, 66v
	atte hynde at corneriū de mynchenlane in ffancherchestrete		
	atte hynde wᵗ oute Crepulgate		85v
Horn	*le horne in Grascherche strete*		29
	atte horne in Aldrisshgatestrete		65
	atte horn	*yn þe pessħ of seynt Gyles*	150
	atte horn in ffletestret		187
	atte horn wᵗ owte Crepulgate		265
Horse	*atte hors in Aldrysshgate strete*		1v
	atte hors wᵗ ynne Algate		85v
	atte hors yn patᵉ nᵉʸ Rowe		303
Horse Head	*in domo Roḃti Lynforde apud horse-hede in la pulterye*		36
	atte horshede	*in poċħ Scī Andree in holborne*	43v
	apud le Horshede	*in poċħ scī Sepulcri*	50v
	atte hors hede yn Bowersrewe		85v
	atte horshede	*yn þe pessħ of white chapeꞇ*	162
	atte horshed wᵗouten Algate		199
Horseshoe	*le horssho fforis Algate*		43
Iron	*atte yroñ atte ffysshstrete ende*		303
Katherine Wheel	*atte katerine whele in Temsestrete*		38
	atte katerine wheꞇ	*in poċħ scī Egidij extra Crepulgate*	65v
	atte katᵉine wheꞇ yn ffleetstrete		224

Headword	House name	Parish	Folio
Key	atte keye en Basynge lane	en poch de aldermarye cherche	1
	atte keye	in poch Sĉe Mᵉ Somᷤsete	29
	atte keye exᵃ Algate		29v
	atte keye iuxᵃ Dowgate		31v
	atte keye in holbourne		37v
	atte keye in Whitecrowchestrete		45
	atte Keye in Colmanstrete		50v
	atte keye	in pochia Mᵉ Magᵭ in ffisshstrete	66
	atte keye	in pochia sc̄i Mich Bassyngeshawe	66
	atte keye wᵗ outen ludgate		86v
	atte keye ny þᵉ brokenwharff		150v
	atte keye yn seynt John strete		151
King's Head	atte kyngeshed yn woodstrete		149
Lamb	a le lambe in Southwerke		6v
	atte lambe in distaffelane		38
	atte lamb in Grobbestrete		40v
	apᵈ lamb in Abechirch lane		43
	atte lamb in strata sc̄i Johis foris lib̄tat'		43
	atte lamb in Martlane	in poch om̄i scôₓ Stanyng	45
	atte Lambe	in poch sc̄i Sepulcri exᵃ Newgate	72v
	atte Lambe apud Baynardescastełł		73
	atte lambe yn holboᵒʳne		233
	atte lambe yn ffaytoᵒʳlane		253v
Lamp	atte lampe extᵃ Bisshoppisgate		37v
	atte Laumpe ex opposito ffratrʾ Minorʾ		73
	atte lampe yn ffletestrete		114
	atte lawmpe wᵗynne Newgate		150v
Lattice	atte latis ageyns þe joynoᵒʳ yn hosier lane beside watlynge strete vpon þe westside		114v
Leaden Porch	atte ledene porche in Smethefeld		1v

Headword	House name	Parish	Folio
Lily	*atte lilie yn Stanynglane*		84v
	atte lilye yn lumbardestrete		113v
Lion	*atte leoñ*	*in poch Sc̄i Botħi iux^{ar}*	36v,
	atte lyon yn Tempstrete	*Byllyngisgate*	187
	atte leon in Aldisshgatestrete		44
	atte leoñ ex^{ar} Bischopysgate iux^{ar} lez barrez		45
	atte leoñ	*in poch om̄j Sc̄oꝛ Berkyng*	50
	ap^d le Lyoñ iuxa Seecollane		50v
	atte leon yn woodstrete		150
Long Entry	*atte longe Entr^)*	*en poche de seynt M^c wlcherche*	1,
	atte longe entr^) ny þe stokkes		149v,
	in domo Witħi harry vocat^) longeentre		40
Maid	*atte Maide*	*in poch sc̄e Mc Colcherche*	1v
	atte Mayde in ffletestrete		66
	atte mayde w^t oute Crepulgate		86
Maiden	*atte maiden yn chepe*		187v
Maiden Head	*atte maidenhed yn tempstrete*		224
Mermaid	*atte Mermayde ex^{ar} Crepulgate*		72v
Mill	*atte Mille in Tempstrete*	*in poch sc̄i laurenc^) pulteneye*	45
	atte Mille yn seynt John strete		85v
	atte Mille w^towten Newgate		199
Mitre	*atte Mitr^) yn Chepe*		165v
Moon	*atte mone extra bisshoppisgate*		37v
New Lion	*atte New leoñ*	*in poch sc̄i Botulphi ex^{ar} Aldrisshgate*	1v
Nun	*atte Nunne ex^{ar} Algate*		30
	atte Noonne ny þe stokkes		166
Pannier	*atte panyer^) en pat^) nost^) rowe*	*poch sc̄i Micħis Corne*	1
	atte Panyer^) in whitecrowchestrete	*in poch sc̄i Egidij ex^{ar} Crepulgate*	31
	atte Panyer^) iux^{ar} le quenehyth		36v
Paul's Head	*atte Paulys hede*	*in poch sc̄e mildrede in Bredestrete*	29

Headword	House name	Parish	Folio
Peacock	atte Pecok ex^a Algate		44v
	atte peĉok yn Aldrisshgatestrete		149
	atte pecok w^t owten Crepulgate		160
Peahen	atte pohenne yn Bisshoppesgatestrete		85v
	atte pohenne w^t owte Algate		253v
Peter & Paul	apud le Peter & Paule	in pochia sc̄i Gregorij	66v
Pewter Pot	atte Peaut'pott' ex^{ia} eccłie sc̄i Andree Cornhyłł		29v
	atte peauterpotte yn Iremongerelane		120v
Pie	atte Pye en la Ryałł		31v
	in domo Iacobi lenegro atte pye iuxta le qwenehythe		36v
	atte Pye in Smythefeld		37v
	atte Pye in holbo^{o}ne		37v
	atte Pye in la more		38
Popinjay	atte Popyngeay	in poch sĉe M^e ffanchirche	66
Purse	atte purs extra Crepulgate		38
Ram	atte Ramb	in poch sc̄i dunstani in ffleetstrete	31v
	in mansione Ric' Braӡo^o ostiler atte Ram in Smethefelde		40
	atte R^{a}me in Southwork		59v
	atte Rambe ny holbo^{o}ne cros		150
Ram's Head	beside þe Rammeshed yn Conyhopp̂lane		120
	atte Rammeshede yn ffancherchestrete		149
Red Cock	atte Rede Cok yn the pultrie		84v
Red Lion	atte rede lyoñ ex^{ia} sc̄m martinū magnū		37v
	atte Rede Lyoun in Woodstrete	in poch Sc̄i Alphegi	72v
Rose	atte Rose in Aldrisshgate strete		1v
	iux^a Rosam apud Crepulgate		30v

Headword	House name	Parish	Folio
	le Rose in Judaismo		31
	atte Rose in whitecrouchestrete		37v
	le Tauerne de le Rose on the hope	*in pochia Sc̄i Nicħi fflesshamles*	43v
	apud le Rose	*in poch Sc̄e Brigide*	65v
	att Rose ny seynt laurence of pounteney		85v
	atte Rose yn Martlane		199
	atte Rose ny wulkeye		265
	atte Rose yn tryllemellestrete		288
Round Hoop	*atte Rondhopp̂ wᵗ owte Crepulgate*		265
St Julian	*atte seynt Julyan beside þe barres yn aldrissħgatestrete*		113v
Saracen's Head	*apud Sarasynshede in fletestrete*		28v
	saresynshede iuxᵃʳ portâ de Gyldehaŧ		43
	in domo vni⁹ Chepster p le Sarasynshede apᵈ Pawlyscheyne		43v
	atte Sarasynshede extra Newgate		73
	atte Saresyneshede wᵗ ynne Algate		84v
Saracen's Head & One Maid	*atte Saresynshede & j mayde [forys struck through] foris Crepulgate*		43v
Savage's Inn	*atte Sauagesyn in ffleetstrete*		65
Scot	*atte Skott ny þe welle þᵗ standeþ yn Bisshopesgatestrete*		162
Scummer	*atte Skomoᵒʳ yn brechenlane*		150v
Seven Stars	*atte vij sterres in Smethefeld*		37v
	atte .vij. Stῤes in la pultr⁾		50v,
	atte .vij. Sterres	*in poch sc̄e Marie Wolchirche*	72v,
	atte vij sterres ny þᵉ Stokkes		149
Ship	*atte Chipp̂ ioust londoñ waŧ*	*en poch de seynt Alffaich*	1
	apud Schyppe apud Byllyngysgate		29
	atte Chypp̂ ad macellas Sĉi Nicħi		31

Headword	House name	Parish	Folio
	atte Shiṗ extra Crepulgate		37v
	atte Chipṗ ex^a Templebarr'		45
	atte Shipṗ yn Tourstrete		149
Sickle	atte Sekełł ny holbo^o ne cros		149v
Snipe	apud Snyte in Estechepe		28v
Squirrel	le sqwyrell in ffanchyrchstrete		30
Star	le sterre in Temsestrete		29
	atte Sterr' in Goldynglane	in poch Sĉi Egidij	44v
	atte Sterr' in ffancherchestrete		45
	atte Sterr' ny Crokedlane		151
	atte Sterr' yn Cornhīłł		161
	atte Sterre yn Estchepe		253
Star & Moon	atte Sterre & le mone	in poch Sĉe M^e vocat' aldermarie Schyrch	36v
Swan	atte Swan	en le poche de seynt Nich fflessh^a mbes	1
	atte Swan	en poch seynt Nich Coldabeye	1
	atte Swan	en Colmanstrete	1
	atte Swan in woodstrete	in poch Sĉi Michis hogene lane	1v
	atte Swan	in poch sĉi Michis in Cornhīłł	1v
	le Swan in Bałłio		30v
	atte Swan	in pochia sĉe Ethelburge in byschopesgatestrete	30v
	atte Swan	in poch sĉī Andree holborñ	30v
	atte swan ex^a algate		31v
	in domo Johis Bayly atte Swan in Siluer Strete		36v
	in domo Wiłłi Payn atte swan iux^a seyntantonyes		36v
	atte Swan iuxta Billingesgate		37v
	in mansione Sturmyn in pissīg lane atte Swan	in pochia sĉi Pancracij	40
	suṗ Corneriû ex^{ıa} sepultur' ecĉie Sĉi Michaelis de Bassyngyshawe ppe le Swan on the hope		43v
	atte Swan ex^a Seynt Elyns		50
	atte Swan infra Newgate		50v

Headword	House name	Parish	Folio
	atte Swanne in Temstrete		73
	atte Swanne in SeintJohnstrete		73
	atte Swan yn Aldrisshgatestrete		84v
	atte Swan yn Old ffisshstrete		121
	atte Swan yn Smythfeld		121
	atte Swan ny lothbury bregge		149v
	atte Swan	*yn þᵉ pessh of þᵉ whitechapell*	162v
	atte Swan yn ffancherchestrete		223v
	atte Swan yn Toᵍ strete		224
Swan & Ship	*in domo Thome Wegge atte le Swan cū le Schypp in Redecrowchestrete*		36
Tabard	*le Tabard in Greschyrch strete*		28
Tankard	*atte Tankard vp vn þe Tourhill*		85
Three Kings	*apud iij Reges exᵃ Algate*		30
Three Legs	*atte iij legges*	*in poch sĉi dunsť in ffleetstrete*	45
Three Nuns	*atte iij Nunnes in Sheteborgh lane* *atte .iij. Noonnes beside þe stokkes*	*in poch Sĉe Marie Wlnoth*	30v, 44v, 114
Trump	*atte Trumpe in Chepe*		29
Two Keys	*atte ij keyes wᵗ outen Bisshopesgate*		85v
Two Nuns	*atte ij Nonnes extra Algate*		65v
Two Stulps	*atte ij stolpes ny Baynerdescastell*		150
Unicorn	*atte Vnycorne* *atte vnycorne wᵗ outen Newgate*	*in poche sĉi Nichi Oloth*	72v 150
Vernacle	*atte vernacle* *atte Vernacle in la Barbican* *atte vernacle ny ffrereaustyns*	*in pochia sĉi Barthi pm*	37v 44v 150v
Vine	*atte vyne ī la Ryole* *atte vyne ny holboᵍne Crosse* *atte vyne wᵗ ynne Bisshoppesgate*		40v 85v 86
Welsh Man	*apud walsshman foris ludgate*		43

Headword	House name	Parish	Folio
White Bear	*atte whyte ber'*	*in poch sĉi Andree holbo⁰ ne*	31
White Bull	*in plano campo ex^a le Whitebole*		50v
White Cock	*atte white Cok*		114v
White Cross	*atte White cros extra Crepulgate*		38
White Culver	*iux^a ffleetbregge apud le white colver'*		50v
White Hart	*atte whiteherte yn knyght rider strete*		161v
	atte whiteherte ny Trenytelane		187v
White Legs	*atte whitelegge in ffleetstrete*		31v
White Lion	*atte white lyoñ*	*in poch sĉi Thome Apłi*	65
	atte whit leoñ yn seynt Joñesstret		253v
	atte white leoñ yn Grascherche strete		265
Whole Bull	*atte hole boole yn estchepe*		104v
Woolsack	*atte wolsak w^t outen Algate*		199v
	atte wollesak yn Smythffeld		233v

APPENDIX 3
STAGECOACH NAMES

Stagecoach names culled from Directories 1828–1844 at http://specialcollections.
le.ac.uk, and Corbett (1891: 300–1).

Terminus or scheduled stop	Name of coach
White Lion Hotel, Stratford	the Union, Oxonian Express, Aurora Day
Red Horse, Stratford	the Rocket, Triumph
Golden Lion Inn, Stratford	Royal Pilot
Duke of Wellington Inn, Stratford	Duke of Wellington, Paul Pry
Shakspeare Inn, Stratford	Britannia
Red Lion, Atherstone	the Royal Mail
Three Tuns, Atherstone	the Herald
New Swan, Atherstone	the Accommodation
Black Boy, Atherstone	the Umpire
Nuneaton	the Alexander, the Magnet
Sutton Coldfield	the Express, the Amity, the Devonshire
Swan, Sutton Coldfield	the Dart
Barley Mow, Solihull	the Royal Express, the Crown Prince, the Regulator, the Telegraph
George Inn, Solihull	the Amicable
Rose & Crown, Tamworth	the Tally-ho
George Inn, Warwick	the Eclipse, the Shamrock, the Coventry Day, the Victoria
Packwood's General Coach and Waggon Offices, Coventry	the Patent Safety Tally-ho, the Greyhound, the New Patent Coach called Peeping Tom, the Rising Sun
City Hotel Coach Office, Coventry	the Wonder, the Albion, the Morning Star, the Times, the Volunteer, the Diligence
Dolphin Inn, Cross Cheaping	the Independent Tally-ho, the Emerald, the Reliance, the Manchester Hero
Cock & Bell, Bury St Edmonds	the Old Bury
Swan, Bury St Edmonds	the Phenomena
Suffolk Hotel, Bury St Edmonds	the Marquis of Cornwallis
King's Head Inn, Beccles	the Star

Terminus or scheduled stop	Name of coach
Falcon, Beccles	the Hope
Angel and Three Tuns, Halesworth	the Shannon
Coach Office, Ipswich	the Blue
Coach & Horses, Ipswich	the Cambridge
Rose & Crown, Sudbury	the Sudbury
Crown, Woodbridge	the Old Blue
Swan, Alresford	the Self Defence
Bridge Inn, Arundel	the Royal Sussex
Norfolk Arms, Arundel	the Comet, the Red Rover, the Defiance
Swan and Castle Hotels, Hastings	the Despatch, the Paragon
King's Head, Horsham	the Accommodation & Sovereign, the Royal William, the Royal Sovereign, the Hero
Half Moon, Petworth	the Duke of Richmond
Red Lion, Marlow	the Industry
Saracen's Head, Newport Pagnall	the Royal Bruce, the Independent, the Courier
Lion Hotel, Wycombe	the Champion, the Aurora, the Blenheim, the Retaliator, the Accommodation Safety, the Thame
Lower Angel, Woolhampton	the Optimus
Red Lion, Hungerford	the Age
Three Swans, Hungerford	the Sociable
Saracen's Head, Maidenhead	the Rival
Three Tuns, Newbury	the Defence
King's Arms, Newbury	the Prince of Wales, the Prince Albert
Crown, Amersham	the Wendover
Saracen's Head, Beaconsfield	the Queen
George, Colnbrook	The Windsor, the Henley
George & Dragon, Princes Risborough	the Live and Let Live
Cross Keys, Princes Risborough	the Worcester
King's Arms, Chumleigh	the Ruby
Castle, Dartmouth	the Subscription
New London Inn, Exeter	the Globe, the Night Mail, the Royal Quicksilver Mail, the Great Western, the Butterfly, the Teign
Old London Inn, Exeter	the Nonpareil, the Nautilus, the Alert
White Lion Coach Office, Sidwell	the Era
George, Hartland	the Emerald
Golden Lion, Honiton	the Forester

Terminus or scheduled stop	Name of coach
White Hart, Oakhampton	the Vivid
Antelope, Dorchester	the John Bull
Berkeley	the Criterion, the Royal Exeter, the Favourite, the Patriot, the Exquisite, the Berkeley Hunt
Bush & Lion Hotels, Bristol	the Fuzileer, the Thistle, the L'Estafette, the Brilliant, the Phoenix, the Celerity, the Cymro, the Royal Dorset
Bath Hotel, Clifton	the Nimrod
George, Cheltenham	the Premier, the Regent
Plough, Cheltenham	the White Hart, the Brunel, the Mazeppa, the Imperial, the Plough Coach
Boat, Dursley	the 'Endeavour'
Heath's Office, Gloucester	the Prince, the Mercury, the Royal
White Hart & Unicorn, Moreton	the Little Wonder
White Hart, Ashby de la Zouch	the Union Alexander
Queen's Head, Ashby de la Zouch	the Commercial
White Hart, Hinckley	the Emperor Alexander
Globe, Leicester	the Queen Caroline
Three Crowns, Leicester	the Leicester Union
George & Stag, Leicester	the Derby Times
Fleur de Lis Inn, Leicester	the Royal Safety
Black Horse, Loughborough	Nelson's Independent
White Lion, Loughborough	the Old Independent
Bull Hotel, Weymouth	the Coronet
Antelope, Dorchester	the South Western
White Hart, Andover	the Plough, the Salisbury
George, Andover	the Swiftsure
King's Arms, Bournemouth	the Bournmouth
White Hart, Fareham	the Anglesey
Dolphin, Havant	the Duke of Richmond
Yelf's Hotel, Ryde	the Felicity
Nag's Head, Lymington	the Original
Red Lion, Petersfield	the Rover
White Horse, Romsey	the Packet
Bridge Inn, Bromyard	the Broxash
Royal Hotel, Ross	the White Lion
Tintern	the Lion
Chapel House, Chipping Norton	the Tantivy, the Day

Terminus or scheduled stop	Name of coach
Angel, Oxford	the Eagle
White Hart, Bath	the L'Hirondelle
Greyhound, Bath	the Dove
George, Castle Cary	the North Devon
Swan, Wells	the Old White Hart Coach
Lansdowne Arms, Calne	the Rory O'More
White Hart, Salisbury	the Light Salisbury, the Little Magnet
White Lion Hotel, Bala	the Sir Watkin
Penrhyn Arms, Bangor	the Queen of Trumps
Cors y Gedol Arms, Barmouth	the Snowdon
Ship, Flint	the Lord Mostyn
King's Head Hotel, Holywell	the Why Not?
Black Lion Inn, Mold	the Owen Glyndwr, the Sir Richard Bulkeley
Bear's Head Inn, Newtown	the Royal Oak, the Nettle
Castle, Brecon	the Collegian
Lion Hotel, Builth	the Lily of the Valley
Swan, Carmarthen	the Monarch
Ivy Bush, Carmarthen	the Picton
Bear, Crickhowell	the Monmouth Hunt
Jones & Herbert's Office, Chester	the Hark Forward, the Vesuvius, the Victory, the Royal George, the Highflier
White Lion, Chester	the Royal Waterloo, the Royal Liverpool, the George the Fourth, the Lady Stanley, the Bang-up
Coach & Horses, Chester	the St. David
Buck & Dog, Stockport	the Traveller, the Nelson
White Lion, Stockport	the Buxton, the Royal Macclesfield, the True Briton
Plough, Stockport	the Independent Potter
John Fell's, Maryport	the Royal Sailor
Crown, Penrith	the New Times
Green Dragon, Workington	the Good Intent
Norfolk Arms, Glossop	the Merry Tradesman
Queen's Head, Chester-le-Street	the Expedition, the Lord Exmouth
Golden Lion, Sunderland	the Collingwood
Commercial Inn, Ashton-under-Line	the Royal Blucher, the Physician, the Glossop Market Coach, the Royal Huddersfield
Ship, Bolton	the North Star, the Longwaist, the Royal Bolton, the Fair Trader

Terminus or scheduled stop	*Name of coach*
Wool Pack, Bolton	the Doctor, the Bolton and Liverpool Union, the Lord Grey
Swan, Bolton	the Royal Neptune
Fleece, Bolton	the Flycatcher
Talbot, Liverpool	the Alliance, the York House Coach, the Sir Walter Scott
Crown, Liverpool	the North Briton, the Earl of Hopetown
Angel, Liverpool	the Invincible
Gorst & Co.'s Office, Liverpool	the Half-Sovereign
Albion, Liverpool	the Erin-go-Bragh
King's Arms, Manchester	the Peveril of the Peak, the Duke of Devonshire, the Miller, the Pacific, the Enterprize, the Marshall, the Perseverance
Royal Hotel, Manchester	the Hawk
Roe Buck, Manchester	the Lark
Crown Inn, Manchester	the Doctor Syntax
Swan with Two Necks, Manchester	the Skipton Union
Talbot, Manchester	the Norfolk, the Commerce
New Boar's Head, Manchester	the Trafalgar
Three Crowns, Manchester	the Queen Ann
Royal Hotel, Manchester	the Duke of Bridgewater
Mosley Arms, Manchester	the Balloon, the Clothier
Swan, Manchester	the Delight
White Horse, Manchester	the Earl of Wilton
Hare & Hounds, Manchester	the Tarrare
Lower Turk's Head, Manchester	the Royal Defence
Buck & Hawthorn, Manchester	the Ancient Briton
Spread Eagle, Salford	the True Blue
Roe Buck, Rochdale	the Superior
Black Swan, York	the Rockingham
Rose & Crown, Aberford	the Providence
King's Head, Barnsley	the Ebor
King's Arms, Beverley	the Queen Adelaide
Tiger, Beverley	the Queen Victoria
Stirling Castle, Bridlington	the Magna Charta
Scarborough Hotel, Dewsbury	the Stag
Rein Deer, Doncaster	the Commander-in-Chief
Cock, Guisborough	the Cleveland
Promenade Inn, Harrogate	the No Wonder
Wellington Inn, Leeds	the Duke of Leeds

Terminus or scheduled stop	Name of coach
Rose & Crown, Leeds	the George IV
Rose & Punch Bowl, Bridgnorth	the Shropshire Hero
Albion, Birmingham	the Young Prince, the Gleaner, the Victoria Spa, the Salopian, the British Queen, the Superb
Swan, Stafford	the Rob Roy
Crown & Cushion, Stafford	the Active
Milton's Head Inn, Nottingham	the Robin Hood
Victoria, Margate	the Herne
White Hart, Newmarket	the Fakenham Hero
Bath	the Beaufort Hunt
Brecon	the Pearl
Hereford	the Tiger
Manchester	the Beehive
Windsor	the Taglioni

SUNNYSIDE GAZETTEER

I list here North British *Sunnyside*s for which there is datable evidence of the name, followed by '*Sunnysides of X*', '*Greens of X*', and *Green(s*. In each case I give the location, the date of the earliest evidence I have noted (if other than on the map), and the national grid reference. Maps are Ordnance Survey unless specified otherwise. Angle brackets are a convention for indicating the precise spelling of a word in a manuscript; asterisks denote an unattested but plausibly reconstructed form.

Historic Northern English Sunnysides

1. Sunnyside, Plawsworth, County Durham, 1857, NZ 26314 47465

Durham XX (includes: Belmont; Framwellgate Moor; Pittington; West Rainton), surveyed: 1857, published: 1861; https://maps.nls.uk/view/102341560#zoom=5&lat=6876&lon=2238&layers=BT

2. Sunnyside, Trimdon, County Durham, 1856, NZ 38133 33001

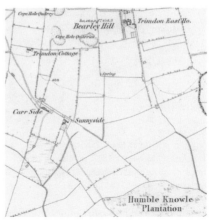

Durham XXXVI (includes: Embleton; Hutton Henry; Sheraton with Hulam; Wingate), surveyed: 1856, published: 1861; https://maps.nls.uk/view/102341656#zoom=6&lat=4236&lon=4810&layers=BT

3. Sunnyside, Iveston, Consett, County Durham, 1857, NZ 14857 50800

Durham XI (includes: Consett), surveyed: 1857, published: 1862; https://maps.nls.uk/view/102341506#zoom=4&lat=2572&lon=13470&layers=BT

4. Sunnyside, Knitsley, Consett, County Durham, 1857, NZ 12804 48264

Durham XVIII (includes: Healeyfield; Lanchester), surveyed: 1857, published: 1861; https://maps.nls.uk/view/102341548#zoom=6&lat=8042&lon=9719&layers=BT

5. Sunnyside, Whitburn, County Durham, 1769, NZ 38649 63421

Detail from Sheet 5, Andrew Armstrong's *Map of Northumberland*, 1769, Whitaker Collection 538, The University Library, University of Leeds

Northern Archaeological Associates (2013–14: 295) says further information on Sunnyside Farm is held in the Durham Diocesan Archive: 'Sunniside Farm NZ 3864 6342. Farm appears on 1839 tithe map and was one of the post-enclosure farmsteads established in the late 17th Century. 18th-century (probably 17th century in origin).'

Sunniside Farm, Sunniside Lane, South Shields NE34 8DY; Google Maps Streetview

6. Sunnyside and Sunnyside Plantation, Whickham Fell, County Durham, 1322, NZ 20680 58688

Sunniside, Whickham Fell, near Lamesley, County Durham, attested as *Sonnyside* in manuscripts of 1322 and 1342 (Mawer 1920: 192; Watts 2004: 590); I have not seen these manuscripts.[1]

Durham VI (includes: Lamesley; Whickham), surveyed: 1857, published: 1862; https://maps.nls.uk/view/102341473#zoom=5&lat=4378&lon=7080&layers=BT

[1] Sir Allen Mawer (1879–1942) was born in Bow in 1879, the eldest son of a commercial traveller in fancy trimmings, and became the founder of the English Place-Name Society. His Nonconformist parents were strongly evangelical and his father was Secretary to the Country Towns Mission, a charitable society (F. M. Stenton in Lapidge 2002: ch. 13).

7. Sunnyside, Seaton, Cumberland, 1864,
   NY 02332 31049

Cumberland LIII (includes: Seaton; Workington),
surveyed: 1864, published: 1867; https://maps.nls.
uk/view/102340845#zoom=5&lat=8660&lon=
12665&layers=BT

8. Sunnyside Tannery, Workington,
   Cumberland, 1864, NY 01478 28812

Cumberland LIII (includes: Seaton;
Workington), surveyed: 1864, published: 1867;
https://maps.nls.uk/view/index.cfm?id=1023408
45#zoom=6&lat=5327&lon=11468&layers=BT

9. Sunnyside, Nichol Forest, Cumberland,
   1863, NY 47628 78479

Cumberland III (includes: Bewcastle; Nichol
Forest), surveyed: 1863, published: 1868; https://
maps.nls.uk/view/102340692#zoom=6&lat=
3711&lon=7531&layers=BT

10. Sunnyside, Haltwhistle,
    Northumberland, 1862, NY 71252 65948

Northumberland XCII (includes: Henshaw;
Melkridge; Plenmeller; Ridley), surveyed: 1862,
published: 1866; https://maps.nls.uk/view/10234
6470#zoom=6&lat=9787&lon=2815&layers=BT

11. Sunnyside, Plainmeller, Unthank,
    Northumberland, 1862, NY 74365 60625

This Sunnyside was the name of a coalmine,
sunk in 1820 (www.aditnow.co.uk/Mines/
Plainmeller-Coal-Colliery_8650/).

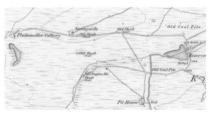

Northumberland XCII (includes: Henshaw;
Melkridge; Plenmeller; Ridley), surveyed: 1862,
published: 1866; https://maps.nls.uk/view/10234
6470#zoom=5&lat=1906&lon=7505&layers=BT

12. Sunnyside, Lambley, Northumberland,
    1861, NY 68632 56881

Northumberland C (includes: Hartleyburn;
Knarsdale; Midgeholme), surveyed: 1861,
published: 1865; https://maps.nls.uk/view/
102346491#zoom=6&lat=5976&lon=13198&
layers=BT

13. Sunnyside, Bedlington,
    Northumberland, 1858–9, NZ 25578
    83199

Ordnance Survey First Series, Sheet 105 NW,
1867; attested earlier on Northumberland
Sheet LXXII (includes: Bedlington; Hepscott;
Stannington), surveyed: 1858–9, published:
1866; https://maps.nls.uk/view/102346413#
zoom=5&lat=6412&lon=11748&layers=BT

14. Sunny Side, Ninebanks, West Allen,
    Northumberland, 1862, NY 73861 57702

This Sunny Side is the name of a fell.

Northumberland CI (includes: Coanwood;
Whitfield), surveyed: 1862, published: 1865;
https://maps.nls.uk/view/102346494#zoom=
5&lat=7122&lon=6597&layers=BT

15. Sunnyside, Great Whittington,
    Corbridge, Northumberland, 1861, NY
    99528 70511

Northumberland LXXXVI (includes: Clarewood;
East Matfen; West Matfen), surveyed: 1860 to
1861, published: 1864; https://maps.nls.uk/
view/102346455#zoom=5&lat=7099&lon=
2335&layers=BT

16. Sunny Side, Cambois, Bedlington
    Parish, Northumberland, 1859,
    NZ 31145 82447

Northumberland LXXIII (includes: Bedlington;
Blyth), surveyed: 1859, published: 1865; https://
maps.nls.uk/view/index.cfm?id=102346416#
zoom=7&lat=5583&lon=5570&layers=BT

17. Sunnyside, Coalcleugh, West Allen, Northumberland, 1833, NY 79954 45231

'George Forster, Sunnyside, Coalcleugh' (Northumberland Poll Book, 1833: 145)

Durham XV (includes: Allendale; Allendale Common), surveyed: 1858, published: 1861; https://maps.nls.uk/view/102341530#zoom= 6&lat=3764&lon=3811&layers=BT

18. Sunnyside Farm, Shildon, Corbridge, Northumberland, 1831, NZ 02474 67458

'TO BE LET, And entered upon the 13th May, 1832, SUNNYSIDE FARM, at Shildon, in the Parish of Corbridge, containing 80 Acres, or thereabouts, in the Occupation of Mr John Charlton' (*The Newcastle Courant*, 31 December 1831).

Northumberland LXXXVI 6″ Ordnance Survey, surveyed 1860 to 1861, published 1864; https:// maps.nls.uk/view/102346455#zoom=6&lat=248 6&lon=5986&layers=BT

19. Sunnyside, Spital, Tweedmouth, Northumberland, 1820, NT 99677 51372

'Town of Spittal frequented for its mineral waters, and sea-bathing quarters – ascend the steep bank of Sunnyside requiring improvement' (Duncan 1820: 8).

'In the field above the quarry at Sunnyside, about a mile south of Berwick' (Winch 1831: 50).

Detail from John Fryer and sons, *Map of the County of Northumberland including the Town and County of Newcastle upon Tyne, the Town and Bounds of Berwick upon Tweed and those parts of the County of Durham situate to the North of the River Tyne*, 1820; The National Archives, MPZ 1/15.

20. Sunnyside, Carham, Northumberland; 1747–55, NT 82672 37319

Labelled *Sunnylaws* on Ordnance Survey maps.

Roy *Military Survey of Scotland*, 1747–55; http:// maps.nls.uk/geo/roy/#zoom=14&lat=55.6367 &lon=-2.3188&layers=roy-lowlands

21. Sunnyside, Shothaugh, Felton,
     Northumberland, 1820, NZ 17218
     99079

John Fryer and sons, *Map of the County of
Northumberland including the Town and County
of Newcastle upon Tyne, the Town and Bounds of
Berwick upon Tweed and those parts of the County
of Durham situate to the North of the River Tyne*,
1820; The National Archives, MPZ 1/15.

22. High and Low Sunnyside, West
     Brunton, Gosforth, Northumberland,
     1786, NZ 20810 70791

1786: 'plaintiff: James Stephen Lushington,
cleric (vicar of Newcastle upon Tyne St
Nicholas); defendant: Robert Coulson of
Sunniside, Gosforth, Newcastle upon Tyne St
Nicholas, Northumberland, yeoman', Durham
Diocesan Records, Durham University Library,
Archives and Special Collections, DDR/EJ/
CCD/3/1786/6. High and Low Sunnyside
farms are marked on Fryer's *Map of the County
of Northumberland* of 1820.

Northumberland LXXXVIII (includes: East
Brunton; Gosforth; Newcastle upon Tyne;
North Gosforth; West Brunton), surveyed: 1858,
published: 1864; https://maps.nls.uk/view/10234
6461#zoom=5&lat=7326&lon=5119&layers=BT

23. Sunnyside, Catton, Allendale,
     Northumberland, 1820, NY 82010
     58459 and NY 82233 58242

'Matthew and John Graham, Sunnyside,
Allendale, Northumberland', *Northumberland
Poll Book*, 1826; shown on Fryer's *Map of
Northumberland*, 1820. The 1865 Ordnance
Survey map of Allendale shows two adjacent
farms with this name, Sunnyside and High
Sunnyside.

Sunnyside and High Sunnyside, Catton, Allendale,
Northumberland CII, 6″ Ordnance Survey, surveyed
1859, published 1865; https://maps.nls.uk/view/1023
46497#zoom=6&lat=8049&lon=4534&layers=BT

24. Sunnyside, Hexham, Northumberland,
     1769, NY 95194 62289

Nurminen (2012) dates this Sunnyside
to 1769. 'John Kirsopp, late of Sunnyside,
Hexham, Northumberland, Farmer, sued,
and in Partnership with, George Kirsopp as
Farmers' (*The London Gazette*, 1835: 1166).

John Fryer and sons, *Map of the County of
Northumberland including the Town and County
of Newcastle upon Tyne, the Town and Bounds of
Berwick upon Tweed and those parts of the County
of Durham situate to the North of the River Tyne*,
1820, The National Archives, MPZ 1/15; image
from http://communities.northumberland.gov.
uk/007193FS.htm

25. Sunnyside, Pauperhaugh, Rothbury, Northumberland, 1725, NZ 09379 97402

4 August 1725, registered copy of will; Ralph Reavely, yeoman, of Sunny Side in the Parish of Rothbury and County of Northumberland; Durham University Library, Archives and Special Collections, Durham Probate Records pre-1858 will register 11, GB-0033-DPRI/2/11, pp. 12–13.

Sheet 5, Andrew Armstrong's *Map of Northumberland*, 1769, Whitaker Collection 538, The University Library, University of Leeds; image from http://communities. northumberland.gov. uk/006946FS.htm

Three more Northern English Sunnysides I pass over, for the following reasons: according to English Place-Name Society volumes, *Sunniside* (present-day spelling) at Crook, County Durham, NZ 1438, was spelt historically <Sonnyngside, Sunnynsyde>; and Sunnyside near Woolsingham, Northumberland, NZ 0535, was historically spelt <Sonnyngside>. These two place-names derive from the name of a man named *Sunna*, so although they are both historical, they are not derived from Old English **sonnig*, Middle English *sunni* 'sunny' + *side* (Jackson (1916: 101), Mawer (1920: 192); I have not seen these manuscripts). Sunny Side, Bellingham, Northumberland, NY 8188, attested in a manuscript of 1769, is spelt *Sundayheugh* in a manuscript of 1325 (Old English *sunnan-dæg* 'Sunday' + Old English *hōh* 'spur of land'), and is shown as Sundaysight on Ordnance Survey maps (Nurminen 2012). Conversely, there are further Northern English Sunnysides visible on Edina Digimap Ancient Roam which may be old, but for which I cannot locate zoomable older maps, such as Sunnyside, Kirklinton, Cumbria, NY 433654; Sunnyside, Ludworth, Durham, NZ 36505 41562.

Historic Scottish Sunnysides

26. Sunnyside, Old Machar, Aberdeenshire, 1602, NJ 93664 07930

'toun and lands callit the Sonye Syde, Spittelhill and croft adiacent to the College Croft' lying within 'the Regalitie of the College of Auld Abd.' 13 November 1602 (Littlejohn 1906: 30).

'Mr. William Moir, son of William Moir, was admitted Burgess of Aberdeen in 1598. He was Dean of Guild of the city in 1606 and 1616, and Treasurer in 1615, etc. He had sasine on two-thirds of Scotstown in 1602, on the remainder of Scotstown in 1620, on Calsayseat in 1603, on Sunnyside and Spittal and crofts beside Calsayseat in 1604, also on land on the east side of the Gallowgate in 1608. . . . Mr. John Moir. He graduated at Marischal College in 1617, was admitted burgess in 1615. He received sasine on land on the east of the Gallowgate in 1615, and on Sunnyside of Spittall in 1626.' Moir (1913: 137).

'Geo. Moir of Scotstown: Spithill, Scotstown, Sunnyside, Old Machar, Aberdeenshire, c.1770', Timperley ed. (1976: 11).

Aberdeenshire, Sheet LXXV (includes: Aberdeen; Newhills; Old Machar), survey date: 1865–7, publication date: 1869; https://maps.nls.uk/view/74425426#zoom=6&lat=6342&lon=8830&layers=BT

27. Sunnyside, Old Machar, Aberdeenshire, 1865–67, NJ 90147 05766

Aberdeenshire, Sheet LXXV (includes: Aberdeen; Newhills; Old Machar), survey date: 1865–7, publication date: 1869; https://maps.nls.uk/view/74425426#zoom=6&lat=3249&lon=3917&layers=BT

28. Sunnyside, Kinmundy, New Machar, Aberdeenshire, 1747–55, NJ 90302 17698

Roy *Military Survey of Scotland*, 1747–55; http://maps.nls.uk/geo/roy/#zoom=15&lat=57.2414&lon=-2.1270&layers=roy-highlands

29. Sunnyside and Nether Sunnyside, Drum, Parish of Drumoak, Aberdeenshire, 1583, NO 79109 99084

'Sunnysyd in Drumneok and Barony of Drum. Sasine dated 26 April 1583. Notary Mr. Gilbert Ross.' (Littlejohn 1904: Part I, p. 377).

'To be Let, for such number of years as shall be agreed on, entry at Whitsunday next 1811, The Following Farms on the Estate of Drum, parish of Drumoak:- 1. The Farm of Sunnyside with Part of Redford, containing about 28 acres infield, 119 outfield, and 155 uncultivated ground.' (*The Aberdeen Journal*, 12 September 12, 1810).

'David Young, 21/02/1826, Farmer at Sunnyside in the Parish of Drumoak', Scottish Wills and Testaments Online, SC1/36/3.

John Thomson's *Atlas of Scotland*, Northern Part of Aberdeen & Banff Shires. Southern Part. Bottom right section, 1832; https://maps.nls.uk/view/74400159#zoom=6&lat=4540&lon=4615&layers=BT

Aberdeenshire, Sheet LXXXV (includes: Drumoak; Maryculter; Peterculter), survey date: 1865, publication date: 1869; https://maps.nls.uk/view/74425436#zoom=6&lat=2983&lon=2850&layers=BT

30. Sunnyside, Drumblade, Aberdeenshire, 1841, NJ 63775 38476

1841 Census. 'James Skinner, 17/09/1863, Farmer Residing at Sunnyside of Glenythan in the Parish of Forgue', Scottish Wills and Testaments Online, SC1/36/53.

Aberdeenshire, Sheet XXVII (includes: Auchterless; Forgue), survey date: 1871, publication date: 1873; https://maps.nls.uk/view/74425329#zoom=6&lat=4201&lon=8305&layers=BT

31. Sunnyside, Leslie, Aberdeenshire, 1841, NJ 60359 24922

1841 Census.

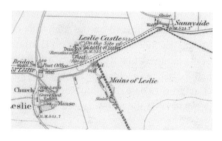

Aberdeenshire, Sheet XLIV (includes: Culsalmond; Insch; Kennethmont; Oyne; Premnay), survey date: 1867, publication date: 1870; https://maps.nls.uk/view/74425346#zoom=5&lat=2991&lon=3283&layers=BT

32. Sunnyside, Parish of Durris, Kincardineshire, 1851, NO 75864 93944

1851 Census.

Kincardineshire, Sheet VI (includes: Banchory-Ternan; Drumoak; Durris), survey date: 1864–5, publication date: 1868; https://maps.nls.uk/view/74427592#zoom=6&lat=2684&lon=9738&layers=BT

33. Sunnyside, Parish of Cluny, Aberdeenshire, 1859-60, NJ 64552 10823

Ordnance Survey Name Book OS1/1/15/13, Valuation Roll 1859–60.

Aberdeen Sheet LXIII.15 (Cluny), survey date: 1865, publication date: 1869; https://maps.nls.uk/view/74479673#zoom=4&lat=2460&lon=6097&layers=BT

34. Sunnyside, Fyvie, Aberdeenshire, 1842,
    NJ 77247 38191

'Miss Eliza Leith, 11/11/1842, Residing at
Sunnyside in the Parish of Fyvie', Scottish
Wills and Testaments Online, SC1/36/19;
Post Office Directory 1852.

Aberdeenshire, Sheet XXVIII (includes:
Auchterless; Fyvie), survey date: 1869–71,
publication date: 1873; https://maps.nls.uk/
view/74425330#zoom=6&lat=4252&lon=14162
&layers=BT

35. Sunnyside of Folla, Parish of Fyvie,
    Aberdeenshire, 1867, NJ 71610 33261

Aberdeen Sheet XXXVI.6 (Fyvie), survey date:
1867, publication date: 1873; https://maps.nls.
uk/view/74480002#zoom=4&lat=2262&lon=43
48&layers=BT

36. Sunnyside, near Braeside of
    Rothmaise, Aberdeenshire, 1747–55,
    NJ 69393 33072

This Sunnyside, sited in between the House
of Rotmays (Rothmaise) and Braerotmays
(Braeside of Rothmaise) to the West, and
Tocherford and Badyfash (Baldyfash) to the
East on Roy's Military Map of 1747–55, is

not marked on Ordnance Survey maps. It
is visible on Roy's map about 2,250 metres
(*c.* 2,460 yards) West of Sunnyside of Folla
(which is not marked on Roy's map).

Roy *Military Survey of Scotland,* 1747–55;
http://maps.nls.uk/geo/roy/#zoom=14&lat=
57.3837&lon=-2.4810&layers=roy-highlands.
From West to East: House of Rotmays,
Braerotmays, Sunnyside, Tocherford, Badyfash

37. North Sunside and Sunnyside, Meikle
    Wartle, Aberdeenshire, *c.*1740, NJ
    72434 30763 and NJ 72020 30501

'James Elphinstone, son of Alexander,
had a disposition of Meikle Warthill from
his father in 1696, and was still living in
1738. He had a sister Katharine, who had
three ploughs of land on the sunnyside of
Meikle Warthill. She married John Gardine
of Bellamore, their contract of marriage
being dated at Braelyne of Glentaner, 1740.'
(Davidson 1878: 412). Only North Sunside
is apparent on the map surveyed 1867–69.

Aberdeenshire, Sheet XXXVI (includes: Daviot;
Fyvie; Meldrum; Rayne), survey date: 1867–69,
publication date: 1873; https://maps.nls.uk/
view/74425338#zoom=6&lat=3102&lon=6911
&layers=BT

Aberdeenshire Sheet XXXVI.SW (includes: Fyvie; Rayne), publication date: 1901, date revised: 1899; https://maps.nls.uk/view/7547393 4#zoom=5&lat=2594&lon=5821&layers=BT

38. Sunside, Kennethmont, Aberdeenshire, 1865–71, NJ 58066 28813

'A large and substantial farm house with offices, garden &c attached, the property of Carlos P. Gordon Esq. of Wardhouse.' Ordnance Survey Name Book OS1/1/46/43.

Aberdeenshire, Sheet XLIII (includes: Auchindoir And Kearn; Clatt; Kennethmont; Leslie), Survey date: 1866, Publication date: 1870; https://maps.nls.uk/view/74425345#zoom =6&lat=8647&lon=13795&layers=BT

39. Sunnyside, Premnay, Insch, Aberdeenshire, 1797–8, NJ 63481 26710

'Jean Milne Sunside', Farm horse tax 1797–8, vol. 7 (ScotlandsPlaces E326/10/7/55).

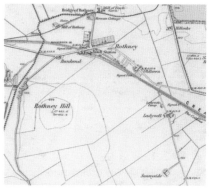

Aberdeenshire, Sheet XLIV (includes: Culsalmond; Insch; Kennethmont; Oyne; Premnay), survey date: 1867, publication date: 1870; https://maps.nls.uk/view/74425346#zoom =5&lat=6003&lon=7786&layers=BT

40. Sunnyside, Cairnbrogie, Tarves, Aberdeenshire, 1867, NJ 85692 27620

Also known as Sunnyside of Cairnbrogie.

Aberdeenshire, Sheet XLVI (includes: Bourtie; Keithhall And Kinkell; Meldrum; Tarves; Udny); survey date: 1867; publication date: 1870; https://maps.nls.uk/view/74425348#zoom= 6&lat=7694&lon=11689&layers=BT

41. Sunnyside, Parish of Udny,
    Aberdeenshire, 1867, NJ 83873 24123

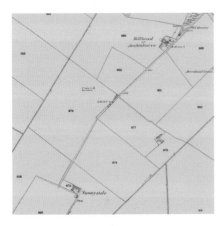

Aberdeen Sheet XLVI.15 (Udny), survey date:
1867, publication date: 1870; https://maps.nls.
uk/view/74480814#zoom=4&lat=4388&lon=
6480&layers=BT

42. Sunnyside of Dudwick, West Ardganty,
    Ellon, Aberdeenshire, 1815, NJ 98098
    37629

'Sunnyside, 32 acres. 1815, James Thomson.'
Godsman (1958: 212). Shown but not
named on older Ordnance Survey maps;
http://canmore.org.uk/site/145368.

Aberdeen Sheet XXXI.13 (Ellon), survey date:
1870, publication date: 1872; https://maps.nls.
uk/view/74479895#zoom=4&lat=9814&lon=
4339&layers=BT

43. Sunnyside of Kemnay, Kintore,
    Aberdeenshire, 1843, NJ 74236 15468

Post Office Directory 1843. The Ordnance
Survey map shows this farm as 'Wreaton', the
name having been changed from 'Sunnyside
of Kemnay' at some point between 1852 and
1864.

Aberdeenshire, Sheet LXIV (includes: Chapel Of
Garioch; Cluny; Kemnay; Kintore; Monymusk;
Skene), survey date: 1864–67, publication date:
1869; https://maps.nls.uk/view/74425415#zoom
=6&lat=8294&lon=9205&layers=BT

44. Sunnyside of Tillyreach, Parish of
    Tough, Aberdeenshire, 1826, ?NJ 58977
    08955

'William Laing, 30/03/1826, Farmer at
Sunnyside of Tillyreach in the Parish of
Tough', Scottish Wills and Testaments
Online, Aberdeen Sheriff Court Inventories,
SC1/36/3.

John Thomson's *Atlas of Scotland*, Northern
Part of Aberdeen & Banff Shires. Southern Part.
Bottom right section, 1832; https://maps.nls.uk/
view/74400159#zoom=6&lat=6082&lon=1372
&layers=BT

I can find no later attestations of Tillyreach in the parish of Tough. Possibly Sunnyside of Tillyreach may be one of the farms marked Southside, Drumend and Steybrae on Ordnance Survey maps, or it may be the farm marked Sunnybrae, as Tillyreach appears to be sited NE of Greenburn on the National Archives of Scotland's *Map of Tillyreach, Tullochvenus, Kintocher and Greenburn holdings*, 1700–1799, Shelfmark RHP13778.

Aberdeenshire Sheet LXXI.NE (includes: Coull; Leochel-Cushnie; Lumphanan; Tough), publication date: 1901, date revised: 1899; https://maps.nls.uk/view/75475748#zoom=5&lat=3685&lon=7316&layers=BT

45. Sunnyside of Luncarty, King Edward, Aberdeenshire, 1747–52, NJ 72635 54649

Canmore Site ID RHP89376, 1779, plans of estate of Castleton.

Roy *Military Survey of Scotland*, 1747–55; http://maps.nls.uk/geo/explore/#zoom=14&lat=57.5764&lon=-2.4251&layers=3

Aberdeenshire, Sheet XI, surveyed: 1870–71, published: 1874; https://maps.nls.uk/view/74425313#zoom=6&lat=8744&lon=5823&layers=BT

46. Sunnyside, Cults, Peterculter, Aberdeenshire, 1865, NJ 88504 03754

Kincardine Sheet III.8 (Banchory Devenick), survey date: 1865, publication date: 1868; https://maps.nls.uk/view/74948025#zoom=5&lat=8482&lon=7704&layers=BT

47. Sunnyside of Drum, Maud, Peterhead, Aberdeenshire, 1621, NJ 89880 46416

'1st February, 1621. — Bond containing reversion of Sunnyside, made by Anna Irvine, daughter of Alexander Irvine of Drum, to her father.' (Forbes Leslie 1909: 159). The building is shown on Ordnance Survey maps but not labelled.

Aberdeenshire, Sheet XXI (includes: New Deer; Old Deer), survey date: 1870, publication date: 1873; https://maps.nls.uk/view/74425323#zoom =6&lat=7207&lon=3736&layers=BT

Sunnyside of Drum, Maud, Peterhead AB42 5RZ; Google Maps Streetview

48. Sunnyside and Sunnyside Cottage, Montrose, Angus, ?1695, NO 71162 61541 and NO 71021 61431

'Jean Anderson, birth 25 August 1695, Sunnyside, Angus (The Church of Jesus Christ of Latter-day Saints, International Genealogical Index (IGI) database, FamilySearch (https://familysearch.org/ark:/ 61903/2:1:MGMM-1LT : accessed 2015-12-04), entry for Jean Anderson) – the IGI database has what look like duplicate entries for Jean Anderson, born 25 August 1695, at

Sunnyside, both in Angus and Alloa, so this may be a transcription error.

Montrose Parish Records, 1834, NRS Reference CH2/943/32, pp. 1–19; *Post Office Directory* 1843.

Forfarshire, Sheet XXVIII (includes: Logie-Pert; Montrose; St Cyrus), survey date: 1862, publication date: 1865; https://maps.nls.uk/view /74426906#zoom=6&lat=5151&lon=6498& layers=BT

49. Sunnyside Cottage, Rhu, Kilcalmonell, Argyllshire, 1841, NR 83893 65365

Census 1841.

Argyllshire, Sheet CCI (includes: Kilcalmonell; South Knapdale), survey date: 1867, publication date: 1873; https://maps.nls.uk/view/74427483# zoom=6&lat=6722&lon=13683&layers=BT

50. Sunnyside, Muirkirk, Ayrshire, 1841,
    NS 72946 29017

1841 Census; Fergusson (1841: 207). *Post Office Directory*, 1851–2.

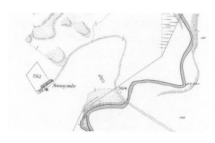

Ayr Sheet XXXI.2 (Muirkirk), survey date: 1856, publication date: 1860; https://maps.nls.uk/view/74963581#zoom=4&lat=9351&lon=8002&layers=BT

51. Sunnyside, Kilmarnock, Ayrshire,
    1851–2, NS 47098 39009

Post Office Directory 1851–2.

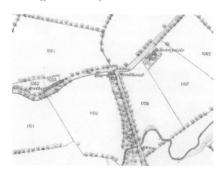

Ayr XVIII.11 (Kilmarnock), survey date: 1856, publication date: 1860; https://maps.nls.uk/view/74930452#zoom=5&lat=5339&lon=9509&layers=BT

52. Sunnyside, Riccarton, Kilmarnock,
    Ayrshire, 1834, NS 42461 34145

'William Armour Sunnyside', Kilmarnock Laigh Kirk Parish Records, 1834 (NRS Reference: CH2/1252/10 pp. 76–85, www.oldscottish.com); 1841 Census.

Ayr Sheet XXIII.5 (Riccarton), survey date: 1857, publication date: 1860; https://maps.nls.uk/view/74937779#zoom=4&lat=3807&lon=12436&layers=BT

53. Sunnyside, Maybole, Ayrshire, 1837,
    NS 30702 10461

Post Office Directory 1837; 'Agnes Henderson, 23/11/1848, Residing at Sunnyside near Maybole', Scottish Wills and Testaments Online, SC6/44/17.

Ayr Sheet XLV.1 (Maybole), survey date: 1856, publication date: 1859; https://maps.nls.uk/view/74935122#zoom=5&lat=3909&lon=3962&layers=BT

54. Sunnyside of Auchenmade, Kilwinning, Ayrshire, 1855–57, NS 35690 48019

'Various modes of spelling: East Auchenmade: Sunnyside of Auchenmade.

Authorities for spelling: Mr (William) Shanks, Kilwinning, occupier, Robert Ferguson, Little Auchenmade.

Description remarks: A far(m) house with Offices etc., the property of Mr Shanks, Kilwinning, and occupied by James Stephen. Mr Shanks the proprietor seems to care little which of the names be given, he thinks either would do.'

(Ayrshire Name Book (1855–1857), OS1/3/41/34)

Ayr XII.6 (Kilwinning), survey date: 1856, publication date: 1858; https://maps.nls.uk/view/74930557#zoom=5&lat=8998&lon=10301&layers=BT

Sunnyside of Auchenmade, Kilwinning, Ayrshire KA13 7RS; Google Maps Streetview

55. Sunnyside, Parish of New Cumnock, East Ayrshire, 1845, NS 56185 11252

Gravestone 'Erected by John Lammie Sunnyside in memory of Margaret Lammie his wife who died 20th March 1845', Auld Kirkyard, New Cumnock (http://newcumnockheritage.com/welcome); *Post Office Directory* 1851–2.

Ayr Sheet XLI.15 (New Cumnock), survey date: 1857, publication date: 1860; https://maps.nls.uk/view/74935251#zoom=4&lat=4656&lon=11956&layers=BT

56. Sunnyside, Parish of Auchinleck, East Ayrshire, 1851–2, NS 61040 21960

Post Office Directory 1851–2.
'Thomas Baird, 12/10/1865, Sometime farmer in Sunnyside, Auchinleck', Scottish Wills and Testaments Online, SC6/46/3.

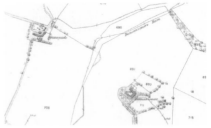

Ayr Sheet XXXVI.1 (Auchenleck), survey date: 1857, publication date: 1860; https://maps.nls.uk/view/74951216#zoom=4&lat=2988&lon=9565&layers=BT

57. Sunnyside, Kirkoswald, Ayrshire, 1851,
NS 23542 09493

1851 Census.

Ayrshire, Sheet XLIV (includes: Kirkoswald;
Maybole), survey date: 1857, publication date:
1859; https://maps.nls.uk/view/74425831#zoom
=6&lat=7236&lon=6179&layers=BT

58. Sunnyside, Dailly, Ayrshire, 1856,
NS 27899 03201

Ayrshire, Sheet L (includes: Dailly; Girvan;
Kirkoswald), survey date: 1856, publication date:
1859; https://maps.nls.uk/view/74425837#zoom
=6&lat=7650&lon=12638&layers=BT

59. Sunnyside, Kilmaurs, Ayrshire, 1851,
NS 40945 41105

1851 Census; Ordnance Survey Name Book
OS1/3/36/51: 'This name applies from Main
Street to Free Church Manse'.

Ayrshire XVII.8 (Kilmaurs), survey date: 1856,
publication date: 1857; https://maps.nls.uk/
view/74930497#zoom=5&lat=7122&lon=15185
&layers=BT

60. Sunnyside, Dalrymple, Ayrshire,
1747–55, NS 35880 14951

 Roy *Military Survey
of Scotland,* 1747–55;
http://maps.nls.uk/geo/
roy/#zoom=14&lat=
55.4066&lon=-
4.6287&layers=
roy-lowlands

61. Sunnyside, Marnoch, Banffshire, 1867,
NJ 56349 53205

Banff Sheet XV.7 (Marnoch), survey date: 1867,
publication date: 1871; https://maps.nls.uk/
view/75067110#zoom=5&lat=3840&lon=10801
&layers=BT

62. Sunnyside, Gamrie, Banffshire, 1836,
     ?NJ 53011 67068 or NJ 77902 61824

Gamrie Parish Records: male heads of families, 1836 (National Archives of Scotland,
Gamrie Kirk Session Records, Minutes and
Accounts 1812–1845, CH2/1051/3 pp. 192–
206): James Ingram, Crofter, Sunnyside;
Alexander Duff, Sunnyside; and Jas. Ingram,
Crofter, Sunnyside (http://www.oldscot-
tish.com/gamrie.html). Sunnyside, Gamrie
is also listed in the 1841 and 1851 censuses. It is not clear whether Sunnyside NJ
53011 67068, is referred to, or the steading
marked *Littlehill* on Ordnance Survey maps
but *Sunnyside* on modern maps, NJ 77902
61824.

Banffshire Sheet III.NW (includes: Cullen;
Fordyce), publication date: 1904, date revised:
1902; https://maps.nls.uk/view/75496740#zoom
=5&lat=3995&lon=5655&layers=BT

There is a similarly north-east-facing bay
named Greenside, Aberdour, Aberdeenshire,
NJ 875653.

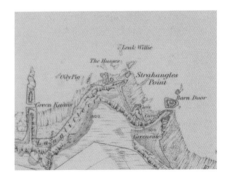

Aberdeenshire, Sheet I, survey date: 1871,
publication date: 1874; https://maps.nls.uk/
view/74425304#zoom=5&lat=5805&lon=13546
&layers=BT

63. Sunnyside, Eccles, Berwickshire, 1772,
     NT 78433 42213

'Mr Dickson, Sunnyside, Eccles,
Berwickshire, 1772', Timperley (1976: 81)
    'George Reid, 08/10/1829, d. 21/10/1827
at Sunnyside, Eccles', Scottish Wills and
Testaments Online, SC60/44/2.

John Thomson's *Atlas of Scotland*, Berwick-shire,
1832; https://maps.nls.uk/view/74400120#zoom
=7&lat=2916&lon=6948&layers=BT

64. Sunnyside, near Auchencrow,
     Coldingham, Berwickshire, 1700–99,
     NT 85262 61380

'George Hood, Sunnyside', *Charting the
Nation*, Work Record ID 0043926, National
Archives of Scotland, Shelfmark RHP14840,
Sketch of the Town and Territory of
Auchincrow (1700–1799); George Hood,

23/07/1821, of Sunnyside, Scottish Wills and Testaments Online, CC15/7/3; 1841 Census.

John Thomson's *Atlas of Scotland*, Berwick-shire, 1832; https://maps.nls.uk/view/74400120#zoom=7&lat=6044&lon=8045&layers=BT

65. Sunnyside or Kersfield Mains, Parish of Coldstream, Berwickshire, 1788, NT 88118 45040

21 August 1788, volume 9: 'Horse Tax, Peter Thomson, Sunnyside, Coldstream Parish' (ScotlandsPlaces, E326/9/9/60).

'Farm in Berwickshire, Banks of the Tweed. To be Let for such a number of years as can be agreed on, and entered to at Whitsunday 1807, Sunnyside or Kersfield Mains, in the parish of Coldstream, consisting of the Fields called Easterfield, Anna, Northcloss, and Mid-park, containing 115 acres or thereby, with the Houses at Sunnyside.' (*Caledonian Mercury*, Monday, 3 November 1806; Issue 13235).

Ordnance Survey Name Book OS1/5/12/16.

John Thomson's *Atlas of Scotland*, Berwick-Shire, 1832; https://maps.nls.uk/view/74400120#zoom=6&lat=3343&lon=8534&layers=BT

Berwick Sheet XXIII.15 (with inset XXIX.3) (Coldstream), survey date: 1858, publication date: 1862; https://maps.nls.uk/view/74944021#zoom=4&lat=9878&lon=5741&layers=BT

Aerial view from Google Maps of Sunnyside, Milnegraden Estate, Coldstream TD12 4HE

Before being bought by Sir David Milne in 1821, the Milnegraden estate was known as Kersfield:

Roy Military *Survey of Scotland*, 1747–55; http://maps.nls.uk/geo/roy/#zoom=14&lat=55.7040&lon=-2.2199&layers=roy-lowlands

66. Sunnyside, Duns, Berwickshire, 1841,
    NT 77992 53621

1841 Census.
'Helen Allan, 02/06/1865, Resided at
Sunnyside near Dunse', Scottish Wills and
Testaments Online, SC60/41/20.

Berwick Sheet XVI.7 (Dunse), survey date: 1857,
publication date: 1862; https://maps.nls.uk/
view/74944129#zoom=5&lat=2232&lon=3674
&layers=BT

67. Sunysyd, Parish of Alloa,
    Clackmannanshire, 1625, NS 88776
    93269

Taylor, McNiven and Williamson (forth-
coming, *Place-Names of Clackmannanshire*),
Elspet Short, 26/03/1625, Relict of John
Burne, Collier in Sunysyd, Parish of Alloway,
Scottish Wills and Testaments Online,
CC21/5/3.

Perth and Clackmannan Sheet CXXXIX.NE
(includes: Airth; Alloa), publication date: 1901,
date revised: 1899; https://maps.nls.uk/view/
75736494#zoom=6&lat=5432&lon=6769&
layers=BT

68. Sunnyside, Airth, Clackmannanshire,
    1482, NS 88800 88439

'Elizabeth Livingstoune swore not to revoke
the alienation made by her to John Bros
of Stanehouse of her half of the lands of
Sunnyside' (*Abstract of Protocol Book of
the Burgh of Stirling*, p. 53). Grid reference
located by John Reid (*Material for a place-
name survey of East Stirlingshire*, http://
www.spns.org.uk/resources09.html), the
building is not named on older Ordnance
Survey maps but Roy's *Military Survey of
Scotland* shows it as 'Greenside', also marked
'Green' on John Thomson's *Atlas of Scotland*,
1832.

John Thomson's *Atlas of Scotland*, Perthshire
with Clackmannan. Bottom right section, 1832;
https://maps.nls.uk/view/74400163#zoom=7&
lat=3709&lon=866&layers=BT

Roy *Military Survey of Scotland*, 1747–55;
http://maps.nls.uk/geo/roy/#zoom=14&lat
=56.0719&lon=-3.7906&layers=roy-lowlands

John Thomson's *Atlas of Scotland*, Stirlingshire, 1832; https://maps.nls.uk/view/74400119#zoom =7&lat=4767&lon=9784&layers=BT

69. Sunnyside Park, Little Denovan, Dunipace, Stirlingshire, 1809, NS 8183

Abridgement of Sasines, Stirlingshire 1781– 1986, 6249. Grid reference located by John Reid (*Material for a place-name survey of East Stirlingshire*). The location (by Denny Bridge, Dunipace) is not named on the 1865 Ordnance Survey map and I have been unable to find it elsewhere. I have not seen the sasine.

70. Sunnyside, Kirkconnel, Dumfries, 1856, NS 76114 11914

Dumfries Sheet VI.10 (With inset VI.14) (Kirkconnel), survey date: 1856, publication date: 1860; https://maps.nls.uk/view/74944750# zoom=5&lat=9875&lon=5759&layers=BT

71. Sunnyside, Parish of Prestonkirk, Haddington, East Lothian, 1805, NT 59527 75407

'James Knox, 27/09/1805, Tenant in Sunnyside, Parish of Prestonkirk near Haddington' Scottish Wills and Testaments Online, CC8/8/136.

'East Lothian. To be Sold, by public voluntary roup, at Sunnyside, upon Saturday the 12th May, 1810, The whole of the valuable Stocking of that Farm, situated in the parish of Prestonkirk.' (*Caledonian Mercury*, 30 April 1810).

John Thomson's *Atlas of Scotland*, Haddington, 1832; https://maps.nls.uk/view/74400130#zoom =6&lat=5516&lon=6547&layers=BT

72. Sunnyside, Tranent, East Lothian; 1747–55; c. NT 43586 72065

Roy *Military Survey of Scotland*, 1747–55; http://maps.nls.uk/geo/roy/#zoom=14&lat= 55.9371&lon=-2.9103&layers=roy-lowlands

73. Sunnyside, Yester, East Lothian, 1841,
     NT 54768 67644

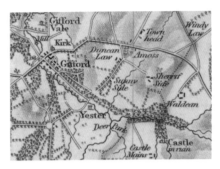

John Thomson's *Atlas of Scotland*, Haddington,
1832; https://maps.nls.uk/view/74400130#zoom
=7&lat=3638&lon=5200&layers=BT

74. Sunnyside, Haddington, East Lothian,
     1752–55, NT 48357 72003

Roy *Military Map of Scotland* 1752–55;
http://maps.nls.uk/geo/explore/#zoom=14&lat
=55.9396&lon=-2.8386&layers=4

John Thomson's *Atlas of Scotland*, Haddington,
1832; https://maps.nls.uk/view/74400130#zoom
=7&lat=4800&lon=3683&layers=BT

75. Sunnyside, Carnock Parish, Fife, 1832,
     NT 01538 90925

John Thomson's *Atlas of Scotland*, Fife with
Kinross Shire. Left side, 1832; https://maps.nls.
uk/view/74400167#zoom=6&lat=7335&lon=
2169&layers=BT

Fife, Sheet 34 (includes: Carnock; Culross;
Saline; Torryburn), survey date: 1854,
publication date: 1856; https://maps.nls.uk/
view/74426851#zoom=6&lat=8265&lon=8346
&layers=BT

Sunnyside, Bickramside, Saline, Fife KY12;
Google Maps Streetview

76. Sunnyside, Torryburn, Saline, Fife, 1841, NT 03892 86795

1841 Census.

Fife, Sheet 34 (includes: Carnock; Culross; Saline; Torryburn), survey date: 1854, publication date: 1856; https://maps.nls.uk/view/74426851#zoom=6&lat=2224&lon=11909&layers=BT

77. Sunnyside, Abbotshall, Fife, 1747–52, NT 25683 91678

'Mary Spence, birth: about 1750, Sunnyside, Abbotshall, Fife' (The Church of Jesus Christ of Latter-day Saints, International Genealogical Index (IGI) database, FamilySearch (https://familysearch.org/ark:/61903/2:1:M29J-3HL : accessed 2015-12-04), entry for Mary Spence).

Roy *Military Map of Scotland*, 1747–55; http://maps.nls.uk/geo/explore/#zoom=15&lat=56.0836&lon=-3.1914&layers=3

78. Sunnyside and Sunnyside Plantation, Auchterderran, Fife, 1747–52, NT 23144 94260

Roy *Military Map of Scotland*, 1747–55; https://maps.nls.uk/geo/explore/#zoom=15&lat=56.1585&lon=-3.1622&layers=3&b=1

Fife, Sheet 31 (includes: Auchterderran; Ballingry; Kinglassie; Kirkcaldy And Dysart; Portmoak), survey date: 1854, publication date: 1856; https://maps.nls.uk/view/74426848#zoom=6&lat=4314&lon=11824&layers=BT

79. Sunnyside Croft, Auchlunies, Kincardine, 1604, NO 88661 99570

Aberdeenshire Sheriff Court, 10 March 1604: 'Killing Salmon in Forbidden Time. In this case about 100 persons were cited from Nether Dee and Feugh sides. Some were acquitted, some convicted, and those who did not appear declared fugitives and denounced to the horn. Among those convicted were John Burnat of Sluie and four other Burnats. There were also three Straquhans. The jury numbered 25, of whom part were from Aberdeen and the others from Deeside. Among the latter were John Irving of Kincowsy (Chancellor), John Collistoun of Auchloonies, John Irving of Sunnyside, Robert Hog of Gellane, Alexander Davidsoune of Brigend.' (Littlejohn, 1906: 17). Also known as Sunnyside of Blairs.

Kincardineshire, Sheet III (includes: Drumoak; Maryculter; Peterculter; Skene), survey date: 1865, publication date: 1868; https://maps.nls.uk/view/74427589#zoom=6&lat=1391&lon=13562&layers=BT

80. Sunnyside, Banchory Devenick, Kincardine, 1865, NJ 91403 00083

Kincardineshire, Sheet IV (includes: Aberdeen; Banchory-Devenick; Nigg), survey date: 1865; publication date: 1868; https://maps.nls.uk/view/74427590#zoom=6&lat=2294&lon=3448&layers=BT

81. Sunnyside of Badentoy, Banchory Devenick, Kincardine, 1865, NO 89968 98064

Kincardine Sheet VIII.1 (Banchory Devenick), survey date: 1865, publication date: 1868; https://maps.nls.uk/view/74948034#zoom=5&lat=2047&lon=2646&layers=BT

82. Sunnyside, Banchory Devenick, Kincardine, 1865, NO 89491 98670

Kincardineshire, Sheet VII (includes: Durris; Fetteresso; Maryculter; Peterculter), survey date: 1865, publication date: 1868; https://maps.nls.uk/view/74427593#zoom=6&lat=9789&lon=15096&layers=BT

83. Sunnyside, Fetteresso, Kincardineshire, 1841, NO 79872 89325

1841 Census.

Kincardine Sheet XI.12 (with inset XI.15) (Fetteresso), survey date: 1864, publication date: 1868; https://maps.nls.uk/view/74949315#zoom =5&lat=8025&lon=14276&layers=BT

84. Sunnyside, Cleish, Kinross, 1841, NT 12553 97419

1841 Census.

'Robert Walls, 18/11/1868, Farmer, Sunnyside, Parish of Cleish', Scottish Wills and Testaments Online, SC22/44/6.

Fife, Sheet 30 (includes: Beath; Cleish; Dunfermline; Kinross), survey date: 1854, publication date: 1856; https://maps.nls.uk/ view/74426847#zoom=6&lat=7967&lon=10283 &layers=BT

85. Sunnyside, Biggar, Lanarkshire; 1734, NT 04286 38401

'The name of Robert Scott, wright in Sunnyside, appears in the Session Records, under date 11th July 1734'... 'The farmhouse consisted of a but and a ben, covered with thatch, and having a dunghill and a garden in front.' (Hunter 1867: 107, 111). Subsequently known as Loaningdale House, Biggar, South Lanarkshire, ML12 6LX.

Roy *Military Survey of Scotland*, 1747–55; http://maps.nls.uk/geo/roy/#zoom=14&lat =55.6445&lon=-3.5669&layers=roy-lowlands

John Thomson's *Atlas of Scotland*, Northern Part of Lanarkshire. Southern Part. Bottom section, 1832; https://maps.nls.uk/view/74400129#zoom =7&lat=6917&lon=8927&layers=BT

86. Sunnyside, Cambusnethan,
    Lanarkshire, 1859, NS 87019 55328

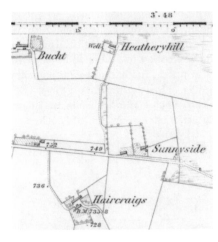

Lanarkshire, Sheet XIX (includes:
Cambusnethan; Carluke; Carstairs), survey date:
1859, publication date: 1864; https://maps.nls.
uk/view/74427708#zoom=6&lat=10422&lon=
7396&layers=BT

87. Sunnyside, Culter, Lanarkshire, 1859,
    NT 01867 34798

Lanarkshire, Sheet XL (includes: Broughton,
Glenholm And Kilbucho; Culter), survey date:
1859, publication date: 1864; https://maps.nls.
uk/view/74427728#zoom=6&lat=9118&lon=
1999&layers=BT

88. Sunnysid (Sunnyside and Little
    Sunnyside), Parish of Hamilton,
    Lanarkshire, c.1583–1614, NS 74740
    51089 and NS 74736 50928

Pont 34 Lanarkshire, c.1583–1614, NS747511
(http://maps.nls.uk/pont/placenames/r-u.
html).

'Jeane Hamiltoun, 06/05/1626, Spouse
to Alexander Wod of Sunnyside, Parish of
Hamilton' Scottish Wills and Testaments
Online, CC10/5/5; Robert Weir of Sunnyside,
Hamilton (ECCO, 1762).

Post Office Directory 1852, Sunnyside,
Larkhall, Hamilton, Lanarkshire.

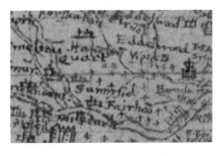

Pont 34, c.1583–1614; http://maps.nls.uk/pont/
view/?id=pont34#zoom=6&lat=4426&lon=
2360&layers=BT

Roy *Military Map of Scotland*, 1752–55;
http://maps.nls.uk/geo/explore/#zoom=15&lat=
55.7390&lon=-3.9890&layers=4

Lanarkshire, Sheet XVIII (includes:
Cambusnethan; Carluke; Dalserf; Dalziel;
Hamilton), survey date: 1859, publication date:
1864; https://maps.nls.uk/view/74427707#zoom
=6&lat=3548&lon=3851&layers=BT

89. Sunnyside, Wishaw, Parish of
    Hamilton, Lanarkshire, 1859, NS
    78179 55319

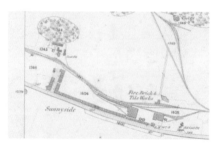

Lanark Sheet XVIII.3 (Cambusnethan), survey
date: 1859, publication date: 1864; https://maps.
nls.uk/view/74952583#zoom=5&lat=7670&lon=
2714&layers=BT

90. Sunnyside Lodge, Parish of Lanark,
    Lanarkshire, 1817, NS 86434 44054

'Died – At Edinburgh, on the 5th inst.
John Gillespie, Esq. of Sunnyside Lodge,
Lanarkshire.' (*The Morning Post*, 9 August
1817)

'At the Manse of Lanark, Alexander
Gillespie, Esq. of Sunnyside, to Miss Jane
Menzies, eldest daughter of the Rev. W.
Menzies, Minister of Lanark.' (*Edinburgh
Magazine and Literary Miscellany*, vol.
80, 398. 27th October 1817. *Gentleman's
Magazine*, vol. 168, 222)

'Sunnyside Lodge' (Duncan 1820: 23);
Post Office Directory 1837.

John Thomson's *Atlas of Scotland*, Northern Part
of Lanarkshire. Southern Part. Top section, 1832;
https://maps.nls.uk/view/74400128#zoom=
7&lat=3250&lon=5230&layers=BT

Lanarkshire, Sheet XXV (includes: Carluke;
Lanark; Lesmahagow), survey date: 1858–59,
publication date: 1864; https://maps.nls.uk/
view/74427714#zoom=6&lat=2917&lon=6843
&layers=BT

91. Sunnyside, Coatbridge, Old Monkland,
    Lanarkshire, 1747–55, NS 73114 65706
    and NS 73194 65664

Anne Webster, christening, 16 June 1758,
Sunnyside, Coatbridge, Lanark (The
Church of Jesus Christ of Latter-day Saints,
'International Genealogical Index (IGI),'
database, *FamilySearch* (https://family-
search.org/ark:/61903/2:1: MP61-6BH:
accessed 2015-12-06), entry for Anne
Webster.)

'Ludovick Baillie, 07/02/1837, Farmer,
Residing in Sunnyside in Parish of Old
Monkland', Scottish Wills and Testaments
Online, SC36/51/13.

Roy *Military Survey of Scotland*, 1747–55;
http://maps.nls.uk/geo/roy/#zoom=15&lat=
55.8683&lon=-4.0275&layers=roy-lowlands

Lanarkshire, Sheet VII (includes: Bothwell;
Cadder; Glasgow; Old Monkland), survey date:
1858–9, publication date: 1864; https://maps.nls.
uk/view/74427696#zoom=6&lat=6061&lon=
14556&layers=BT

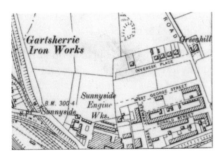

Lanarkshire Sheet VII.NE (includes: Cadder; Old
Monkland), publication date: 1899, date revised:
1897; https://maps.nls.uk/view/75650688#zoom
=5&lat=1669&lon=7416&layers=BT

92. Sunnyside, Crawfordjohn, Lanarkshire,
1832, NS 87270 22863

1841 Census; 'Hugh Murdoch, 14/09/1847,
Farmer at Sunnyside, Crawfordjohn', Scottish
Wills and Testaments Online, SC36/48/33.

John Thomson's *Atlas of Scotland*, Northern Part
of Lanarkshire. Southern Part. Bottom section,
1832; https://maps.nls.uk/view/74400129#zoom
=7&lat=5751&lon=4766&layers=BT

93. Sunnyside, Shotts, Lanarkshire, 1832,
NS 75489 58406

John Thomson's *Atlas of Scotland*, Northern Part
of Lanarkshire. Southern Part. Top section, 1832;
https://maps.nls.uk/view/74400128#zoom=7&
lat=4005&lon=6511&layers=BT

Lanarkshire, Sheet XII (includes: Bothwell;
Cambusnethan; Dalziel; Shotts), survey date:
1859, publication date: 1864; https://maps.nls.
uk/view/74427701#zoom=6&lat=3902&lon=
11689&layers=BT

94. Sunnyside, Glencorse, Midlothian,
    1852, NT 24438 62366

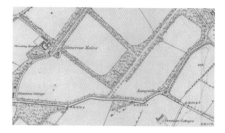

Edinburghshire, Sheet 12 (includes: Glencorse;
Lasswade; Penicuik), survey date: 1852,
publication date: 1854; https://maps.nls.uk/
view/74426712#zoom=6&lat=5202&lon=8240
&layers=BT

95. Sunnyside, Kirknewton, East Calder,
    Midlothian, 1851, NT 11517 64745

1851 Census.

Edinburghshire, Sheet 11 (includes: Currie;
Penicuik), survey date: 1852, publication date:
1853; https://maps.nls.uk/view/74426711#zoom
=6&lat=8077&lon=3962&layers=BT

96. Sunnyside, Liberton, Parish of
    Edinburgh, Midlothian, 1785, NT
    28354 70116

Now Liberton Golf Club, previously
Kingston Grange *c.*1850, previously
Sunnyside House built 1785–7 for Patrick
Inglis (Canmore ID 153306, Site Number
NT27SE 4140). Architect Robert Adam
(http://portal.historic-scotland.gov.uk/hes/

web/f?p=PORTAL:DESIGNATION:::::DES
:LB28083).

'On Monday last Rear-Admiral Inglis
died at Sunnyside, in Scotland' (*World*, 17
October 1791). 'Patrick Inglis, 07/04/1818,
Sir, Bart., of Sunnyside, Inventory; Trust
Disposition, Settlement', Scottish Wills and
Testaments Online, SC70/1/17.

John Thomson's *Atlas of Scotland*, Edinburgh
Shire. Top right section, 1832; https://maps.nls.
uk/view/74400125#zoom=7&lat=2371&lon=
3323&layers=BT

Edinburghshire 004.13 (includes: Edinburgh;
Newton), publication date: 1895, revised: 1893;
http://maps.nls.uk/view/82877610

97. Sunnyside, Shawfair, Newton,
    Midlothian, 1665, NT 31748 70642

'they will, in quest of Honour, repair to the
Dominions of Chawfair and Sunnyside'
(Thomas St. Serfe, 1665, *The remarkable
prophesies in order to the present times the
one of Gilpine Girnigo, one of the heritable
poets of the old Thanes of Gilliquhimnee: the
other of Sir Tristram, Clerk of the Kitchin to
the Knights of King Arthur's Round Table*);

228 *Sunnyside*

Records of the Parliaments of Scotland 12 June 1672 ([1672/6/73]); Timperley (1976: 232) 'Christian Spence, 20/01/1737, Late Residenter at Sunnyside, Parish of Newtoun, and Relict of Archibald Miller, Baxter in Canongate', Scottish Wills and Testaments Online, CC8/8/99; 'Jas. Wauchope of Edmonston: Sunnyside, Shawfair, Newton', 1771 valuation rolls, Timperley (1976: 232).

Roy *Military Survey of Scotland*, 1747–55; http://maps.nls.uk/geo/roy/#zoom=15&lat= 55.9238&lon=-3.0998&layers=roy-lowlands

98. Sunnyside, Newlands, Peebleshire, 1832, NT 17953 51627

1841 Census; 1852 Census (Sunnyside, Leadburn, Peebles)

John Thomson's *Atlas of Scotland*, Edinburgh Shire. Bottom left section, 1832; https://maps.nls.uk/view/74400126#zoom=6&lat=3418&lon= 10695&layers=BT

99. Sunnyside, Kirkurd, Peebleshire, 1747–55, NT 11323 44338

Roy Military Survey of Scotland, 1752–55; http://maps.nls.uk/geo/roy/#zoom=15&lat= 55.6982&lon=-3.4088&layers=roy-lowlands

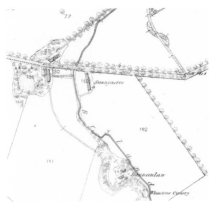

Peebles Sheet VII.16 (Kirkurd), survey date: 1857, publication date: 1859; https://maps.nls.uk/view/74954654#zoom=5&lat=8542&lon= 13726&layers=BT

100. Sonysyd, Barony of Tulliallan, Perthshire, 1619, NS 93383 89151

1619, *Registrum Magni Sigilli Regum Scotorum* vii no. 2017 (barony of Tulliallan; Vol. 1, 564), 1306-1668; 'Farms of the Estate of Tulliallan, &c. In the County of Perth. To be Let, and entered to at Martinmas 1808, Overtoun, possessed by Robert Stein, Esq. of Kilbagie, consisting of about 158 Acres. Sunnyside, possessed also by Mr Stein, consisting of about 50' (*Caledonian Mercury*, 17 March 1808).

Perth and Clackmannan Perthshire Sheet CXL.14 (Combined), survey date: 1861, publication date: 1866; https://maps.nls.uk/view/74479301#zoom=4&lat=9593&lon=6983&layers=BT

101. Wester Sunnyside and Easter Sunnyside, Fowlis Wester, Perth and Kinross, 1835, NN 97295 24443 and NN 97533 24495

'Lord Lynedoch Sunnyside' (Gloag 1835: 109)

Perth and Clackmannan Sheet XCVI.7 (Fowlis Wester), survey date: 1864, publication date: 1867; https://maps.nls.uk/view/74957921#zoom=4&lat=9656&lon=11323&layers=BT

102. Sunnyside, Barrhead, Neilston, Renfrewshire, 1852, NS 49959 58635

Post Office Directory 1852.

Renfrewshire, Sheet XII (includes: Eastwood; Neilston; Paisley), survey date: 1858, publication date: 1864; https://maps.nls.uk/view/74428239#zoom=6&lat=1611&lon=10410&layers=BT

103. Sunnyside, Cathcart, Renfrewshire, 1858, NS 58581 59684

Renfrewshire, Sheet XIII (includes: Carmunnock; Cathcart; Eastwood; Glasgow; Govan; Rutherglen), survey date: 1858, publication date: 1863; https://maps.nls.uk/view/74428240#zoom=6&lat=3415&lon=8429&layers=BT

104. Sunnyside, Invergordon, Rosskeen Parish, Ross & Cromarty, 1869, NH 71160 68513

'Malcolm, Andrew, corn factor, Sunnyside, Invergordon' *Inverness Advertiser*, 12 February 1869.

Ross-shire & Cromartyshire (Mainland), Sheet LXVI (includes: Cromarty; Kilmuir Easter; Resolis; Rosskeen), survey date: 1872, publication date: 1880; https://maps.nls.uk/view/74428390#zoom=7&lat=6713&lon=5601&layers=BT

105. Sonnyesyde, Melrose, Roxburghshire,
     1590, NT 52055 34052

Williamson (1942: 59).

Roxburghshire, Sheet VII (includes: Caddonfoot;
Galashiels; Melrose; Selkirk), survey date: 1859,
publication date: 1863; https://maps.nls.uk/
view/74428467#zoom=6&lat=8278&lon=13454
&layers=BT

106. Sonnyesyde, Cavers, Roxburghshire,
     1590, NT 52912 13818 and Sunnyside
     Hill, 1858, NT 52368 13363

Williamson (1942: 59).
Post Office Directory 1843.

Roxburgh Sheet XXV.08 (Combined), survey
date: 1858, publication date: 1863; https://maps.
nls.uk/view/74479534#zoom=4&lat=4987&
lon=12527&layers=BT

107. Sunnyside Hill, Morebattle,
     Roxburghshire, 1859, NT 83367
     25229

Sunnyside Hill has a medieval cultivation terrace: https://canmore.org.uk/site/343752/
sunnyside-hill.

Roxburgh Sheet XVII.9 (Morebattle), survey
date: 1859, publication date: 1863; https://maps.
nls.uk/view/74986414#zoom=4&lat=8364&
lon=5859&layers=BT

108. Sunnyside Cottage, Campsie,
     Stirlingshire, 1859, NS 67233 76454

Stirlingshire, Sheet XXVIII (includes: Campsie;
Fintry; Kilsyth; Kirkintilloch), survey date: 1859,
publication date: 1865; https://maps.nls.uk/
view/74430877#zoom=6&lat=3044&lon=8116
&layers=BT

109. Sunneside, Camelon, Falkirk, Stirlingshire, 1482, NS 87613 80452

Abstract of Protocol Book of the Burgh of Stirling, page 301, quoted in Stevenson (1897: 30): '1482. April 20. Elisabeth Levingstoun, spouse of Robert Calenter of Dinate, daughter and one of the heirs of the late John Levingstoun of Athingrye, swore not to revoke the alienation made by her to John Bros of Stanehouse of her half of the lands of Sunneside.'

Post Office Directory 1837.

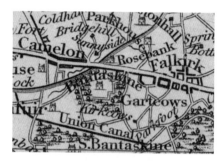

John Thomson's *Atlas of Scotland*, Stirlingshire, 1832; https://maps.nls.uk/view/74400119#zoom=8&lat=3650&lon=9459&layers=BT

110. Sunnyside, St Ninians, Stirlingshire, 1860, NS 79356 91716

Stirling Sheet XVII.7 (Combined), survey date: 1860, publication date: 1865; https://maps.nls.uk/view/74479580#zoom=5&lat=5027&lon=12510&layers=BT

111. Sunnyside, St Ninians, Stirlingshire, 1860, NS 84654 90655

'A small cottage, thatched and in good repair' Ordnance Survey Name Book OS1/32/27/25

Stirling Sheet XVIII.9 (St. Ninians), survey date: 1860, publication date: 1865; https://maps.nls.uk/view/74984256#zoom=4&lat=9664&lon=13929&layers=BT

Shown but not labelled on Thomson's map, unless the 'S' stands for 'Sunnyside of Thorsk'.

John Thomson's *Atlas of Scotland*, Stirlingshire, 1832; https://maps.nls.uk/view/74400119#zoom=7&lat=5129&lon=8946&layers=BT

112. Suny Side, Muiravonside, Stirlingshire, 1747–55, NS 90063 74426

A lost placename; Suny Side is marked as *Boxtonrighead* on Ordnance Survey maps, a division of the steading marked *Bokston* on Roy's *Military Survey of Scotland*.

Roy *Military Survey of Scotland*, 1747–55; http://maps.nls.uk/geo/roy/#zoom=14&lat=55.9610&lon=-3.7542&layers=roy-lowlands

113. Sunnyside, Bathgate, West Lothian, 1775, NS 98332 70279

'James Walker, 06/06/1775, Farmer at Sunnyside, in the Parish of Linlithgow' Scottish Wills and Testaments Online, CC8/8/123
    1841 Census.

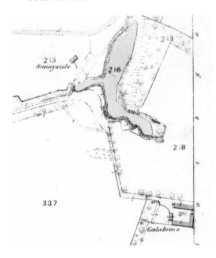

Linlithgow Sheet IX.2 (Bathgate), survey date: 1854, publication date: 1856; https://maps.nls.uk/view/74963063#zoom=5&lat=4876&lon=14487&layers=BT

114. Sunnyside, Ythzies, Tarves, Aberdeenshire, 1832, NJ 88660 30681

John Thomson's *Atlas of Scotland*, Northern Part of Aberdeen & Banff Shires. Southern Part. Top right section, 1832; https://maps.nls.uk/view/74400157#zoom=7&lat=1685&lon=5948&layers=BT

115. Sunnyside, Linlithgow, 1832, NT 03500 77601

John Thomson's *Atlas of Scotland*, Linlithgowshire, 1832; https://maps.nls.uk/view/74400118#zoom=7&lat=5874&lon=6491&layers=BT

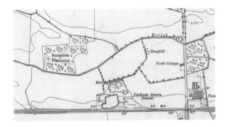

Linlithgowshire Sheet nIV (includes: Abercorn; Dalmeny; Ecclesmachan; Kirkliston; Linlithgow), publication date: 1922, date revised: 1913; https://maps.nls.uk/view/76342875#zoom=6&lat=5842&lon=2428&layers=BT

116. Sunnyside, Slamannan, Stirlingshire,
     1832, near NS 84796 72417

John Thomson's *Atlas of Scotland*, Stirlingshire,
1832; https://maps.nls.uk/view/74400119#zoom
=7&lat=2401&lon=9239&layers=BT

FURTHER SUNNYSIDES IN THE GB1900 GAZETTEER

There are many further Sunnysides in the GB1900 gazetteer (http://geo.nls.uk/maps/gb1900), which is to be expected, as the period covered, 1890–1914, is when the name began to spread. Not included in the Sunnyside Gazetteer above are the following Sunnysides, which may be old since they appear on earlier maps but are unlabelled.

Sunnyside, Knowhead, Alford, Aberdeenshire, 1899, NJ 6041 2154

This farm is depicted on earlier maps but not labelled Sunnyside until the 1899 revision; http://canmore.org.uk/site/173102. Included in the GB1900 Gazetteer.

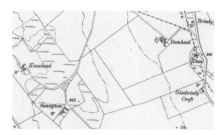

Aberdeenshire Sheet LIII.NW (includes: Keig; Leslie; Premnay), publication date: 1901, date revised: 1899; https://maps.nls.uk/view/7547533 9#zoom=5&lat=3099&lon=2537&layers=BT

Sunnyside, Drum, Fife, 1894, NO 044008

This farm is depicted on earlier maps but not labelled Sunnyside until the 1894 revision. Included in the GB1900 Gazetteer.

Fife and Kinross Sheet XXV.NE (includes: Fossoway; Kinross), publication date: 1897, date revised: 1894; https://maps.nls.uk/view/7563317 8#zoom=5&lat=3871&lon=1735&layers=BT

Sunnyside Strip, Athelstaneford, Haddingtonshire, 1893, NT 553781

The strip of trees is depicted on earlier maps but not labelled Sunnyside Strip until the 1893 revision. Included in the GB1900 Gazetteer.

Haddingtonshire Sheet V.SE (includes: Athelstaneford; Haddington; Prestonkirk), publication date: 1895, date revised: 1893; https://maps.nls.uk/view/75632034#zoom= 5&lat=4900&lon=5629&layers=BT

OTHER SUNNYSIDES

There are present-day Sunnysides that are not labelled on older Ordnance Survey maps but which may nevertheless be old, such as Sunnyside, Stevens Burn, New Deer, Turriff AB53 6TY, NJ 86896 50191, which is shown but not named on older maps.

There are Orkney and Shetland Sunnysides predating 1900, but I have been unable to ascertain dates for the following:

Sunnyside, Parish of Kirkwall & St Ola, Orkney, HY 419107. Ordnance Survey Name Book OS1/23/12/32 (1879–80).

Sunnyside, Quinnifeneth/Queenafinieth, Parish of Harray, Orkney, HY 310148. Ordnance Survey Orkney Sheet CI (includes: Birsay and Harray; Firth; Stenness), publication date: 1903, date revised: 1900.

Sunnyside, Unst, Shetland, HP 647134. Ordnance Survey Name Book OS1/31/23/42 (1877–8).

There are historic Sunnysides I have been unable to identify, such as:

Records of the Parliaments of Scotland to 1707 [1685/4/92] (rps.ac.uk), 23 April 1685: 'Torquhandallochy, Mill of Cattie, Belhangie, Sunnyside'. The other locations are in the Parish of Birse, Aberdeenshire; there is a Sunnyside at Marywell, Parish of Birse, but I cannot ascertain whether it is the same one.

'Robert Pearson, 23/05/1836, of Sunnyside, Farmer at Bankhead, Parish of Moneydie, Perth Sheriff Court, SC49/31/21' (Scottish Wills and Testaments Online). Bankhead is marked on John Thomson's *Atlas of Scotland* (Perthshire with Clackmannan. Bottom right section) in between farms named Nether Ballondie and Growen, where the farm named Marybank is marked on the Ordnance Survey map (OS1/25/58/15).

The 1841 and 1851 censuses show Sunnysides I have not identified in Lightburn, Shettleston, Lanarkshire (although there is a Green there, no. 16 in the Green gazetteer below); at Stracathro, Forfarshire (although there is a Green there, no. 12 in the Green gazetteer below), and in Sorn, Ayrshire.

The 1852 *Post Office Directory* lists Sunnyside, Newmills, Ayrshire, which I cannot identify (although there is a Greens nearby, no. 3 in the Green gazetteer).

'Sunnyside of X'

Where possible I give the Gazetteer number, but not all of the following Sunnyside of Xs appear in the Sunnyside Gazetteer above as I have been unable to date and locate them all. Sunnysides added in late nineteenth-century and early twentieth-century Ordnance Survey revisions may be previously overlooked historic Sunnysides, or they may be modern names, and await investigation.

1. Sunnyside of Airth, Stirlingshire; no. 67; NS 88800 88439
2. Sunnyside of Altries, Maryculter, Kincardineshire; possibly near Altries House, Maryculter, OS1/19/15/29 (Kincardineshire OS Name Book 1863); perhaps the farm at NO 8420 9895 ('Back Mains') or another nearby.
3. Sunnyside of Auchenmade, Kilwinning, Ayrshire; no. 54, NS 35690 48019
4. Sunnyside of Auchmunziel, New Deer, Turriff; depicted on 1871 Ordnance Survey map of Aberdeenshire XX.8 (New Deer) but not named; NJ 87213 46448
5. Sunnyside of Badentoy, Portlethen, Aberdeen; no. 81, NO 89968 98064
6. Sunnyside of Blairs, Maryculter, Kincardineshire; no. 79, NO 88661 99570
7. Sunnyside Of Cairnbrogie, Tarves, Aberdeenshire; no. 40, NJ 85692 27620
8. Sunnyside Of Collonach, Strachan, Banchory, Kincardine; labelled 'Sunnyside' on Ordnance Survey map Kincardineshire Sheet IX.SW (includes: Banchory-Ternan; Strachan), date revised 1901, publication date 1904; https://maps.nls.uk/view/75632713 #zoom=5&lat=4950&lon=2100&lay ers=BT; but no name or building is depicted on that site on the earlier Ordnance Survey map Kincardineshire V.16 (Strachan), survey date: 1865, publication date: 1866; NO 6871 9389
9. Sunnyside of Cook, Crudie, New Byth, Turriff, Aberdeenshire; shown but not named on Ordnance Survey map Aberdeenshire VI.13 (King Edward), survey date: 1870, publication date: 1871; https://maps.nls.uk/view/7448 0218#zoom=5&lat=9955&lon=114 69&layers=BT; named on Ordnance Survey map Aberdeenshire VI.13 (King Edward), revised: 1901, publication date: 1902; https://maps.nls.uk/view/8 2860549#zoom=4&lat=9571&lon=110 70&layers=BT
10. Sunnyside Of Drum, Maud, Peterhead; no. 47, NJ 89880 46416
11. Sunnyside of Dudwick, Ellon, Aberdeenshire; no. 42, NJ 98098 37629
12. Sunnyside of Folla, Rothienorman, Inverurie, Aberdeenshire; no. 35, NJ 71610 33261
13. Sunnyside of Littlefolla, Rothienorman, Inverurie, Aberdeenshire; E326/10/1/24, Farm Horse Tax 1797–8, vol 1 'Leslie Durno Sunside James Durno little Follow'; 'George Morrison, born 8 May 1876, Sunnyside of Littlefolla, Fyvie, Aberdeenshire'. Backhill of Little Folla (http://canmore.org.uk/site/174840) was a steading about 100m south-west of Backhill of Folla; presumably Sunnyside of Littlefolla was nearby, possibly coterminous with Burnside of Littlefolla. Perhaps near NJ 7123 3411
14. Sunnyside of Gight, Methlick, Ellon, Aberdeenshire; labelled Burnside of Gight on Ordnance Survey map Aberdeenshire 029.07 (includes: Fyvie; Methlick; Monquhitter), publication date: 1901, revised: 1899; NJ 84000 40999
15. Sunnyside of Glenythan, Ythanwells, Aberdeenshire; no. 30, NJ 63775 38476

16. Sunnyside of Kemnay, Kintore, Aberdeenshire; now known as Wreaton Farm, name changed between 1852 and 1864; no. 43, NJ 74236 15468

17. Sunnyside of Meikle Warthill, Aberdeenshire; no building shown on Ordnance Survey map Aberdeenshire XXXVI.14 (Rayne), survey date: 1867, publication date: 1868; but shown and marked 'Sunside' on Ordnance Survey map Aberdeenshire XXXVI.14 (Chapel Of Garioch; Daviot; Rayne), revised: 1899, publication date: 1901; NJ 72020 30501

18. Sunnyside of Leslie, Leslie, Insch, Aberdeenshire; no. 31, NJ 60359 24922

19. Sunnyside Of Lethenty, Fyvie, Turriff, Aberdeenshire; shown but not named on Ordnance Survey map Aberdeenshire XXIX.5 (Fyvie), survey date: 1869, publication date: 1869; NJ 80498 40996

20. Sunnyside of Luncarty, King Edward, Aberdeenshire; no. 45, NJ 72635 54649

21. Sunnyside Of Redhill, Rothienorman, Aberdeenshire; marked but not named on Ordnance Survey map Aberdeenshire XXVII.16 (Auchterless), survey date: 1871, publication date: 1872; NJ 68501 36867

22. Sunnyside of Slacks, Greens, New Deer, Turriff; shown but not named on Ordnance Survey map Aberdeenshire XX.7 (New Deer & Monquhitter – Combined), survey date: 1870, publication date: 1873; NJ 85582 46608

23. Sunnyside of Threepwood, Laigh Threepwood, Beith, Ayrshire; shown but not named on Ordnance Survey map Ayrshire VIII.3 (Beith), survey date: 1855, publication date: 1856; NS 38847 55360

24. Sunnyside of Tillyreach in the Parish of Tough, Aberdeenshire; no. 44

25. Sunside of Rayne, Rayne, Aberdeenshire, NJ 70213 29571, is labelled 'Southside', 'a newly erected dwellinghouse and farmsteading', OS1/1/77/43 pg 43. The name may or may not be old.

Gazetteer of 'Greens of X'

1. Greens of Achorties, Keith, Banffshire, 1869; NJ 43529 48352

2. Greens of Addie, Rathven, Banffshire, 1867; NJ 44187 59711

Banff Sheet VIII.6 (Rathven), survey date: 1867, publication date: 1871; https://maps.nls.uk/view/75067326#zoom=5&lat=2658&lon=9925&layers=BT

Banff Sheet XX.2 (Keith), survey date: 1869, publication date: 1872; https://maps.nls.uk/view/75067074#zoom=4&lat=2475&lon=5915&layers=BT

3. Greens of Afforsk, Blairdaff, Inverurie, Aberdeenshire, 1866–7; NJ 6955 1912, Canmore ID 172778

Aberdeenshire, Sheet LIV (includes: Chapel Of Garioch; Inverurie; Kemnay; Kintore), survey date: 1866–7, publication date: 1869; https://maps.nls.uk/view/74425406#zoom=6&lat=3231&lon=1857&layers=BT

4. Greens of Airth, Stirlingshire, 1860; NS 90193 87552

'Greens of Airth' (*The Glasgow Herald*, 21 April 1864).

Stirling Sheet XVIII.16 (Airth), survey date: 1860, publication date: 1865; https://maps.nls.uk/view/74968833#zoom=4&lat=2546&lon=6960&layers=BT

5. Greens of Allt-Sean-Gharaidh, Watten, Caithness, 1871; ND 25452 48352

Ordnance Survey Name Book OS1/7/12/176: 'This is a large portion of rough green Pasture, situated by the side of Allt-an-Sean Ghaiadh, it is well known by this name'.

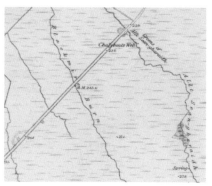

Caithness, Sheet XXIV (includes: Watten; Wick), survey date: 1871, publication date: 1877; https://maps.nls.uk/view/74426581#zoom=5&lat=6088&lon=2692&layers=BT

6. Greens of Allathan, Monquhitter, Aberdeenshire, 1640; NJ 82597 46860

Mains of Greens, Mill of Greens, Auldtown of Greens, Inchgreen, Greenfield, Ordnance Survey Name Book OS1/1/63/51: 'This name is applied to a fertile district on the eastern side of the parish.'

Robert Gordon's *Map of Scotland*, 1640: Aberdeen, Banf, Murrey &c. to Inverness: [and] Fra the north water to Ross / Robertus Gordonius a Strathloch describebat 1640; https://maps.nls.uk/view/00000356#zoom=7&lat=3586&lon=5593&layers=BT

Robert Gordon/Joan Blaeu *Atlas of Scotland*,
Duo Vicecomitatus Aberdonia & Banfia, 1654;
https://maps.nls.uk/view/00000453#zoom=7&
lat=4408&lon=5695&layers=BT

Roy *Military Survey of Scotland*, 1747–55;
http://maps.nls.uk/geo/roy/#zoom=14&lat=
57.5073&lon=-2.2508&layers=roy-highlands

John Thomson's *Atlas of Scotland*, Northern Part
of Aberdeen & Banff Shires. Southern Part. Top
right section, 1832; https://maps.nls.uk/view/
74400157#zoom=6&lat=4189&lon=5188&
layers=BT

7. Greens of Aucharnie, Ythanwells,
   Forgue, Huntly, Aberdeenshire, 1871;
   NJ 6380 3965

http://canmore.org.uk/site/159874. Lies
north of no. 30, Sunnyside, Ythanwells.

Aberdeenshire, Sheet XXVII (includes:
Auchterless; Forgue), survey date: 1871,
publication date: 1873; https://maps.nls.uk/
view/74425329#zoom=6&lat=6007&lon=8503
&layers=BT

8. Greens of Auchmacleddie, Strichen,
   Fraserburgh, Aberdeenshire, 1870; NJ
   92184 58415

Aberdeenshire, Sheet VII (includes: Strichen;
Tyrie), survey date: 1870 Publication date: 1874;
https://maps.nls.uk/view/74425310#zoom=5&
lat=5203&lon=6307&layers=BT

9. Greens of Auchmahoy, Strathdon, Aberdeenshire, 1867 NJ 37358 10293

Ordnance Survey Name Book OS1/1/81/186 'a portion of mossy ground'.

Aberdeenshire, Sheet LXIX (includes: Glenmuick, Tullich And Glengairn; Strathdon), survey date: 1867, publication date: 1869; https://maps.nls.uk/view/74425420#zoom=6&lat=9154&lon=12096&layers=BT

10. Greens of Auchmedden, Aberdour, Aberdeenshire, 1870; NJ 83497 58294

Ordnance Survey Name Book OS1/1/2/83 'Applies to a Small Croft with Offices attached'.

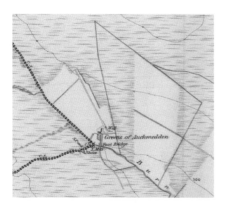

Aberdeenshire, Sheet VI (includes: Aberdour; Gamrie; King Edward; Tyrie) Survey date: 1870–71 Publication date: 1874; https://maps.nls.uk/view/74425309#zoom=6&lat=4680&lon=8059&layers=BT

11. Greens of Bad na Imireach, Logie Coldstone, Aberdeenshire, 1868; NJ 40852 08895

Ordnance Survey Name Book OS1/1/56/41 'a tract of mossy ground a short distance north from Craig Glas'

Aberdeenshire, Sheet LXX (includes: Logie-Coldstone; Tarland; Towie) Survey date: 1868 Publication date: 1870; https://maps.nls.uk/view/74425421#zoom=5&lat=7157&lon=3047&layers=BT

12. Greens of Bedlaithen, Gartly, Aberdeenshire, 1866; NJ 4515 3295

Ordnance Survey Name Book OS1/1/36/36: 'this name applies to piece of green marshy ground, situated on the north-east side of the Burn of Bedlaithen'

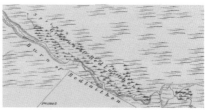

Aberdeen Sheet XXXIII.6 (Gartly), survey date: 1866, publication date: 1874; https://maps.nls.uk/view/74480017#zoom=4&lat=2388&lon=13295&layers=BT

13. Green of Badlormie, Lanarkshire
     1747–55; c.NS 8744 6732

http://canmore.org.uk/site/46716

Roy *Military Survey of Scotland*, 1747–55;
http://maps.nls.uk/geo/roy/#zoom=14
&lat=55.8958&lon=-3.8535&layers=
roy-lowlands

14. Greens of Blairock, Rathven,
     Banffshire 1867; NJ 48764 62475

Banffshire, Sheet VIII (includes: Deskford;
Grange; Keith; Rathven), survey date: 1867,
publication date: 1871; http://maps.nls.
uk/view/74426493 and Banffshire, Sheet
II (includes: Rathven), survey date: 1867,
publication date: 1870; https://maps.nls.uk/
view/74426487#zoom=6&lat=1342&lon=14686
&layers=BT

15. Greens of Bogbuie, Strathdon,
     Aberdeenshire; NJ 350081

Grid reference supplied by Watson (2013:
291): 'rough field up Carvie'. Not shown on
Ordnance Survey maps.

16. Greens of Bogside, Elgin, Morayshire,
     1747–55; NJ 19134 56310

Roy *Military Survey of Scotland*, 1747–55;
http://maps.nls.uk/geo/roy/#zoom=14&lat=
57.6203&lon=-3.2629&layers=roy-highlands

Elgin, Sheet XII (includes: Birnie; Dallas; Elgin),
survey date: 1870, publication date: 1874;
https://maps.nls.uk/view/74426739#zoom=
5&lat=3147&lon=8946&layers=BT

17. Greens of Carnwath, South
     Lanarkshire, 1747–55; NT 01556 47138

Roy *Military Survey of Scotland*, 1747–55;
http://maps.nls.uk/geo/roy/#zoom=14&lat=
55.7191&lon=-3.6065&layers=roy-lowlands

18. Greens of Cook, Crudie, New Byth,
Aberdeenshire, 1901; NJ 80914 56756

Aberdeenshire 006.13 (includes: King Edward),
publication date: 1902, revised: 1901; https://
maps.nls.uk/view/82860549#zoom=4&lat=9097
&lon=11999&layers=BT

19. Greens of Coxton, St Andrews
Lhanbryd, Morayshire, 1871; NJ 25077
60740

Elgin, Sheet XIII (includes: Elgin; Rothes;
Speymouth; St Andrews Lhanbryd; Urquhart),
survey date: 1871, publication date: 1874;
https://maps.nls.uk/view/74426740#zoom=6&
lat=9597&lon=4134&layers=BT

20. Greens of Crynoch, Maryculter,
Kincardineshire, 1865; NO 86683
97367

Kincardineshire, Sheet VII (includes: Durris;
Fetteresso; Maryculter; Peterculter)
Survey date: 1865, Publication date: 1868;
https://maps.nls.uk/view/74427593#zoom=6&
lat=7915&lon=10922&layers=BT

21. Greens of Dipple, Speymouth,
Morayshire, 1747–55; NJ 33202 57572

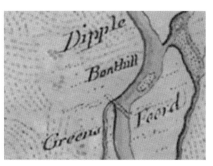

Roy *Military Survey of Scotland,* 1747–55;
http://maps.nls.uk/geo/roy/#zoom=14&lat=
57.5994&lon=-3.0760&layers=roy-highlands

22. Greens of Dunain, Peterhead,
    Aberdeenshire, 1747–55; NJ 97177
    55154

Roy *Military Survey of Scotland*, 1747–55;
http://maps.nls.uk/geo/roy/#zoom=14&lat=
57.5706&lon=-1.9737&layers=roy-highlands

23. Greens of Ethie, Inverkeilor,
    Forfarshire, 1859; NO 68734 47817

Forfar Sheet XLI.9 (Inverkeilor), survey date:
1859, publication date: 1865; https://maps.nls.
uk/view/74946490#zoom=5&lat=2724&lon=
8202&layers=BT

24. Greens of Feithhill, Fortrie, Turriff,
    Aberdeenshire, 1900; NJ 6611 4374

http://canmore.org.uk/site/166701

Banffshire 022.15 (includes: Forgue;
Inverkeithny), publication date: 1901, revised:
1900; https://maps.nls.uk/view/82870695#zoom
=4&lat=5574&lon=12074&layers=BT

25. Greens of Gardyne, Kirkden,
    Forfarshire, 1832; NO 57841 51928

Greens of Gardyne, Forfar, Angus, DD8
2TT is labelled 'North Mains' on Ordnance
Survey maps. Ordnance Survey maps
show a smaller dwelling labelled 'Greens'
to the north, NO 57802 52409. Ordnance
Survey Name Book OS1/14/57/3 (1857-
16) says 'Greens of Gardyne: A small one
story dwelling house with outbuilding
garden and lands attached the property of
Mr. Lyall of Gardyne. North Mains: A few
wooden building answering the purpose of
a farm steading the property of Mr. Lyall of
Gardyne'. John Thomson's *Atlas of Scotland*
shows 'Greens of Kirkden' at this point, NE
of Guthrie, with Gardyne south of Guthrie.

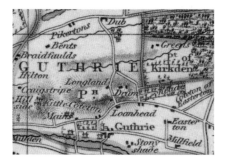

John Thomson's *Atlas of Scotland*, Northern Part of Angus Shire. Southern Part. Bottom section, 1832; https://maps.nls.uk/view/74400150#zoom =7&lat=6794&lon=8550&layers=BT

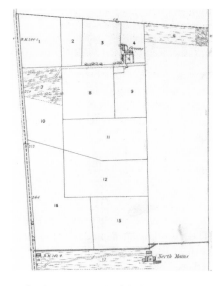

Forfar Sheet XXXIX.4 (Kirkden), survey date: 1859, publication date: 1865; https://maps.nls. uk/view/74946649#zoom=3&lat=8361&lon= 15838&layers=BT

26. Greens of Gaval, Old Deer, Aberdeenshire, 1747–55; NJ 98262 50958

Roy *Military Survey of Scotland*, 1747–55; http://maps.nls.uk/geo/roy/#zoom=14&lat= 57.5585&lon=-1.9600&layers=roy-highlands

27. Greens of Glenbeg, Mortlach, Huntly, Moray, Banffshire, 1868; NJ 4051 3761

Ruined building in area of land southwest of Glenbeg (Moray Archaeology Service Sites and Monuments Record NJ43NW0065)

Banffshire, Sheet XXV (includes: Botriphnie; Mortlach); survey date: 1868–9, publication date: 1872; https://maps.nls.uk/view/74426509# zoom=5&lat=1787&lon=15087&layers=BT

28. Greens of Glennieston, Gartly,
    Aberdeenshire, 1868; NJ 56709 34191

Aberdeen Sheet XXXIV.7 (Gartly)
Survey date: 1868 Publication date: 1874; https://
maps.nls.uk/view/74480031#zoom=4&lat=5879
&lon=14397&layers=BT

29. Greens of Harystone, Kildrummy,
    Aberdeenshire, 1867; NJ 44253 23480

Aberdeen Sheet LI.2 (Kildrummy); survey date:
1867, publication date: 1870; https://maps.nls.
uk/view/74480105#zoom=5&lat=7912&lon=
13067&layers=BT

30. Green of Invermay, Forteviot,
    Perthshire,1832; NO 05053 16348

John Thomson's *Atlas of Scotland*, Perthshire
with Clackmannan. Bottom right section, 1832;
https://maps.nls.uk/view/74400163#zoom=7&
lat=6571&lon=2795&layers=BT

31. Greens of Lochhill, Urquhart,
    Morayshire, 1870; NJ 29787 64171

Elgin Sheet VIII.11 (Urquhart), survey date:
1870, publication date: 1874; https://maps.nls.
uk/view/75202556#zoom=5&lat=9015&lon=
10983&layers=BT

32. Greens of Lepshiel, Glen Cova,
    Aberdeenshire; NO 265793

Unnamed on Ordnance Survey maps, Watson
(2013: 83) and Watson and Murray (2015:
112) report that this is the name of a grassy
glen bottom where the Burn of Loupshiel
enters the River South Esk.

33. Greens of Luchray, Fourdoun,
    Kincardineshire, 1863–4; NO 6948
    8251

Ordnance Survey Name Book OS1/19/9/8:
'The green sloping land on the east side of
Burn of Inchray and south-east of White
Hill'.

Kincardineshire, Sheet XV (includes: Fordoun;
Strachan), survey date: 1863–4, publication date:
1868; https://maps.nls.uk/view/74427601#zoom
=5&lat=4708&lon=13809&layers=BT

34. Greens of Lurgbrae, Grange,
    Banffshire, 1866; NJ 5051 5734

Ordnance Survey Name Book OS1/4/16/27:
'a small portion marshy land the name
appears to have arisen from its being con-
stantly green.'

Banffshire, Sheet IX (includes: Deskford;
Fordyce; Grange; Ordiquhill), survey date: 1866;
publication date: 1871; https://maps.nls.uk/
view/74426494#zoom=6&lat=3195&lon=1652
&layers=BT

35. Greens of Middlehill, Monquhitter,
    Aberdeenshire, 1970; NJ 82783 50020

Aberdeenshire, Sheet XII (includes: Aberdour;
King Edward; Monquhitter; New Deer); survey
date: 1870; publication date: 1874; https://maps.
nls.uk/view/74425314#zoom=5&lat=1936&lon=
7008&layers=BT

36. Greens of Middleton, Inverurie,
    Aberdeenshire, 1838; NJ 7293 2233

http://canmore.org.uk/site/124771: 'shown
on Walker and Beattie's estate plan of 1838'.

Aberdeenshire, Sheet LIV (includes: Chapel Of
Garioch; Inverurie; Kemnay; Kintore), survey
date: 1866–7, publication date: 1869; https://
maps.nls.uk/view/74425406#zoom=5&lat=8219
&lon=7187&layers=BT

37. Greens of Morinsh, Inveravon,
    Morayshire, 1869; NJ 2125 3116

Ordnance Survey Name Book OS1/4/17/135:
'a small green portion of moorland hence
the name given it is situated on the lands of
Ballindalloch'.

Banffshire, Sheet XXX (includes: Aberlour;
Inveravon; Mortlach), survey date: 1869,
publication date: 1872; https://maps.nls.uk/
view/74426512#zoom=6&lat=1719&lon=1994
&layers=BT

38. Greens of Murkle, Caithness, 1747–55;
     ND 1647 6858

Roy *Military Survey of Scotland*, 1747–55;
https://maps.nls.uk/geo/roy/#zoom=15&lat=
58.6008&lon=-3.4335&layers=roy-highlands

39. Greens of Oakenhead, Lossiemouth,
     Morayshire, 1857; NJ 23926 67997

Scottish Wills & Testaments 11 April 1857
'Greens of Oakenhead in parish of Drainie'.
Marked as Easter Greens on Ordnance
Survey maps.

Elgin Sheet III (includes: Urquhart), survey date:
1870, publication date: 1872; https://maps.nls.
uk/view/74426728#zoom=5&lat=1437&lon=
2899&layers=BT

40. Greens of Paithnick, Grange,
     Banffshire, 1832; NJ 47611 54093

John Thomson's *Atlas of Scotland*, Northern Part
of Aberdeen & Banff Shires. Southern Part.
Top left section, 1832; https://maps.nls.uk/view/
74400156#zoom=7&lat=5411&lon=10541&
layers=BT

41. Greens of Pulwhite, Culsalmond,
     Aberdeenshire, 1868–71; NJ 6678 3225

http://canmore.org.uk/site/165650: 'the
steading appears to have been removed
before the end of the 19th century.'

Aberdeenshire, Sheet XXXV (includes:
Culsalmond; Forgue; Insch), survey date:
1868–71, publication date: 1873; https://maps.
nls.uk/view/74425337#zoom=6&lat=4657&lon=
12974&layers=BT

42. Greens of Rora, Longside,
     Aberdeenshire, 1869–70; NK 0634
     5080

Ordnance Survey Name Book OS1/1/57/13
'Applies to a Number of Crofts in the lands
of Rora.'

Aberdeenshire, Sheet XIV (includes: Crimond;
Longside; Lonmay; Old Deer; St Fergus), survey
date: 1869–70, publication date: 1872; https://
maps.nls.uk/view/74425316#zoom=6&lat=3829
&lon=13333&layers=BT

43. Greens of Rothes, Rothes, Morayshire, 1747–55; NJ 27830 50103

Roy *Military Survey of Scotland*, 1747–55; https://maps.nls.uk/geo/roy/#zoom=14&lat=57.5392&lon=-3.1834&layers=roy-highlands

Elgin, Sheet XVIII (includes: Boharm; Rothes; Speymouth; St Andrews Lhanbryd), survey date: 1871, publication date: 1874; https://maps.nls.uk/view/74426745#zoom=6&lat=3410&lon=8091&layers=BT

44. Greens of Savoch, Auchnagatt, Ellon, Aberdeenshire, 1868–70; NJ 91700 38938

Aberdeenshire, Sheet XXX (includes: Ellon; New Deer; Old Deer; Tarves), survey date: 1868–70, publication date: 1873; https://maps.nls.uk/view/74425332#zoom=6&lat=5749&lon=6542&layers=BT

45. Greens of Shandford, Fern, Forfarshire, 1863; NO 49558 63938

Forfarshire, Sheet XXVI (includes: Brechin; Careston; Fern; Menmuir) Survey date: 1863 Publication date: 1865; https://maps.nls.uk/view/74426904#zoom=5&lat=8035&lon=3041&layers=BT

46. Greens of Warbellton, east of Nether Warburton, near NO 73755 63181

John Thomson's *Atlas of Scotland*, Northern Part of Angus Shire. Southern Part; https://maps.nls.uk/view/74400151#zoom=7&lat=1197&lon=10996&layers=BT

47. Greens of Woodend, Botriphnie,
    Banffshire, 1747–55; NJ 39343 44674

There are further 'Greens of X' which I have
been unable to locate on older maps, such
as Greens of Burgie, Forres, Morayshire, NJ
089572.

Roy *Military Survey of Scotland*, 1747–55;
http://maps.nls.uk/geo/roy/#zoom=14&lat=
57.4845&lon=-3.0056&layers=roy-highlands

Green(s

These are steadings named with the simplex form, or the premodified simplex form, *Green(s,
X Green(s*. The Ordnance Survey name books for Scotland record 62 places named *Grian-*
with a suffix of some sort: *Grianan, Grianain, Grianach, Grianal*, and so on. They occur
substantially in the Gaelic-speaking regions: Argyllshire, Sutherland, Ross & Cromarty,
Inverness-shire, and sporadically in Aberdeenshire, Morayshire and Perthshire. Several are
the names of mountains rather than settlements and I have not included them here.

1. Greens, Banchory, Kincardineshire,
   1832; NO 70302 99773

2. Cuthelton Greens, Denny, Stirlingshire,
   1747–55; NS 80204 81811

John Thomson's *Atlas of Scotland*, 1832,
Kincardine Shire; https://maps.nls.uk/view/7440
0134#zoom=7&lat=7652&lon=5258&layers=BT

Roy *Military Survey of Scotland*, 1747–55;
https://maps.nls.uk/geo/roy/#zoom=15&lat=
56.0216&lon=-3.9199&layers=roy-lowlands

3. Greens, Darvel, Ayrshire, 1832; NS 56952 40530

John Thomson's *Atlas of Scotland*, Northern Part of Ayrshire. Southern Part. Top right section, 1832; https://maps.nls.uk/view/74400169#zoom =7&lat=4593&lon=3499&layers=BT

4. Easter Greens and Wester Greens, Edinkillie, Morayshire, 1871; NJ 04113 49579 and NJ 03726 49404

Elgin Sheet XVI (includes: Dallas; Edinkillie; Rafford), survey date 1871, publication date: 1874; https://maps.nls.uk/view/74426743#zoom =6&lat=1996&lon=2121&layers=BT

5. Greens, Errol, Perthshire, 1747–55; near NO 21834 25037

Roy *Military Survey of Scotland*, 1747–55; https://maps.nls.uk/geo/roy/#zoom=15&lat= 56.4097&lon=-3.2549&layers=roy-highlands

6. Greens, Kinmundy, Aberdeenshire, 1747–55; NJ 89071 18996

Roy *Military Survey of Scotland*, 1747–55; https://maps.nls.uk/geo/roy/#zoom=15&lat= 57.2524&lon=-2.1570&layers=roy-highlands

7. East Greens, Kirkintilloch, Dumbartonshire, 1859; NS 65543 73199

Dumbarton Sheet XXIV.12 (Kirkintilloch), survey date: 1859, publication date: 1864; https://maps.nls.uk/view/74941111#zoom=4& lat=8391&lon=13403&layers=BT

8. Greens, New Castleton, Roxburghshire, 1747–55; NY 48316 86734

Roy *Military Survey of Scotland*, 1747–55; https://maps.nls.uk/geo/roy/#zoom=15&lat= 55.1718&lon=-2.8088&layers=roy-lowlands

9. Greens, New Monkland, Lanarkshire, 1832; NS 76114 71806

John Thomson's *Atlas of Scotland*, Northern Part of Lanarkshire. Southern Part. Top section, 1832; https://maps.nls.uk/view/74400128#zoom=7&lat=6824&lon=7285&layers=BT

10. Green, North Lanarkshire, 1747–55; NS 73611 69859

Roy *Military Survey of Scotland*, 1747–55; https://maps.nls.uk/geo/roy/#zoom=16&lat=55.9055&lon=-4.0302&layers=roy-lowlands

11. Greens, Shotts, North Lanarkshire, 1832; NS 84629 67071

John Thomson's *Atlas of Scotland*, Northern Part of Lanarkshire. Southern Part. Top section, 1832; https://maps.nls.uk/view/74400128#zoom=7&lat=5257&lon=8055&layers=BT

12. Greens, Stracathro, Forfarshire, 1832; NO 58761 67100

John Thomson's *Atlas of Scotland*, Northern Part of Angus Shire. Southern Part. Top section, 1832; https://maps.nls.uk/view/74400151#zoom=7&lat=1798&lon=8540&layers=BT

13. Greens, Tough, Aberdeenshire, 1899; NJ 6265 1134

Aberdeenshire Sheet LXIII.SW (includes: Leochel-Cushnie; Tough), publication date: 1901, date revised: 1899; https://maps.nls.uk/view/75475526#zoom=6&lat=2138&lon=6647&layers=BT

14. Green, Wishaw, Lanarkshire, 1747–55; NS 78712 53917

Roy *Military Survey of Scotland*, 1747–55; https://maps.nls.uk/geo/roy/#zoom=16&lat=55.7680&lon=-3.9374&layers=roy-lowlands

15. Green, Tillicoultry, Clackmannanshire, 1832; near NS 93464 97090

John Thomson's *Atlas of Scotland*, Perthshire with Clackmannan. Bottom right section, 1832; https://maps.nls.uk/view/74400163#zoom=7&lat=4191&lon=1413&layers=BT

16. Green, Lightburn, Shettleston, Lanarkshire, 1832; NS 64115 64326

John Thomson's *Atlas of Scotland*, Northern Part of Lanarkshire. Southern Part. Top section, 1832; https://maps.nls.uk/view/74400128#zoom=7&lat=6485&lon=4730&layers=BT

As with Sunnyside, this list of historic Scottish 'Greens of X' and Green(s is unlikely to be exhaustive; further Greens listed in the GB1900 gazetteer may be old.

SELECT BIBLIOGRAPHY

Manuscripts

British Library, Cotton MS Cleopatra A VI, Croniques de London 1259–1343.

British Library, Cotton MS Galba E ii, Cartulary of St Benet of Hulme Abbey.

British Library, Cotton MS Faustina B VIII, Cartulary of Malmesbury Abbey.

British Library, Harley MS 3656, Cartulary of Newnham Priory.

Guildhall Library, CLC/L/BF/A/021/MS05440, William Porlond's Book.

Guildhall Library, MS 34048/1, MS Merchant Taylors' Company Accounts 1397–1445.

London Metropolitan Archives, CLA/007/EM/02/A/041, Bridge House Deed.

London Metropolitan Archives, CLA/007/EM/02/B/029, Bridge House Deed.

London Metropolitan Archives, CLA/007/EM/02/G/045, Bridge House Deed.

London Metropolitan Archives, CLA/007/FN/02/003, 1460–84, Bridgemasters' Annual Accounts and Rental, volume 3.

London Metropolitan Archives, CLA/007/EM/04/6a, Nominal and Topographical Indexes to Bridge House Deeds Portfolios A–K.

London Metropolitan Archive, CLA/006/AD/04/004, City of London Commissioners of Sewers and Pavements. 1767. 'Minutes of Public Meetings for Implementing the New Act for Improving the Streets of London etc.' *Proceedings* 1766–1767.

London Metropolitan Archives, CLA/024/01/01/009, Early Mayors Court Roll I.

London Metropolitan Archives, CLA/024/01/02/002, Plea & Memoranda Roll A 1b.

London Metropolitan Archives, CLA/024/01/02/004, Plea & Memoranda Roll A 3.

London Metropolitan Archives, CLA/024/01/02/006, Plea & Memoranda Roll A 5.

London Metropolitan Archives, CLA/024/01/02/008, Plea & Memoranda Roll A 7.

London Metropolitan Archives, CLA/024/01/02/018, Plea & Memoranda Roll A 17.

London Metropolitan Archives, CLA/024/01/02/024, Plea & Memoranda Roll A 23.

London Metropolitan Archives, CLA/024/01/02/025, Plea & Memoranda Roll A 24.

London Metropolitan Archives, CLA/024/01/02/026, Plea & Memoranda Roll A 25.

London Metropolitan Archives, CLA/024/01/02/028, Plea & Memoranda Roll A 27 (i).

London Metropolitan Archives, CLA/024/01/02/31, Plea & Memoranda Roll A 30.

London Metropolitan Archives, CLA/024/01/02/051, Plea & Memoranda Roll A 50.

London Metropolitan Archives, CLA/040/02/002 (old ref Miscellaneous Roll FF), Pleas of Nuisance, Miscellaneous Roll.

London Metropolitan Archives, CLA/040/02/003, Pleas of Nuisance, Miscellaneous Roll.

London Metropolitan Archives, CLC/313/B/001/MS25504, St Paul's Cathedral MS Liber L.

London Metropolitan Archives, CLC/313/L/D/001/MS25125/030, 031, 032, 033, 1393–6, MSS Account Rolls of the Collectors of Rents in London and its Suburbs, Dean & Chapter of St Paul's Cathedral, London.

London Metropolitan Archives, CLC/313/L/H/001/MS25121, St Paul's Cathedral deeds nos. 111, 113, 184, 232, 608, 680, 693, 729, 852, 941, 962, 1074, 1123, 1233, 1265, 1519, 1770, 1772.

London Metropolitan Archives, CLC/313/N/006/MS25345, Court Roll of the Prebendal Manor of Finsbury.

London Metropolitan Archives, COL/AD/01/001, Letter-Book A.

London Metropolitan Archives, COL/AD/01/002, Letter-Book B.

London Metropolitan Archives, COL/AD/01/003, Letter-Book C.

London Metropolitan Archives, COL/AD/01/004, Letter-Book D.

London Metropolitan Archives, COL/AD/01/005, Letter-Book E.

London Metropolitan Archives, COL/AD/01/006, Letter-Book F.

London Metropolitan Archives, COL/AD/01/007, Letter-Book G.

London Metropolitan Archives, COL/AD/01/008, Letter-Book H.

London Metropolitan Archives, DL/C/B/004/MS09171/001, Register of Wills.

London Metropolitan Archives, microfilm X109/400–424. Deeds Enrolled in the Court of Husting (HR).

London Metropolitan Archives, microfilm X109/425. Maude, R. F., F. J. Craller and H. Trotter. 1885–1907. Court of Husting: Deeds and Wills: Index of Names and Places. Vol. 5. 'Tenements'.

The National Archives, C 146/765, Chancery, Ancient Deeds

The National Archives, C 136/85, Chancery, Inquisitions Post Mortem.

The National Archives, C 134/5, Chancery, Inquisitions Post Mortem.

The National Archives, C 135/48, Chancery, Inquisitions Post Mortem.

The National Archives, C 136/88, Chancery, Inquisitions Post Mortem.

The National Archives, C 47/4/4, Chancery Miscellanea, Bundle 4, Wardrobe Books.

The National Archives, C 145/163, Chancery, Miscellaneous Inquisitions.

The National Archives, C 145/232, Chancery, Miscellaneous Inquisitions.

The National Archives, C 145/259, Chancery, Miscellaneous Inquisitions.

The National Archives, C 145/261, Chancery, Miscellaneous Inquisitions.

The National Archives, C 54/212, Chancery and Supreme Court of Judicature, Close Rolls.

The National Archives, C 54/225, Chancery and Supreme Court of Judicature, Close Rolls.

The National Archives, C 66/83, Chancery and Supreme Court of Judicature, Patent Rolls.

The National Archives, C 66/95, Chancery and Supreme Court of Judicature, Patent Rolls.

The National Archives, C 66/154, Chancery and Supreme Court of Judicature, Patent Rolls.

The National Archives, C 66/159, Chancery and Supreme Court of Judicature, Patent Rolls.

The National Archives, C 66/173, Chancery and Supreme Court of Judicature, Patent Rolls.

The National Archives, C 66/175, Chancery and Supreme Court of Judicature, Patent Rolls.

The National Archives, C 66/243, Chancery and Supreme Court of Judicature, Patent Rolls.

The National Archives, C 66/278, Chancery and Supreme Court of Judicature, Patent Rolls.

The National Archives, C 66/319, Chancery and Supreme Court of Judicature, Patent Rolls.

The National Archives, C 66/332, Chancery and Supreme Court of Judicature, Patent Rolls.

The National Archives, C 66/489, Chancery and Supreme Court of Judicature, Patent Rolls.

The National Archives, E 40/1935 A, Exchequer, Treasury of Receipt, Ancient Deeds.

The National Archives, E 40/1668, Exchequer, Treasury of Receipt, Ancient Deeds.

The National Archives, E 40/1783, Exchequer, Treasury of Receipt, Ancient Deeds.

The National Archives, E 40/2559, Exchequer, Treasury of Receipt, Ancient Deeds.

The National Archives, E 101/502/14, Exchequer, King's Remembrancer, Accounts Various.

The National Archives, E 179/144/2, Exchequer, King's Remembrancer, Particulars of Account relating to Lay and Clerical Taxation.

The National Archives, E 179 144/3, Exchequer, King's Remembrancer, Particulars of Account relating to Lay and Clerical Taxation.

Westminster Abbey Muniments Book 11.

Westminster Abbey Muniments 13431.

Westminster Abbey Muniments 13764.

Westminster Abbey Muniments 13993.

Westminster Abbey Muniments 16232.

Westminster Abbey Muniments 17083.

Westminster Abbey Muniments 17476.

Westminster Abbey Muniments 17588.

Westminster Abbey Muniments 17610.

Westminster Abbey Muniments 17634.

Westminster Abbey Muniments 17640.

Westminster Abbey Muniments 17644.

Westminster Abbey Muniments 17665.

Westminster Abbey Muniments 17702.

Westminster Abbey Muniments 17706.

Westminster Abbey Muniments 24567.

Westminster Abbey Muniments 26924.

Westminster Abbey Muniments 26924B.

Westminster Abbey Muniments 26938.

Westminster Abbey Muniments 26999.

Printed and Online References

Alexander, William M. 1952. *The Place Names of Aberdeenshire*. Third Spalding Club. Aberdeen: Aberdeen University Press.

Allen, Michael. 2011. *Charles Dickens and the Blacking Factory*. Oxford: Stockley Publications.

Archaeologia Cambrensis, the Journal of the Cambrian Archaeological Association 14, 1868, 3rd series. London: J. Russell Smith.

Ashmore, Owen. 1982. *The Industrial Archaeology of North-west England*. Manchester: Manchester University Press.

'Aunt Clara' (Clarissa Woolloton). 1862. 'Rambles at Sunnyside; or, A Week with my Godchildren'. New ed. London: W. Wells Gardner.

Austin, David, Mac Dowdy and Judith Miller. 1997. *Be Your Own House Detective*. London: BBC Books.

A-Z London Street Atlas. 1995. 3rd ed. No place: Geographers' A-Z Map Co. Ltd.

Bankton, Andrew Macdowall, Lord. 1752. *An institute of the laws of Scotland in civil rights: with observations upon the agreement or diversity between them and the laws of England*. Edinburgh: A. Kincaid and A. Donaldson.

Barron, Caroline M. 2000. 'London 1300–1500.' In D. M. Palliser (ed.). *The Cambridge Urban History of Britain*. Vol. 1. *600–1540*. Cambridge: Cambridge University Press. 395–440.

Barrow, G. W. S. 1973. *The Kingdom of the Scots*. London: Edward Arnold.

Bateman, Henry. 1859. 'The Substance of a Lecture on the History and Objects of the New Church College Delivered in the School Room of the New Church Society, Devonshire-street, Islington, London, on Tuesday, 8th November, 1859'. In: *Ritualism; Ecclesiastical and Revealed*. 1868. No editor. London: Longmans, Green & Co.

Bayley, Johnathan, Rev. Dr. 1884. *New Church Worthies: or, Early but Little-Known Disciples of the Lord in Diffusing the Truths of the New Church*. London: James Speirs.

Bebbington, David W. 2011 [1992]. *Victorian Nonconformity*. Eugene, Oregon: Cascade.

Beebe, Ann. 2003. 'Elizabeth Stuart Phelps (1815–1852).' In Denise D. Knight (ed.) *Writers of the American Renaissance: an A–Z Guide*. Westport, Connecticut: Greenwood Press. 292–9.

Beresford, Camilla, David Mason, John D. Stewart and Jenifer White. 2008. *Durability Guaranteed: Pulhamite Rockwork – Its Conservation and Repair*. London: English Heritage Publications.

Betjeman, John. 1932. *Mount Zion; Or, in Touch with the Infinite*. London: James Press.

Betjeman, John. 1994. In Lycett-Green, Candida (ed.). *Letters: Volume One, 1926 to 1951*. London: Methuen.

Betjeman, John. 1929. *Lord Mount Prospect*. In Guest (ed.) 2006 [1978]. *The Best of Betjeman*. London: John Murray.

Biddle, Martin and D. J. Keene. 1976a. 'The Early Place-Names of Winchester.' In Biddle, Martin (ed.). *Winchester in the Early Middle Ages: An Edition and Discussion of the Winton Domesday*. Oxford: Clarendon. 231–40.

Biddle, Martin and D. J. Keene. 1976b. 'Winchester in the Eleventh and Twelfth Centuries: Private Houses.' In Biddle, Martin (ed.). *Winchester in the Early Middle Ages: An Edition and Discussion of the Winton Domesday*. Oxford: Clarendon. 337–48.

Binfield, Clyde. 1977. *So Down to Prayers: Studies in English Nonconformity 1780-1920*. London: J. M. Dent & Sons Ltd.

Blanch, William Hartnett. 1875. *Ye Parish of Camberwell A Brief Account of the Parish of Camberwell, its History and Antiquities*. London: E. W. Allen.

Blayney, Peter W. M. 1990. 'The Bookshops in Paul's Cross Churchyard'. *Occasional Papers of the Bibliographic Society* 5. London: Bibliographical Society.

Blayney, Peter W. M. 2013. *The Stationers' Company and the Printers of London, 1501–1557*. Cambridge: Cambridge University Press.

Bloch, Michael (ed.). 1986. *Wallis & Edward : Letters 1931–1937: the Intimate Correspondence of the Duke and Duchess of Windsor*. London: Weidenfeld & Nicolson.

Blondé, Bruno, Peter Stabel, Jon Stobart and Ilja Van Damme (eds). 2006. *Buyers and Sellers: Retail Circuits and Practices in Medieval and Early Modern Europe*. Turnhout: Brepols.

Blunt, John Henry. 1874. *Dictionary of Sects, Heresies, Ecclesiastical Parties and Schools of Religious Thought*. London, Oxford and Cambridge: Rivingtons.

Bolin, Sture. 2008. 'Scandinavia'. In M. M. Postan (ed.) *The Cambridge Economic History of Europe*. Vol. 1, The Agrarian Life of the Middle Ages. Cambridge: Cambridge University Press.

Bonta, Marcia. 1985. 'Graceanna Lewis: Portrait of a Quaker Naturalist.' *Quaker History*, 74/1, 27–40.

Boulton, D'Arcy Jonathan Dacre. 1987. *The Knights of the Crown: The Monarchical Orders of Knighthood in Later Medieval Europe, 1325–1520.* Woodbridge: Boydell and Brewer.

Boulton, D'Arcy Jonathan Dacre. 1995. 'Classic knighthood as nobiliary dignity: the knighting of counts and kings' sons in England, 1066–1272.' In Stephen Church and Ruth Harvey. *Medieval Knighthood V: Papers from the Sixth Strawberry Hill Conference 1994.* Woodbridge: Boydell and Brewer. 41–100.

Boyle's Fashionable Court and Country Guide, and Town Visiting Directory. 1861. London: Court Guide Office, 50a Pall-Mall.

The British Chronologist; comprehending every Material Occurrence, Ecclesiastical, Civil, or Military, relative to England and Wales, from the Invasion of the Romans: interspersed with Processions at Coronations, Instalments of the Military Honours, Marriages, Funerals of Sovereigns, &c. &c. 1789. vol 2. London: J. Lackington.

Britnell, Richard. 2004. 'Fields, farms and sun-division in a moorland region, 1100–1400'. *Agricultural History Review*, 52/1, 20–37.

Butlin, R. A. 1964. 'Northumberland Field Systems.' *Agricultural History Review* 12, 99–120.

Caine, W. S. 1890. *Picturesque India, a Handbook for European Travellers.* London: G. Routledge and Sons.

Cantor, Geoffrey. 1991a. *Michael Faraday Sandemanian and Scientist.* Basingstoke: Macmillan.

Cantor, Geoffrey. 1991b. 'Dissent and Radicalism?: The Example of the Sandemanians'. *Enlightenment and Dissent*, Aberystwyth: University College of Wales. 3–20.

Carlin, Martha. 1987. Topographical Index to *St Botolph Aldgate Gazetteer (Minories, East Side; Holy Trinity Minories).* Centre for Metropolitan History, Institute of Historical Research, University of London: typescript.

Carlin, Martha. 1990. 'Four Plans of Southwark in the Time of Stow.' *London Topographical Record* 26, 15–56.

Carlin, Martha. 2013. 'The Host.' In Stephen Rigby and Alastair J. Minnis (eds). *Historians on Chaucer: The 'General Prologue' to the Canterbury Tales.* Oxford: Oxford University Press. 460–80.

Carlyle, Thomas. 1864. *History of Friedrich II of Prussia, Called Frederick the Great.* Volume 4. London: Chapman and Hall.

Cary, John. 1828. *Cary's New Itinerary: or an Accurate Delineation of the Great Roads, both Direct and Cross throughout England and Wales.* 11th ed. London: G. & J. Cary.

Chadwick, Hector Munro. 1949 [2013]. *Early Scotland: The Picts, the Scots and the Welsh of Southern Scotland.* Cambridge: Cambridge University Press.

Chambers, W. (ed.). 1872, 1909. *Charters and Documents relating to the Burgh of Peebles with extracts from the Records of the Burgh, AD 1165–1710.* 2 vols. Edinburgh: Scottish Burgh Record Society.

Chapman, J. B. W. and H. C. Johnson (eds). 1957. *Calendar of Inquisitions Miscellaneous (Chancery) Preserved in the Public Record Office.* Vol 4. 1377–1388. London: Her Majesty's Stationery Office.

Chapman, J. B. W. and Hunnisett, R. F. (eds). 1963. *Calendar of Inquisitions Miscellaneous (Chancery) Preserved in the Public Record Office.* Vol 6. 1392–1399. London: Her Majesty's Stationery Office.

Chew, Helena M. and William Kellaway (eds). 1973. *London Assize of Nuisance, 1301–1431: A Calendar*. London: London Record Society 10.

Christmas, Captain Walter. 1914. Translated by A. G. Chater. *King George of Greece*. New York: McBride, Nast & Company.

Clarke, Charles. 1864. *A Box for the Season A Sporting Sketch*. London: Chapman and Hall.

Coates, Richard. 1982/3. 'English medieval Latin *bellerīca'. *Journal of the English Place-Name Society* 15, 20–3.

Coates, Richard. 1984. 'Coldharbour: for the last time?' *Nomina* 8, 73–8.

Cogan, Thomas. 1794. *The Rhine: or, a journey from Utrecht to Francfort; chiefly by the borders of the Rhine, and the passage down the river, from Mentz to Bonn: described in a series of letters, written from Holland, to a Friend in England, in the years 1791 and 1792*. London: G. Woodfall for J. Johnson.

Cooke, Mrs Robert. 1908. *A History of the New Jerusalem Church, Kearsley, (1808–1908)*. Farnworth: Robert Cooke Ltd.

Cooksey, Pamela (ed.). 2011. *The Large and Small Notebooks of Joseph Wood A Yorkshire Quaker (1750–1821)*. Volumes 1–3. High Flatts: High Flatts Quaker Meeting. www.woodbrooke.org.uk/data/files/CPQS/Volume_3.pdf.

Cooper, Brian. 2008. 'Contribution to the study of a euphemism in the intimate lexis of Slavonic and Germanic Languages'. *Transactions of the Philological Society* 106/1, 71–91.

Corbett, Edward. 1891. *An old coachman's chatter: with some practical remarks on driving by a semi-professional*. 2nd ed. London: Richard Bentley & Son.

Cowper, William. 1782. *Poems*. London: Printed for J. Johnson. ESTC T14895.

Cox, Montagu H. and G. Topham Forrest (eds). 1931. *Survey of London*. Vol 14. St Margaret, Westminster, Part III: Whitehall II. London: London County Council.

Cox, Barrie. 1994. *English Inn and Tavern Names*. University of Nottingham: Centre for English Name Studies.

Cox, Richard A. V. 2007. 'The Norse Element in Scottish Place-names: syntax as a chronological marker.' *The Journal of Scottish Name Studies* 1, 13–27.

Cramond, William. (ed.) 1903. *The Records of Elgin, 1234–1800*. Vol 1. Aberdeen: New Spalding Club.

Crawford, Barbara E. 1987. *Scandinavian Scotland*. Leicester: Leicester University Press.

Crawford, Barbara E. (ed.) 1995. *Scandinavian Settlement in Northern Britain: Thirteen Studies of Place-Names in their Historical Context*. Leicester: Leicester University Press.

Davidson, the Rev. John. 1878. *Inverurie and the Earldom of the Garioch; a Topographical and Historical Account of the Garioch from the earliest times to the Revolution Settlement, with a genealogical appendix of Garioch families flourishing at the period of the revolution settlement and still represented*. Edinburgh: David Douglas.

Dickens, Charles. 1837. *The Posthumous Papers of the Pickwick Club*. London: Chapman and Hall.

Dickens, Charles. 1853 [2003]. *Bleak House*. New York: the Penguin Group.

Dickinson, H. W. 1939. *Matthew Boulton*. Cambridge: Cambridge University Press.

Dixon, Robert M. W. 1997 [2002]. *The Rise and Fall of Languages*. Cambridge: Cambridge University Press.

Directory to noblemen and gentlemen's seats, villages etc. in Scotland: giving the counties in which they are situated, the post-towns to which each is attached, and the name of the resident, etc. [With a map.]. 1857. Edinburgh: Sutherland and Knox; London: Simpkin, Marshall & Co.

Dodgshon, R. A. 1975. 'Scandinavian Solskifte and the Sun-Wise Division of Land in Eastern Scotland', *Scottish Studies* 19, 1–2 [1–24].

Dodgshon, R. A. 1987. 'The landholding foundations of the open-field system'. In T. H. Aston (ed.) Landlords, Peasants and Politics in Medieval England. Cambridge: Cambridge University Press, 6–32.

Dodgshon, R. A. 1988. 'The Scottish farming township as metaphor.' In L. Leneman (ed.), *Perspectives in Scottish Social History: Essays in Honour of Rosalind Mitchison*. Aberdeen: Aberdeen University Press, 69–82.

Donnelly, J. 2000. 'In the territory of Auchencrow: long continuity or late development in early Scottish field-systems?' *Proceedings of the Society of Antiquaries of Scotland* 130, 743–772.

Douglas Woodward, C. 2009. *The Vanished Coaching Inns of the City of London.* London: Historical Publications Ltd.

Duncan, James. 1820. *The Scotch Itinerary, Containing the Roads through Scotland, on a New Plan. With Copious Observations for the Entertainment of Travellers.* 2nd ed. Glasgow: James Lumsden and Son.

Dwelly, Edward. 1901–11. *Illustrated Gaelic-English Dictionary.* Glasgow: Glairm Publications (Dwelly-d): www.cairnwater.co.uk/gaelicdictionary/index.aspx?Language=en

Eagen Johnson, Kathleen and Timothy Steinhoff. 1997. *Art of the Landscape: Sunnyside, Montgomery Place and Romanticism.* Tarrytown, NY: Historic Hudson Valley Press.

Eckert, Penelope and Étienne Wenger. 2005. 'Communities of Practice in Sociolinguistics'. *Journal of Sociolinguistics.* Volume 9, Issue 4, 582–89.

Edward, Duke of Windsor. 29 May 1950. 'A King's Story'. Part II. *Life.* 62–86.

Ekwall, Bror Eilert. 1947. *Early London Personal Names.* Lund: Gleerup.

Ekwall, Bror Eilert. 1954. *Street-Names of the City of London.* Oxford: Clarendon.

Ekwall, Bror Eilert (ed.). 1951. *Two Early London Subsidy Rolls.* Lund: Gleerup.

Ellis, Alexander J. 1889. *On Early English Pronunciation.* London: The Philological Society.

Endelman, Todd M. 1994. 'The Frankaus of London: A Study in Radical Assimilation 1837–1967'. *Jewish History* 8/1–2: 117–54.

Faherty, Duncan. 2007. *Remodeling the Nation: the Architecture of American Identity, 1776–1858.* Lebanon, New Hampshire: University of New Hampshire Press.

Falkland, Henry Cary, Viscount. 1680. *The History of the life, reign, and death of Edward II, King of England, and Lord of Ireland.* London: Printed by J.C. for Charles Harper, Samuel Crouch and Thomas Fox. Wing / F313.

Faulkenburg, Marilyn Thomas. 2001. *Victorian Conscience: F. W. Robertson.* New York: Peter Lang.

von Feilitzen, Olof. 1976. 'The Personal Names and Bynames of the Winton Domesday'. In Biddle, Martin (ed.). *Winchester in the Early Middle Ages: An Edition and Discussion of the Winton Domesday.* Oxford: Clarendon. 143–230.

Fergusson, John. 1841. 'Geological and Mineralogical Report upon Muirkirk Coal-Field, in the County of Ayr.' In *Prize Essays and Transactions of the Highland and Agricultural Society of Scotland,* New Series, volume 7. Edinburgh: William Blackwood and Sons. 205–22.

Flatrès, Pierre. 1977. 'Breton Settlement Names: A Geographical View'. *Word* 28:1–2, 63–77. DOI: 10.1080/00437956.1977.11435849

Flower, C. T. (ed.). 1947. *Calendar of Close Rolls, Henry VI: Volume 6, 1454–1461*. London: His Majesty's Stationery Office.

Forster, E. M. 1910. *Howards End*. London: Edward Arnold.

Forsyth, Katherine. 1997. *Language in Pictland: the case against 'non-Indo-European Pictish'*. Studia Hameliana 2. Utrecht: De Keltische Draak.

Foster, Joseph. 1885. *Men-at-the-Bar: A Biographical Hand-list of the Members of the Various Inns of Court, Including Her Majesty's Judges, Etc.* 2nd ed. London and Aylesbury: Hazell, Watson and Viney, Ltd.

Freeman, Linton C., 1978. 'Centrality in Social Networks: Conceptual Clarification'. *Social Networks* 1, 215–39.

Fulk, R. D. 1992. *A History of Old English Meter*. Philadelphia PA: University of Pennsylvania Press.

Gaffney, Victor. 1960. *The Lordship of Strathavon: Tomintoul under the Gordons*. Aberdeen: Third Spalding Club.

Gardiner, B. W. 1860. *Royal Blue Book; Fashionable Directory, & Parliamentary Guide*. London: B. W. Gardiner & Son.

Gardner, Kevin J. 2014. 'Strange Deliberations: John Betjeman and Protestant Nonconformity'. *Christianity and Literature* 63/2. 225–56.

Garrioch, David. 1994. 'House Names, Shop Signs and Social Organisation in Western European Cities 1500-1900.' *Urban History* 21/1, 20–48.

Gelling, Margaret and Ann Cole. 2003. *The Landscape of Place-Names*. Donington: Shaun Tyas.

Glinert, Ed. 2008. *The Manchester Compendium A Street-by-Street History of England's Greatest Industrial City*. London: Penguin.

Gloag, William (ed.). 1835. *Rentall of the County of Perth, by Act of the Estates of Parliament of Scotland, 4th August, 1649; Contrasted with the Valuation of the Same County, 1st January, 1835*. Perth: Morisons.

Godsman, James. 1958. *A History of the Burgh and Parish of Ellon, Aberdeenshire*. Ellon: W. and W. Lindsey.

Goering, Nelson. 2016. 'Early Old English Foot Structure.' *Transactions of the Philological Society* 114/2, 171–97.

Göransson, Sölve. 1961. 'Regular Open-Field Pattern in England and Scandinavian Solskifte'. *Geografiska Annaler* 43B, 80–104.

Gould, Jeremy. 2011. 'Landscapes and Gardens of the Long Weekend.' In Steven Parissien (ed.) *Stanley Spencer and the English Garden*. London: Compton Verney in association with Paul Holberton Publishing. 54–75.

Gover, J. E. B., Allen Mawer and F. M. Stenton. 1942. *The Place-Names of Middlesex apart from the City of London*. English Place-Name Society 18. Cambridge: Cambridge University Press.

Guest, John (ed.). 2006 [1978]. *The Best of Betjeman*. London: John Murray.

Harben, Henry A. 1918. *A Dictionary of London; being Notes Topographical and Historical Relating to the Streets and Principal Buildings in the City of London*. London: Herbert Jenkins.

Harding, Vanessa. 2008. *People in Place: Families, Households and Housing in Early Modern London*. London: Centre for Metropolitan History.

Hardy, Dennis and Colin Ward. 1984. *Plotlands Phenomenon, Arcadia for All, The Legacy of a Makeshift Landscape.* London: Mansell.

Harland, John (ed.). 1865. *Court Leet Records of the Manor of Manchester A.D. 1586–1602*, Vol. 2. Chetham Society vol 65. Manchester: Chetham Society.

Harley, Rodney and J. B. W. Chapman, (eds). 1937. *Calendar of Inquisitions Miscellaneous (Chancery) Preserved in the Public Record Office.* Vol 3. London: His Majesty's Stationery Office.

Hart, Colonel H. G. 1871. *The New Annual Army List, Militia List, and Indian Civil Service List.* London: John Murray.

Hart, Colonel H. G. 1899. *The New Annual Army List, Militia List, and Indian Civil Service List.* London: John Murray.

Harvey, I. M. W. 1988. *Popular Revolt and Unrest in England During the Second Half of the Reign of Henry VI.* University College of Wales Aberystwyth: PhD thesis.

Haslam, Jeremy. 2010. 'The Development of London by King Alfred: A Reassessment.' *Transactions of the London and Middlesex Archaeological Society* 61, 109–44.

Heal, Sir Ambrose. 1925. *London Tradesmen's Cards of the XVIII Century An Account of their Origin and Use.* London: B. T. Batsford.

Heal, Sir Ambrose. 1927. 'The Trade Cards of Engravers.' *The Print Collector's Quarterly* 14/3, 1–34.

Heal, Sir Ambrose. 1929. 'Street Numbers in London', in *Notes and Queries* 156, May 18, 354–6.

Heal, Sir Ambrose. 1931. *Old London Bridge Tradesmen's Cards and Tokens.* Originally published in Gordon Home. *Old London Bridge.* London: John Lane, The Bodley Head. 308–31.

Heal, Sir Ambrose. 1933. 'Samuel Pepys, his Trade-Cards.' *The Connoisseur* 92, 165–71.

Heal, Sir Ambrose. 1939. 'London Shop-Signs other than those given by Larwood and Hotten in their "History of Signboards"'. *Notes and Queries* 176, 1–76.

Heal, Sir Ambrose. 1942. *Notes and Queries* August 15, 100–1.

Heal, Sir Ambrose. 1947. *The Signboards of Old London Shops.* London: B. T. Batsford.

Heal, Sir Ambrose. 1948. '17th century Booksellers' & Stationers' Trade Cards'. *Alphabet and Image* 8, 51–63.

Heal, Sir Ambrose. 1972 [1935]. *The London goldsmiths, 1200–1800: a record of the names and addresses of the craftsmen, their shop-signs and trade-cards.* Newton Abbot: David and Charles Reprints.

Hilton Price, F. G. 1895. 'The Signs of Old Fleet Street to the End of the Eighteenth Century'. Address read to the Royal Archaeological Institute.

Hitchcock, Henry-Russell. 1958 [1977]. *Architecture: Nineteenth and Twentieth Centuries.* Harmondsworth: Penguin.

Hobbs, Richard, Judith Swaddling, James Graham-Campbell and Sonja Marzinzik. 2011. The 'William Allen Box': A Victorian Gentleman's Collection of Antiquities and Curios.' *The Antiquaries Journal* 91, 283–321.

Holt, Hazel. 1990. *A Lot to Ask: A Life of Barbara Pym.* Dutton.

Hooper, Janet. 2002. *A Landscape Given Meaning: An Archaeological Perspective on Landscape History in Highland Scotland.* University of Glasgow: PhD thesis.

Horovitz, David. 2003. *A Survey and Analysis of the Place-names of Staffordshire.* 2 vols. University of Nottingham: PhD thesis.

House of Commons. *Journal of the House of Commons.* Volume 29. 1803. London: H. M. Stationery Office.

Hunter, William. 1867. *Biggar and the House of Fleming.* Edinburgh: William Paterson.

Hurditch, Charles Russell. 1896. (ed.). *Footsteps of Truth.* New Series, vol XIV. London: John F. Shaw & Co.

Hutton, William. 1835. *The History of Birmingham.* 6th ed. Birmingham: James Guest.

Immonen, Visa. 2014. 'Fondling on the kitchen table – artefacts, sexualities and performative metaphors from the 15th to the 17th centuries'. *Journal of Social Archaeology* 14/2, 177–95.

Innes, Cosmo (ed.). 1837. *Liber Sancte Marie de Melros. Munimenta Vetustiora Monasterii Cisterciensis de Melros.* Vol 2. Edinburgh: Bannatyne Club 59.

James, Alan G. (n.d.) *The Brittonic Language in the Old North: A Guide to the Place-Name Evidence*: www.spns.org.uk/bliton/BLITON2014ii_elements.pdf

James, Frank A. J. L. 1996. *The Correspondence of Michael Faraday, volume 3: 1841–1848.* London: The Institution of Engineering and Technology.

James, Frank A. J. L. 2008. *The Correspondence of Michael Faraday, volume 5: 1855–1860.* London: The Institution of Engineering and Technology.

Johnson, Janet. 2009. *Sunniside Conservation Area Character Appraisal and Management Strategy.* Sunderland: Sunderland City Council: www.sunderland.gov.uk/CHttpHandler. ashx?id=7948&p=0

Johnston, James B. 1904. *The Place-Names of Stirlingshire.* 2nd ed. Stirling. R. S. Shearer and Son.

Johnston, James B. 1940. *The Place-Names of Berwickshire.* Edinburgh: The Royal Scottish Geographical Society.

Jordan, Richard. 1925 [1974]. *Handbook of Middle English grammar: Phonology.* Trans. Joseph Crook. Berlin: Mouton.

Jubb, Michael. 1984. *Cocoa and Corsets: A Selection of late Victorian and Edwardian Posters and Showcards from the Stationers' Company Copyright Records Preserved in the Public Record Office.* London: Her Majesty's Stationery Office.

The Intellectual Repository, and New Jerusalem Magazine. September 1859. Vol VI, No. 69. London: The General Conference of the New Church.

Keene, Derek. 1985a. *Survey of Medieval Winchester.* 2 vols. Oxford: Clarendon.

Keene, Derek. 1985b. *Cheapside before the Great Fire.* No place: Economic and Social Research Council.

Keene, Derek. 1995. 'London in the Early Middle Ages 600–1300', *London Journal* 20/2, 9–21.

Keene, Derek. 2006. 'Sites of Desire: Shops, Selds and Wardrobes in London and other English Cities, 1100–1550.' In Blondé, Stabel, Stobart and Van Damme (eds). 125–55.

Keene, Derek. 2008. 'Tall Buildings in Medieval London: Precipitation, Aspiration and Thrills.' *London Journal* 33/3, 201–15.

Keene, Derek and Vanessa Harding (eds) 1985. *A Survey of Documentary Sources for Property Holding in London before the Great Fire.* London: London Record Society 22.

Keene, Derek and Vanessa Harding (eds). 1987 [1994]. *Historical Gazetteer of London Before the Great Fire Cheapside; Parishes of All Hallows Honey Lane, St Martin Pomary, St Mary Le Bow, St Mary Colechurch and St Pancras Soper Lane.* London: Centre for Metropolitan History. British History Online: www.british-history.ac.uk/no-series/ london-gazetteer-pre-fire

Kelly, Susan E. (ed.). 2004. *Charters of St Paul's, London.* Oxford: The British Academy at the Oxford University Press.

Kime, Wayne R. 1977. *Pierre M. Irving and Washington Irving: A Collaboration in Life and Letters.* Waterloo, Ontario: Wilfrid Laurier University Press.

Kingsford, C. L. 1916. 'Historical Notes on Medieval London Houses.' *London Topographical Record* 10, 44–144.

Kingsford, C. L. 1917. 'Historical Notes on Medieval London Houses.' *London Topographical Record* 11, 28–82.

Kingsford, C. L. 1920. 'Historical Notes on Medieval London Houses.' *London Topographical Record* 12, 1–67.

Kingsley, Charles. 1855. *Glaucus; or, the Wonders of the Shore.* 2nd ed. Cambridge: Macmillan & Co.

Koch, John T. (ed.). 2006. *Celtic Culture A Historical Encyclopedia.* Volume 1: A–Celti. Santa Barbara, California: ABC Clio.

Lapidge, Michael (ed.). 2002. *Interpreters of Early Medieval Britain.* Oxford: Oxford University Press for the British Academy.

Larwood, Jacob and John Camden Hotten. 1866. *The History of Signboards.* Piccadilly: John Camden Hotten.

Larwood, Jacob and John Camden Hotten. 1951 [1866]. *English Inn Signs.* London: Chatto and Windus.

Lee-Whitman, Leanna. 1982. 'The Silk Trade: Chinese Silks and the British East India Company'. *Winterthur Portfolio* 17, 1 (Spring). 21–41.

Leslie, Lieutenant Colonel Jonathan Forbes. 1909. *The Irvines of Drum and Collateral Branches.* Aberdeen: The Aberdeen Daily Journal Office.

Liber Feodorum: The Book of Fees commonly known called Testa de Nevill, reformed from the earliest MS, by the Deputy Keeper of the Records. 1920–31. Preface by Sir Henry Maxwell-Lyte. 3 vols. London: His Majesty's Stationery Office.

Lillywhite, Bryant. 1972. *London Signs.* London: George Allen & Unwin.

Littlejohn, David (ed.). 1904, 1906. *Records of the Sheriff Court of Aberdeenshire.* 2 vols. Aberdeen: The Spalding Club.

Loudon, John Claudius. 1837. *The Gardeners Magazine and Register of Rural and Domestic Improvement.* Vol. 3. London: Longman, Brown, Green and Longmans.

Macafee, Caroline and A.J. Aitken. 2002. 'A history of Scots to 1700' in *A Dictionary of the Older Scottish Tongue* vol. XII, xxix–clvii. (www.dsl.ac.uk/about-scots/history-of-scots/characteristics, accessed 27 November 2018).

McEwan, John A. 2016. *Seals in Medieval London 1050–1300: A Catalogue.* London: London Record Society extra series vol. 1. Woodbridge: The Boydell Press.

Mackenzie, Eneas and Marvin Ross. 1834. *An Historical, Topographical, and Descriptive View of the County Palatine of Durham.* Vol. 2. Newcastle upon Tyne: Mackenzie and Dent.

McLean, Ruari. 1963. *Victorian Book Design and Colour Printing.* London: Faber & Faber.

MacMichael, J. Holden. 1904. 'The London Signs and their Associations', *The Antiquary* 40, 216–18.

MacMichael, J. Holden. 1906. 'The London Signs and their Associations', *The Antiquary* 42, 183–7.

Martin, Martin. 1716 [1999]. *A Description of the Western Islands of Scotland, circa 1695.* Edinburgh: Birlinn.

Mason, Emma (ed.). 1988. *Westminster Abbey Charters, 1066–c.1214.* London: London Record Society 25.

Mason, R. H. 1853. *Mason's Court Guide and General Directory for Brentford, Kew, Ealing, Isleworth, Twickenham, Teddington, Richmond, Kingston, Hampton, &c., &c.* 1853. Greenwich: Mason.

Matthews, Derek, Malcolm Anderson and John Richard Edwards. 1998. *The Priesthood of Industry: The Rise of the Professional Accountant in British Management.* Oxford: Oxford University Press.

Mawer, Allan, Sir. 1920. *Place-Names of Northumberland and Durham.* English Place-Name Society. Cambridge: Cambridge University Press.

Maxwell Lyte, H. C. 1890. *A Descriptive Catalogue of Ancient Deeds in the Public Record Office.* Vol 1. London: Her Majesty's Stationery Office.

Maxwell Lyte, H. C. 1913. *Calendar of the Close Rolls Preserved in the Public Record Office: Edward III.* London: His Majesty's Stationery Office.

Maxwell Lyte, H. C. 1914. *Calendar of the Close Rolls Preserved in the Public Record Office: Richard II. A.D. 1381-1385.* Vol 2. London: His Majesty's Stationery Office.

Maxwell Lyte, H. C. 1925. *Calendar of the Close Rolls Preserved in the Public Record Office: Richard II. A.D. 1392-1396.* Vol 5. London: His Majesty's Stationery Office.

Meadows. Cecil A. 1957. *Trade Signs and their Origin.* London: Routledge and Kegan Paul.

Meecham Jones, Simon. 2018. 'Code-switching and contact influence in Middle English manuscripts from the Welsh Penumbra – Should we re-interpret the evidence from *Sir Gawain and the Green Knight?*'. In Päivi Pahta, Janne Skaffari and Laura Wright (eds). *Multilingual Practices in Language History: English and Beyond.* Berlin: Mouton de Gruyter, 97–120.

Miles, Joyce C. 1972. *House Names Around the World.* Newton Abbot: David and Charles. 117.

Miles, Joyce C. 2000. *Owl's Hoot: How People Name their Houses.* London: John Murray.

Milroy, Lesley. 1980. *Language and Social Networks.* Oxford: Basil Blackwell.

Moir, Alexander L. 1913. *Moir Genealogy and Collateral Lines, with Historical Notes.* Lowell, MA: the author.

The Monthly Observer and New Church Record. 3/33. London: Hodson & Son.

The Monthly Observer and New Church Record. 7/83. London: Hodson & Son.

Morpurgo Davies, Anna. 2002. 'Anna Morpurgo Davies'. In Keith Brown and Vivien Law (eds). *Linguistics in Britain Personal Histories.* Publications of the Philological Society 36.

Murray, John (Iain Moireach). 2014. *Reading the Gaelic Landscape / Leughadh Aghaidh na Tire.* Dunbeath: Whittles Publishing Ltd.

Murray, K. M. Elisabeth. 1977. *Caught in the Web of Words: James A. H. Murray and the Oxford English Dictionary.* New Haven: Yale University Press.

Myhill, Olwen. n.d. Indexes to Derek Keene and Vanessa Harding (eds). 1987 [1994]. Topographical Index to *Historical Gazetteer of London before the Great Fire, Part 1: Cheapside,* Vol II. Centre for Metropolitan History, Institute of Historical Research, University of London: typescript.

Nevell, Michael. 2008. 'The Archaeology of Industrialisation and the Textile Industry: the Example of Manchester and the South-western Pennine Uplands During the 18th Century (Part 1)', *Industrial Archaeology Review* 30/1, 33–48.

The New-Church Magazine 21/45. London and Edinburgh.

New, Elizabeth. 2008. 'Representation and Identity in Medieval London: the Evidence of Seals'. In Matthew Davies and Andrew Prescott (eds). *London and the Kingdom: Essays in Honour of Caroline M. Barron.* Donington: Shaun Tyas. 246–58.

Newbigging, Thomas. 1893. *History of the Forest of Rossendale.* 2nd. ed. Rawtenstall: J. J. Riley.

Newman, Edward. 1840. *A History of British Ferns.* London: J. Van Voorst.

Nicolaisen, W. F. H. 1976. *Scottish Place-Names, their Study and Significance.* London: B. T. Batsford Ltd.

The Northumberland Poll Book; Containing a List of the Freeholders who Voted at the Contested Elections for the County of Northumberland. 1826. Alnwick: W. Davison.

The Poll Book of the Contested Election for the Southern Division of Northumberland. 1833. Newcastle on Tyne: Hernaman and Perring.

Northern Archaeological Associates and The Cleadon Village Atlas Team. 2013–14. *The Cleadon Village Atlas: The Geology, History, Archaeology and Ecology of a Village.* Northern Archaeological Associates Ltd: http://cleadon-village.co.uk/atlas-final.pdf

Nurmi, Arja, Jukka Tyrkkö, Anna Petäjäniemi and Päivi Pahta. 'The Social and Textual Embedding of Multilingual Practices in Late Modern English: A Corpus-based Analysis.' In Päivi Pahta, Janne Skaffari and Laura Wright (eds). 2018. *Multilingual Practices in Language History: English and Beyond.* Berlin: Mouton de Gruyter, 171–98.

Nurminen, Terhi Johanna. 2012. *Hill-Terms in the Place-Names of Northumberland and County Durham.* Newcastle University: PhD Thesis.

O'Brien, Patrick, Trevor Griffiths, and Philip Hunt. 1991. 'Political Components of the Industrial Revolution: Parliament and the English Cotton Textile Industry, 1660–1774'. *Economic History Review* 44/3, 395–423.

Ogborn, Miles. 1998. *Spaces of Modernity: London's Geographies, 1680–1780.* London, New York: The Guilford Press.

Okasha, Elisabeth. 2011. *Women's Names in Old English.* Farnham: Ashgate.

Padel, Oliver. 2014. 'Change and Development in English Place-Names: What Counts as Corruption?' *Quaestio Insularis* 15, 1–21.

Papers Relating to Military Operations in Affghanistan : Presented to both Houses of Parliament, by Command of Her Majesty, 1843. London: T. R. Harrison.

Papson, Don and Tom Calarco. 2015. *Secret Lives of the Underground Railroad in New York City. Sydney Howard Gay, Louis Napoleon and the Record of Fugitives.* Jefferson, North Carolina: McFarland and Co.

Paul, James Balfour and John Maitland Thomson (eds). 1882–1894. *The Register of the Great Seal of Scotland.* Vols 5–8. Edinburgh: H. M. General Register House.

Pegge, Samuel. 1814. *Anecdotes of the English language; chiefly regarding the local dialect of London and its Environs.* 2nd ed. London: J. Nichols, Son, & Bentley.

Pevsner, Nikolaus. 1969. *The Buildings of England: Lancashire. 2 The Rural North.* Harmondsworth: Penguin.

Phillips, Henry. 1823. Sylva florifera. *The Shrubbery, Historically and Botanically treated, with observations on the formation of Ornamental and Picturesque Scenery.* 2 volumes. London: Longmans, Hurst, Rees, Orme and Brown.

Pigot, James and Co. 1828. *National Commercial Directory for 1828–9.* London and Manchester: J. Pigot & Co.

Post Office London Directory, June.1846. London: Kelly & Co. Facsimile edition. 1994. King's Lynn: Michael Winton.

Post Office London Directory.1848. London: W. Kelly & Co.

Post Office London Directory. 1851. London: W. Kelly & Co.

Post Office Directory of London, with Essex, Hertfordshire, Kent, Middlesex, Surrey and Sussex.1852. London: W. Kelly & Co.

Post Office London Official Directory for 1855. London: W. Kelly & Co.

Post Office Edinburgh and Leith Directory.1856–7. Edinburgh: Ballantyne and Co.

Post Office London Directory. 1858. London: W. Kelly & Co.

Post Office London Suburban Directory.1860. London: W. Kelly & Co.

Post Office London Directory.1863. London: W. Kelly & Co.

Post Office London Suburban Directory 1865. London: W. Kelly & Co.

Post Office Directory of the Six Home Counties: Essex, Herts, Middlesex, Kent, Surrey & Sussex.1870. London: Kelly & Co.

1872. *Post Office London Suburban Directory*. London: Kelly & Co.

Post Office Directory of Surrey.1878. London: Kelly & Co.

Poussa, Patricia. 1995. 'Ellis's "Land of Wee": a historico-structural re-evaluation'. *Neuphilologische Mitteilungen* 96, 295–307.

Presland, C. H. *p.*1984. *'All Our Yesterdays'. The Story of a Family*. http://preslandhistory. co.uk/story_of_a_family_chapter_2.html

Rachleff, Allison S. 2011. *Historic and Natural Districts Inventory Form*, Division for Historic Preservation New York State Parks and Recreation: South End Historic District. www. newnybridge.com/documents/study-documents/section106/c10.pdf

Railway Gazette International 87, July–December 1947.

Ramsey, Sherwood. 1913. *Historic Battersea; Topographical, Biographical*. Battersea: G. Rangecroft & Co.

Raven, James. 2007. *The Business of Books: Booksellers and the English Book Trade 1450–1850*. New Haven, Connecticut: Yale University Press.

Reaney, P. H. 1935. *The Place-Names of Essex*. English Place-Name Society 12. Cambridge: Cambridge University Press.

Reaney, P. H. and R. M. Wilson (eds). 1991 [1995]. *A Dictionary of English Surnames*. 3rd ed. Oxford: Oxford University Press.

Registrum Magni Sigilli Regum Scotorum A. D. 1306–1668. 1882–1914. Editors: v.1, J. M. Thomson; v.2, J. B. Paul; v.3, J. B. Paul and J. M. Thomson; v.4–9, J. M. Thomson; v.10, J. H. Stevenson and W. K. Dickson; v.11 J. H. Stevenson. 11 vols. Edinburgh: H. M. Treasury.

Riley, H. T. (ed.). 1868. *Memorials of London Life in the 13th, 14th and 15th Centuries*. London: Longmans, Green.

Riley, James. 1979. *A Brief History of the Primitive Methodist Church in Crawshawbooth*. No place, no publisher.

Ritchie, James Ewing. 1870. *The Religious Life of London*. London: Tinsley Brothers.

Robinson, William. 1840. *The History and Antiquities of the Parish of Tottenham in the County of Middlesex*. Vol. 1. Tottenham: G. S. Coventry.

Robson's London Directory, Street Key, Classification of Trades, and Royal Court Guide and Peerage: Particularizing the Residences of 70,000 Establishments in London and Its Environs, and Fifteen Thousand of the Nobility and Gentry, Also an Extensive Conveyance

List, Alphabetical List of Public Carriers, Together With the Street Guide. 1842. London: Robson & Co.

Ross, A. 2008. *Literature review of the history of grassland management in Scotland.* Scottish Natural Heritage Commissioned Report No. 313. Edinburgh: Scottish Natural Heritage.

Russell, Paul. 1995 [2013]. *An Introduction to the Celtic Languages.* London: Routledge.

St Giles, Camberwell, Surrey. Tenth Annual Report of the Vestry of their Proceedings under the Metropolis Local Management Act. 1866. Camberwell: E. Billing and Son.

St Serfe, Thomas, Sir. 1665. *The remarkable prophesies in order to the present times the one of Gilpine Girnigo, one of the heritable poets of the old Thanes of Gilliquhimnee: the other of Sir Tristram, Clerk of the Kitchin to the Knights of King Arthur's Round Table.* Amsterdam [i.e. Edinburgh]: Printed by Joacim Nosche. Wing (2nd ed.) / G789A.

Salter, H. E. 1929. *Cartulary of Oseney Abbey.* Vol. 2. Oxford: Clarendon.

Salzman, L. F. 1952. *Building in England Down to 1540, A Documentary History.* Oxford: Clarendon.

Sandeman, John Glas and David Peat. 1895. *The Sandemanian Genealogy.* Edinburgh: George Waterston and Sons.

Sandnes, Berit. 1997. 'The Bu of Orphir, Burn of Gueth – a Gaelic Pattern in Orkney Place-Names?' *Northern Studies* 32: 125–8.

Saunders, Ann (ed.). 1997. *The Royal Exchange.* London Topographical Society 152. London: London Topographical Society.

Saunders, Ann. (ed.). 2007. *The A to Z of Edwardian London, with an Introduction by M. H. Port.* London: London Topographical Society publication no. 166.

Savage, W. H. 1833. *The Vulgarisms and Improprieties of the English Language.* London: T. S. Porter.

Schofield, John. 1994. *Medieval London Houses.* New Haven and London: Yale University Press.

Scott, Clement and Cecil Howard. 1891. *The Life and Reminiscences of E. L. Blanchard.* London: Hutchinson and Co.

Sedgefield, W. J. 1915. *The Place-Names of Cumberland and Westmoreland.* Publications of the University of Manchester, English Series 7. Manchester: Manchester University Press and London: Longmans, Green & Co.

Seed, John. 2014 [1992]. 'From "middling sort" to middle class in late eighteenth- and early nineteenth-century England'. In M. L. Bush (ed.). *Social Orders and Social Classes in Europe Since 1500: Studies in Social Stratification.* Hoboken: Taylor and Francis. 114–35.

Sharp, Sir Cuthbert. 1851 [1816]. *History of Hartlepool.* Hartlepool: John Proctor.

Sharp, J. E. E. S. and A. E. Stamp. 1909. *Calendar of Inquisitions Post Mortem: Volume 7, Edward III.* London: His Majesty's Stationery Office.

Sharpe, Reginald R. (ed.). 1889. *Calendar of Wills Proved and Enrolled in the Court of Husting, London: Part 1, 1258–1358.* London: Her Majesty's Stationery Office.

Sharpe, Reginald R. (ed.). 1890. *Calendar of Wills Proved and Enrolled in the Court of Husting, London: Part 2, 1358–1688.* London: Her Majesty's Stationery Office.

Sharpe, Reginald R. (ed.). 1899. *Calendar of Letter-Books Preserved Among the Archives of the Corporation of the City of London at the Guildhall. Letter-Book A. Circa A. D. 1275–1298.* London: Corporation of London.

Sharpe, Reginald R. (ed.). 1900. *Calendar of Letter-Books Preserved Among the Archives of the Corporation of the City of London at the Guildhall. Letter-Book B. Circa A. D. c.1275–c.1312.* London: Corporation of London.

Sharpe, Reginald R. (ed.). 1901. *Calendar of Letter-Books Preserved Among the Archives of the Corporation of the City of London at the Guildhall. Letter-Book C. Circa A. D. 1291–1309.* London: Corporation of London.

Sharpe, Reginald R. (ed.). 1902. *Calendar of Letter-Books Preserved Among the Archives of the Corporation of the City of London at the Guildhall. Letter-Book D. Circa A. D. 1309–1314.* London: Corporation of London.

Sharpe, Reginald R. (ed.). 1903. *Calendar of Letter-Books Preserved Among the Archives of the Corporation of the City of London at the Guildhall. Letter-Book E. Circa A. D. 1314–1337.* London: Corporation of London.

Sharpe, Reginald R. (ed.). 1904. *Calendar of Letter-Books Preserved Among the Archives of the Corporation of the City of London at the Guildhall. Letter-Book F. Circa A. D. 1337–1352.* London: Corporation of London.

Sharpe, Reginald R. (ed.). 1905. *Calendar of Letter-Books Preserved Among the Archives of the Corporation of the City of London at the Guildhall. Letter-Book G. Circa A. D. 1352–1374.* London: Corporation of London.

Sheppard, F.H.W. (ed.). 1966. *Survey of London: Volumes 33 and 34, St Anne Soho. British History Online* (www.british-history.ac.uk/survey-london/vols33–4/pp1–19, accessed 31 January 2018).

Sheppard, J. 1973. 'Field Systems of Yorkshire'. In A. R. H. Baker and R. A. Butlin (eds). *Studies of Field Systems in the British Isles.* Cambridge: Cambridge University Press. 145–87.

Slater, John. 1986. *Sunnyside House: A History of the Manchester Diocesan Conference and Retreat House.* Manchester: Manchester Diocesan Board of Finance.

Smith, John. 1866. *Ferns: British and Foreign: the History, Organography, Classification and Enumeration, with a Treatise on their Cultivation, &c., &c.* London: Robert Hardwicke.

Smith, Robert (ed.). 1843. *The Friend: A Religious and Literary Journal* vol. 16. Philadelphia: Joseph and William Kite.

Smith, Stevie. 1984 [1949]. 'A London Suburb'. *Me Again. Uncollected Writings of Stevie Smith.* London: Virago, 104.

Statistical Society. 1877. *The Journal of the Statistical Society* 40. London: Edward Stanford.

Stevenson, Brian and Stanley Warren. September 2013. 'In Search of the Victorian-era Microscope Slide Makers "J&TJ"'. *Micscape Magazine* 215: www.microscopy-uk.org.uk/mag/artsep13/bs-sw-JTJ.pdf

Stevenson, J. H. (ed.). 1897. *The Scottish Antiquary or Northern Notes and Queries.* Vol. 11. Edinburgh: George P. Johnston.

Stoddart, John. 1801. *Remarks on Local Scenery and Manners in Scotland during the Years 1799 and 1800.* Vol 1. London: William Miller.

Strachey, John (ed.). 1771. *Rotuli Parliamentorum, ut et petitiones, et placita in Parliamento.* Vol. 3, 1377–1411. London.

Straker, Samuel and Sons. 1863. *Strakers' Annual Mercantile, Ship & Insurance Register.* London: S. Straker and Sons.

Straker Brothers. 1950. *The House of Straker 1800–1950*. London: Straker Brothers Limited.

Suburban Life, the Countryside Magazine. 1908. New York: Suburban Press.

Taylor, Simon. 1995. *Settlement Names in Fife*. University of Edinburgh: PhD thesis.

Taylor, Simon. 2004. 'Scandinavians in Central Scotland –By Place-Names and their Context'. In Gareth Williams and Paul Bibire (eds) *Sagas, Saints and Settlements*. Leiden: Brill, 125–46.

Taylor, Simon, with Gilbert Márkus. 2006. *Place-Names of Fife* Vol. 1 (West Fife between Leven and Forth). Donington: Shaun Tyas.

Taylor, Simon, with Gilbert Márkus. 2008. *Place-Names of Fife* Vol. 2 (Central Fife between Leven and Eden). Donington: Shaun Tyas.

Taylor, Simon, with Gilbert Márkus. 2009. *Place-Names of Fife* Vol. 3 (St Andrews and the East Neuk). Donington: Shaun Tyas.

Taylor, Simon, with Gilbert Márkus. 2010. *Place-Names of Fife* Vol. 4 (North Fife between Eden and Tay). Donington: Shaun Tyas.

Taylor, Simon, with Gilbert Márkus. 2012. *Place-Names of Fife* Vol. 5 (Discussion, Glossaries, Texts). Donington: Shaun Tyas.

Taylor, Simon. 2014. 'Aa the airts: directional words in Scottish place-names'. Paper given to the Cognitive Toponymy Symposium, University of Copenhagen, 4 June 2014. http://cogtop.org/en/symposiums/symposium-1-2/simon-taylor-aa-the-airts-directional-words-in-scottish-place-names/.

Taylor, Simon, Peter McNiven and Eila Williamson. Forthcoming. *Place-Names of Clackmannanshire*.

Thomas, A. H. 1926. *Calendar of the Plea and Memoranda Rolls of the City of London*. Vol 1, 1323–1364. London: His Majesty's Stationary Office.

Thompson, G. and Charlotte Matthews. 2013. *Historic Building Recording of a Number of Heritage Features at Paddington Railway Station, Praed Street, City of Westminster, London, W2 1HQ*. Brockley: Pre-Construct Archaeology.

Timperley, Loretta R. (ed.). 1976. *A Directory of Landownership in Scotland c. 1770*. Scottish Record Society, New Series, 5.

Town, Matthew. 2006. *North Pennines Archaeology Newcastle Project Designs and Client Reports No. CP/291/06, 'The Place', West Sunniside, Sunderland, Tyne and Wear*. Newcastle upon Tyne: North Pennines Archaeology.

Trippier, J. M. 2007. *Crawshaw Hall, Burnley Road, Crawshawbooth: An Historic Building Survey*. Bolton: J. M. Trippier Archaeological and Surveying Consultancy: http://archaeologydataservice.ac.uk/archiveDS/archiveDownload?t=arch-943-1/dissemination/pdf/jmtrippi1-203354_1.pdf

Trippier, J. M. 2008. *Archaeological Building Survey of Outbuildings at Crawshaw Hall, Crawshawbooth, Rossendale*. Bolton: J. M. Trippier Archaeological and Surveying Consultancy: http://archaeologydataservice.ac.uk/archiveDS/archiveDownload?t=arch-943-1/dissemination/pdf/jmtrippi1-61795_1.pdf

Trudgill, Peter. 2010. *Investigations in Sociohistorical Linguistics: Stories of Colonisation and Contact*. Cambridge: Cambridge University Press.

Trudgill, Peter, Daniel Schreier, Daniel Long & Jeffrey P. Williams. 2004. 'On the reversibility of mergers: /w/, /v/ and evidence from lesser-known Englishes'. *Folia Linguistica Historica* 24/1–2: 23–45.

Turin, Luca. 2006. *The Secret of Scent: Adventures in Perfume and the Science of Smell*. London: Faber and Faber.

Watson, Adam. 2013. *Place Names in Much of North-East Scotland: Hill, Glen, Lowland, Coast, Sea, Folk*. Paragon: Rothersthorpe.

Watson, Adam and Ian Murray. 2015. *Place Name Discoveries on Upper Deeside and the Far Highlands*. Paragon: Rothersthorpe.

Watts, Victor, (ed.). 2004 [2010]. *The Cambridge Dictionary of English Place-Names*. Cambridge: Cambridge University Press.

Watts, Victor. 2007. *The Place-Names of County Durham*, Part I. ed. Paul Cavill. Nottingham: English Place-Name Society.

Way, Twigs. 2009. *Garden Gnomes: A History*. Botley: Shire Publications Ltd.

Webb, Sidney and Beatrice. 1922. *English Local Government: Statutory Authorities for Special Purposes*. London: Longmans, Green and Co.

Weinstein, Rosemary. 1985. 'Medieval Houses in St Giles Cripplegate and St Botolph Bishopsgate.' *London Topographical Record* 25, 13–32.

Whittingham, Sarah. 2012. *Fern Fever: The Story of Pteridomania*. London: Frances Lincoln.

Whittington, G. 1973. 'Field Systems of Scotland'. In Alan R. H. Baker and Robin Alan Butlin (eds). *Studies of Field Systems in the British Isles*. Cambridge: Cambridge University Press. 530–79.

Whyte, Ian D. 2001 [2007]. 'Economy, Primary Sector'. In Michael Lynch (ed.). *The Oxford Companion to Scottish History*. Oxford: Oxford University Press. 206.

Willems, Klaus. 2000. 'Form, Meaning, and Reference in Natural Language: A Phenomenological Account of Proper Names.' *Onoma* 35, 85–119.

Williamson, May G. 1942. *The Non-Celtic Place-Names of the Scottish Border Counties*. University of Edinburgh: PhD thesis: www.spns.org.uk/MayWilliamsonComplete.pdf

Wilson, Walter. 1810. *History and Antiquities of the Dissenting Churches in London, Westminster, and Southwark, including the Lives of their Ministers, from the Rise of Nonconformity to the Present Time*. Vol. 3. London: printed for the author.

Winch, Nathaniel John. 1831. *Flora of Northumberland and Durham*. Newcastle: T. and J. Hodgson.

Woollacott, Ron. 2006. *The Victorian Catacombs at Nunhead*. London: Friends of Nunhead Cemetery.

Woollacott, Ron and Michèle Louise Burford. 2014. *Buried at Nunhead. Nunhead Notables Volume 3*. London: Friends of Nunhead Cemetery.

Wright, Arnold (ed.). 1907. *Twentieth Century Impressions of Ceylon: its history, people, commerce, industries, and resources*. London: Lloyd's Greater Britain Publishing Co.

Wright, Laura. 1992. 'OED's tabard, 4 (?).' *Notes and Queries*. 39/2 New Series. 155–7.

Wright, Laura. 2006a. 'On the Global Dissemination of Medical Writing: Medicines Required by a Sea-surgeon in 1715'. In Maurizio Gotti and Françoise Salager-Meyer (eds). *Advances in Medical Discourse Analysis: Oral and Written Contexts*. Linguistic Insights Studies in Language and Communication, Volume 45. Bern: Peter Lang. 457–82.

Wright, Laura. 2006b. 'Street addresses and directions in mid-eighteenth-century London newspaper advertisements.' In Nicholas Brownlees (ed.). *News Discourse in Early Modern Britain*. Selected papers of the Conference on Historical News Discourse 2004. Linguistic Insights Studies in Language and Communication, Vol. 30. Bern: Peter Lang. 199–215.

Wright, Laura. 2007. 'On some Middle English Colour Terms, including *pink*'. In Gabriella Mazzon (ed.). *Studies in Middle English Forms and Meanings*. Studies in English Medieval Language and Literature 19. Frankfurt: Peter Lang. 57–72.

Wright, Laura. 2010a. 'A pilot study on the singular definite articles *le* and *la* in fifteenth-century London mixed-language business writing'. In Richard Ingham (ed.). *The Anglo-Norman Language and its Contexts*. York: York Medieval Press and The Boydell Press, 130–42.

Wright, Laura. 2010b. 'Eighteenth-Century London Non-Standard Spellings as Evidenced by Servants', Tradesmen's and Shopkeepers' Bills'. In Nicholas Brownlees, Gabriella Del Lungo and John Denton (eds). *The Language of Public and Private Communication in a Historical Perspective*. Cambridge: Cambridge Scholars Publishing, 161–90.

Wright, Laura. July 2011. 'The Nomenclature of some French and Italian Fireworks in Eighteenth-Century London'. *The London Journal* 36/2 July, 109–39.

Wright, Laura. 2012. 'On variation and change in London medieval mixed-language business documents'. In Merja Stenroos, Martti Mäkinen and Inge Særheim (eds), *Language Contact and Development around the North Sea*. Amsterdam/Philadelphia: John Benjamins, 99–115.

Wright, Laura. 2013. Judith A. Jefferson and Ad Putter (eds) 'Mixed-Language Accounts as Sources for Linguistic Analysis'. *Multilingualism in Medieval Britain (c. 1066–1520): Sources and Analysis*. Turnhout: Brepols, 123–36.

Wright, Laura. 2017a. 'Kiss Me Quick: on the Naming of Commodities in Britain, 1650 to the First World War'. In Esther-Miriam Wagner, Bettina Beinhof and Ben Outhwaite (eds). *Merchants of Innovation: the Language of Traders*. Berlin: Mouton. 108–31.

Wright, Laura. 2017b [2016]. 'From Lavender Water to Kiss Me, You Dare!: Shifting Linguistic Norms in the Perfume Industry, 1700–1900'. In Giovanni Iamartino and Laura Wright (eds). *Textus English Studies in Italy: Late Modern English Norms and Usage*, 29/3, 147–76.

Wright, Laura. 2017c. 'On the East India Company vocabulary of St Helena in the late 17th and early 18th century'. *World Englishes* 36/4, 522–40. doi: 10.1111/weng.12286.

Wyld, Henry Cecil. 1920 [1956]. *A history of modern colloquial English*. 3rd ed. Oxford: Blackwells.

Young, Robyn. 2014. '"Truth, Like Roses, Often Blossoms Upon A Thorny Stem." Graceanna Lewis 1821–1912'. *Chester County Day 74*: http://content.yudu.com/Library/A32sa7/74thAnnualChesterCou/resources/36.htm

General Online Resources

Ancestry: www.ancestry.co.uk

Anglo-Saxons.net: www.anglo-saxons.net

Anglo-Saxon Charters: www.aschart.kcl.ac.uk

The Association of British Counties Gazetteer of British Place Names: www.gazetteer.org.uk/search.php?type=co&place=sunnyside

Bathurst, John. 1999/2000. 'Laindon Memories'. Laindon and District Community Archive: www.laindonhistory.org.uk/page_id__714_path__0p29p21p37p59p24p.aspx)

British Book Trade Index: www.bbti.bham.ac.uk

Census of England, 1861 and 1871: www.nationalarchives.gov.uk/records/census-records.htm

Charting the Nation, Work Record ID 0043926, Sketch of the Town and Territory of Auchincrow (1700–1799): https://images-teaching.is.ed.ac.uk/luna/servlet/detail/UoEcha~1~1~322508~103440:Sketch-of-the-Town-and-Territory-of?amp;qvq=w4s:/who/Hood

Clyde Built Ships: http://www.clydeships.co.uk

Le Conservatoire International des Parfums: www.osmotheque.fr/

Documents of Early England Dataset: http://deeds.library.utoronto.ca/

Dictionary of the Scots Language: http://www.dsl.ac.uk/

The Dictionary of the Older Scottish Tongue: http://dsl.ac.uk/

Eighteenth Century Collections Online (ECCO): http://gdc.gale.com/products/eighteenth-century-collections-online

Early English Books Online (EEBO): http://eebo.chadwyck.com

The Electronic Sawyer Online Catalogue of Anglo-Saxon Charters: www.esawyer.org.uk

Gale Cengage Learning newspaper archive databases: (17th–18th Century Burney Collection Newspapers; 19th Century British Library Newspapers; The Illustrated London News Historical Archive, 1842–2003; The Times Digital Archive, 1785–2008): www.gale.com/primary-sources/historical-newspapers

Grace's Guide to British Industrial History: www.gracesguide.co.uk

Historical Directories of England and Wales: http://leicester.contentdm.oclc.org/cdm/landingpage/collection/p16445coll4

House of Commons Parliamentary Papers: http://parlipapers.chadwyck.co.uk

International Genealogical Index: https://familysearch.org/search/collection/igi

Irving, Washington. 1835. *Abbotsford*: http://digital.nls.uk/jma/gallery/title.cfm?id=65&seq=5

Oxford Dictionary of National Biography: http://www.oxforddnb.com

Oxford English Dictionary Online: www.oed.com

The Prosopography of Anglo-Saxon England: http://www.pase.ac.uk/

Placenames Database of Ireland: http://www.logainm.ie/7740.aspx

The Proceedings of the Old Bailey Online: www.oldbaileyonline.org

Records of London's Livery Companies Online: http://www.londonroll.org

Records of the Parliaments of Scotland to 1707: http://rps.ac.uk

Scotland's Places: http://www.scotlandsplaces.gov.uk

Scottish Post Office Directories: http://digital.nls.uk/directories

Scottish Wills and Testaments Online: http://www.scottishdocuments.com/opwills.asp

INDEX

Page numbers in **bold** refer to tables and boxes; page numbers in *italics* refer to figures; 'n' after a page number indicates the footnote number.